UNDERSTANDING
WALL
STREET

FIFTH EDITION

UNDERSTANDING WALL STREET

FIFTH EDITION

Jeffrey B. Little and Lucien Rhodes

New York   Chicago   San Francisco
Lisbon   London   Madrid   Mexico City   Milan
New Delhi   San Juan   Seoul   Singapore
Sydney   Toronto

ISBN-13: 978-0-07-163322-2
ISBN-10:   0-07-163322-7

This publication is designed to provide accurate and authoritative information in regard to the subject matter covered. It is sold with the understanding that neither the author nor the publisher is engaged in rendering legal, accounting, or other professional service. If legal advice or other expert assistance is required, the services of a competent professional person should be sought.

*—From a Declaration of Principles jointly adopted
by a Committee of the American Bar
Association and a Committee of Publishers*

McGraw-Hill books are available at special quantity discounts to use as premiums and sales promotions, or for use in corporate training programs. To contact a representative please e-mail us at bulksales@mcgraw-hill.com.

This book is printed on acid-free paper.

To
Helen T. Walbran
Years Ahead of Her Time

Contents

Preface

When *Understanding Wall Street* was first published more than thirty years ago, we never imagined that it would eventually become a "classic," available in four languages—English, Spanish, Russian, and Chinese. Moreover, with the passing of time, the original work has been enhanced with each new version. This Fifth Edition is no exception.

In this book's early days, explaining the financial pages of a newspaper was paramount. This is no longer true. Today, investors can quickly find all the necessary information on the Internet. So, the facts are the same, but the lessons here are totally different.

In addition, the changes on Wall Street have been never-ending with the introduction of new products. Just since the Fourth Edition alone, the popularity of exchange traded funds (ETFs) has exploded, requiring new sections.

The collapse of the real estate market in 2007 and the subsequent meltdown of the entire financial system is now part of this text. And any investor today who can-not explain the term "credit default swap" is missing an important link between Wall Street and Main Street.

Initially, *Understanding Wall Street* was intended mainly as a "primer," since the stock market is rarely taught in high school. And even on the college level, investment courses are typically selected only by students with specialized business interests. Today, this book is no longer just a primer. In fact, many Wall Street professionals are also using it as an everyday reference.

Finally, it is interesting to note how the audience for *Understanding Wall Street* has shifted over the years. This has, of course, been largely influenced by the maturing baby boomer generation. The millions of people who now own shares of stock through their retirement plans suddenly have a "need to know."

So, armed with a reasonable degree of common sense, along with the immense quantities of timely information available today, we believe it is still possible to be a successful investor—with the guidance of this new book.

1 | What Is a Share of Stock?

Introduction

Every business day, billions of shares of stock are bought and sold. How did these shares originate, and how are their prices determined? For shares to be traded from one person to another, a company must be created. How does it begin? Where does the money come from?

In this chapter, The NewBrite Lighting Company is born and its officers confront the problems that all successful corporations must solve. Directors are elected, shares are issued, profits are reinvested in the business, and dividends are declared. In the process, the reader will see capitalism at work and will gain an appreciation for a great system that has produced the most advanced economy in the world.

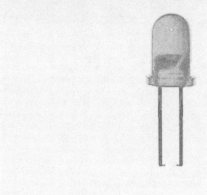

The NewBrite Lighting Company

Johnston W. "Jack" Campbell, a young inventor, has just created a brighter, more efficient LED lighting fixture with a superior design. Encouraged by his family and friends, he decides to turn his hobby of improving lights into a full-time business rather than sell his patents to a large lighting company.

Although Jack has savings that could be put into the venture, the amount is far short of the total capital necessary. He estimates that the total cost for the factory, machinery, and initial money required for product inventory to be approximately $2 million.

These "assets" (the factory, machinery, inventory, and remaining capital) would be used to produce the units and maintain the new business. The more fixtures Jack can produce using these assets, the more profitable the business would be.

Jack has calculated that if he could make and sell at least 100,000 units annually, it would cost about $20 to manufacture each unit. In addition, he estimates the sales and marketing expenses for each fixture to be roughly $10.

Since each new lighting fixture would be sold to his customers at the competitive price of $35, his profit (before paying federal, state, and local taxes) would be exactly $5 per unit.

ONE NEWBRITE UNIT		
	Selling Price	$35.00
Less	Cost of Manufacturing, Materials, Salaries, Labor, Other Direct Costs	$20.00
	"Gross Profit"	**$15.00**
Less	Advertising Expenses, Sales Commissions, Other Expenses	$10.00
	Profit Before Taxes	**$ 5.00**

Jack believes that his new enterprise would be beneficial in several ways. Thousands would enjoy using the lights, many people in his community would be earning a living by making and selling the fixtures, and the company would contribute to the welfare of his community, state, and country through the payment of taxes. If Jack could, indeed, manufacture and sell 100,000 light fixtures, this activity would no longer be a hobby; it would be a sizable business.

Now Jack faces a major problem. Where will he get almost $2 million for the factory, machinery, and working capital? He is unable to borrow such a large amount without collateral.

100,000 NEWBRITE UNITS		
Total Sales		**$3,500,000**
Less	Cost of Manufacturing, Materials, Salaries, Labor, Other Direct Costs	**$2,000,000**
	"Gross Profit"	**$1,500,000**
Less	Advertising Expenses, Sales Commissions, Other Expenses	**$1,000,000**
	Profit Before Taxes	**$ 500,000**
Less	Federal, State, Local Taxes	**$ 240,000**
Net Profit or "Earnings"		**$ 260,000**

Jack decides to find other investors, frequently called "venture capitalists," who might also see the potential for his idea and be willing to risk some capital to get the venture started.

To interest others, Jack must divide his new business into smaller pieces to give the investors some ownership. Jack realizes, too, that relinquishing some ownership means that he would no longer be entitled to all the profits. However, he is willing to do this to secure the help of others.

After exploring the advantages and disadvantages of the various legal forms of business, he decides to establish a "corporation." The principal reason for choosing a corporation rather than a partnership or any other form is *financial liability*. Jack learned that no matter which legal structure is used, creditors always have first claim on the assets if the business fails. However, a corporation, as a legal entity, limits the financial risk of the owners to the amount of capital invested. In other words, stockholders owning shares in a corporation are not liable for more than they invest.

Jack forms the corporation under the laws of his state, names it "The NewBrite Lighting Company," and selects a few individuals to act as the board of directors until the first annual meeting of stockholders. At that time, the board of directors will be formally elected by the stockholders.

The directors decide to "issue" 250,000 shares of stock of the 400,000 total possible shares authorized by the company's founding charter (when the company was organized, this number was determined to be the most appropriate for the company's needs). The 250,000 shares are divided between Jack and the venture capitalists in proportion to their agreed-upon ownership, determined by the contributions of each. Jack still owns a

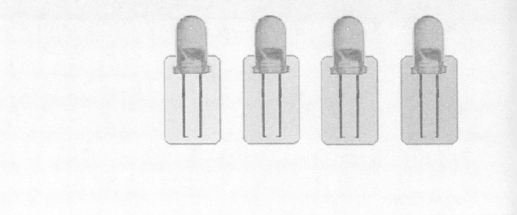

meaningful amount because of his importance to the company, his fixture patents, and his initial capital. Now it can be said that he and the venture capitalists are, indeed, "stockholders in common."

Each stockholder is a part owner of the company, with the extent of ownership depending upon the number of shares held (someone who holds 50 of the total 250,000 shares issued owns 1/5,000 of the entire company, whereas a person who owns 10,000 shares owns 1/25 of the company). The remaining 150,000 shares could be issued by the directors at a later date if the company finds it necessary. However, at the present time, the ownership of the company is divided into 250,000 pieces. In other words, there are 250,000 shares outstanding of 400,000 shares authorized.

The members of the board of directors, including Jack, are elected by all the stockholders to oversee the affairs of the company. Each share outstanding, according to the company's charter, is entitled to an equal vote in the annual election of the directors.

The NewBrite Lighting Company is now a "private" corporation owned solely by its small group of founders. However, later they might allow the public to participate. If so, stock would be sold to these new investors through the company's "Initial Public Offering" (or "IPO"). But, first, the company needs to establish a "track record" before "going public."

Most of the initial $2 million has been contributed in the form of "equity capital" by the venture capitalists. To raise the remaining capital, the company decides to go into debt. If the corporation were to borrow this money, expecting to repay it in a relatively short period of time, a bank could be approached for a loan. If it needs the money for a longer time period, a few years or more, the company might consider selling bonds.

The NewBrite Lighting Company, being a young, unproven business, would probably be unable to issue bonds backed solely by its word or good name (bonds of this type are called "debentures"). Lenders are usually reluctant to loan money to a new firm without security. Consequently, the company might be asked to put up some property as collateral (bonds of this type are often called "mortgage bonds").

Although The NewBrite Lighting Company would have to pay interest on the money it borrows, present holders would not have to give up any of their ownership, as Jack did when the new stock was issued for equity capital.

On the other hand, the lenders (the bondholders) do have first claim on the

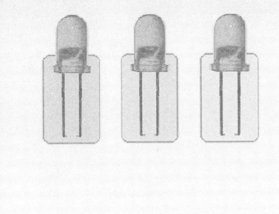

company's property if the company fails to repay the debt (such a failure is called a "default").

The Importance of Profits Why would Jack and his associates risk their personal savings to build a factory to manufacture the lights? They could have deposited their money into a bank account rather than investing in the new enterprise. The money would have been safe, and the bank would have paid them interest. Why would anybody be willing to risk money—let alone $2 million—to start The NewBrite Lighting Company? The answer is simple: *profits*.

Jack and his associates saw an opportunity to make a good profit on each fixture manufactured if the company met its business objectives. The stockholders also saw the possibility of increasing their profits in later years if more light fixtures could be manufactured and sold. In short, Jack and his associates figured that they could achieve a much better return on their money by investing in the new venture than by receiving interest from the bank.

Now time has passed; Jack's projections were accurate, and the venture has been successful. According to the statement of income in its recent Annual Report to stockholders, The NewBrite Lighting Company sold 100,000 units last year, resulting in a net profit, also called earnings, of $260,000—just as Jack had anticipated. The stockholders of the company are now entitled to divide this money among themselves. Since there are 250,000 shares outstanding, dividing the earnings of $260,000 equally means that, for every share held, a stockholder would be entitled to $1.04 ($260,000 divided by 250,000 shares). This calculation is called "earnings per share."

If, next year or the year after, the company increases its production and earns, for example, $500,000, the calculation would be $2.00 per share ($500,000 divided by 250,000 shares outstanding).

Each year, the directors of the company must decide what to do with the earnings. If the company were to distribute part or all of last year's $260,000 earnings to its stockholders, this cash payment would be called a "dividend." The size of the dividend declared by the directors each year would most likely be determined by the amount of profits available. However, regardless of the total amount declared, each share would receive an equal dividend. A stockholder owning a larger number of shares would, of course, receive a larger dividend check from the company.

The directors of The NewBrite Lighting Company might declare only a small dividend, or maybe none at all. If most or all of the $260,000 net profit is used to increase the size of the factory, hire more people, or add to the company's research program to design better fixtures, the stockholders might enjoy higher earnings and bigger dividends in later years without having to invest any additional capital. This growth process is called "internal financing."

At the board meeting, the directors declare a dividend of $0.26 per share, or a total of $65,000 (one-fourth of the earnings). In effect, the $0.26 per share dividend represents a 25% payout of the $1.04 earnings per share. The remaining $195,000 that is not paid out will be reinvested in the business. These "retained earnings" will also enhance the financial condition of the company, expressed by reports that are released to shareholders periodically.

FINANCIAL REPORTS

The NewBrite Lighting Company, like most companies, will regularly provide financial reports to its shareholders and other people who might be interested, including lenders and potential investors. Financial reports will be discussed in detail later.

However, for the purposes of this discussion, generally speaking, two important reports are always included in the company's year-end Annual Report to shareholders:

1. The *Balance Sheet* shows what the company owns, what it owes, and the value of the remaining amount, called "stockholders' equity" (i.e., the net worth of the stockholders' ownership), at the end of the year.

2. The *Statement of Income* indicates The NewBrite Lighting Company's sales, costs, and profits earned during the year.

Obviously the stockholders will be watching the company's earnings progress closely. As they examine the profitability of the business, they will be asking two basic questions:

1. How much profit was produced by each sales dollar?

2. How much profit was produced by each dollar of stockholders' equity?

A typical U.S. company today earns only 7%, or approximately 7 cents profit, after taxes, from each sales dollar. This profit also represents about 14 to 15% of each dollar of stockholders' equity.

> *There are two requirements for success on Wall Street. One you have to think correctly; and secondly, you have to think independently.*
>
> —BENJAMIN GRAHAM

Clearly, profits are important to everyone in our economic system. Without profits to spur individual initiative and encourage investment, factories would not be built, people would not be using better products, and many more workers would be looking for employment.

The Stock Price Once a company's stock has been issued and is outstanding, how is the market price determined? To answer this question, there is an old Wall Street saying: "A stock is worth only what someone is willing to pay." Although the saying is somewhat shortsighted, there is some truth to it. A stockholder wanting to sell shares in The NewBrite Lighting Company, for example, could sell them for no more than the price someone else would be willing to pay.

Stock is rarely sold back to the company, since the company's financial resources are tied up in the business. If the firm is prospering and the outlook is bright, there could be many eager investors ready to buy the shares at the asking price, or maybe higher. A large demand to buy could lead to higher bids for the stock. On the other hand, if the business outlook is unfavorable, anxious buyers might be scarce. Perhaps the asking price would have to be reduced to attract buyers. The price is determined simply by the supply/demand situation at that moment.

There are many factors to consider when estimating a value for the stock. However, an investor is most interested in the company's earnings outlook, dividend prospects, and financial condition. The stock price revolves around these three fundamental factors as investors compare the stock to all other investment opportunities.

Two Wall Street terms that are used frequently to appraise stocks are "price/earnings ratio" and "dividend yield." They are not as complicated as they sound.

PRICE/EARNINGS RATIO

The "P/E ratio," or "P/E multiple," as it is also called, simply describes the relationship between the stock price and the earnings per share. It is easily calculated by dividing the price of the stock by the earnings per share figure. For example, if the price of the stock happens to be $30 and the annual earnings per share is $1.50, the P/E ratio is 20 ($30 divided by $1.50 per share).

DIVIDEND YIELD

The "dividend yield," often just called the "yield," represents the annual percent return that the dividend provides to the in-

NBZ Declares First Dividend!

vestor. Yield is calculated by dividing the annual cash dividend per share by the price of the stock. If a company pays an annual cash dividend of $0.60 per share and the stock price happens to be $30, the annual return, or dividend yield, is 2.0% ($0.60 per share divided by $30).

Although a low P/E ratio is considered desirable, it is a common mistake to assume that a stock with a low P/E ratio is automatically more attractively priced than another stock that has a higher P/E.

A stock with a P/E ratio of 8.0 times earnings, for example, is not necessarily a better value than one with a P/E multiple of, say, 20.0 if the future profits of the first company grow much more slowly or maybe not at all, compared with the second company. A higher P/E ratio implies, but does not necessarily mean, greater investment risk.

The same applies to the dividend yield. A stock paying a dividend that yields a return of, say, 7.0% is not necessarily more attractive than another stock with a lower dividend yield of 2.0%, for example. How secure or safe is the dividend? What is the chance that the dividend will be increased in the future? How much of the company's profit is being paid out as a cash dividend to shareholders rather than being reinvested in the business for future growth? These and other related questions must be considered.

Of course, the P/E ratio and the dividend yield never remain constant. The P/E ratio increases and the dividend yield declines when the stock price moves higher.

Conversely, the P/E ratio declines and the dividend yield increases when the stock price declines. Moreover, the P/E ratio and dividend yield will also vary as the company's earnings and dividends increase or decrease.

Over a period of days, weeks, or months, the price of a stock can fluctuate widely depending upon the direction of the overall stock market or news items affecting the company or its industry. Sometimes a stock will rise or fall at random for no apparent reason. Any number of circumstances or events can influence the confidence of investors and the delicate supply/demand balance of buyers and sellers. However, to repeat, over an extended time period—a few years or longer—the stock price will most likely rise or fall in line with the company's earnings, dividends, and financial condition.

Accountability With the administration and ownership of corporations come many responsibilities and at different levels.

The executives of a company, appointed by the "Board of Directors," have obligations to the firm—to its customers, to its employees, and especially to the "shareholders," who are the owners. In effect, the board members, who are elected by the owners, are "caretakers" of the owners' property—primarily denoted by the Shareholders' Equity on the balance sheet and the good name that goes with it.

This is a democratic system. Shareholders who are unhappy with the management of the company or with its actions can vote for a change. The owners always have the final say. If they do nothing, they have no one else to blame but themselves.

Why Do People Buy Stocks? Where should that extra money go? Into the bank? Bonds? Real estate? Or art? Or will the stock market provide the best possible return? While each individual has a different investment objective, stocks are bought for one primary reason: to make money!

An individual can participate in the stock market in three ways.

INVESTING

This is generally the most successful approach because time can be used to ad-vantage. An investor buys shares to be a part owner of the company and to obtain at least an adequate return on the investment (enough to justify the risk and enable the investor to keep ahead of the rising cost of living). The investment time horizon is usually a few years or longer.

SPECULATING

The speculator is willing to assume great risk for a potentially great reward. Being a part owner is not important to the speculator, since the time horizon is to be no longer than necessary.

TRADING

A trader attempts to take advantage of small price changes and is less interested in the intrinsic value of the shares. Stock certificates are merely pieces of paper to be bought or sold for a profit within a short period of time—sometimes weeks, days, hours, or even minutes.

In Wall Street parlance, the term "trader" is often used synonymously with the term "speculator," which is okay. However, it is best not to confuse the terms "trader" and "investor." They are quite different.

Whether investing, speculating, or trading, a stockholder makes money by

MARKET TRENDS:
"In bear markets, they never let you out.
In bull markets, they never let you in."

receiving *dividends* from the company, usually paid quarterly, and/or by obtaining *capital appreciation* if the stock is sold at a price higher than the original price paid. Each day the stockholder can calculate the theoretical profit or loss on a piece of paper (hence, the popular terms "paper profit" and "paper loss"), but a profit or loss is not, as they say, "realized" until the stock is actually sold.

The stock market can be different things to different people. An older person, for example, might invest in stocks with the objective of obtaining a high, but fairly secure, dividend yield. A middle-aged couple might prefer buying only higher-quality stocks with an investment objective of growth and modest dividend returns. A young investor, on the other hand, could be less interested in a current dividend return. Instead, he or she might be willing to assume greater risk and buy shares of small, rapidly growing companies for maximum capital appreciation.

In any case, it is important for an investor to use only as much stock market capital as he or she can safely afford, to identify a realistic investment objective, and to know what to expect from each dollar invested.

Many years ago, a popular slogan was used by brokerage firms to attract the small investor. "Own a Share of America," they used to say. With as little as a few thousand dollars of extra cash, inexperienced investors would buy shares of companies without any knowledge of their business activities, management, or investment potential.

Perhaps this explains why the "small investor" is so underrated by Wall Street professionals. Many market observers figure that stock prices are too high once the "average Joe" is fully invested. Conversely, they believe that prices have finally reached attractive levels once the public, frightened by the possibility of further losses, has finished its selling in disgust. The small investor, as the stereotype goes, will then swear off this form of "gambling" and vow never to return to the Wall Street arena again.

For many nonprofessional investors, this is, indeed, a vicious cycle that will most likely continue for generations to come. But there have also been wise, patient individuals who have regularly invested modest amounts of money successfully over the years. Because they have taken the time to learn the basics of investing, they now have meaningful investment portfolios.

Stocks will always fluctuate, and there will always be uncertainties. But as long as

Stocks Soar

there are innovative men and women striving to profit from new ideas, to build new products, or to offer new services, company values will rise. The profit opportunity for a long-term investor is no less promising today than it was five years ago, ten years ago, or fifty years ago!

Common-Sense Investing Today's financial news is replete with dramatic headlines of every kind—big swings in stock prices, program trading, company failures, large corporate mergers, and so on. To those who do not follow the busy day-to-day happenings of Wall Street, it appears confusing and intimidating, and many would-be investors become discouraged. Actually, for most people, investing in the stock market can be a simple process. It can be educational, challenging, and, with a little patience, very rewarding.

Many investment ideas have been identified by combining common sense with personal knowledge and using each observation as a starting point. "This new restaurant chain has just opened. It has a better menu and faster service than any other of its kind. Can I buy shares and be a part owner of this business?"

Or, "This product is poorly constructed and inferior to its competition— I'd never want to own stock in this outfit."

Or, "Just a few weeks ago, I saw Jack Campbell demonstrate a new, more efficient lighting fixture. It adjusts color and brightness unlike any other. It is, indeed, superior in every way! Perhaps The NewBrite Lighting Company is a great investment idea!"

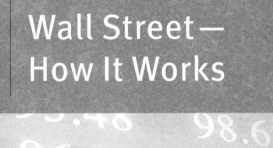

2 | Wall Street—How It Works

Introduction

Nearly 400 years ago, Wall Street was an insignificant dirt path. Since then, history has changed that dirt path into the financial center of the world. Yet Wall Street, perhaps the most famous of all streets, might also be the least understood.

Many people are frightened away by the apparent complexities of investing. They never learn of Wall Street's colorful history or its role in the American economy so the way stocks are bought and sold remains a mystery.

Wise investing is indeed a challenge that requires serious study, but a stock market transaction is much less complicated than buying or selling a car or a boat.

This chapter will provide a glimpse into the past and a description of Wall Street today, including the recent successor entities of NYSE Euronext and Nasdaq OMX.

Wall Street Defined Wall Street is a street in New York City, pointing straight from Franklin D. Roosevelt Drive near the East River to the old Trinity Church. But this is not the Wall Street people refer to when they ask, "How does Wall Street work?" or "What does Wall Street say?" That Wall Street is a marketplace.

Specifically, it is a marketplace where the merchants, agents, and customers of finance meet to buy and sell stocks and bonds. It is composed of all the individual marketplaces and the total community of interests that maintains them, and it is regulated closely by the Securities and Exchange Commission (SEC), created by the Securities Exchange Act of 1934.

Thus, the name Wall Street is a short, convenient reference to the exchanges where stocks are traded in a two-way auction process—the New York and American stock exchanges of NYSE Euronext, the nationwide network of broker/dealers that is known as the Nasdaq over-the-counter (OTC) system, and the regional stock exchanges. This reference also includes the brokerage firms and their employees, and a variety of investors, both individual and institutional.

Wall Street can also be defined with added precision according to its two major functions: to provide both a "primary" market and a "secondary" market. Through the primary market, corporations sell their stocks and bonds directly to the public, thereby obtaining the money that they need for expansion. The process of bringing a stock issue to the market for the first time is called "going public." The term "initial public offering" (IPO) is more commonly used today.

After a company has gone public, its shares are traded in the secondary market, which provides investors with an adequate number of bids to buy and offers to sell, as well as an opportunity to buy or sell shares at any time. In the secondary market, stock prices rise or fall according to supply and demand.

Each person using the Wall Street marketplace has one objective: to make money. The buyer is seeking to obtain an adequate investment return from a higher stock price, through dividend payments, or both. The seller, on the other hand, may already have a capital gain or loss and would like to free the money for investment elsewhere. These efforts, in total, form a fundamental economic process that creates new industries, new jobs, and a higher standard of living.

A Short History The dirt path took its name from a wall of brush and mud built alongside it shortly after New York was founded as a Dutch trading post in 1609. The wall, later improved with a wooden fence, was built to keep cows in and Indians out. Although little is known about the wall's success with cows, by 1626, Indians were certainly allowed to enter the early business community—at least long enough to sell Manhattan for $24 and some beads. The street, however, quickly became a center of commercial activity because it connected the docks serving the Hudson River trade at one end with the East River importing business at its other end.

Early merchants had many interests. They bought and sold commodities such as furs, molasses, and tobacco; they traded in currencies; they insured cargos, and speculated in land. They did not, however, formally invest in stocks and bonds, for even as late as George Washington's inauguration, Wall Street had no securities exchange. In fact, this country's first stock exchange was established in Philadelphia in 1790.

In 1789, the first Congress of the United States met in Federal Hall on Wall Street, the place where George Washington had been inaugurated as president earlier that year. Its first order of business was to authorize the issue of $80 million in government bonds to cover the cost of the war. Two years later, bank stocks were added to government bonds when Alexander Hamilton, then secretary of the treasury, established the nation's first bank, the Bank of the United States, and offered shares to the public.

Now there were securities to trade, but still no organized market existed on Wall Street. Investors, by word of mouth, indicated their interest in any available issue through Wall Street coffeehouses or by advertising in newspapers. As the list of securities grew with more bank stocks and newly formed insurance companies, a need for an organized market developed.

By early 1792, Wall Street was enjoying its first bull market. Several merchants, encouraged by the increased activity, kept a small inventory of securities on hand that they would sell over the counter like any other wares. Today's Nasdaq electronic over-the-counter system got its name from this early form of trading. Business was booming. Some days as many as 100 bank shares would be traded.

Wall Street businessmen began to schedule stock and bond auctions, as they did for commodities. Soon, several leading merchants organized a central auction at 22 Wall Street, where securities were traded daily at noon. Customers of the

newly formed "Stock Exchange Office," or their agents, left securities with the auctioneers, who received a commission for each stock or bond sold. A customer's agent, or broker, would also receive a commission for shares purchased.

With predictable ingenuity, some businessmen came to the auction only to listen. They noted the prices and, after the auction, would offer the same securities, but at reduced commission rates. Even auction members traded in this after-hours market.

On March 21, 1792, concerned Wall Street leaders met at Corre's Hotel to establish an improved auction market that would also better serve their own interests. On May 17, 1792, twenty-four men signed a document they called "The Buttonwood Agreement," in which they agreed to trade securities only among themselves, to maintain fixed commission rates, and to avoid other auctions. These men are considered to be the original members of the New York Stock Exchange.

For a while, the new brokers' union met under the aging buttonwood tree that faced 68 Wall Street, but they soon moved indoors when the Tontine Coffee House at the northwest corner of Wall and William Streets was completed in 1793. They prospered and moved to larger quarters in what is now 40 Wall Street. On March 8,

1817, the members adopted a formal constitution, creating the New York Stock and Exchange Board. Every morning a list of all the stocks to be auctioned was read to the assembled board members, who would then make bids and offers while seated. Only members were allowed to trade, and the privilege of sitting at the auctions cost $25. The fee was later raised to $400. To this day, a member of the NYSE is said to own a "seat," although he or she is never seated while trading.

The board moved several times until it took space in a building located at the present NYSE site in 1863, the year the New York Stock Exchange became the official name (the building occupied by the NYSE

Tontine Coffee House, 1793

today was completed in 1903). About the time the Civil War was drawing to a close, NYSE members were prohibited from trading at the "Evening Exchange," which led to an adjustment in the landscape.

Brokers who were not able to afford a seat on the board (often affectionately referred to as the "Big Board"), or who were simply refused membership, often found it difficult to make a living. In poor markets, many went bankrupt. Others drifted away to take odd jobs elsewhere, only to return for another try when business improved.

In the mid-nineteenth century, Wall Street was throbbing with activity. Gold had been discovered in California, and the country turned its attention to the West. Mining stocks and railroad shares were especially popular. Many issues that the board considered too speculative were eagerly traded by nonmembers. Few could afford office space, so they traded in the street. By the late 1870s, the corner of William and Beaver Streets filled daily with brokers shouting out orders to buy and sell. They were called "curbstone brokers," and their market was known as "The Curb."

In the early 1890s, when The Curb was moved to Broad Street for more room, many brokers used offices in the nearby Mills Building. There, telephone clerks took orders and shouted them to the bro-kers below. But with several hundred brokers being called, more or less simultaneously, shouting soon proved futile. A system of hand signaling was developed (parts of which are still used today) to convey price and volume information to the waiting brokers. Clerks would lean out the windows of the Mills Building or balance precariously on an outside ledge, working their fingers furiously. The brokers below often wore brightly colored or otherwise distinctive clothing, allowing the clerks to spot them in the crowd. Although it looked like pandemonium, the brokers knew that certain stocks were traded at specific landmarks, usually lampposts. Action was brisk in any kind of weather.

In 1908, Emanuel S. Mendels, Jr., a leading curbstone broker, organized the Curb Market Agency, which developed trading rules but had little enforcement power. In 1911, Mendels and his advisors drew up a constitution and formed the New York Curb Market Association.

One of the most colorful spectacles in American business ended on the morning of June 27, 1921. Edward McCormick, the Curb Market's chairman, led the curbstone brokers in a march up Wall Street to their newly completed building on Trinity Place behind Trinity Church. They sang "The Star Spangled Banner" and went in-

side to begin their first session on the new trading floor. Inside, each trading post was marked by a lamppost that, interestingly, resembled those left behind on the street.

In 1953, the New York Curb Exchange, as it was called after 1928, was named the American Stock Exchange. Now in full circle, after 143 years, the Amex was acquired by NYSE Euronext in 2008.

The Primary Market The investment process begins with a primary market. Its focal point is the "investment banker," an important member of the Wall Street community who specializes in raising the capital that businesses require for long-term growth. He guides a company into the public marketplace and generally helps the company in its dealings with Wall Street.

Assume, for example, that a company has enjoyed several years of business success and is now ready to expand. The firm's management has determined that several million dollars will be needed for plant expansion. An investment banker is contacted to explore financing alternatives, including the possibility of going public.

Before recommending a specific method of financing, the investment banker must consider several factors, such as general economic conditions, the Wall Street market environment, and the

company's particular circumstances, including its financial condition, earnings history within its industry, and business prospects. These and other factors would also be used to establish an offering price.

In this case, a public offering of common stock would be appropriate, as opposed to a form of debt obligation.

The investment banker agrees to "underwrite" the issue by buying all the shares for resale at a preestablished price per share. If the issue were larger, the risk could be spread by inviting other investment bankers to join in an underwriting group or "syndicate." At the time of sale, the syndicate usually invites other security dealers to join it in a selling group, and together they sell the new shares to the public at a set price. Before a new issue can be sold, however, the company must comply with the full disclosure requirements of the Securities and Exchange Commission (SEC).

In a registration statement filed with the SEC, the company lists the essential facts of its financial condition and operations. These facts must also be printed in a "red herring," later called a "prospectus," that members of the selling group must give to every buyer or potential buyer.

The company pays all underwriting costs, allowing the buyer to purchase the

stock free of any commissions or other charges. The price is temporarily supported by the investment banker—in general, this is the only time a stock price is ever fixed. After that, the shares are traded as usual, according to supply and demand, in the secondary market.

The Secondary Market Just as a corporate treasurer works closely with an investment banker in the primary market, the main contact for most investors in the secondary market is the "registered representative," still periodically referred to as the "stockbroker" or just the "broker."

The formal title indicates that this person is "registered" with the SEC and "represents" the firm's brokers and dealers who actually execute a customer's order on the trading floor of an exchange or in the Nasdaq market. This "rep" does not buy from or sell to the customer, but rather acts on the customer's behalf as an agent.

Both the registered representative and the brokerage firm are compensated by a "brokerage commission," charged each time a stock is bought or sold.

In the Nasdaq OTC market, a customer may pay either a "markup" or "markdown" or a commission, depending on how the order is handled. A markup is an amount added to the purchase price, while a markdown is subtracted from the sales price by the broker/dealer. The actual markup or markdown must conform to the Financial Industry Regulatory Authority (FINRA) regulations limiting the amount that may be charged. FINRA regulates the securities industry under the supervision of the Securities and Exchange Commission.

Prior to 1975, an investor could expect to pay a predetermined minimum commission based on the number of shares involved and the price for any stock listed on an exchange. This system of minimum fixed commission rates was abandoned on May 1 ("May Day") of that year, ending a practice that began when the first members of the NYSE agreed to charge fixed rates in 1792. At the SEC's direction, commission charges on all orders were made fully negotiable. Thus, it is now possible for an investor, who previously had no choice but to pay a fixed commission under a set schedule, to bargain with brokers for the lowest commission rate, although stiff competition tends to keep the rates low.

Of course, major financial institutions, such as pension funds, banks, insurance companies, and mutual funds, have the greatest bargaining power because of the large amounts of stock in each order that they place. If the transaction is for 10,000

The New York Stock Exchange
in session just after the Civil
War and 100 years later

shares or more, it is referred to as a "block" trade and has an even lower per-share transaction cost. Orders of this type account for the majority of activity on the exchanges today.

In addition to varying commission rates, brokerage firms, also called "brokerage houses," differ by the types of services they offer. The main office of a large NYSE member firm, for example, usually includes trading departments for exchange-listed stocks, OTC stocks, and various types of bonds; a research department where securities analysts appraise the investment potential of securities; an underwriting department for new issues; a corporate finance department for investment banking; and appropriate record-keeping departments for account maintenance and securities safekeeping. Other firms may offer only a few of these services, and still others specialize strictly in order execution.

All firms must, however, conform to extensive SEC requirements as well as additional exchange or OTC rules. Cash and securities held in custody are usually insured by the Security Investors Protection Corporation (SIPC, a federal corporation) and by other insurance companies.

Finally, brokerage firms can be differentiated on the basis of their exchange memberships and by the source of their commission income. Only licensed members are allowed to execute orders on the exchange trading floor. In days past, to become a member, a brokerage firm had to buy a "seat," an expression that recalls the days when brokers paid $25 for the privilege of being seated during the stock auctions.

The number of NYSE members who own seats (1,366) has remained unchanged since 1953. Since there is a limited number available, seats, like stocks, have had their own auction market. By 1929, the price of a seat had risen to $625,000, but it then dropped to $17,000 in 1942. Recently, the price reached about $4 million (although, today, this trading privilege is referred to as an "annual trading license").

Firms without licenses are called "nonmember" firms. Their orders for exchange-listed stocks must be processed through a member firm or be executed in the so-called Third Market (buying and selling exchange-listed stocks in the OTC market).

A brokerage firm doing most of its commission business with individual investors is referred to as a "retail house," while a firm emphasizing institutional business by servicing mutual funds, pension funds, insurance companies, and banks is called an "institutional house." This distinction is less clear today than it was years ago because of crossover functions and similar capabilities via the Internet.

Just as brokerage firms differ, the markets are also different in terms of both listing requirements and methods of execution.

When a stock is "listed" on an exchange, it means that the stock has been accepted for trading there. The term recalls the "list" of stocks that was read to the assembled brokers at the daily auctions more than a century ago. Before its stock can be listed, a company must meet certain minimum listing requirements.

Each exchange has its own minimums. For a company to be among the 4,000 listed on the NYSE, for example, it must have shareholders' equity of $60 million; pretax earnings of at least $10 million over three years; a total of 1.1 million outstanding shares; and 400 round-lot shareholders.

The Nasdaq market requires similar, but less stringent, requirements before a company is accepted for quotation in the computerized National Association of Security Dealers Automatic Quotation System (abbreviated Nasdaq and pronounced "naz-dak"). In general, the company must have $30 million of equity and $18 million of market value with an operating history of two years, and at least 400 round-lot share-holders. On both Nasdaq and the NYSE, a company can be "delisted" if it falls below certain minimum requirements.

Years ago, the net effect of the various listing requirements was to attract the oldest, largest, and best-known companies to the New York Stock Exchange; smaller and younger companies to the Amex; and the newest, least-seasoned companies to the Nasdaq market. This is not as true currently. Many large, well-known firms, such as Microsoft, Apple Computer, Intel, and others, have not sought NYSE listing by their own choice.

Today, NYSE Euronext brings together six cash equities exchanges in five countries and six derivatives exchanges. It is a world leader in equities, bonds, and derivatives.

Moreover, the Amex is now part of NYSE Euronext. And a Nasdaq listing is no longer regarded as just a low-priced "penny stock" selling for less than $1. Also, today, many of the most active issues can be traded on alternative exchanges, still often referred to as the "third market."

A company can be listed on more than one exchange. Dual listings are common on the regional exchanges, where transactions in dually traded issues are usually based on current NYSE prices. Many companies listed on regional exchanges

The old Edison "dome" stock ticker is now a relic of the past.

are local businesses in that area, but the regional exchanges are being absorbed into the NYSE and Nasdaq systems. Moreover, today's markets are global in scope, and many companies are listed on overseas exchanges, just as a great many foreign companies are listed here.

Only a few regional equity exchanges remain—the Boston, Chicago, and National exchanges—but it can still be said that they improve the liquidity of the marketplace. Of course, all are registered with the SEC.

Also, the various markets (the Nasdaq, Boston, Chicago, and National exchanges) are all linked with NYSE Euronext. The order execution methods in the different markets are still different, although they are much more similar today than at any time in the past as a result of computers, automation, and the electronic devices that are now being used.

How the System Works After opening an account with a brokerage firm, a process similar in many ways to opening a bank account, the investor is free to buy or sell stocks through any exchange, including the Nasdaq (OTC) market.

The following example of a NYSE floor transaction represents the traditional way in which stocks have been bought and sold for well over a century. Actually, the system has been altered and enhanced markedly in recent years. But visualize how the inherent forces of supply and demand influenced the price with this "open outcry" system.

A shopkeeper in Atlanta, Georgia, goes to his local brokerage firm, one of 200 NYSE members, and places a "market order" to buy 100 shares (the standard unit of trading, commonly called a "round lot") of the XYZ Company. A market order is an order to be executed as soon as possible at the best price available. At about the same time, a teacher in Denver, Colorado, places a market order with her local broker, also a member firm, to sell 100 shares of XYZ stock. The orders are quickly sent to the trading departments of the respective firms, then transmitted directly to the floor of the NYSE. The firms' "floor brokers," employees located on the trading floor, receive the orders and proceed immediately to the "trading post" where XYZ is being bought and sold. Each listed stock is traded at one of 11 posts, and each stock has a "specialist" assigned to it. The specialist's primary function is "to ensure a fair and orderly market" in each assigned stock by buying and selling for his own account in the absence of competing bids and offers. (For years, there were roughly 450 specialists, each responsible for

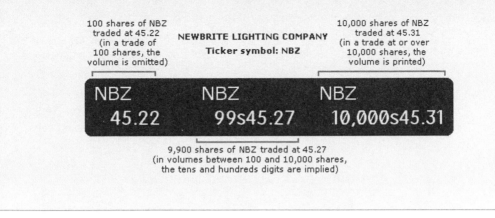

100 shares of NBZ traded at 45.22 (in a trade of 100 shares, the volume is omitted)

NEWBRITE LIGHTING COMPANY
Ticker symbol: NBZ

10,000 shares of NBZ traded at 45.31 (in a trade at or over 10,000 shares, the volume is printed)

NBZ 45.22   NBZ 99s45.27   NBZ 10,000s45.31

9,900 shares of NBZ traded at 45.27 (in volumes between 100 and 10,000 shares, the tens and hundreds digits are implied)

about six stocks, and they were employed by seven firms. Some big stocks had specialists devoted solely to them.)

At the post, the brokers enter the "crowd," a group of two or more brokers who also have orders for XYZ. "How's XYZ?" asks the broker representing the Atlanta shopkeeper. "Thirty and forty to thirty-fifty," someone—usually the specialist—responds. This is the current "bid and asked" quotation. This means that $30.40 is the best bid, the most anyone in the crowd is then willing to pay; and $30.50 is the best offer, the lowest price at which anyone will sell. The difference between the two is called the "spread."

The shopkeeper's broker would try to get a better price than the offer, by saying, "30 and 45 for one hundred." If there is no response, the broker could raise the bid, but would also risk losing the best asking price. Perhaps at $30.45, the teacher's broker hollers, "Sold," feeling that it is the best price he can expect at that time. The transaction is completed, and the customers can be notified by their registered representatives within a minute after the order was first sent to the floor. The company's stock symbol, usually an abbreviation of the name, and the execution price of the trade are both printed immediately on the consolidated ticker tape (see the example given

here), which is displayed electronically in brokerage offices throughout the country.

If there had been no offers to sell stock when the floor broker representing the Atlanta customer arrived at the post, the specialist would have filled the order himself by selling stock from his own account. Similarly, if the broker had a sell order and there were no bids, the specialist would have bought the stock for his own account.

The specialist's bid and asked quotation reflects the orders in his "specialist's book," a notebook containing special types of customer orders for each assigned stock. Orders in the specialist's book cannot be executed immediately because they are "away from the market," that is, they are above or below the price at which the stock is currently being traded. The specialist, or his specialist firm, must always have enough capital on hand to buy 2,000 shares of any stock he has been assigned. In discharging his responsibility to preserve a fair and orderly market, the specialist attempts to keep the spread narrow and to minimize any sharp price fluctuation, either up or down.

When the specialist trades for his own account, he is said to be acting as a "dealer," much like the dealers in the OTC market. A dealer acts as a principal in a transaction, buying stock from and sell-

The high-tech, high-touch
market model of the NYSE
combines the expertise of
Direct Market Maker (DMM)
with the automated fast
executions of electronic
trading.

ing it to a customer. A broker, on the other hand, only represents a customer as a middleman or agent.

In early 2001, as an SEC directive, the exchanges ended the quaint, Spanish-derived price system of quoting stocks in "eighths" of a dollar. Since then, stocks have been quoted in decimals (pennies), with narrower spreads as a result.

Moreover, this traditional system utilizing the specialist has changed considerably in recent years. In 1976, the New York Stock Exchange introduced the "Designated Order Turnaround" ("DOT") system. DOT, later improved and renamed "SuperDOT," is an electronic order-routing system that allows member firms to transmit orders directly to the specialist post. Thus, member firms' market and day limit orders up to specified sizes are transmitted by SuperDOT. With the narrow spreads that are common today, orders can be filled almost immediately and at prices that are in line with customer expectations. Presently, including SuperDOT, the NYSE can handle 10 billion shares daily.

Before the opening bell to begin the day's trading, SuperDOT continuously pairs buy and sell orders and presents the preopening balance to the specialist, who then uses the imbalance to determine the opening price. In addition, the specialist's

book is no longer a pencil and pad, but a touch-screen electronic display book. The book is activated simply by touching the display screen at the appropriate places.

The specialist acts as a dealer when an investor wants to buy or sell from 1 to 99 shares, called an "odd lot." On the NYSE, an odd-lot order with a price limit is processed by computer and is executed automatically at the next round-lot price struck at the post. The specialist receives periodic reports indicating how many odd-lot shares have been added to or subtracted from his inventory. For this service, the specialist charges the customer a small fraction (typically 1/8 point) per share, traditionally called the "odd-lot differential." Odd-lot orders without a price limit are immediately executed at the NYSE bid or offer price without any odd-lot differential.

(Note: Today, most orders on the NYSE take place between customers without any capital participation by the market maker. Also, nearly all trades take place at less than $0.05 from the last sale.)

If the Atlanta shopkeeper wanted to buy 100 shares of an OTC stock rather than an exchange-listed stock, the order would have been sent to the firm's OTC desk.

The individuals at this desk are referred to as "broker/dealers" because they

can act in either capacity, depending on the circumstances.

The shopkeeper's order may be filled directly from the firm's inventory if the broker/dealer "makes a market" in the stock. In this case, the broker/dealer acts as a principal, or, in other words, as a dealer. As a market maker, the dealer maintains an inventory of the stock, must be prepared to buy or sell at least 100 shares at any time, and must announce bid and asked prices continuously. The OTC trading department, through the registered representative, quotes a single "net price" to the customer, which includes the dealer's markup. The customer is free to negotiate for a lower price. The order is completed as soon as the customer and the dealer agree.

If the broker/dealer does not make a market in the stock and the stock is quoted in the Nasdaq System, the broker/dealer interrogates the system's computer by typing the trading symbol of the stock onto a keyboard attached to an electronic display screen. The names and the bid and asked quotations of all market makers in that stock instantly appear on the screen.

The broker/dealer then calls the market maker offering the best quote, negotiates a price, and buys the stock for the customer. The broker/dealer has acted as a broker or agent and charges the customer a commission.

If the stock is not among the almost 4,000 stocks currently being quoted on Nasdaq, the broker/dealer will have to negotiate a price with one of the market makers listed in the "pink sheets," a daily list of all OTC market makers and their quotes published by the National Quotation Service. The process takes longer but is otherwise identical to a Nasdaq System trade.

The OTC market is the largest securities market in the country. Although it does not meet in any one central place, OTC broker/dealers are connected by the computer of the Nasdaq System and by telephone. Traded in the OTC market are almost all federal, state, municipal, and corporate bonds; almost all new issues; most mutual funds; several foreign stocks; and nearly 30,000 domestic stocks. The aggregate dollar volume of the OTC market exceeds the dollar volume executed on all stock exchanges combined.

NYSE ARCA

NYSE Euronext operates the completely electronic exchange NYSE ARCA, which was acquired with the 2006 acquisition of

Archipelago. Currently, this platform is best known for trading "exchange-traded funds" (ETFs)—e.g., the S&P 500 with the symbol SPY—even though equities trade there as well, especially Nasdaq issues.

THE NYSE "NEXT GEN" MARKET

One key component of the NYSE "Next Generation" Market at the New York Stock Exchange is the "Broker Booth Support System" ("BBSS"). This order-management system enables member firms to interface quickly with the trading floor via SuperDOT.

The NYSE "e-Broker" is a wireless, hand-held tool that enables floor brokers to submit and manage quotes and orders, as well as to track order executions.

NYSE Euronext also provides a direct electronic connection with NYSE member firms to speed the execution of customer orders.

DESIGNATED MARKET MAKERS

The traditional specialist firm has been replaced by what NYSE Euronext calls the "designated market maker" ("DMM"). No longer will these specialists have an exclusive right to make a market in any assigned security. Now, DMMs can com-

pete with other exchange members for trades, rather than just assist them.

In short, to compensate for their greater obligations, DMMs have greater incentives.

The NYSE has been trying to retain the "human element" on the floor, but in this electronic age in recent years, this has been somewhat difficult to do.

PROGRAM TRADING

Computerized "program trading" has increased in recent years and now represents approximately one-third of NYSE daily volume. Program trades, which typically involve a computer-directed trade of a basket of stocks that is immediately and automatically executed, have been a controversial subject. In general, the net result of this activity tends to increase the volatility of stocks overall, but also adds to their liquidity. And there are some controls.

CIRCUIT BREAKERS

The stock market crash in 1987 was a rude awakening for Wall Street. Considering the numerous economic "safety nets" that had been installed since the Depression years, many people believed that a crash similar in magnitude to 1929

would be an unlikely event. This was proved false in October 1987.

So, following the example of the Tokyo exchange with its trading suspensions, a series of rules was adopted to allow the markets to "take a breath" during a highly emotional period. Later, in the "Manias, Fads, and Panics" chapter, it will be shown how market psychology and momentary fear can almost feed on themselves to create chaotic conditions.

In response to this need, "circuit breakers" were set based on the price levels of the Dow Jones Industrial Average, and these rules will change with higher or lower prices.

Applied under extreme conditions, these circuit breakers can halt all trading when the Dow Industrial Average declines by 10%, 20%, or 30%.

Under circuit-breaker limits, trading can be halted for one hour if the Dow declines 10% before 2 p.m. (the halt is 30 minutes if the decline occurs between 2 and 2:30 p.m., and there is no trading halt after 2:30).

If the Dow declines by 20% before 1 p.m., trading will be halted for two hours (the halt is one hour if the decline occurs between 1 and 2:00 p.m. and is for the remainder of the day if the drop occurs after 2 p.m.).

A 30% drop will halt trading for the day, regardless of when it occurs.

Market historians argue as to what extent these rules might have altered the course of history in either 1929 or 1987. Clearly, these rules will never change marketplace emotions, but they should prove to be a calming factor, nonetheless. Time will tell.

Who Buys Stock? Common stock ownership is broadly separated into two categories, individual and institutional, even though institutions invest on behalf of individuals through pensions, trusts, profit-sharing plans, and mutual funds.

In 1952, an early industry census revealed that stock ownership was under 10 million. Ten years later, a similar census indicated the number of shareowners to be close to 17 million.

In recent years, investor surveys have placed the number of individuals who own shares, either directly or indirectly, at approximately 84 million, divided almost equally between men and women.

Although stockholder characteristics vary widely, it is generally believed that the average shareowner has a median age in the mid- to upper forties and that about two-thirds have had education beyond high school.

To the surprise of some, according to the latest surveys, not more than 20% of all shareowners have a family income above $100,000. Also, a majority of shareholders have investments in IRA-type accounts, 401(k)s, or Keogh accounts.

Today, the Internet probably accounts for more than half of all retail trades, and, of course, this activity has been increasing steadily. Yet the number of very active traders, including day traders, is still relatively small.

During the past several decades, institutional investors have steadily replaced individuals as the most important factor in the stock market. It is estimated that, overall, U.S. institutional investors now own about $7 trillion, or nearly 60%, of outstanding equities. The holdings of foreign institutions, private funds, and certain other funds are also considerable.

The largest institutional investors, judged by the market value of their holdings, have been uninsured pension funds, investment firms, nonprofit institutions, insurance companies, common trust funds, and mutual savings banks.

One of the most important developments in recent years has been the introduction of exchange-traded funds (ETFs), pioneered by the American Stock Exchange, now part of NYSE Euronext. These relatively new investment instruments, explained in a later chapter, have become very popular; they currently number about 800, and they represent an increasing portion of overall daily volume.

The Future In the years ahead, as we move further into the twenty-first century, a global market network will be operating that will encompass all of the world's major stock markets, including those in the United States, Europe, Japan, and other countries.

The technological developments of the past forty years and the organizational efforts that began as far back as the 1970s are continuing to this day. The markets will be even more efficient, with minimal duplication, and worldwide orders to buy and sell will be routed and filled on a timely basis. Indeed, investors will eventually be able to locate the best bid and asked prices, no matter where they might be or whatever the time of the day.

This process of change is continuing and should reach fruition within the next ten years. In due course, Wall Street may once again hear the words spoken in 1921 by Edward McCormick. Just before the curbstone brokers went inside for the first time, he said: "The die is cast. The old order is gone forever."

3 | Analyzing Your Company

Introduction

The company with the best-performing stock over the long run—ten or twenty years—almost always has a superior record of earnings, dividends, and improved financial condition. An individual investor will find it easier to identify such a company once the rudiments of security analysis are mastered.

The unfortunate situations that investors have encountered in recent years, including inadequate transparency and creative accounting, have placed a dark cloud over all fundamental analysis. This is discouraging to those who take this business seriously because activities of this type do not represent typical corporate culture or behavior.

This chapter will show how to read corporate financial statements and will highlight the most important analytical concepts used by successful long-term investors.

VALUE STOCKS:
"Growth stocks without the growth"

Getting to Know the Company "What is this company's business?" is the first question an investor should ask. The president of a diversified company might answer, "Oh, we're in business to make money" or "We make motorbikes, golf clubs, tennis balls, and football helmets." Yet, like a ship, a company must have a charted course to follow. An answer such as: "We manufacture and sell high-quality sporting goods to the leisure-time market" would indicate that the company has a corporate strategy. Before anything else, an investor should know the corporate purpose and have confidence that management also knows it.

There are various ways an investor can become acquainted with a company. First, and most important, is through the firm's literature: past annual reports and 10-Ks, quarterly interim reports, management speeches, and press releases. This information can be obtained free of charge by visiting the company's Internet Web site or by writing to the company's secretary. The firm's address and/or phone number can be found online, or it can be obtained from sources in the public library or from representatives of most brokerage offices.

Research reports written by securities analysts at brokerage firms provide an-other way to learn about a company. The typical brokerage report ordinarily focuses on an analysis of a company's current earnings prospects but rarely provides the necessary insight into the industry, the competition, or the company's management. However, these reports can help an investor better understand current operations and problems. The investor should read the reports, extract factual information, and avoid unsubstantiated assumptions. The investment decision should be made by the investor alone after studying all the information available.

The development of the Internet in recent years has created an excellent way for prospective shareholders to become "tuned in" to the company's current operations and its prospects. Immediately after an earnings release, many companies sponsor an online conference call. Usually only analysts and current stockholders are permitted to ask questions during this management presentation, but the details and information, as well as officer candor, can be very valuable in most cases.

A fourth way to learn about a corporation is by attending its annual meeting when it is convenient. Depending on company policy, it may be possible to attend without being a stockholder—that is, as a "guest." A phone call or letter to the company's secretary will answer this question.

Annual meetings can be very interesting because the corporate executives want to make a favorable impression. At the same time, investors are trying to look beneath the executives' smooth or clumsy presentations for any indication of management talent or weakness. Company presentations become increasingly valuable as the investor gains experience through exposure to different companies.

The annual meeting is usually held at or near the corporate headquarters, although many large, widely held firms accommodate stockholders by holding the meeting in a different city each year.

In most cases, the annual meeting is scheduled for the same day every year according to the company's bylaws. The date, time, and location of the annual meeting normally can be found on the inside cover of the annual report or in a variety of other places, including online or at the public library.

One major order of business at the annual meeting is the election of the company's directors by the stockholders. A few weeks prior to the meeting, the company will mail a "proxy statement" to each stockholder. The stockholder reviews the proxy material, decides how to vote on the election of directors and other proposals, fills out the proxy, and returns it to the company to be counted like any other election ballot.

The business portion of the meeting usually takes only a few minutes, but it can continue for an hour or so, depending on the length of the stockholders' question-and-answer period. Sometimes the annual meeting also includes a tour of the company's offices or factories. In fact, several companies, such as Berkshire Hathaway, are well known for holding stimulating annual meetings. If it is possible to attend, an investor will find a well-organized annual meeting an interesting and worthwhile experience.

Financial Statements The annual report, usually published a few months after the company's fiscal year ends, is the best place to begin the analysis of a company. The typical report contains the President's Letter to Stockholders, which outlines the events of the past year and the present status of the corporation. The body of the report explains the company's business operations in greater detail. Located in the back is the financial section, the most revealing part of any annual report. This section contains three important financial statements:

- The Income Statement
- The Balance Sheet
- The Statement of Cash Flows

The "Income Statement" presents the company's business results for the year. It shows, in dollar terms, the company's sales, costs, and earnings (profits) over the past twelve months compared with the preceding twelve-month period.

The "Balance Sheet" presents the company's financial condition at the end of the year by listing (1) what the company owns (assets such as cash, inventory, factories, equipment, and so on), (2) what the company owes (liabilities such as short-term bank borrowings and long-term debt), and (3) the "stockholders' equity," which is the difference between the assets and the liabilities. Said another way, on every Balance Sheet, the *Total Assets* figure is always equal to the sum of the company's *Total Liabilities* figure and the *Stockholders' Equity* figure.

The "Statement of Cash Flows," also called the "Sources and Applications of Funds Statement," is best described as a bridge between the Income Statement and the Balance Sheet. It explains exactly how the company's financial position changed during the year. In short, the Statement of Cash Flows outlines how the company financed its growth during the year (i.e., the "sources," where the money came from, and the "applications," where the money went).

All three statements are accompanied by a series of footnotes that explain the figures in greater detail. Sometimes these footnotes contain significant information and are worth reading. In addition, there is a table showing several years of financial history. This table generally includes Income Statement data, Balance Sheet data, and supplementary statistics that can further help an investor understand the company and its background.

Finally, the financial section contains a report submitted by an independent accounting expert indicating that the statements were prepared in accordance with generally accepted accounting principles and that the financial statements present, fairly and on a consistent basis, the financial position of the company for the years noted. The investor should read it to check for any "qualifications" that the auditors considered important and be wary of the company if its financial reports have any such qualifications.

To better understand the example to follow, an investor should be familiar with several terms.

ON THE INCOME STATEMENT

The term "sales" is used to describe the total dollar amount received for the products sold to customers during the period. "Cost of products sold," sometimes called "cost of sales," represents the cost of manufacturing these products. These costs include raw materials, wages, salaries, fuel, and other direct production costs. The difference between the company's sales and its cost of sales is called "gross profit." "Selling, general, and administrative expenses" include officers' salaries, sales commissions, advertising spending, research and development expenses, and other general expenses. The term "depreciation" is often used to describe the gradual decline in the value of assets such as buildings and equipment. Depreciation is not a cash outlay. Nevertheless, it is another cost of operating the business because of the reduction in the service life of the property. Assets of this type are typically in use for more than a year, and, therefore, an estimated portion of their original cost is recognized as they are "used up." The "operating profit" is calculated by deducting cost of sales, SG&A expenses, and depreciation from the sales figure.

Once all costs and expenses have been deducted from all revenues, the profit that a company achieves before paying taxes (federal, state, local, and foreign) is called "profit before taxes." The profit that a company earns after deducting taxes is referred to as "net earnings."

ON THE BALANCE SHEET

The Balance Sheet is divided into three major parts: "assets," or what the company owns; "liabilities," or what the company owes; and the difference between them, known as "stockholders' equity." The company's assets and liabilities can be either "current" or "long-term." "Current" refers to any time within twelve months from the date of the Balance Sheet, whereas "long-term" refers to any time period beyond twelve months.

"Current assets" are assets that are expected to be converted to cash within twelve months. "Current liabilities" are obligations that will be paid within twelve months. Among the important items included in current assets besides cash and securities are "accounts receivable" (money owed to the company, primarily by its customers) and "inventories" (raw materials, work in process, supplies, and finished products ready to be sold).

"Current liabilities" include an "accounts payable" figure that represents money that the company owes to raw material suppliers and others in the normal course of business. A "notes payable" figure in the current liabilities section indicates that the company is obligated to pay a debt, often to a bank or a supplier, within twelve months.

One important term that is used frequently is "working capital," which is simply the excess of current assets over current liabilities. In the example to follow, the working capital of the XYZ Company is $630 ($946 current assets less $316 current liabilities). Sometimes current liabilities exceed current assets, although this rarely happens with good companies. When this does occur, it is said that the company has "negative working capital."

"Long-term debt" is debt that the company will have to repay sometime beyond twelve months after the date of the Balance Sheet. The footnotes to the annual report explain in greater detail the types of obligations and exactly when the debt is due for repayment. The company's long-term debt could be in the form of bank debt, mortgage bonds, debenture bonds (bonds issued solely on the credit of the company, rather than being secured by property), or other types of obligations.

"Stockholders' equity," sometimes called "net worth," represents the value of the stockholders' ownership in the company, and it is defined as total assets less total liabilities. Included in the stockholders' equity figure would be the amount of money that has been invested directly into the company and all earnings reinvested in the business up to the date of the Balance Sheet.

When a stockholder calculates the amount of equity behind each share, the result is called "book value." This number is determined by dividing the amount of stockholders' equity by the average number of shares outstanding.

In addition to common stock, many companies have "preferred stock" outstanding. As the name implies, these shares have preference over common stock in the payment of dividends and in the event of corporate liquidation. If preferred stock is outstanding, any amount to which preferred shareholders are entitled must first be deducted from total stockholders' equity before calculating the book value of the common.

Frequently an investor will see the term "par value" applied to common stock. Par value is an arbitrary amount that is placed on the stock certificate; it has no relation to the market price of the stock or its liquidation value. The term is used principally for bookkeeping purposes. To avoid confusion, many companies simply place an arbitrary stated value on the stock and call it "no-par value stock."

When reading financial statements, you can expect to see three additional terms used often:

The first is "Generally Accepted Accounting Principles," or "GAAP," which refers to a list of reporting standards that have been established by the Financial Accounting Standards Board, an oversight group for the accounting profession.

Another is "pro forma." This term refers to financial statements that do not include items that are deemed nonrecurring.

A third popular term is "restructuring," which refers to the reorganization of a company's operations or organization. In most cases, it is a nonrecurring charge.

The Basics of Analysis How the three financial statements are constructed, how they relate to one another, and how the company's fundamental story is told can be seen in the example of the XYZ Company, a hypothetical, well-managed firm, on the next two pages.

The most effective means of analyzing a company is to study its record over the past few years and to compare it to other well-managed companies, preferably in the same industry or with the same financial characteristics. Companies and industries are very different. A retailer will differ from a pharmaceutical company or an airline. An electric utility will differ from a computer manufacturer or a fast-food company. *However, each company and its management have one thing in common with every other company: an obligation to achieve the best possible investment return for the owners of the business* (the stockholders).

When one individual buys a share of stock from another individual, the investor is acquiring a share of ownership in the business and a part ownership of the company's equity. This equity, which belongs to the stockholders, is entrusted to the management. The management has an obligation to invest this money wisely, taking into consideration the company's opportunities, its expertise, and the degree of risk the stockholders are willing to assume.

One of the most important calculations in security analysis is determining the company's "return on equity" ("ROE"). This ratio indicates the rate of return that the company's executives have been able to achieve on the equity entrusted to them. A return of much less than 10% is generally regarded as unsatisfactory.

Using the example of the XYZ Company, as shown, the return on equity is calculated by dividing the net earnings figure ($184, located on the Income Statement) by the stockholders' equity figure ($1,150, located on the Balance Sheet).

The economic repercussions of a stock market crash depend less on the severity of the crash itself than on the response of economic policymakers....

—Federal Reserve
Chairman
Ben S. Bernacke

XYZ Company Income Statement For the Year Ended December 31		
REVENUES		
Sales to Customers	$2,225	
Interest Income	12	
Royalty and Other Income	15	
Total Revenues		2,252
COSTS AND EXPENSES		
Cost of Products Sold	1,100	
Selling, General, and Administrative Expenses	755	
Depreciation	69	
Other Expenses	18	
TOTAL COSTS AND EXPENSES		1,942
PROFIT BEFORE TAXES		310
Less:		
Federal, State, and Foreign Taxes		126
NET EARNINGS		$184

XYZ Com Balance Sheet as		
ASSETS		
Current Assets		
Cash	$ 38	
Marketable Securities	200	
Accounts Receivable	288	
Inventories	397	
Other Current Assets	23	
Total Current Assets		946
Long-Term Assets		
Property, Plant and Equipment	528	
Other Assets	77	
Total Long-Term Assets		605
TOTAL ASSETS		$1,551

Return on Equity

Net earnings divided by stockholders' equity

pany
of December 31

LIABILITIES

Current Liabilities

Accounts Payable	$ 99	
Loans and Notes Payable	88	
Other Current Liabilities	129	
Total Current Liabilities		316
Long-Term Debt		85

STOCKHOLDERS' EQUITY

Common Stock	145	
Retained Earnings	1,005	
Total Stockholders' Equity		1,150
TOTAL LIABILITIES & EQUITY		$1,551

Retention Rate

Net earnings less
dividends, divided by
net earnings

XYZ Company
Source and Application
of Funds Statement

SOURCE OF FUNDS

Net Earnings	$184	
Depreciation of Property	69	
Other Sources	7	
Provided by Operations		260
Increase in		
Long-Term Debt	13	
Proceeds from Employee's		
Stock Options	4	
Proceeds from the		
Sale of Property	3	
Provided by Outside Sources		20
TOTAL		280

APPLICATION OF FUNDS

Additions to Property, Plant,		
and Equipment	$136	
Cash Dividends Paid	49	
Decrease in		
Long-Term Debt	10	
Other Applications	10	
TOTAL		205
INCREASE IN		
WORKING CAPITAL		$ 75

Reinvestment Rate   =   Return on Equity   X   Retention Rate

The return on equity of the XYZ Company is therefore 16%. To be more precise, it is preferable, when calculating return on equity, to use the average equity over the past year, since the company's $184 income was earned over the prior twelve months, whereas the equity figure on the Balance Sheet is a year-end figure. Average equity is calculated by averaging the year-beginning and year-ending stockholders' equity figures. Nevertheless, the idea is the same.

Another important calculation is the "retention rate," or, in other words, the percentage of net earnings being reinvested in the business rather than being paid out as dividends. The retention rate is easily calculated from the Statement of Cash Flows by dividing the amount of net earnings reinvested in the business (net earnings less dividends) by the net earnings figure. Last year, for example, the retention rate for XYZ Company was 73%, or $184 less $49 divided by $184.

Of course, the retention rate can also be found by using the earnings per share and dividends per share figures. Most analysts do it this way.

A company that grows entirely by reinvesting its earnings in the business is said to be "self-financing." Generally speaking, the most successful companies today are self-financing, which can be particularly important when outside capital is more difficult to obtain and during inflationary or deflationary periods.

Both the return on equity and the retention rate calculations are very important to an analyst because they provide a clue to the company's internal growth rate potential for earnings (analysts refer to this growth potential as the "reinvestment rate"). A company can grow only by either (1) plowing earnings back into the business or (2) obtaining new debt or equity capital from outside the company.

The reinvestment rate is simply the product of the return on equity and the retention rate, as shown in the formula.

The internal growth potential for the XYZ Company is therefore

Reinvestment Rate		Return on Equity		Retention Rate
↓	=	↓	X	↓
11.7%	=	16%	X	73%

It can be seen from the formula that a company can improve its reinvestment rate by either increasing its return on equity, expanding its retention rate, or a combination of both.

The retention rate is influenced directly by the company's dividend policy and can be adjusted at will by management, while improving the return on equity is a more complex task, as illustrated later.

Any substantial enhancement or deterioration of a company's reinvestment rate can influence the market performance of its stock. Consequently, every serious investor should understand this formula and recognize its limitations.

At certain times, the formula can be misleading. For instance, a low-quality company can achieve a high return on equity simply by showing a profit with a small amount of equity (perhaps the result of many unprofitable years). For this reason, it is advisable to also calculate the company's "return on total assets" (net income divided by the total assets).

When both return on equity and return on assets are high, the reinvestment rate can be used with greater confidence.

In addition to the reinvestment rate formula, there are many other statistical calculations that can be applied when analyzing companies. Here are a few, using the figures from the XYZ Company.

Operating Profit Margin (Income Statement)

$$\text{Operating Profit Margin} = \frac{\text{Operating Profits}}{\text{Sale}}$$

$$13.5\% = \frac{\$301}{\$2,225}$$

This calculation tells an investor how profitable the company's products are to manufacture and sell. An operating profit margin of less than 8% for manufacturing companies is usually regarded as being unsatisfactory.

Pretax Profit Margin (Income Statement)

$$\text{Pretax Profit Margin} = \frac{\text{Profit before Taxes}}{\text{Total Revenues}}$$

$$13.8\% = \frac{\$310}{\$2,252}$$

The pretax profit margin, or pretax margin, as it is often called, shows how profitable the company's operations have been, taking into account all sources of income and all costs, before paying income taxes.

Tax Rate (Income Statement)

$$\text{TaxRate} = \frac{\text{Taxes}}{\text{Profit before Taxes}}$$

$$40.6\% = \frac{\$126}{\$310}$$

The tax rate calculation shows the percentage of profits paid to federal, state, local, and foreign governments—usually in the form of income taxes. Most often, a company's tax rate will be in the 30% to 45% range. However, the tax rate could be lower for several reasons. Perhaps the company has a plant in a foreign country with an extremely low tax rate, or perhaps the company has taken advantage of various tax credits (allowances for unprofitable operations in previous years or incentives established by the government for one reason or another).

Net Profit Margin (Income Statement)

$$\text{Net Profit Margin} = \frac{\text{Net Earnings}}{\text{Total Revenues}}$$

$$\downarrow \qquad \qquad \downarrow$$

$$8.2\% = \frac{\$184}{\$2,252}$$

The net profit margin measures a company's profitability after all costs, expenses, and taxes have been paid. For many U.S. companies, 8% is typical.

Current Ratio (Balance Sheet)

$$\text{Current Ratio} = \frac{\text{Current Assets}}{\text{Current Liabilities}}$$

$$\downarrow \qquad \qquad \downarrow$$

$$3.0 = \frac{\$946}{\$316}$$

The current ratio is one measure of a company's financial strength. A ratio of 2.0 or higher is desirable, although a somewhat lower current ratio might still be considered healthy if current assets are mostly cash or if the business is cash-oriented. A

ratio of more than 5.0 could indicate that business volume is not meeting expectations or that the company's assets are not being employed to their best advantage.

Another current relationship is the ratio of cash and equivalents (e.g., marketable securities) to current liabilities. This is sometimes called the "acid test ratio." The acid test ratio of XYZ Company last year was 75% ($38 + $200 divided by $316).

CAPITAL STRUCTURE

The capital structure, frequently called "capitalization," is the total amount of money invested in a company, including both bonds (long-term debt) and equity. The capital structure of the XYZ Company, for example, is as follows:

Capitalization (Balance Sheet)

Long-Term Debt	$ 85	7%
Stockholders' Equity	1,150	93%
Total Capitalization	$1,235	100%

The XYZ Company is conservatively managed, judging by the low amount of debt within the total capital structure. This is a desirable quality, since it permits management greater flexibility during difficult economic times. Unless the company is a utility or is in a finance-oriented

"Analysts are much smarter in bull markets."

business, the general rule is: the greater the proportion of debt, the greater the risk to the stockholders.

One of the notable trends in years past was the so-called leveraged buyout. Typically, management would have the company assume substantial amounts of debt, with the money being used to buy stock from the shareholders, often for the benefit of management. It is best to avoid becoming a creditor in a leveraged buyout.

The more recent trend has been the repurchase of shares in the open market. This, of course, will reduce the number of outstanding shares and can be good for stockholders in many ways—but not always. It depends on the amount of money involved, the source of the funds and, most important, the purchase price. For buybacks, there are many questions stockholders should be asking. Here are just a few:

- Are the buybacks for the benefit of *all* the shareholders, or just to benefit the executives holding stock options?

- What is the source of the money? Is this the best use of the money, or should the cash be reinvested in the business?

- How many shares are outstanding, and what is the average daily trading

volume? Once in a while buybacks can benefit a stock's price markedly.

By judging the amount of money involved and the likely price range for the purchases, and by comparing the buyback price with the per share book value, the investor can answer many of these key questions.

Cash Flow (Statement of Cash Flows)

$$\text{Cash Flow} = \text{Net Income} + \text{Depreciation}$$
$$\$253 = \$184 + \$69$$

Cash flow can be helpful in the analysis of profit trends and in measuring a firm's ability to finance its construction programs. It is especially meaningful when comparing companies because not all of them depreciate their assets at the same rate. It can be seen from the Statement of Cash Flows how important the cash flow items of net income and depreciation can be. Depreciation is regarded as a source of capital because it is a noncash expense on the Income Statement.

"Free cash flow" ("FCF") is an alternative and similar way to view the health of a company. Securities analysts frequently use "discounted cash flow" and "discounted free cash flow" models to esti-

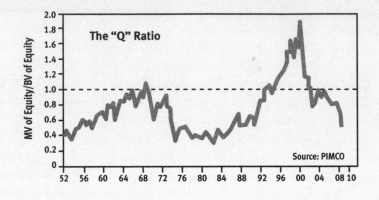

The "Q" Ratio

Source: PIMCO

mate the current market value of the stock. Applying this approach, however, depends on the many assumptions that go into the model as well as the type of company being analyzed. Also see the table in Chapter 6, "Growth Stocks," to better understand and appreciate this "discounting" approach.

The definition of free cash flow is profits after taxes, *plus* depreciation/amortization, less the total of dividends, capital expenditures, required debt repayments, and any other scheduled cash outlays. It is also sometimes loosely defined as "cash flow, plus after-tax interest, plus any noncash decrease in net working capital."

EARNINGS PER SHARE

This number is probably watched more closely by the financial community than any other investment statistic. It is calculated by dividing net earnings by the average number of shares outstanding.

Using the XYZ Company as an example, if net earnings last year happened to be $184 million and the company had 40 million shares outstanding, the earnings per share of the XYZ Company would be $4.60 per share. Sometimes the number of shares outstanding changes during the year. When this occurs, the earnings per

share calculation is usually based on the average number of shares outstanding during the year rather than the number of shares outstanding at year end.

The earnings per share number can be calculated another way, which, once more, illustrates a relationship between the company's financial statements:

Earnings per Share		Return on Equity		Book Value per Share
↓		↓		↓
$4.60	=	16%	X	$28.75

As this section and the next illustrate, there are many ways to analyze a company and to value its shares.

Other Analytical Concepts The importance of management's attaining a high return on the stockholders' investment cannot be overemphasized. Whenever additional money is invested in the business, either as new capital or as reinvested earnings, the stockholders expect to see an increase in revenues.

Sales growth is important, but its meaning is lost if each incremental sales dollar does not produce the profit to justify the new investment. For these reasons, an investor should watch for trends in sales, profit margins (as well as return on equity), and, of course, overall earnings growth.

THE PROFITABILITY OF SELECTED INDUSTRIES

Industry	ROE%				
Aerospace	16%	Conglomerates	12%	Office Equipment	17%
Airline	NIL	Drugs	19%	Paper	16%
Automotive	15%	Electronics	15%	Railroads	8%
Banks	11%	Food Processing	16%	Retailing (non food)	13%
Beverages	15%	Food Retailing	13%	Steels	8%
Broadcasting	20%	Machinery	14%	Textiles & Apparel	13%
Building Materials	12%	Metals & Mining	7%	Tire & Rubber	9%
Chemicals	15%	Natural Resources	14%	Utilities	11%

THE PEG RATIO

Many Wall Street analysts apply a very useful rule of thumb. They compare the company's P/E multiple to its long-term growth rate (this calculation is called "price to earnings growth" or simply "PEG"). Thus, a stock that sells at a P/E ratio of 18 with an EPS growth rate of 15% has a PEG of 1.2, which is not too far above the desirable 1.0 figure. A PEG of more than 2.0 is considered high.

SALES GROWTH

A sales increase or decline can occur in any or all of these three ways: (1) an increase or decline in the absolute number of units sold; (2) higher or lower selling prices for each unit; (3) if a company's products are sold overseas, an increase or decline in the values of currencies between countries. These factors should be recognized when sales growth is being monitored or estimated.

Another effective method of measuring a company's sales progress is watching for a trend in "equity turnover" (sales divided by average stockholders' equity). The level of equity turnover often reflects the type of business in which the company is engaged. As a general rule, companies with high profit margins usually have a low equity turnover, while companies with low profitability usually have a high equity turnover. A trend, either up or down, could be important.

PROFITABILITY

Sales growth loses significance if it is not translated into earnings "at the bottom line." Growing net earnings is, of course, the primary means of increasing stockholders' equity. When sales advance more rapidly than costs and expenses, profit margins expand, and vice versa. As explained earlier, profit margins can be analyzed in many ways, with the "operating profit margin," the "pretax profit margin," and the "net profit margin" being among the most popular.

"EBITDA" (earnings before interest, taxes, depreciation, and amortization) gained a measure of fame during the Internet craze when analysts who were unable to justify equity valuations used it as a measure of a stock's value because the company was not profitable. While EBITDA is a valuable analytical tool, it cannot be a substitute for net earnings. After all, the investor's objective is to identify companies that grow their ability to pay dividends. EBITDA is only a small step in that direction.

RETURN ON EQUITY

A company can improve its return on equity by increasing its equity turnover, its profitability, or both, as the formula for the XYZ Company demonstrates:

Return on Equity		Net Profit Margin		Equity Turnover
↓	=	↓	X	↓
16%	=	8%	X	2.0

For the XYZ Company to improve its return on equity from 16% to, say, 18%, management would have to either attain a net profit margin closer to 9% or increase the equity turnover to more than 2.2, or a combination of the two.

Return on equity is not the same for every industry, as the table above illustrates. In recent years, the average return on equity for the major industries in the United States has been just over 14%.

Some industries are regarded as "growth" industries, while others are referred to as "basic" industries. Generally speaking, growth companies have consistently superior profitability, usually require less money to build a new plant (i.e., they are less capital-intensive), and usually have a better return on the money invested. But within each industry, some companies are consistently more profitable and have more promising futures than others.

Regardless of the industry, for long-term success in the stock market, it is always better to buy shares of a company in which financial progress can be expected. That is, the company should be enjoying steady improvement in revenues, along with healthy and expanding profit margins. It should also hold the promise of higher dividends in the future, and it should have a financial condition (i.e., Balance Sheet) that can support these expectations.

ENTERPRISE VALUE

One calculation that investment analysts use to compare companies, especially within different industries, is the company's "enterprise value." The calculation is very straightforward: "total market value of the stock" *plus* the company's "total debt outstanding" *less* the "cash and equivalents" on the Balance Sheet.

TANGIBLE BOOK VALUE

Earlier in this chapter, the term "book value" was explained. However, in most cases where it is applicable, analysts will deduct "intangible" assets noted on the Balance Sheet. Thus, they arrive at a more conservative calculation of book value.

Intangible assets are nonphysical assets such as trademarks, patents, copyrights, and "goodwill" (usually the result of accounting differences following mergers or acquisitions). A "tangible book value" per share calculation is preferable when it is measured against the stock price.

DISCOUNTING VALUES

The subject of discounting values was introduced briefly in the discussion of cash flow earlier in this chapter.

When the current earnings per share of a stock is multiplied by a selected P/E ratio, one arrives at a target price for the stock. If this multiple is applied to *future* earnings, one can arrive at a *future* target price. For example, if the current EPS is $2.00 and the selected P/E ratio is 15 times earnings, the current target price is $30. If the EPS five years from today is estimated to be $3.50 (a growth rate of 12% annually), and the stock is expected to be 15 times earnings at that time, the target price becomes $52.50. This is for the stock five years from today. What is that $52.50 price worth *today*, not five years from now?

The answer to this question depends on the annual "rate of return" that is desired from that investment for the next five years. In this case, if the expected rate of return is

15%, the "present value," as it is called, is $26.09. This number can be found in any "Present Value Table" or with most of today's hand calculators. However, if the desired rate of return is, say, 16% rather than 15%, the present value is only $24.99.

Most analysts apply this basic concept to many financial items—earnings, dividends, and cash flow are the most common.

Investment Analyst as a Career? On Wall Street, the term "analyst" typically refers to an investment analyst (or Wall Street analyst or securities analyst) who works for a broker/dealer (the "sell side") or for an institution such as a mutual fund, a bank, an insurance company, or an investment counsel firm (the "buy side").

An analyst position is usually classified as either a "fundamentalist" (one who studies the details of a company and its industry), or a "technical analyst" (one whose specialty is charts and indicators to determine the potential supply and demand for the stock itself). A good fundamental analyst will understand and appreciate technical analysis, and vice versa.

To become an investment analyst, it is necessary to meet the requirements of the Financial Industry Regulatory Authority, better known as FINRA. This is the largest nongovernmental regulator of nearly

5,000 brokerage firms, 170,000 branch offices, and about 650,000 registered securities representatives. The chief role of FINRA is to offer protection for investors within the U.S. capital markets.

A registered investment analyst must pass the grueling Series 86 and Series 87 tests as well as the Series 7 (a test that all salespeople must pass). In lieu of the Series 86 test, Levels I and II of the Chartered Financial Analyst (CFA) or Chartered Market Technician (CMT) program will be accepted for exemption.

Conclusion Statistical analytical concepts are important, to be sure, but there are many questions that must also be answered during the selection process:

- What is the company's primary business, and is it *the* leader in its industry?

- Will there be good demand for the company's products or services in the years ahead?

- Who are the principal competitors, and can the company compete?

- Will product prices be under pressure?

- What are the strengths and weaknesses of management? Does management have a good record of accomplishments, and what are its goals?

- Does management recognize its responsibilities to the stockholders of the company?

Here is one good rule to follow: if the story and the numbers that go with it appear "too good to be true"—use extreme care.

In recent years, many questions have been raised regarding accounting and the earnings produced by various accounting procedures. Lock six accountants into one room, and they will later emerge with ten "correct" answers. For example, one point of discussion could be employee stock options and how they should be recorded. The added expense for options is likely to be greater for a technology stock, for instance, than for a consumer products stock. Also, pension funding is a continual controversy. Thus, security analysis should be approached with a modest degree of common sense.

Despite these shortcomings, once the statistical methods outlined in this chapter become routine, the investor should find security analysis an enjoyable challenge. Success in the stock market will come more easily if you take the time to analyze your company.

4 Reading the Financial Pages

Introduction

This is the only chapter in this book that should begin, "*Once upon a time.*" It illustrates how the world has changed in such a short period! When the first edition of this book rolled off the press, "Reading the Financial Pages" was one of its most crucial segments. That is no longer true.

A few years ago, it was unimaginable that the *Wall Street Journal* and the *New York Times* daily newspapers, historic in their own way, could become nothing more than tabloids of investment-oriented features, with limited stock tables that hold little, if any, interest. Business editors, if they still exist today, must be embarrassed that the weather maps in their newspapers often command greater prominence.

How did this happen? Well, the Internet is the primary reason. Anyone who is interested in the stock market today has rapid access to the Internet, with its substantial, practical, and timely information. With just a click of the mouse, any required data are readily available online, including from the excellent Web site WSJ.com. At this writing, *Barron's* (a weekly) is the only remaining financial domestic newspaper of any consequence.

However, much of the earlier version of this chapter is being retained here, not out of nostalgia, but because investors who are familiar with this material will not be lost in cyberspace. The information is essentially the same; only the medium has changed.

THE ORIGINAL 12 STOCKS IN THE DOW INDUSTRIAL AVERAGE

American Cotton Oil	Laclede Gas
American Sugar	National Lead
American Tobacco	North American
Chicago Gas	Tennessee Coal & Iron
Distilling & Cattle Feeding	U.S. Leather Preferred
General Electric	U.S. Rubber

The Dow Jones Averages The Dow Jones Industrial Average is by far the most popular single indicator of day-to-day market direction. Charles H. Dow, one of the founders of Dow Jones Company and the first editor of the *Wall Street Journal,* is credited with the original 1884 calculations of what are still, to this day, the most widely followed stock market averages in the world. It was his intention to express the general level and trend of the stock market by using the average prices of a few representative stocks.

In 1896, there were two Dow Jones averages. Most important at the time was the Dow Jones Railroad Average, composed of 20 rail stocks. The other average, containing 12 stocks representing all other types of businesses, was called the Dow Jones Industrial Average (DJIA). In 1916, the Industrial Average was increased to 20 stocks, and twelve years later, in 1928, it was increased to 30 stocks, the same number used today.

A third average, the Dow Jones Utility Average, was established as a 20-stock average in 1929 (later reduced to 15 stocks, as it is today). The three averages—the 30 Industrials, now regarded as the most important; the 20 Transportations, revised and renamed to include airlines and trucking stocks; and the 15 Utilities—together make up the fourth average, the 65-stock Dow Jones Composite.

Over the years, the widely followed Dow Jones Industrial Average has changed considerably, with many substitutions. Fewer than 20 of the 30 stocks that were on it in 1928 remain, and of the present stocks, only General Electric was included in Dow's original computation. The tables above show the original 12 issues and the 30 equities, along with the ticker symbols, that are currently being used.

The Industrial Average is simply an average of the prices of these 30 stocks. However, whenever one of the companies in the group declares a stock split or a stock dividend (explained later), the divisor has to be decreased accordingly to maintain comparability. Today, the divisor, instead of being 30, is about 0.1250. This means that for every one dollar that each DJIA stock advances or declines, the average moves about eight points.

With the passing of time, the level of the DJIA has increased, mainly reflecting the growth of the companies in the average. From 1915 to about 1925, the Industrials fluctuated around the 100 mark. During the economic boom of the late 1920s, the Dow Industrials rose to a September 3, 1929, peak of 386.10.

Alcoa (AA)	CocaCola (KO)	Intel (INTC)	ProctGamb (PG)
AmerExp (AXP)	Disney (DIS)	JohnsJohns (JNJ)	3M Co (MMM)
AT&T (T)	DuPont (DD)	JPMorgan (JPM)	Travelers (TRV)
BankAmer (BAC)	ExxonMobl (XOM)	KraftFoods (KFT)	UnitedTech (UTX)
Boeing (BA)	GenlElect (GE)	McDonalds (MCD)	Verizon (VZ)
Caterpillar (CAT)	HewlettPk (HPQ)	Merck (MRK)	WalMart (WMT)
Chevron (CVX)	HomeDepot (HD)	Microsoft (MSFT)	
CiscoSys (CSCO)	IBM (IBM)	Pfizer (PFE)	

The sharp stock market plunge in late 1929 and the steep decline early in the Great Depression took the DJIA back to as low as 40.56 in July 1932—down 89%!

The DJIA remained in the 100–200 range throughout the late 1930s and during the decade of the 1940s. It advanced from under 200 to above 700 in the post–World War II bull market. Following a sharp setback in 1962, the index continued to climb to the "Magic 1,000" mark, reached for the first time in early 1966. It is interesting to note that IBM was replaced in the Dow Jones Industrial Average by American Telephone in 1939. Had this substitution not been made, the DJIA would have crossed the 1,000 mark four years before it did.

The 1966–1982 period brought several sharp swings in the stock market, taking the Dow Industrials on a roller-coaster ride that few investors at that time will ever forget. The most dramatic drop occurred in the two-year period 1972–1974. In only twenty-two months, the DJIA dropped 45%, from 1,067 to 570, one of the steepest declines in its history, though nothing like 1929–1932.

Beginning in 1982, the Dow began a climb that pushed the average to 2,747 in 1987. The crash that year resembled the panic in 1929, but the economic climates were very different. In both cases, a great many stocks lost more than 40% of their market value in just a matter of days. The rapid recovery after the 1987 stock market crash was but one more reminder of Wall Street's famous quote: "The stock market will fluctuate." In 1988 the Dow resumed its advance, and the average reached almost 12,000 in January 2000, before encountering the most substantial multiyear bear market since 1974. The next major bear market occurred following the 14,280 peak on October 11, 2007.

Once the Dow Jones Industrial Average is calculated, the result is expressed in terms of "points" rather than "dollars."

When the news commentator announces:

"The market was up 72 points today to close at 8,585," what is really being said is: "The Dow Jones 30 Industrial stocks averaged 8,585 when calculated at 4 p.m. today (the end of the NYSE trading session), which is an increase of 72 points from the 8,513 calculation at the close of the session yesterday."

The DJIA is frequently criticized because a higher-priced stock such as IBM tends to have a greater influence on the average than a lower-priced stock such as Disney. In addition, some people would prefer a broader list than just 30 or 65 stocks. As a result, other market barometers are also watched closely. One of these is the Standard & Poor's 500 Index, which was first calculated in 1957. Weighted according to the market value of each security in it, the S&P 500 accounts for more than 80% of the dollar market value of all stocks listed on the New York Stock Exchange. Generally speaking, a market capitalization of at least $3 billion is required to be included in the S&P 500. However, it should be noted that the DJIA stocks are among the most important issues in the S&P 500. Another index, the New York Stock Exchange Index, was initiated in 1966. It includes all listed stocks on the Big Board and, like the Dow averages, the S&P 500, and other indexes, it is calculated by computers continuously throughout the trading day.

The Dow Jones Industrial Average is an important benchmark for investors in more than one way. Not only does it provide a means of indicating the overall direction of stock prices, but it can also be used as a guide to relative values. The DJIA has its own earnings and dividends figures, which are averages of the earnings and dividends of the component companies. (See the appendix.) These statistics are readily available and can be used by investors as a basis for comparison with

individual stocks. Similar calculations are also available for the other Dow averages and the Standard & Poor's indexes.

For investors who want to "buy or sell shares" in the broad market indexes such as the S&P 500, there are exchange-traded funds (or ETFs), which are discussed later. Anyone who wants to invest directly in the Dow Jones Industrial Average can do so through an ETF called "Diamonds" (the ETF symbol is DIA). Many newspapers now have columns devoted to ETFs.

The Stock Tables In years past, just as a minute is divided into sixty seconds, a foot into twelve inches, or a gallon into four quarts, Wall Street once used the quaint Spanish system of dividing a stock dollar into fractions of eight or, as they say, "eighths of a point," with each eighth of a dollar having a value of 12.5 cents. For example, a share of stock priced between $30 and $31 was quoted as 30⅛, 30¼, 30⅜, 30½, 30⅝, 30¾, or 30⅞, which is another way of saying $30.125, $30.25, $30.375, $30.50, $30.625, $30.75, or $30.875. Since April 2001, however, stocks have been traded with the fractions of share prices quoted in cents.

An individual can buy one share or many shares, although the broker's commission charge is proportionately lower

| YTD | 52-WEEK | | | | Yield | | VOL. | | NET |
% CHG.	High	Low	STOCK (Symbol)	DIV	%	PE	100's	CLOSE	CHG.
−18.1	42.78	21.05	Thor Ind (THO)	0.04	0.1	12	4012	28.35	0.29
−0.2	21.33	16.20	Thornburg Mtg (TMA)	2.32	11.6	8	2362	20.18	−0.37
−30.3	16.42	3.47	Three-Five (TFS)		. . .	def	1078	5.15	−0.18
2.1	131.55	105.50	3M (MMM)	2.48	2.0	25	18019	125.83	0.75
−8.9	45.70	23.38	Tidewater (TDW)	0.60	2.1	16	5478	28.03	−0.29
−1.7	41.00	19.40	Tiffany (TIF)	0.16	0.7	19	2943	23.22	0.40
−8.4	45.95	25.80	Timberland (TBL)		. . .	13	3467	32.28	−0.25

when a larger number of shares is bought or sold. An investor who buys 100 shares of stock at $48.72 per share pays $4,872.00 total, before a brokerage commission is added for executing the order. (The fee is calculated in the same manner and deducted from the total when the stock is sold.) This fee can vary widely, roughly from $10 to $100, depending upon the brokerage firm's commission table.

If this company's stock were listed on the New York Stock Exchange, the transaction or "trade" would appear next to the company's name on the NYSE Composite table for that day. If the stock were listed on the American Stock Exchange (Alternext), listed on a regional exchange, or traded in the over-the-counter markets (traded on the Nasdaq System or not listed on an exchange), the transaction would be recorded either in a composite table or in an appropriate table elsewhere.

Each line of the daily stock table tells a different story. As an example, assume that, years ago, a long-term stockholder of the 3M Company happened to be reading a copy of the *Wall Street Journal* or some other major daily newspaper. 3M is the well-known manufacturer of Scotch Tape and thousands of other products. Its stock is listed on the New York Stock Exchange and is usually found alphabetically in the "T" section of most stock tables with the heading "New York Stock Exchange Composite Transactions." Since this shareholder has been watching 3M's stock for many years, its exact location on any stock table then (or on any computer screen today) can be found quickly.

The three columns to the left of the company's name show the price range of the stock over the preceding 52 weeks and its percent change (+2.1%) since the beginning of the current year. On this day, before any subsequent stock splits, 3M closed at $125.83, up $0.75 from the close on the preceding day. During the session, 1,801,900 shares (referred to as "volume") were bought and sold. And with every trade, there was a buyer and a seller.

The "MMM" notation immediately to the right of the company's name is the stock's ticker symbol. The figure to the right of the symbol is the company's estimated annual dividend per share (based on the last quarterly or semiannual payment rate).

This expected dividend of $2.48 is higher than the $2.40 per share that 3M holders received twelve months earlier, and about 50% greater than the dividend that was paid to this shareholder when the stock was first purchased nine years earlier.

The most active stocks and
volume statistics usually appear
in a special highlight section.

Fortunately, 3M's earnings have improved over the years, and the company's directors have increased the dividend periodically—which explains why the stock has more than doubled in value during this period.

The stock's current 2.0% dividend yield is indicated on the stock table. Although a 2.0% yield does not appear especially exciting right now, this patient, long-term shareholder is satisfied. As a result of increased earnings and dividends over the years, the stock price is much higher now than it was when the stock was purchased, and today's $2.48 dividend represents an annual return of more than 5% on the original investment made nine years earlier. This investor is also encouraged by the fact that 3M has paid dividends every year, continuously, since 1916. Management is obviously conscious of this enviable record.

The price/earnings ratio, also called the P/E multiple, measures the relationship between the current price of the stock and 3M's earnings per share. The company recently reported $4.99 per share for the past twelve months. The P/E is calculated by dividing the current price of the stock by the earnings per share. Based on the closing price of 3M ($125.83) and the most recent four quarters of earnings reported by the company (not shown in the table), 3M's P/E ratio is 25.2, as it appears, rounded to 25, in the middle column. In this case, it can be said that 3M was selling at roughly 25 times earnings.

It should be noted that the P/E ratio will fluctuate whenever the stock's price (or earnings per share) rises or declines.

Investors can also quickly calculate that 3M is currently paying its shareholders just under half of its earnings (i.e., a 49.7% payout) in the form of a cash dividend.

The stock of 3M is listed not only on the New York Stock Exchange, but also elsewhere, including the Boston, Chicago, Cincinnati (now National), and Philadelphia exchanges. As indicated earlier, 1.8 million shares were traded yesterday. Because the New York Stock Exchange is the largest exchange, most of these shares were probably traded on the trading floor in New York, but from these figures, the reader cannot be sure.

Stock Market Activity On the first or second page of many daily newspapers that have a financial section, a special market activity segment appears. It shows total shares traded, or the "volume," and it highlights the ten or fifteen most active

Most Active Issues				Diaries			
	Volume	Close	Chg		Tues	Mon	Wk Ago
AT&T Wrlss	40,621,500	7.23	+0.22	Issues traded	3,442	3,421	3,451
Pfizer	38,935,400	31.12	+0.88	Advances	2,185	650	1,093
GenlElec	34,672,100	33.01	−1.11	Declines	1,097	2,633	2,197
ExxonMobl	33,783,300	34.66	+0.55	Unchanged	160	138	161
Wyeth	28,229,800	37.70	+1.03	New highs	53	47	101
Citigroup	24,325,100	35.46	−0.42	New lows	44	23	34
Xerox	22,812,100	9.43	−0.15	Adv vol (000)	983,564	743,006	332,912
NortelNtwks	20,114,700	3.18	+0.03	Decl vol (000)	360,234	500,535	929,865
LucentTch	18,311,200	2.10	−0.05	Total vol (000)	1,345,897	1,245,649	1,324,872
EMC Corp	14,328,900	8.98	−0.22	Closing Tick	+83	−77	+22
TX Instr	12,983,400	18.18	+1.07	Closing Arms (trin)	0.65	1.43	1.89
Sprint PCS	12,266,700	4.68	+0.29	Block trades	23,453	21,651	20,443

stocks of the day and those that have gained or lost the most during the session. Volume is important, but investors should not be concerned if a particular stock is or is not on the most active list. A stock can rise or fall on high or low volume.

The number of shares traded during the day is totaled by each exchange after it closes. However, the total volume reported by the New York Stock Exchange is the figure used most often by commentators to describe the day's market activity.

In the early 1920s, a very active day on the New York exchange was a total of 1,500,000 shares traded. By the late 1920s, daily volume of 4,000,000 shares was not unusual. The panic in October 1929 produced several days of high volume (the record of 16,410,000 shares of October 30, 1929, was not surpassed for nearly forty years). Since the 1950s, volume has steadily increased, principally because of a larger number of companies and shares, not to mention greater activity by institutions (mutual funds, pension funds, insurance companies, and banks). The single-day record of 608 million shares traded on October 20, 1987, is no longer viewed with awe. Only ten years later, the record was set at 1.2 billion shares. Today, a 1.2-billion-share session is considered to be a "slow" day.

Market Breadth Besides watching stock market averages, a general market trend can be determined by monitoring the "market breadth" numbers that can be found in tables like the "Market Diary" column. These figures, which are available for both the NYSE and other markets, show the number of *stocks* that advanced or declined for the day, the number of *shares* that advanced or declined, and the number of stocks that reached new high or low prices in the past 52 weeks.

When the ratio between advancing and declining issues is compared to the ratio of advancing and declining volume, a so-called ARMS Ratio is created. Generally, an ARMS reading of under 1.00 indicates buying demand and a reading above 1.00 suggests selling pressure.

Some statistics have only limited value on a day-to-day basis. But they become more significant as trends are established over a period of time. Seasoned observers like to see the market breadth figures improve whenever the more widely followed averages move higher. The subject of market breadth will be explored in greater detail later. (See Chapter 13, "The Principles of Technical Analysis.")

To have most stocks participate in the advancing market trend is regarded as a

3M Beats Q4 Views, Raises Q1

"confirmation" and a "healthy sign" that the upward trend might continue.

Wall Street professionals often say, "It is a market of stocks rather than a stock market," and, to a great extent, this is true. A company's business prospects will always be the most powerful influence on its stock's price action. And it is not unusual to see a stock, or a group of stocks, contrarily hit new highs in a bear market or sink to new lows in a bull market.

However, a broad stock market advance or decline can have an important effect on an individual stock. For this reason, it pays to keep abreast of the technical condition and trend of the overall market.

Earnings Reports To repeat, over the long term—a few years or longer—the price of a stock will most likely rise or fall in line with the company's earnings progress, dividends, and financial condition. There is a tendency for investors to anticipate future earnings reports, which, in turn, places importance on earnings announcements and how investors perceive these figures.

A company usually reports its sales and earnings results every three months. In most cases, the figures are available a few weeks after the quarter ends. A majority of companies, but not all, end their business year on December 31, the end of the regular calendar year. If a company uses December 31 (rather than a "fiscal year" that ends on another date), the first quarter will close on March 31, the second quarter on June 30, and the third quarter on September 30. These quarterly results are referred to as "interim reports." A company's year includes three interim reports and one annual report.

A quarterly interim report is available to each shareholder almost immediately after the close of the quarter. However, many of the pertinent figures will frequently appear over the news wires and in the newspaper a few days before shareholders actually receive the report. Sometimes the earnings report is better or worse than Wall Street analysts expect, and this can produce an immediate positive or negative price change in the stock. Although most long-term investors do not buy or sell stocks solely on the basis of quarterly results, short-term traders are often influenced by these reports.

Most major newspapers once devoted a great deal of space to sales and earnings announcements. Today, few do. The *Wall Street Journal* gives some coverage to the specific numbers in a daily column entitled "Digest of Corporate

Fourth-Period Earnings at 3M Rose 34%, Helped by Solid Sales

Dow Jones Newswires

ST. PAUL, Minn.—Manufacturer 3M Co. said fourth-quarter earnings rose 34% from a year earlier, helped by solid overall sales and cost-cutting measures.

The company said it had net income of $511 million, or $1.29 a share, compared with $381 million, or 96 cents a share, a year earlier.

In October, 3M said it expected to earn between $1.25 and $1.30 a share for the period.

The company, a component of the Dow Jones Industrial Average, has a product line that includes such consumer products as household tape and Post-it notes, as well as industrial abrasives and adhesives. The company's results often are viewed as an indicator of economic trends because other manufacturers buy many 3M products.

In 4p.m. New York Stock Exchange composite trading, 3M shares fell 68 cents to $125.64.

3M's sales for the quarter increased 7.3% to $4.14 billion from $3.86 billion a year earlier. The company said sales volumes increased 14% in its transportation, graphics and safety businesses; 4.6% in industrial products; 4.5% in consumer and office supplies; 3.6% in health care; and 2.2% in electronics and communications operations. U.S. sales rose 1.8% to $1.84 billion, the company said.

For the year, 3M said net rose 38% to $1.97 billion, or $4.99 per share, compared with $1.43 billion, or $3.58 a share. Sales for the year rose 1.7% to $16.33 billion from $16.05 billion for 2001.

The company invested more than $1 billion in research and development in 2002, said Chairman and Chief Executive W. James McNerney Jr.

The company said it expects earnings of between $1.38 and $1.43 a share for the first quarter and full-year earnings of between $5.80 and $6.00 a share.

Digest of Corporate Earnings Reports

COMPANY	PERIOD		REV (mill)	% CHG	INC CT OP (mill)	NET (mill)	% CHG	PER SHARE CURR	PREV	% CHG
Thornburg Mtge	Q12/31		...	...	...	35.2	64	.67	.65	3.1
TMA (N)	▲	Yr	...	...	120.0	120.0	105	2.59	2.09	24
3M Co	Q12/31		4,138	7.3	...	511.0	34	1.29	.96	34
MMM (N)	▲	Yr	16,332	1.7	...	a1,974	38	4.99	3.58	39
a-Includes nonrecurring net charges of $108,000,000.										
Tidewater Inc	Q12/31		163.1	−10	...	23.6	−30	.42	.60	−30
TDW (N)	▼	9 mo	482.0	−14	...	a70.0	−35	1.24	1.92	−35
a-Includes one-time gain of $4,875,000.										
Tredegar Corp	Q12/31		176.9	−1.4	a1.98	1.98	...	.05	(.12)	...
TG (N)	P	Yr	737.4	−3.4	a6.20	(2.53)	...	(.07)	.25	...
a-Includes nonrecurring gains of $3,705,000 in the quarter and $2,263,000 in the year.										
Tropical Sprtswre	13wk12/28		99.0	−10	...	(5.02)	...	(.45)	.38	...
TSIC (Nq)	L									

*Wall Street people learn nothing
and forget everything.*

—BENJAMIN GRAHAM

Earnings Reports," usually found in the "Marketplace" section.

If there is a significant story, newspapers will provide details. The formats that newspapers use can differ—and some tables are easier to interpret than others.

The fourth-quarter announcement for the 3M Company was a good example. The story that appeared in the *Wall Street Journal* at that time appears on the right, along with 3M's Earnings Digest figures.

This brief report tells the reader that in the three-month period ending December 31, 3M's revenues increased 7.3% to just over $4.13 billion, compared with about $3.85 billion in the same quarter a year earlier. It also shows that 3M enjoyed profits of $511 million in the quarter, or $1.29 per share, comparing favorably with $381 million, or $0.96 per share, the year before.

Today, stories and a table identical to the one shown here can be found on the Internet immediately after the company makes its report pubic. This newspaper story and others like it will normally appear in a format similar to this.

The initial stories, most often written by news agencies, are typically based on the company's official news release, found in a readily available report submitted by the company to the SEC. This document,

which offers the greatest amount of detail, is known as an 8-K Report and can be found in the SEC's Edgar database. Companies use the 8-K report to satisfy "full disclosure" requirements.

The company's annual numbers (earnings of $4.99 per share on revenues of $16.3 billion) were, of course, also part of this announcement. And, as many better-managed companies do, 3M released rough guidelines for the next quarter and for the year to come.

Once in a while it is necessary for a company's management to revise its projections, either up or down, as the year progresses. And this announcement could come before the quarterly release. If it is negative, this so-called earnings warning could hurt the stock price temporarily. However, as a rule, long-term investors should not make rash portfolio decisions based solely on interim reports, although the firm's progress should be monitored.

Of course, not all companies have the benefit of publicity with each quarterly report, but 3M is a widely held blue chip.

Investors frequently interpret a company's interim report positively when the quarterly comparison is better than the preceding quarterly comparison and view it negatively when the reverse occurs.

Worldwide > Our Company > Investor Relations >

Investor Relations

Investing in 3M
⊞ Stock Information
⊞ Financial Information
▷ SEC Filings
▷ Earnings Estimates
⊞ Corporate Governance

Webcasts & Presentations
▷ Calendar of Events
▷ Quarterly Earnings
▷ Investor Presentations

Contact Information
▷ Contact Us
▷ Sign Up for Email Alerts
▷ Transfer Agent
▷ FAQ

Webcast
Q4 2008 3M Company
Earnings Conference Call
Thursday, January 29,
2009 at 9:00 a.m. ET

Investor Tool Kit

▤ Print-friendly

✉ E-mail this page

📶 RSS Feeds

✉! Receive E-mail Alerts

📋 2008 Annual Report

Upcoming Events

January 2009

Sun	Mon	Tue	Wed	Thu	Fri	Sat
				1	2	3
4	5	6	7	8	9	10
11	12	13	14	15	16	17
18	19	20	21	22	23	24
25	26	27	28	29	30	31

3M Corporate News

3M Library Systems Announces Space-Saving Automated Materials Handling System

Affordable three-bin system features small footprint, options for inductionDENVER, Jan 23, 2009 (BUSINESS WIRE) -- (Booth #1032)--3M

More Stories >>

Featured Presentations

2009 Outlook Meeting

2008 3M Investor Conference

Related Links

3M Technologies
Social Responsibility
3M Facts

Analyst's Research Report

The format of the investment research report varies, but the content remains essentially the same.

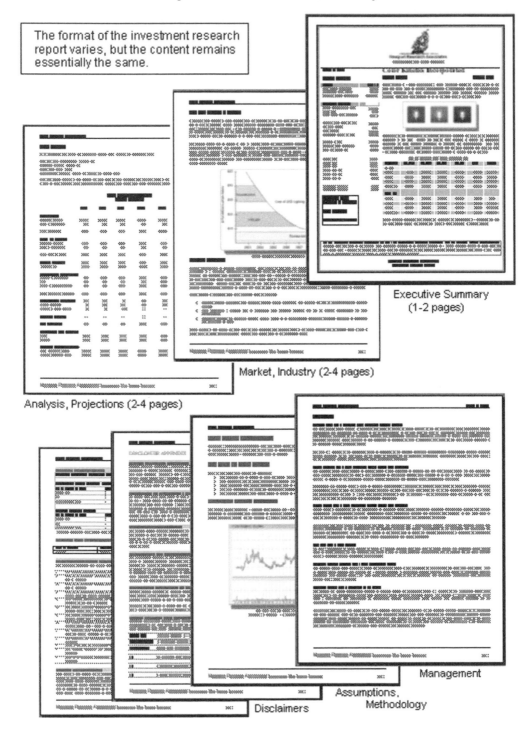

Executive Summary
(1-2 pages)

Market, Industry (2-4 pages)

Analysis, Projections (2-4 pages)

Management

Assumptions, Methodology

Disclaimers

Dividend Announcements

Dividends Reported

COMPANY	PERIOD	AMT	PAYABLE DATE	RECORD DATE
REGULAR				
AGL Resources Inc	Q	.27	3-01	2-14
BankcorpRhodeIsl	Q	.14	3-11	2-18
BectonDickinson	Q	.10	3-31	3-10
BostonFed Bancorp	Q	.16	2-20	2-06
CNB Florida Bcshs	Q	.05	2-07	1-28
Carrollton Bcp	Q	.09	3-03	2-13
Crane Co	Q	.10	3-12	3-03
DPL Inc	Q	.235	3-01	2-14
Diamond Offshore	Q	.125	3-03	2-03
Eastern Co	Q	.11	3-14	2-21
ElkCorp	Q	.05	2-27	2-10
Ethan Allen Inter	Q	.08	4-15	4-10
Fahnestock Viner A	Q	b.09	2-28	2-14
FarmersCapBank	Q	.32	4-01	3-01
FstCitznBncshrs A	Q	.25	4-07	3-17
FirstBank CorpMI	Q	.19	3-14	2-28
HF Fin'l	Q	.115	2-18	2-04
Hibernia Corp A	Q	.15	2-20	2-07
HsohldInt1$4.30pf	S	2.15	3-31	2-28
Int'lBusMach	Q	.15	3-10	2-10
KanCityLifeIns	Q	.27	2-24	2-10
Knight-Ridder	Q	.27	2-24	2-12
MeadWestvaco Corp	Q	.23	3-03	2-07
Neub&Berm Inc	Q	.075	2-19	2-07
NJ Resources	Q	.31	4-01	3-14
NiagMohawk 3.60%pf	Q	.90	3-31	3-10
NiagMohawk 3.90%pf	Q	.975	3-31	3-10
NiagMohawk adjpfD	Q	.863125	3-31	3-10
Norfolk Southern	Q	.07	3-10	2-07
Oregon Trail Finl	Q	.11	2-28	2-14
Peabody Energy	Q	.10	3-05	2-11
Pennichuck Corp	Q	.195	3-03	2-14
Potash Corp Saskat	Q	.25	5-15	4-17
Schering-Plough	Q	.17	2-28	2-07
Sthn Missouri Bcp	Q	.14	2-28	2-14
Sun Bancorp-PA	Q	.165	3-07	2-21
TECO Energy	Q	.355	2-15	2-07
Teleflex Inc	Q	.18	3-14	2-25
UnitedStates Steel	Q	.05	3-10	2-19
WVS Finl Corp	Q	.16	2-27	2-10
Weis Markets	Q	.30	3-11	3-04
IRREGULAR				
Chesterfield Finl	Q	.06	3-03	2-14
Guaranty Financial	-	.075	2-10	1-29
Health Mgmt Assc A	Q	.02	3-03	2-07
FUNDS, REITS, INVESTMENT COS, LPS				
Correctional Props	Q	.40	3-04	2-14
Cousins Properties	Q	.37	2-24	2-10
DreyfusStratMuniBd	M	.051	2-28	2-13
Hancock(J)PatGlbDv	M	.081	2-28	2-07
HealthCarePropInv	Q	.83	2-20	2-06
Hlth CarePrp pfA	Q	.492188	3-31	3-17
Hlth CarePrp pfB	Q	.54375	3-31	3-17
Hlth CarePrp pfC	Q	.5375	3-31	3-17
HealthcareRltyTr	Q	.61	3-06	2-14
Highwoods Props	Q	.585	2-24	2-10
Highwoods Props B	Q	.50	3-17	3-03
Highwoods Props D	Q	.50	4-30	4-01
Oil ServiceHOLDRs	-	.01375	3-05	2-03

COMPANY	PERIOD	AMT	PAYABLE DATE	RECORD DATE
MerLyUtilHGi DRs	-	.002	4-02	3-14
Penn VA ResLP	Q	.50	2-14	2-04
Plum Creek Co Inc	Q	.35	2-28	2-14
TCW/DW Trm2003	M	.047	2-21	2-07
STOCKS				
Central Coast Bncp		10%	2-28	2-14

INCREASED

COMPANY	PERIOD	AMOUNTS		PAYABLE DATE	RECORD DATE
		NEW	OLD		
AmerHomeMtge	Q	.10	.05	4-17	4-03
Bank of Montreal	Q	b.33	b.30	2-27	2-12
City National Corp	Q	.205	.195	2-18	2-05
Comerica Inc	Q	.50	.48	4-01	3-15
CommunityBkMrkVA	Q	.07	.04	3-01	2-11
McClatchy Co	Q	.11	.10	4-01	3-12
NASB Financial	Q	.17	.15	2-28	2-07
Port Fin'l Corp	Q	.20	.18	2-21	2-07
Praxair Inc	Q	.215	.19	3-17	3-07
R&G Fin'l pfB	Q	.0985	.092	3-27	3-21
SterlingBcsh TX	Q	.045	.04	2-21	2-07
TransCanada Pipns	Q	b.27	b.25	4-30	3-31
WA Banking Company	Q	.07	.065	2-26	2-10
Wells Fargo Co	Q	.30	.28	3-01	2-07
Woodward Governor	Q	.24	.2325	3-03	2-17
Wrigley(Wm) Jr	Q	.22	.205	5-01	4-15

SPECIAL

COMPANY	PERIOD	AMT	PAYABLE DATE	RECORD DATE
Methanex Corp	Q	b.25	2-14	2-06

XTRA

COMPANY	PERIOD	AMT	PAYABLE DATE	RECORD DATE
SouthwestGasCorp	Q	v.215	3-03	2-18

v-Amount has been changed. Reflects $.01 from redemption of rights.
A-Annual, M-Monthly, Q-Quarterly, S-Semi-annual.
b-Payable in Canadian funds. c-Corrected. h-From income. k-From capital gains.
r-Revised. t-Approximate U.S. dollar amount per American Depositary Receipt/Share before adjustment for foreign taxes.

Stocks Ex-Dividend

COMPANY	AMOUNT	COMPANY	AMOUNT
AT&T CapPINES8.125	.50781	MerLynAmgen7%	.7946
AbbeyNatl7.25%Nts	t.453125	NY Community Bncp	.25
AffiliatedMgrPRIDE	.375	NewfieldFlnlquipsA	.8125
Alberto CulverA	.105	ONEOK	.166
Alberto CulverB	.105	PNM Resources	.22
BNP Resident Prep	.25	Pall Corp	.09
Banco BradescoADS	t.019582	Pengrowth Engy Un	b.70
Borg-Warner Inc	.18	Pinnacle West Cap	.425
Citigrp Inc	.20	Russell Corp	.04
Cleco Corp	.225	Southern Co	.3425
ColgatePalm	.18	Sovereign Bcp	.025
CntySanDiegoPINES	.561458	Staten Island Bncp	.13
Diamond Offshore	.125	Sussex Bancorp	.07
Dow Jones & Co	.25	Toys R Us EqUn	.781
Eaton Corp	.44	Union Planters	.3334
EqtyOfficeProp pfB	.65625	Vornado Rlty Tr	.68
Everest ReCapTRUPS	.496076	Wausau-Mosinee Pap	.085
HartfordFinlCorpUn	.75	Wilmington Trust	.255
Mkt2000+ HOLDRs	.006	Winn-Dixie Stores	.05
Oil ServiceHOLDRs	.01375	Wireless Telecom	.02
MerLyUtilHOLDRs	.099325		
Horton (DR) Inc	.07	t-Approximate U.S. dollar amount per American Depositary Receipt/Share before adjustment for foreign taxes.	
Kimco Rlty depshsA	.484375		

				−H—H—H—					
36	27⅛	HackW	2.48	7	1	32⅝	32⅝	32⅝	− ⅛
18⅝	14¾	HallFB	.60	13	74	17⅝	17⅜	17½	+ ⅛
17¼	13¾	HallPrt	.80a	7	5	15¼	15⅛	15¼	− ⅛
166	133½	Hallibtn	1.68	13	373	155½	153	153⅜	+ ¾

Before the "when issued" period 3/24

				−H—H—H—					
36	27⅛	HackW	2.48	7	3	32⅞	32½	32½	− ⅛
18⅝	14¾	HallFB	.60	13	40	17½	17¼	17½	.....
17¼	13¾	HallPrt	.80a	7	18	15½	15⅛	15¼	.....
166	133½	Hallibtn	1.68	13	230	152½	150¾	151½	−1⅞
....	....	Hallibtn	wi	...	1	51⅛	51⅛	51⅛	.....

The new stock's first day of trading 3/25

Stated a little differently, investors like to see earnings improve—especially at an increasing rate. Also, much can depend on the numbers that analysts have been expecting.

As the next page illustrates, investors should visit a company's Internet Web site.

FINDING WELL-MANAGED COMPANIES

"Earnings growth," although desirable, does not by itself define a well-managed company. Equally important are "revenue growth" and the many management decisions required to attain it. The earnings report can be one clue to finding a well-managed company.

Firing thousands of top-notch workers in the name of "productivity" in order to maintain a dividend or to meet a quarterly profit target does not necessarily indicate superior management. This is especially true if the company should be investing in research, developing new products, modernizing its production facilities, or hiring new salespeople. Long-term holders become familiar with their company over time and can recognize the possibility of important fundamental changes when they occur.

In the 14 years from 1988 to 2002, 3M has effectively doubled its earnings (EPS growth of only 5% annually) by introducing new and innovative products. Also, 3M improved its profitability through greater productivity. The company's revenue growth has been a meager 3% per year. This time frame included the recession in 1990–1991 as well as the recession in 2001–2002, plus a negative currency trend. So, informed 3M Company shareowners found that quarterly release to be encouraging. In each cycle, investors should be watching to see how a company meets its challenges.

Dividends and Stock Splits Each quarter, a company's board of directors meets to decide how much, if any, of the company's earnings will be paid to stockholders as a cash dividend. If a dividend is "declared," the directors will also set a "date of record." This means that stockholders who are on record as owning the stock on or before that date are entitled to this dividend. Anyone buying the stock after that date would have to wait for the next declaration to receive a dividend. As a result, the stock's market price is reduced by the amount of the dividend on the day after the date of record. To say it another way, the stock is "ex-dividend" after that date.

			— H—H—H —						
36	27⅛	HackW	2.48	7	5	32¾	32¼	32¾	.....
18⅝	14¾	HallFB	.60	12	10	17⅝	17	17	− ⅝
17¼	13¾	HallPrt	.80a	6	2	14⅝	14⅝	14⅝	− ⅛
166	133½	Hallibtn	1.68	13	155	152¼	150⅜	150¾	− ¾
52⅛	48¼	Hallibtn	wi	...	60	50⅞	50½	50¾	+ ⅛

The last day of the "when issued" period 4/29

			— H—H—H —						
36	27⅛	HackW	2.48	7	4	33	32½	33	+ ¼
18⅝	14¾	HallFB	.60	12	35	17⅛	16½	16¾	− ¼
17¼	13¾	HallPrt	.80a	7	11	15⅜	14¾	15⅜	+ ¾
52⅛	48¼	Hallibtn	.56	13	562	50¼	49¾	50¼	− ½

The "new" stock is trading alone 4/30

When a company's earnings improve, the directors might raise the regular dividend rate, or perhaps declare an "extra dividend." This term is not to be confused with the term "ex-dividend." On the other hand, if the company's earnings trend is unfavorable, the dividend could be reduced or omitted entirely. Dividend declarations, good or bad, are sometimes found in a special dividend section of the newspaper.

Perhaps the directors of a corporation will want to conserve cash but still reward the stockholders. In this instance, the directors might declare a "stock dividend." As an example, a stockholder who owns 100 shares of a company that declares a 10% stock dividend would receive another 10 shares from the company—although the value of all 110 shares would be the same as that of the 100 shares held initially. The pie is simply being divided into eleven pieces rather than ten. If the company's per share cash dividend rate remains the same, the stockholder has, in effect, been given increased future dividend income. However, if the dividend rate is cut to adjust for the stock dividend or if the company does not pay a regular cash dividend and has no intention of doing so, then the stockholder has received absolutely nothing new. In this case, the directors of the company should explain their action to the stockholders.

Much the same can be said about a "stock split," regardless of how the stock is divided—2 for 1, 3 for 1, 3 for 2, or whatever. For example, if XYZ Company has 20,000,000 shares outstanding and the directors declare a 2 for 1 stock split, there would be 40,000,000 shares, or twice as many, outstanding after the split. If the stock price happened to be $50 before the split, it would be $25 after. At the same time, the earnings per share figure is also halved. A stockholder 100 shares before the split would, of course, own 200 shares after it, but the total value would be the same (similar to holding two nickels instead of one dime). In other words, unless the dividend is increased, the stockholder receives nothing new when a company's stock is split.

There is, however, a school of thought that a lower-priced stock becomes more "marketable," or more attractive to the investing public. To a certain degree, this is true. Primarily for psychological reasons, some investors prefer owning stock in multiples of 100 shares, called "round lots," rather than any amount less than 100 shares, called "odd lots." There is a common belief held by many investors that 600 shares of a $5 stock will appreciate in

Microsoft's 2 for 1 Stock Split

5.8	29.75	18.32	+	MicrosSys MCRS	...	26	z82802	23.72	0.97
26.4	21.78	4.66	+	Microsemi MSCC	...	dd	1731	7.70	−0.18
−6.6	65	41.41		Microsoft MSFT .16p	...	28	401698	48.30	1.31
2.0	24.30	23.10		Microsoft wi MSFTV n	...	...	z3550	23.98	0.56
37.9	32.40	4.20		MicroStrat MSTR	...	10	3695	20.83	1.27
−33.3	2.32	0.01		MicroStratw n	...	...	14	0.04	...
−13.9	3.55	0.88		MicrotekMed MTMD	...	16	156	2.05	−0.03
−39.9	16.69	1.52		Microtune TUNE	...·	dd	2122	1.88	0.03
8.5	13.68	2.64		Micrvisn MVIS	...	dd	624	5.77	−0.11

February 18

value more rapidly than 200 shares of a $15 stock or 10 shares of a $300 stock. While it is true that a lower-priced stock is often more volatile, the company's earnings progress is, by far, a more important influence on the future value of the stock.

Inexperienced investors can be misled by stock splits—or, for that matter, by low-priced stocks in general. A $20 stock is not necessarily a better buy than a $40 stock. In fact, higher-priced stocks are frequently among the leading companies in their industries.

For example, there is IBM in the office equipment industry, Johnson & Johnson in the health-care field, and so on. While these stocks have split at one time or another, the managements of these and other leading companies are probably fully aware of the informal status of having their shares appear at a "respectable" price.

Normally, when a company—especially an important company—announces a stock split, the newspapers reveal the necessary details. The *Wall Street Journal* places an "s" after the company's stock symbol to denote "split" and then an "n" once the new shares trade on a split basis. Note on the next page how the *Journal* presented Microsoft's latest 2 for 1 split.

Years ago, a split rarely went undetected. There was a transitional period of at least a week or so between the time the "old" shares were being traded and the time the new, split shares were trading. During this transition, the split stock would be trading on a "when-issued" basis, which meant that the shares had been authorized by the corporation but had not yet been issued or delivered.

The illustrations given here show how a split used to appear in the newspaper, using the sequence of Halliburton Company's 3 for 1 stock split of years ago as an example. Today, the stock split ceremony is fast and less formal, but the behind-the-scenes process remains exactly the same.

As the NYSE explains it, "Ordinarily, the date fixed for settlement of when-issued contracts is the fourth business day after the mailing of split shares. When-issued trading itself terminates on the mail date."

In Wall Street parlance, a "stock dividend" involves the distribution of less than 25% of the outstanding shares. A "partial stock split" is the distribution of 25% or more, but less than 100%, of outstanding shares. A "stock split" involves the distribution of 100% or more of the outstanding stock.

After a nasty bear market, the price of a stock can be taken to an unacceptable level. In such a case, the board of directors might declare a "reverse stock split."

4.8	29.75	18.32	+	MicrosSys MCRS		...	25	1332	23.50	−0.22
29.9	21.78	4.66	+	Microsemi MSCC		...	dd	1174	7.91	0.21
−3.4	32.50	20.71		Microsoft MSFT	.08p	...	29	560722	24.96	0.81
39.1	31.80	4.20		MicroStrat MSTR		...	10	3784	21	0.17
33.3	2.32	0.01		MicroStratw n		...	...	18	0.08	0.04
−13.1	3.55	0.88		MicrotekMed MTMD		...	16	368	2.07	0.02
−39.6	16.69	1.52		Microtune TUNE		...	dd	3573	1.89	0.01
9.4	13.68	2.64		Micrvisn MVIS		...	dd	z54265	5.82	0.05

February 19

Shares that have fallen to penny-stock levels could face delisting procedures or simply be shunned by the investment community. Thus, a reverse split might be appropriate. For example, a 1-for-10 reverse split would raise the share price of a $1.25 stock to $12.50. The effect is just the reverse of a stock split, as explained earlier. However, because the circumstances are not entirely positive, reverse splits rarely help stocks regain their upside momentum immediately.

Short Interest One popular Wall Street trading technique is "short selling" or "selling a stock short." When an investor expects a stock to rise, it is purchased, with the intention of selling it later at a higher price. On the other hand, if the investor expects the price to decline, the shares can legally be "sold short" by borrowing them from a broker and then immediately selling them on the open market. The short seller must buy back an equivalent number of shares later, hopefully at a lower price. Once the stock is repurchased, the same number of shares is repaid to the broker. The profit, or the difference between the price at which the stock was sold and the price at which it was later purchased, belongs to the short seller (less commissions and taxes, of course).

At mid-month, each exchange announces its short-interest figures. This is a list of companies, showing, individually, the number of shares of each that had been sold short and were still short as of the indicated date, usually the fourteenth or fifteenth. For the most part, these are shares that must be repurchased in the future. It can be said that a high short interest is both bearish (because many people believe that stock prices will be declining) and bullish (because these shares must be repurchased at some future date, and thus represent potential buying power).

Mutual Funds Today the number of mutual funds is greater than the number of stocks, so finding mutual fund quotations is not a difficult task. Because of the diversification of their portfolios, mutual funds are much less volatile than individual stocks. So reviewing their prices every day may not be necessary—but reading the table is easy.

Because there are so many of them, the *Wall Street Journal* and the *New York Times* offer only limited lists of mutual funds. *IBD* (*Investor's Business Daily*) is much more generous, but it might require a magnifying glass and a ruler. The next page illustrates a small portion of a typical daily table.

T. Rowe Price Associates, the high-quality investment firm in Baltimore, has a family of no-load mutual funds, and its offerings are typically found under the heading "Price Funds." For example, an investor who owns two TRP funds, the Capital Appreciation Fund and the New Era Fund, could see the following in a newspaper:

FUND	NAV	NET CHG	YTD %RET	3-YR %RET	FUND	NAV	NET CHG	YTD %RET	3-YR %RET
P Q					PionFdC p	28.62	0.32	-4.1	-10.8
					Pitcairn Funds				
PBHG Funds					DivValue	8.23	0.10	-2.9	NS
CliprFoc	12.97	0.21	-1.9	14.3	TaxExBd	10.70	-0.01	-0.3	NS
EmgGro	8.44	0.13	0.6	-35.5	**Preferred Group**				
Growth	13.90	0.18	-2.0	-30.6	AssetA	9.97	0.11	-2.3	-6.1
IRACapPres	10.00	...	0.3	5.7	FxdIn	10.59	...	0.3	9.2
LrgCpGr	14.67	0.17	-0.9	-20.8	IntlVal	9.99	-0.03	-3.9	-7.2
LrgCpVl	9.90	0.15	-2.7	-2.2	LgCpGwth	8.44	0.13	-1.5	-21.6
LrgCp20	10.97	0.12	-1.8	-29.2	ST Gov	10.12	...	...	7.1
MidCpVal	12.43	0.18	-2.7	3.8	Value	14.48	0.18	-3.0	-4.7
SelEq	15.43	0.15	-4.2	-36.1	**Price Funds**				
SmlpVl	13.63	0.07	-2.9	-2.7	Balanced	15.24	0.09	-1.7	-2.9
TechCom	7.52	0.10	0.8	-51.2	BlChip	21.57	0.32	-1.7	-13.2
PIMCO Fds Admin MMS					CA Bond	11.01	-0.02	-0.8	8.3
CapAppAd p	12.38	0.18	-1.3	-9.9	CapApp	14.11	0.13	-0.7	11.4
PIMCO Fds Admin PIMS					DivGro	16.20	0.20	-3.3	-4.4
HiYldAd p	8.67	0.02	2.4	1.9	EmgMktB	10.45	0.01	0.9	12.1
LDurAd p	10.27	0.01	0.2	7.6	EmMktS	10.10	0.04	-1.2	-13.9
LTrmGvt n	10.92	-0.01	-1.0	13.7	EqInc	19.15	0.25	-3.2	1.3
RealRetAd p	11.30	-0.03	0.5	NS	EqIndex	23.11	0.30	-2.4	-13.2
ShortTrmAd p	10.00	...	0.3	5.0	Eurcpe	11.93	0.01	-7.4	-16.6
StockPIAd p	7.60	0.09	-2.1	-12.0	FinSvcs	16.32	0.17	-2.6	6.4
TotRtAd p	10.67	...	0.3	10.5	FL Inter	11.11	-0.01	-0.5	7.3
TRII Ad p	10.27	...	0.2	10.3	ForEq	9.99	...	-6.1	-19.2
PIMCO Fds Instl MMS					GNMA	9.87	-0.01	0.1	9.5
CapApp	12.57	0.18	-1.2	-9.7	Growth	18.28	0.27	-1.6	-10.3
EmgComps	15.68	0.19	-1.0	1.4	Gr&In	16.70	0.20	-2.4	-5.7
MdCp	15.33	0.19	-1.6	-5.8	HelSci	14.52	0.20	0.1	-2.3
Renaissance	13.74	0.14	-6.5	6.4	HiYield	6.34	-0.01	1.8	2.7
RCM LCGwth	9.84	0.13	-2.6	-17.4	InstHiYld	9.98x	-0.02	1.6	NS
RCM MidCap	1.83	0.03	-1.1	-17.7	N Inc	8.90	-0.01	0.4	9.1
PIMCO Fds Instl PIMS					IntlBond	9.54	-0.01	2.9	6.8
EmMktsBd	9.33	0.03	1.4	19.6	IntDis	15.99	-0.08	-0.4	-20.6
FrgnRd	10.69	...	1.3	9.7	IntlStk	8.33	...	-6.2	-19.6
GlblRd	10.03	0.01	2.5	9.7	InstSmCap	9.12	0.09	-3.9	NS
HiYld	8.67	0.02	2.4	2.1	Lat Am	6.98	0.02	-7.1	-11.0
LowDur	10.27	0.01	0.2	7.9	MCapGro	30.48	0.41	-1.8	-5.0
LowDurII	9.99	...	0.2	7.8	MCapVal	14.70	0.12	-2.0	10.3
LTUSG	10.92	-0.01	-1.0	13.9	MCEqGr	14.94	0.20	-2.0	-5.1
ModDur	10.33	0.01	0.3	10.3	MD Short	5.29	...	0.2	5.1
MuriRd	10.17	...	-0.3	8.9	MD Bond	10.79	-0.02	-0.6	8.6
RealRtnl	11.30	-0.03	0.5	13.1	MediaTel	14.48	0.18	0.3	-19.1
ShortT	10.00	...	0.3	5.2	N Amer	21.77	0.30	-1.3	-16.0
StkcPLS	7.74	0.09	-2.0	-11.7	N Asia	5.74	0.03	2.7	-17.3
TotRt	10.67	...	0.3	10.8	New Era	19.57	0.25	-5.1	2.8
					N Horiz	16.17	0.16	-2.6	-12.3

On this day, the Capital Appreciation Fund had a net asset value (NAV) of $14.11, which was $0.13 above the NAV for the previous day and down 0.8% since the beginning of the year. The New Era Fund reported a net asset value of $19.57, a $0.25 gain from the prior day and down 5.1% since the beginning of the year. For these funds, the trailing three-year annualized returns were 11.4% and 2.8%, respectively.

Business News In addition to the most popular *Wall Street Journal*, there are many newspapers that offer business news in detail. One of these is *Investor's Business Daily*. Although this paper is directed more toward traders than toward investors, and its stock tables are arranged in a very awkward manner, the additional statistics and analytical insights make the newspaper worth its competitive price.

The social, economic, and political circumstances of different markets are never exactly the same, although "old-timers" occasionally cite similarities. Nevertheless, an investor can be well informed about the financial events of the day by focusing on two principal subjects: "the business cycle" and the status of "inflation" or "deflation."

THE BUSINESS CYCLE

Described as the expansion or contraction of the economy as a whole, the business cycle has an important influence on the profit trends of most companies. To keep abreast, there are eight key items that the investor should watch:

1. Trends in consumer confidence and spending

2. Actions by the Federal Reserve Board (FRB) to tighten or ease the supply of money

3. The trend of interest rates (the "Treasury bill rate" and the "prime lending rate" are good benchmarks)

4. The government's Index of Leading Indicators

5. Tax increases or tax cuts

6. The accumulation or liquidation of business inventories

7. Capital expenditure plans of businesses for new plant and equipment

8. Government spending for defense and social needs

Today, business is more global than ever before. The business cycle in the United States will be influenced to an ever-increasing extent by international trade opportunities, currency exchange rates between countries, and competing products and services from abroad.

INFLATION OR DEFLATION

Inflation, the declining value of money as a result of rising prices, is caused, many economists believe, by excessive government spending. This subject should be closely monitored because it influences, and is influenced by, the business cycle. Moreover, and most important, inflation has a direct impact on the investment environment. A rising or declining inflation rate can shift the balance of investment returns between stocks, bonds, and other alternatives.

In this regard, investors should watch the Consumer Price Index (see the appendix) and the Producer Price Index. The government announces the monthly figures for each on or about the middle of the following month. In addition, the Commodity Research Bureau (CRB) Index and the prices of gold, silver, and oil are all good indicators for measuring inflation.

The effect of deflation, or declining prices, mostly as a result of excessive competition or lack of demand, is best exem-

House Approves Compromise Bill

plified by the economic conditions of the early 1930s.

As a general rule, the operating results of most companies can be hurt badly in an environment of high inflation or steep deflation, especially if the company has little or no ability to control its prices.

Historically, the most positive environment for equities has been during periods with a declining rate of inflation (economists call this "disinflation"). The three periods in U.S. history when this environment was most prevalent (measured by year-to-year changes in the CPI) were in the decade of the 1920s, the1981 to 1986 period, and the 1991 to 2001 period.

Over the long term, investors can probably assume that inflation will persist, although held in check temporarily by a decline in business activity, as seen recently, or by tough Fed policies (i.e., sharply higher interest rates). In its present form, the U.S. political system promotes inflation.

POLITICS AND THE STOCK MARKET

Harry Truman once said: "The buck stops here." Not so with Congress. Under the present circumstances, a responsible fiscal policy is nearly impossible because members of Congress will always find new programs on which to spend our fiat currency "for the benefit of their constituents." Politicians, of course, are motivated by the desire to be reelected, and they are more apt to be reelected if they deliver what they promised on the campaign trail. This is true for Republicans and Democrats alike.

There are two political measures that could help solve this problem—although neither is likely to be enacted without a crisis to force the issue:

1. Some effective means of restraining pork barrel legislation now that the line-item veto has been struck down by the Supreme Court.
2. A constitutional amendment that requires the federal budget to be balanced every year, including limits on spending. Any exceptions should be made only in cases of dire economic circumstances.

Unfortunately, both solutions are remote. If history is any guide, politicians never relinquish power willingly, and, given a choice, they would prefer not to be held accountable for their budget decisions.

When it comes to politics and the stock market, there is a general misconception regarding "the party in power." The U.S. Constitution places the burden of finance on Congress: "All Bills for raising Revenue shall originate in the House of Representatives; but the Senate may propose or concur with Amendments as on other Bills." The president can propose legislation, but can halt congressional spending only temporarily. Therefore, the direction of the stock market depends mostly on the party that controls Congress.

Among other times, Republicans controlled both houses of Congress during the entire decade of the 1920s and from November 1994 until May 2001. Since then, the two parties have held control alternately.

Conclusion Long-term shareholders must continuously maintain a steady perspective and beware of excessive "news minutiae." Between the promotional financial channels on TV, the Internet, magazines, and daily newspapers, investors can be misled by unimportant news items and can be "whipsawed" if they attempt to catch every short-term cycle. When each so-called critical financial story breaks, the long-term implications of its details will need to be weighed.

To benefit from this new input, it will be necessary for the investor to first develop a long-term economic picture on which to base an investment strategy. Then, each day, the investor must decide how this new information relates to it. This personal scenario will change only gradually—and rarely will it be altered dramatically from one month to the next. But without this framework, it will be easy for the investor to "miss the forest for the trees," as they say, making success in the stock market that much more elusive.

Finally, the investor should be alert for unusual opportunities. History contains many examples of how unexpected events can affect stock prices. By definition, unexpected events cannot be predicted, but they sometimes present an opportunity to profitably buy or sell against the emotions of the crowd.

Beyond the emotions of the day, however, the keys to investment success are often found behind the headlines and between the lines of the financial news stories.

5 | Investing and Trading

Introduction

Noted financier Bernard Baruch once said, "There is no investment which does not involve some risk and is not something of a gamble." Indeed, most experienced investors can immediately recognize the relationship between the risk level of a security and the reward it promises.

Because individuals' investment needs and objectives are different, their risk and reward expectations are different and their approaches to the stock market are different.

This chapter will help the new investor enter the Wall Street arena. It will aid in the selection of a stockbroker and provide guidelines to help the investor establish a realistic investment objective. In addition, it examines many market details that serious investors should know. Explanations of the margin account, of bear market strategies, hedges, exchange-traded funds (ETFs), arbitraging, a preliminary look at taxes, investment clubs, and mutual funds are among the numerous topics discussed.

Family Financial Planning Financial advisors unanimously recommend against buying common stocks, preferred stocks, or long-term bonds at least until

1. Some money has been set aside to meet emergency family needs for a few months or longer.

2. An adequate property, health, and life insurance plan has been established.

3. Provision has been made for other obvious needs, such as a home and education.

Any money that is earmarked for investing (including a retirement nest egg) should be referred to as "risk capital"— no matter how conservative the intended investment program might be. Although the degree of risk can be controlled to a great extent, an investor should use only capital that can be called "discretionary." Moreover, most advisors often recommend against committing the entire amount at any one time or to any single investment. A flexible investment program provides considerable peace of mind.

Besides money, time is also a factor. Managing a portfolio properly requires a certain amount of time and effort. Surveys have shown that dedicated investors can spend six to twelve hours, or more, each month on investment work.

Tax-free retirement programs can be administered in various ways. Here, most individuals will require some honest and practical advice. There is no better time to begin than now.

For specific, personal advice on family financial planning, one approach might be to consult an attorney or an accountant, both of whom are somewhat impartial observers. But the fact is, nearly everyone today is trying to sell something financial.

How much risk capital can or should be made available will be revealed by a well-organized financial plan. With this family program complete, a personalized "investment objective" can then be established to determine the types of investments most suitable under the circumstances. Here, a good stockbroker, sometimes called an "account executive," can be worth his or her weight in gold.

The Stockbroker Over the past thirty years, millions of workers in the United States have encountered evolutionary shifts in their industries. People in the steel, auto, and textile fields have seen such a shift firsthand. High-tech employees who rode the boom-and-bust dot-com bubble in Silicon Valley saw it happen. And, recently, the investment community has been turned upside down, forcing Wall Street workers, including analysts and stockbrokers, into a notable defensive posture.

Historically, the economic well-being of this group has been influenced primarily by the trend in stock prices. This time, however, the change will not be temporary, and things will never be the same as they once were.

Recently, about 5,100 firms and 660,000 "brokers" were registered with FINRA. It appears that these numbers have already peaked and are likely to decline in the years ahead for the reasons explained earlier. In fact, it can now be said that the traditional stockbroker is a dying breed.

Most account executives nowadays are emphasizing "financial services," which can include other products, such as insurance. So, these professionals have been moving into the twenty-first century sporting more esoteric titles, and with a much broader perspective. While we may still affectionately call them "stockbrokers," in most cases today, their employers will probably apply terms such as "financial consultant" or "asset manager."

Searching for a good stockbroker is much like looking for a family doctor. Expertise, personality, and reputation are all important qualifications.

Quite often, a broker is referred by family, friends, or business associates. It is best to begin the search with a candidate list of two or three people. The choice would be made following individual "interviews" (but nothing more than friendly conversations).

The person selected should be employed by a reputable brokerage firm, preferably a NYSE member firm, and should have the necessary experience, or access to it. As a broker for a member firm, this individual is most likely the graduate of an extensive training course and has passed several comprehensive tests (including the Series 7, administered by FINRA). Then he or she is a registered professional.

The rules and code of ethics are strict. Among the many regulations, a broker is forbidden to guarantee any customer against a loss and cannot share in the profits or losses of any customer's account or receive rebates to secure business.

Every broker interviewed will most likely appear to be a friendly person in a busy, almost hectic environment. The choice may be difficult. It is not unusual for a broker to have hundreds of customers, although probably no more than

An artist's rendering of
trading on the New York
Stock Exchange in 1850

ten or twenty of them will be considered extremely active. A broker is obviously on the phone often and cannot devote too much time to any one client, so the interview should be brief—perhaps in the evening.

Other items to consider during the interviews are personality, investment philosophy, the quality of the firm's research, other services, and, of course, the level of commission rates and fees. Often, brokers have areas of special interests or specific investment talents. It is particularly beneficial when the broker-client relationship is compatible in this regard.

Sometimes, but not often, paperwork or "computer glitches" in the "back office" of an otherwise well-managed brokerage firm can result in clerical errors. Discussions with people who are using the brokerage firm being considered could be one way to check the frequency of this possible inconvenience.

Once all interviews have been completed and the selection has been made, a conference should be held between the customer and the broker to review the client's investment objective. If personal finances are discussed, the topics might include age and family circumstances, income, personal debt, interest payments, insurance coverage, and inheritance, if

any. Again, all family financial planning should be completed beforehand.

The brokerage firm charges a commission each time stock is bought and sold. The stockbroker, an employee of the firm, will receive a portion of that fee.

For example, the commission on the purchase or sale of, say, 200 shares of a $25 stock, a $5,000 investment, is typically about $75 to $125 (1.5% to 2.5%). Of this, the broker normally receives about 35 to 40%. Note, too, that a registered representative's income increases if customers buy and sell stock more frequently. For the customer, this is almost always counterproductive. This practice, taken to an extreme, is called "churning" and can result in severe penalties for the broker and for the firm if it encourages the practice. This is not usually a problem, however. Stockbrokers know that it is to their own advantage in the long run for each customer to be a successful investor.

Stockbrokers should not be judged by the short term price action of any stocks they recommend or do not recommend (they can neither control stock prices nor consistently predict them). They should be judged primarily by the type and quality of the service they provide in return for the commission dollars and/or salary they are being paid.

To use a stockbroker most effectively, the investor should

- Be considerate and call only when necessary rather than just to "chat." Then the stockbroker will return a call promptly, thinking that it must be important. To be fair, a small-commission customer should not demand a large slice of the broker's time.

- Listen to the stockbroker's advice. The ultimate decision to buy or sell, however, should rest entirely with the customer—who should also assume the credit or the blame for each decision.

- Be explicit when placing an order or giving instructions to minimize any misunderstandings. This is important because most business is conducted over the phone when a computer is not used.

- Look to the stockbroker as a valuable information source. The customer should feel free to ask for research reports and other investment data. In most cases, this information, along with account access, is available via the brokerage firm's Web site. The broker can help here too.

- Build a research library at home. Old stock guides, investment handbooks, annual reports, and other research material kept in home files will make the task of searching for information later much easier. Of course, a computer is essential today.

Discount Brokers Most investors do not have the time. They also want or need the extra assistance and the stockbroker relationship that a so-called full service brokerage firm can provide. However, firms that offer cut rate commissions, referred to as "discount brokers," are worth considering if the investor expects to be independent and active. Either way, commission costs should not be onerous.

An individual who trades only a few times each year might not find the substantially lower cost worthwhile, considering all the services required. Also, in most cases, discount brokers post a minimum level of activity below which an account maintenance fee could be charged. But for an active, independent investor trading fifteen or twenty times or more each year, the savings could be sizable.

Ever since fixed commission rates were abolished—and now with Internet access—the selection of a discount broker has been made very easy. They are in every city. And as with other aspects of investing, if a discount broker is being con-

sidered, it would be wise to investigate the firm and its background.

Opening an Account Opening a brokerage account is no more difficult than opening a charge account at a local store or a checking account with a bank. In fact, they are similar in many ways. The client must demonstrate a satisfactory credit rating, certain financial responsibilities must be met, the account can be personal or joint, and a monthly statement is usually mailed to the customer.

The typical retail brokerage office is a large room with ten to twenty desks for the brokers, often designated "the boardroom." Years ago, customers could stand or sit to watch a ticker tape that displayed stock prices. This is no longer true. Today, most investors use a home computer or a local library with its reference books, various subscriptions, and other investment material. Libraries also offer computers for those patrons who want online stock quotes and news sources.

Depending upon the policy of the firm, or that of the office manager, it is not always necessary to have an account with a brokerage firm to visit the office. However, it is inadvisable to walk in unannounced and interrupt the daily routine of an office.

For more about online brokers and their services, see Chapter 10, "The Internet."

The day on which a share of stock is bought or sold is called the "trade date." The customer (and the brokerage firm) must deposit the required cash and/or securities into the account on or before the third business day after the transaction takes place. This deadline is known as the "settlement date." Saturdays, Sundays, and holidays are not included.

Once the brokerage firm has been paid in full for stock purchased, the stockholder can request any one of three procedures:

1. The stock can be "transferred and shipped." This means that the name of the owner is transferred onto the stock certificate and it is mailed to the designated address. This process, usually involving a transfer agent (e.g., a bank), normally takes about two weeks. The stockholder must then find a safe place to keep the certificate. If it is lost or destroyed, it can, with some effort, be replaced.

2. The stock can be "transferred and held." This means that the certificate is prepared, as in the first case, but it is kept for the owner in the brokerage firm's vault. If the stock is sold later,

the owner must sign a "stock power" permitting its transfer to the new owner.

3. The stock can be held in "street name." In this instance, the stock is safely held by the broker in the broker's name for the customer's convenience. All dividends, which would otherwise be mailed directly from the company to the stockholder, are credited to the account or forwarded, as the customer directs. Corporate reports and proxy statements (used for voting) are forwarded to the customer.

The monthly statement mailed to the customer is similar to a bank statement in appearance. It shows, in addition to other data, a beginning balance, all transactions made during the period, a final cash balance, and stock positions at the end of the period. Stock held in the account at the date of the statement is said to be "long"; stock owed in the account by the customer is said to be "short."

There are two basic types of accounts: a cash account and a margin account. Many brokerage customers today have both.

The cash account, by far the most popular, is used when securities are bought or sold in a direct cash transaction. In a cash account, every transaction is concluded on or before the settlement date. If stock has been purchased, the customer has paid for it in full, the customer's broker has paid the seller's broker, and the shares have been credited to the buyer's account . . . all occurring within three business days.

A margin account, which will be explained in greater detail later, allows the customer to borrow from the broker part of the amount needed to purchase or sell securities. The minimum New York Stock Exchange requirement is $2,000 to open a margin account in which most types of securities can be bought and sold. The margin account, like the cash account, requires that all transactions be concluded by the settlement date, but a customer who is buying or selling "on margin" need not deposit more than the required amount by that time. The broker will extend some credit to the customer based on the amount of cash and/or securities in the account. For this service, the customer pays an interest charge to the broker.

Because a minor does not have the legal power to contract in his or her own name, opening a brokerage account is limited to adults. Until the mid 1950s, giving securities to minors and having shares registered in a minor's name presented complications. Since then, to deal with this problem, all states have adopted laws that are similar in most cases to the 1956 Uniform Gifts to Minors Act, sponsored by the brokerage industry. Under these laws, minors can own securities in special "custodial accounts" if the minor also has an adult custodian (most likely an adult family member). The laws are different in many states. It is, therefore, advisable to know the legalities and their possible disadvantages before a custodial account is opened.

Professional Counsel A professional investment advisor is worth considering if an individual has a large sum of money to invest, say $100,000 or more, and has neither an interest in mutual funds (explained later) nor the time to devote to personal portfolio management. Advisory fees, which are usually tax deductible, vary. The fee is typically 1% to 1.5% annually on portfolios up to about $200,000. Thereafter, the cost declines proportionately. The investor must still pay brokerage commissions, but may designate a stockbroker, give the counselor freedom to select the broker, or instruct that orders be executed at the lowest possible commission rate.

Most investment counselors work closely with several stockbrokers and a few banks to obtain their services. Commissions directed to brokers (typically for research services) are referred to as "soft dollars."

In addition to investment counselors, the trust departments of many banks also offer professional services. These services frequently include both portfolio management and custodial functions, for essentially the same 1% to 1.5% fee structure. Most investment counselors and banks have either in-house investment research or, as in most cases, the ability to obtain it elsewhere. Custodial functions, such as safekeeping of securities, dividend or interest collection and disbursements, and other accounting tasks, are handled primarily by banks.

The recommended approach, at least initially, for those who employ professional money management services would be a "nondiscretionary" account, with the understanding that the advisor has some freedom in managing the portfolio. With such an account, the investor will be involved, can learn more about the investment process, and will be in a better position to evaluate the style and talents of the portfolio manager.

Investment Objectives Selecting an objective that best meets an individual's personal financial needs is difficult. There are often many confusing alternatives.

Market Ends Higher

Generally speaking, portfolios are managed for income, capital appreciation, or safety, or some combination thereof.

RISK AND REWARD

Perhaps the most basic of all Wall Street concepts is: "The greater the expected return, the greater the investment risk." In effect, this "risk/reward ratio," as it is often called, places a desire to preserve capital at one end of the spectrum and a desire to maximize return at the other end. Evidence of this principle has been documented in several thorough studies of historical rates of investment return. The table presented on the next page is based on these findings. It shows, in very general terms, the typical risk/reward choices that investors have had over the past several decades. Throughout this period, the rate of inflation averaged 2% to 4% annually. Also see the appendix.

It is important to note that this risk/reward table can change dramatically from one month to the next as investors respond to changes in interest rates or inflation. For example, given an inflation rate of 5.5%, Treasury bills at 4.5%, savings accounts at 5.0%, and corporate bonds at 7.5%, one might conclude that a share of stock should provide a return of at least 10% to be competitive for the investor's dollar. Today, it might be less than that.

With the higher interest and inflation rates experienced in past years, it is easy to see why investors have become more sensitive to these relationships.

Each category in the table also obviously has its own risk/reward scale, and all opportunities are related to one another. There are, for example, many low-quality bonds that provide a better return (also with greater risk) than the typical high-quality stock.

SELECTION AND TIMING

To be successful on Wall Street, every investor must find a satisfactory combination of two key variables: "investment selection" and "timing." While it may sound elementary and trite, an investor must make the proper selection at the proper time to obtain the best possible results. A wrong selection at the wrong time can be costly, and mixed results can be obtained with any other combination.

As a general rule, investment selection and investment timing are inversely important. When the investment horizon is longer, selection becomes more important than timing. But timing is far more criti-

Investment	Degree of Risk	Annual Return (Reward)
Treasury Bill	Smallest degree of risk. Only the government has the power to print money. The return is usually just enough to offset inflation.	2.5–3.5%
Government Bond	High degree of safety. Adjusted for inflation, the return is modest.	3.0–4.0%
Savings Account	Greater risk than government bonds, although funds are insured by the government. Little protection against higher rates of inflation.	3.5–4.5%
Corporate Bond	More risk than a savings account. Priority over common stock if there is a business failure. Adjusted for inflation, the return is modest.	4.0–5.0%
Share of Stock	The highest degree of risk due to possible business failure. The return includes about 4% from dividends. Some protection from inflation.	7.0–9.0%

MARKET TIMING:
"Timing is for eggs."

cal when the horizon is shorter. For example, the common stock of Deere & Co., a leading manufacturer of farm equipment, was quoted in 1998 at half of its $32 high only months earlier (adjusted for splits). Had the stock been purchased months before at $25, any serious investor would have been disappointed with the 40% "loss," but might have seen it as an opportunity to buy more. On the other hand, a trader in 1998 would have viewed the situation differently and might have sold the stock, even at a loss. Ten years later, in 2008, the stock price hit $90 before plunging again. If the company is growing, time works in favor of the investor.

TOTAL RETURN

Securities analysts often compare investment opportunities by estimating the total capital appreciation, plus dividend (or interest) return, that each investment provides annually. This calculation, expressed as a total annual percentage figure, is referred to as "total return."

Done properly, total return takes into account possible tax consequences—especially when tax-free investments are under consideration. Because taxes are personal and unique to each investor, they are excluded in the examples to follow.

Future capital appreciation of a stock is difficult to estimate. To make the process easier, analysts include in their total return calculations the assumption that today's price/earnings ratios will not be changing in the future. This means that the estimated growth rate of earnings per share can be used in place of the capital appreciation estimate. Thus, a stock with a projected earnings per share growth rate of 8% and a current dividend yield of 3% is offering a "total return" of 11% before taxes.

Using this total return approach, an investor can immediately see what each investment offers. A hypothetical comparison is illustrated here.

	POSSIBLE CAPITAL APPRECIATION	DIVIDEND OR INTEREST YIELD	TOTAL RETURN
"X" Growth Stock (Earnings Per Share Growth + Div. Yield)	10%	2%	12%
"Y" Income Stock (Earnings Per Share Growth + Div. Yield)	7%	5%	12%
"Z" Corporate Bond (Bond Discount to Maturity + Int. Yield)	2%	7%	9%*
Savings Account	0%	5%	5%
Treasury Bill	4%	0%	4%

* Also called "yield to maturity."

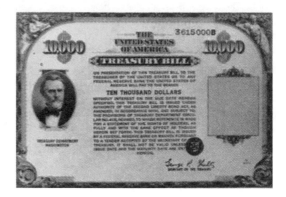

In this case, an investor comparing total return opportunities must make a value judgment between the highly assured 4% return on the Treasury bill, a reasonably safe 5% return on the savings account, a less certain 9% return on the bond, and a much less certain 12% return from either stock. To repeat, taxes must also be taken into consideration.

Finally, when comparing individual stocks of similar quality that offer the same total return, investors should realize that a growth stock probably offers both higher initial market risk and greater reward over time than a slower growing, higher yielding stock. In the preceding example, both stocks promise the same total return of 12%, but, based on the "bird in the hand" argument, there might be greater assurance of obtaining 12% from the income stock initially than from the growth stock. However, patient investors will find that the future earnings increases of the growth stock will, within a few years, produce superior investment results overall.

The Margin Account In a land of credit cards and financial conveniences, and with more than 80 million investors, it is somewhat surprising that there are only a few million margin accounts in use.

While it is true that the margin account is sometimes complex and definitely not for everybody, its application extends well beyond the simple function of buying securities on credit. The margin account is a tool that provides flexibility for the serious investor.

Upon opening a margin account and submitting the normal credit information, the investor will be asked to sign a margin agreement and loan consent that will permit the brokerage firm to pledge or lend securities carried within the account. In addition, the margin account will be subject to various rules, including, as mentioned earlier, an initial minimum requirement of the NYSE, an initial margin requirement established by Regulation T of the Federal Reserve Board (FRB), and maintenance requirements enforced by the brokerage firm.

The initial margin requirement is the minimum percentage of total value that investors must deposit to purchase or sell securities in a margin account. The initial margin requirement for stocks (not all stocks qualify) has been raised twelve times and lowered ten times since the FRB was given power to regulate security credit under the Securities Exchange Act of 1934. The margin requirement since

1934 has been as low as 40% (1937) and as high as 100% (1946). The most recent board action was in January 1974, when the initial margin requirement was lowered from 65% to 50%. In other words, to make a $10,000 stock purchase in a margin account today, an investor must put up, within three days, at least $5,000 collateral, rather than the $6,500 required before.

There is an easy way to calculate the amount of marginable securities that can be bought with a specific amount of cash available:

Add two zeros and divide by the margin number.

By applying this simple formula, an investor can quickly see that $6,000 cash will buy $8,571 worth of marginable securities when the margin requirement is 70% ($6,000 + 00 divided by 70), $10,000 when the margin is 60% ($6,000 + 00 divided by 60), or $12,000 when the margin is 50% ($6,000 + 00 divided by 50).

Using the figures in the last case as an example, if the margin requirement is 50% and the investor deposits $6,000 cash collateral, a decision to purchase, say, $9,000 of marginable stock would be recorded in the margin account in this manner:

$9,000	Current market value
3,000	Debit balance
$6,000	Current equity
4,500	Required margin (50% x $9,000)
─────	
$1,500	Excess margin (can be withdrawn or invested)

The $1,500 excess margin, if invested, has a "buying power" of $3,000 (i.e., $1,500 + 00 divided by 50), which, with the $9,000 already invested, would take the account up to its marginable limit of $12,000.

The "debit balance" is money that the investor owes to the brokerage firm. For this service, the investor is charged an interest rate somewhat above the prime rate charged by banks. This cost should not be disregarded. Normally based on a daily average of the debit balance, the interest cost can fluctuate from month to month as interest rates swing. For example, several years ago, when the prime rate rose to about 12%, an investor's annual cost of carrying a debit balance could have been 14% or more. This is a high price to pay for stock market capital.

A margin account provides leverage that can expand or contract an investor's equity position quickly as the figures on the next page demonstrate.

The curbstone brokers filling orders during a blizzard in the early 1900s

Continuing the earlier example, if the market value of the portfolio climbed 22%, from $9,000 to $11,000, the investor's equity would increase by 33% and buying power would be 67% greater.

$11,000	Current market value
3,000	Debit balance
$ 8,000	Current equity
5,500	Required margin (50% x $11,000)
$ 2,500	Excess margin ($5,000 buying power)

If, instead of rising, the value of the portfolio declined 22% to $7,000, the results would be quite different. In this case, equity declines 33% and buying power drops 67%.

$7,000	Current market value
3,000	Debit balance
$4,000	Current equity
3,500	Required margin (50% x $7,000)
500	Excess margin ($1,000 buying power)

At most brokerage firms, the margin account is the responsibility of a centralized back office department called the margin department. With the help of computers, every account is reviewed daily to keep the firm's brokers and customers informed regarding certain guidelines.

The first is a check to see whether a margin customer's equity is above or below the current federal initial margin requirement, as explained earlier. If it has fallen below, the account is considered "restricted." In a restricted account, the investor has no additional buying power and cannot withdraw more than 30% of any sale proceeds. The remaining 70% would be retained to reduce the debit balance.

Another guideline that is closely watched is the maintenance requirement set by the New York Stock Exchange (NYSE) or by the brokerage firm itself, which sometimes has a requirement that is stricter than that of the exchange. The NYSE maintenance requirement states that a customer's equity may at no time be less than 25% of the market value of the securities carried (brokerage firms often set a 30% or 35% limit). If equity does drop below this level, the account is said to be "undermargined," and the customer will be asked to put up more margin. This is known as a "margin call." If more collateral is not deposited, the broker will sell the securities.

The margin department will establish more than one type of margin account for a customer who uses margin for other specific reasons, such as selling stock short, buying or selling convertible bonds, buying or selling nonconvertible bonds, and so on. Moreover, margin requirements often vary for different types of securities. There are, in other words, many details that investors should learn before using a margin account extensively. This information can be obtained from most brokerage firms or by writing to

NYSE Euronext
11 Wall Street
New York, New York 10005

"Playing the Market" There are several tools and strategies that can lend versatility to an investment program and, in some cases, make stock market investing more profitable. While many of these techniques are not appropriate for most conservative long term portfolios, serious investors should at least be aware of the alternatives available.

TYPES OF ORDERS

The "market order" to buy or sell is the most widely used type of order. It is simply an instruction to the broker and others involved to buy or sell stock at the best possible price once the order reaches the trading post or trading desk. Normally, a market order is executed at a price that is reasonably close to the quote obtained before the order was entered. If the stock is volatile, however, the final price could be better or worse than expected. A market order transaction can be completed and reported back to the broker very quickly. In most cases, a confirmation is mailed to the investor within 24 hours.

The "limit order" is an instruction to buy or sell a stated amount of stock at a specific price (or better). When the target price is not within the current market quote, it is said to be "away from the market," and it will be entered on the specialist's book beneath any similar orders received earlier. So, if there are, as they say, "shares ahead of you," the limit order may not be executed instantly or maybe not at all at that price.

The "stop order," called a "stop loss order" many years ago, is a trading tool designed to protect a profit or prevent further loss if the stock begins to move in the wrong direction. This idea is based on the ageless Wall Street advice, "Let your profits run; cut your losses short." The stop order becomes a market order once the stock trades at or through a certain price, known as the "stop price." If the stop price is reached, there is no guarantee that the executed price will be as favorable.

It is possible, for example, to place an order to sell 100 shares of XYZ at 54 "stop" and later receive notice that your stock was sold at 53.50. Except in technical analysis situations, the stop price should not be placed too close to the current market price, since many stocks can randomly fluctuate 15% or more in a brief period of time. Long-term investors will probably not be using the stop order in the normal course of investing.

The "stop limit order" is a stop order and limit order combination. Like the stop order, it is a trading tool that requires extreme care. A stop limit order to buy means, "As soon as a trade occurs at this top price or higher, the order becomes a limit order to buy." A stop limit order to sell works the same way. As soon as a trade occurs at the stop price or lower, the order becomes a limit order to sell.

Each order to buy or sell may be entered for a single trading day, week, or month, or it may be an "open order," also called a "good 'til canceled (GTC) order." An open order will remain in force until it is canceled by the investor. However, the investor does have an obligation to keep the broker informed on the status of every open order because the exchange specialist must receive confirmation at regular intervals. Not all brokerage firms accept stop orders or GTC orders for unlisted stocks.

DOLLAR COST AVERAGING

There are no magic formulas to stock market investing, but one approach that is widely used and frequently successful is dollar cost averaging. Dollar cost averaging involves purchasing the same dollar amount of stock at regular intervals, regardless of price. As a result, more shares are bought when the price is low than when the price is high. Dollar cost averaging usually works well when the investor

1. Has an investment horizon of at least several years.

2. Selects a company that has favorable growth prospects that could lead to a rising stock price over the long term.

3. Selects a high-quality stock that, preferably, pays a dividend.

4. Is willing to continue the program relentlessly—barring any major change in the company's long-term outlook.

As a real-life example of dollar cost averaging, the table given here shows the result of a ten-year investment program. The name of the stock is not important. This stock's price performance was especially disappointing in this specific time frame, and it was selected for this reason.

Year	Annual Price Range	Shares Bought	Shares Owned at Year End	Average Price	Estimated Annual Dividend Check
1	$29.63–20.38	80	80	$25.00	$ 25
2	26.50–19.25	90	170	23.50	106
3	30.25–23.13	75	245	24.50	251
4	38.25–26.13	63	308	26.00	422
5	37.50–22.63	70	378	26.50	594
6	32.75–21.88	77	455	26.38	664
7	47.75–29.25	52	507	27.63	571
8	48.63–30.75	57	564	28.38	633
9	40.75–29.75	57	621	29.00	702
10	46.38–32.63	56	677	29.50	770

During the period, the company's earnings record was erratic, but profits did grow from $2.79 per share in year 1 to $3.08 per share in year 10. At the same time, the dividend was increased from $0.69 per share to $1.20 per share. In the beginning, the stock price was $29. At the end, it was just above $42.

This table illustrates the result of investing $500 quarterly throughout the ten year period. The program was accomplished by buying the rounded number of shares that $500 would purchase each time. After ten years, the total capital invested was $20,000 before commissions (probably much less than $200).

If profits grow, dividends can become more important as time passes. Had the investor continued the program shown here, nearly half of the annual $2,000 investment would have been contributed by dividends five years later.

Investors who use dollar cost averaging will see the best results if the company's profits and dividends are expected to be growing over an extended period of time. And, as with any mechanical approach, the results should be monitored periodically.

Better still, today many companies offer direct dividend reinvestment plans (called "DRIPs"). By reinvesting dividends without transaction costs, an investor can enjoy the huge benefit of compounding values. See Chapter 6, "Growth Stocks," for even more dramatic dividend examples.

EXCHANGE-TRADED FUNDS (ETFS)

Perhaps the most attractive investment vehicle created in recent years is the "exchange-traded fund," known as an ETF. It is a basket of securities designed to track an index, whether it is a broad market, an industry sector, or an international stock. ETFs are fairly liquid and trade on an exchange much like stocks.

This clever idea was pioneered by the American Stock Exchange in early 1993 with the introduction of the Standard & Poor's Depositary Receipt (SPDR, better known as "Spider"). It now trades on the NYSE ARCA platform with the ticker symbol SPY, and it represents about 1/10 the value of the S&P 500.

Another notable ETF is the Dow Jones Industrial Average fund ("Diamonds" with the ARCA symbol DIA). Also very popular is QQQQ, which tracks the value of the Nasdaq 100 Index (about 1/40 value).

Over the years, most mutual fund portfolio managers have been unable to match the performance of the S&P 500 and the DJIA. So, introducing an investment that moves in lockstep with each average has been a compelling alternative to a managed fund.

An ETF offers diversification, lower costs (regular brokerage commissions apply), all-day trading (most mutual funds can be purchased or redeemed only at day-end prices), tax efficiency, and dividend opportunities. As with mutual funds, ETFs also offer hedging possibilities.

It is important to read the prospectus of any ETF (normally available on the Internet via the ETF sponsor) before investing.

Exchange-traded funds will be discussed in greater detail later in this chapter.

BEAR MARKET STRATEGIES

Stock prices will tend to rise over the very long term. They always have. Yet, since World War I, there have been no fewer than ten major bear markets in which stocks declined dramatically. In the bear markets of 1929–1932, of 1972–1974, in 1987, and, of course, in both 2000 and 2007, the market values of a great many stocks were sliced by more than half. Also, as a general rule, prices usually drop faster than they rise. Experienced investors realize that the "disasters" that seem to occur frequently in bear markets can be devastating to the long-term performance of any portfolio. While most people are merely trying to preserve capital or hedge in a bear market, the risk-oriented trader regards severe market weakness as an opportunity to make a meaningful profit.

There are several ways to make money in a bear market.

Buying Exchange-Traded Funds

There are many ETFs available to meet this need, as explained shortly. ETFs are a good tool.

Buying Contra-Market Stocks

When the market (measured by the averages or any broad list) is advancing or declining, a contra-market stock will be moving in the opposite direction. It is usually among an industry group that has attracted special attention for one reason or another. A contra-market stock is especially noticeable during a bear market when everything else is dropping. Each bear market is different. In years past, the groups that outperformed the market were oil and gas in 1946; pharmaceuticals, food, and tobacco in 1957; gold briefly in 1962; and coal and automobile replacement parts in 1969–1970. One of the worst bear markets since the 1930s occurred in 1973–1974, when gold, sugar, steel, and fertilizer stocks were in favor.

During the bear market of the early 2000s, gold stocks performed very well.

Once a bear market has ended, contra-market stocks do not follow a definite pattern. Sometimes they continue rising; sometimes they turn down immediately. In any case, the investor should investigate the industry and the company before buying. It is not advisable to buy a stock simply because it is going up when other stocks are declining.

Buying Put Options

A "put option" is a contract to sell 100 shares at a definite price within a specified time limit. The put option buyer (who expects the stock price to decline in the short term) purchases the right to "put" the stock to someone else under the terms of the contract.

There are two primary reasons for buying a put option in a bear market: (1) as a leveraged, high-risk vehicle to obtain a quick capital gain, or (2) as a defensive hedge against a stock that the investor does not want to sell for various reasons, usually taxes. Normally, buying a put is not the best way to profit from a bear market.

Writing Call Options

A "call option" is a contract to buy 100 shares at a definite price within a specified time limit. A call option buyer (one who expects the stock to go up in the short term) purchases the right to "call" the stock from someone else under the terms of the contract. Thus, an investor who owns 100 shares of stock and believes that its price will remain flat or go down can write a call option against those shares and sell that option to someone who believes that the stock price will be going up.

Writing a call option when the investor does not own the stock is referred to as "writing a naked call option." The writer of a naked call option can profit only by the amount received from the option buyer, but can lose much more. In other words, the writer is a speculator who is willing to bet that the stock will not rise within the time limit of the contract. Writing a naked call option is, obviously, a very high risk undertaking and is not recommended for most investors.

Short Selling

Selling a stock short is one of the best ways for investors to profit in a bear market. Of course, this approach is not appropriate for everyone, and there is an additional risk involved.

In effect, the normal sequence of the purchase and sale is reversed. When stock is sold short, the brokerage firm either lends the stock to the customer or borrows it for the customer, who then sells it in the open market. Eventually the same number of shares will have to be repurchased (this is referred to as "short covering") and be returned to the lender. If the repurchase price is lower because the stock dropped as expected, the short seller will make a profit. If the price is higher, the short seller will need to deposit more money to cover the same number of shares and will suffer a loss.

There is a special risk to short selling. Stock that is bought "long" in the regular way cannot drop below zero, and therefore cannot lead to a loss greater than the total investment. But a stock that has been sold short could, theoretically, produce unlimited losses. There is no ceiling to a stock's appreciation potential. Therefore, the fear of being "squeezed" can make the short seller a more restless investor. To limit this potential loss, the short seller can use a stop order or, preferably, purchase a call option as a hedge against the position.

Unless the investor is experienced with short selling, it is best not to short a stock that (1) has a favorable fundamental outlook (i.e., has earnings gains or an improving profit trend), (2) has already suffered a large price decline of, say, 60% or more, (3) has been strong technically

(e.g., the price should not be above its average price of the prior 200 days), or (4) could be a likely candidate for a merger.

It is also worth noting that ETFs, like stocks, can be sold short. However, borrowing the shares may prove difficult and not worth the effort. As a general rule, it is better to buy ETFs designed for down markets than to sell short those intended for bull markets.

In the earlier discussion of margin, short selling was not explained in any detail to avoid confusion. It is more complicated. A short seller must know three things to calculate the current equity figure in the margin account:

1. The initial credit (deposit)

2. The stock's current market value

3. The net proceeds of the short sale

Current equity can be found by using the two-step formula shown above.

As an example, assume that an investor sells short 100 shares of Baltimore Buggy Whip at $70 after depositing $5,000 cash into the margin account. The formula would read

$$.714 = \frac{\$7,000 + \$5,000}{\$7,000} - 1.000$$

$$\$5,000 = .714 \times \$7,000$$

Step 1.

$$\text{Current Margin} = \frac{\text{Proceeds} + \text{Deposit}}{\text{Market Value}} - 1.000$$

Step 2.

$$\text{Current Equity} = \text{Current Margin} \times \text{Market Value}$$

If the stock declines to $55, the short sale becomes profitable and current equity increases:

$$1.182 = \frac{\$7,000 + \$5,000}{\$5,500} - 1.000$$

$$\$6,500 = 1.182 \times \$5,500$$

On the other hand, if Baltimore Buggy Whip had advanced to $85, the short seller's equity would have been reduced:

$$.412 = \frac{\$7,000 + \$5,000}{\$8,500} - 1.000$$

$$\$3,500 = .412 \times \$8,500$$

As the stock rises, the current margin drops, which, in turn, reduces current equity. At $85 and a current margin of 41%, the investor is probably unhappy, but is still safe from a margin call. If the brokerage firm's maintenance requirement happens to be 35% on short sale transactions, a margin call for an additional deposit would be issued if the stock advances to $89.

TAXES

Tax laws are complicated. To make matters worse, they are always changing. When tax problems are encountered, it is advisable to seek the help of a qualified accountant. In fact, many of the strategies suggested in this book will require professional tax guidance.

Active investors are constantly faced with tax decisions. This is especially true now, because tax reforms in 1986 and later in 1997 changed the way in which investors must treat capital gains when filing income taxes. The 60% capital gain deduction for individuals, estates, and trusts has been eliminated. Under these laws, all capital gains, whether short term or long term, are now being treated as ordinary income. However, while it is possible for tax rates to be higher than the 15% and 28% brackets into which most families will fall, the tax rate for capital gains cannot, by law, exceed 20% (or 10% if the taxpayer is in the 15% tax bracket).

Again, it should be stressed that tax rules change often and that a professional tax advisor or accountant should be consulted before investment decisions are made.

If an individual would like to continue investing in the stock market and wants to establish a tax loss, there are basically three things that can be done:

1. Sell the stock outright and repurchase it after 31 or more days.

2. Purchase an equal number of shares (called "doubling up") and sell the original holdings 31 days later.

Change is the investor's only certainty.

—T. Rowe Price

3. Sell the stock and immediately replace it with another stock.

Prior to 1997, investors who wanted to postpone profits from one year to the next could use a technique called "shorting against the box." This transaction was essentially the same as normal short selling, except that the short position would be covered by similar shares that were already in the account rather than borrowing them from the broker. This is no longer allowed. Still, investors should avoid waiting until December to work out a tax strategy.

ARBITRAGE

On Wall Street, the term "arbitrage" refers to the simultaneous purchase and sale of two different securities that have a close relationship (e.g., a convertibility of one security into the other) to take advantage of a disparity in their prices. This activity can apply to equivalent securities trading in different markets, securities with convertible features, or securities involved in mergers, tender offers, recapitalizations, or corporate divestitures.

A "merger arbitrageur," sometimes known as the riverboat gambler of Wall Street, will risk a substantial loss in an attempt to make a small, quick profit. Purchasing one stock and selling the other short eliminates all risk, except a possible change in the agreement that reduces the terms of the merger (an unusual situation) or a termination of the proposal (a much more likely event). In other words, if the proposed merger is completed, a smart merger arbitrageur will almost always make a profit. If the marriage is not consummated, however, the purchased stock could decline sharply and the shorted stock could rise, producing a substantial loss.

Hundreds of viable arbitrage opportunities arise each year. Therefore, anyone entering this arena can afford to be patient and should select and research the situation carefully.

There are several brokerage firms that specialize in arbitrage activity and make a point of being well informed. The spreads, therefore, tend to be fairly representative of the risk involved.

An individual who is willing to assume the risks of merger arbitrage should establish a list of personal criteria and concentrate on only the mergers that meet those standards. For example, it might be advisable for the acquired company to be high quality, medium sized, and in a growing field that is different from that of the acquiring company. In such a case, there could easily be other suitors, and the chance of government intervention would be less.

Because the risks in merger arbitrage are high, the investor should either make an effort to become knowledgeable about the companies involved—or simply avoid merger arbitrage altogether.

Investment Clubs An individual who is seeking fun, education, and perhaps a little profit can join or start an investment club. Typically, this is a group of 10 to 15 friends who meet once a month to manage their collective investment portfolio. The monthly contribution from each member is pooled and is often invested in growth stocks using dollar cost averaging. Dividends and capital gains are reinvested in most cases.

About 92,000 members (only a fraction of a larger, unknown number established in the United States) belong to the National Association of Investors Corporation (now called "BetterInvesting"), founded in 1951.

The NAIC is a nonprofit organization that provides guidance and literature to its membership. Individuals may be NAIC members for a modest annual fee, or clubs may belong for a similar annual payment plus a small per-member fee. Further information on investment clubs or on the NAIC may be obtained by contacting

BetterInvesting
P.O. Box 220
Royal Oak, MI 48068
Toll-free: (877) 275-6242
www.better-investing.org

BetterInvesting also offers online courses and useful investment information for the small investor.

Investment Companies Being part owner of a portfolio that is managed by professionals is a good alternative for individuals who

1. Have neither an interest in security analysis nor the time to manage their own portfolios.

2. Do not want to pay an investment advisor.

3. Are willing to forgo some capital appreciation potential to obtain a professionally managed portfolio.

There are two kinds of funds that investment companies manage: "open end funds," also called "mutual funds," and "closed end funds."

An open end fund deals directly with investors and always stands ready to sell or buy its shares at the current net asset value. Stated differently, an investor can buy shares from a mutual fund (subscribe) or sell shares to the fund (redeem) at any time. As a result, money flows into or out of a mutual fund when investors subscribe for or redeem shares. A closed end fund, on the other hand, has a fixed number of shares outstanding, and investors buy or sell them in the open market like any stock.

Because the market price of a closed-end fund share will rise or fall according to its supply and demand, its price can be at a premium or, most likely, a discount to its net asset value at any time.

Therefore, if the investor wants the market value of each share to reflect directly the net asset value of the fund's portfolio, an open end fund is preferable to a closed end fund.

A mutual fund can be either a "load fund" or a "no load fund." When an investor buys a load fund, a sales charge (called the "load") is normally deducted from the investment immediately to compensate the salesperson who sold the fund. This fee is typically 6% or more and is usually charged one time, up front. A no load fund is bought directly from the invest-ment company, and the investor is not charged a fee, although both types of funds also charge investors for operational expenses. Otherwise, load funds and no load funds are comparable in terms of their operations and investment performance.

At least once a year, *Business Week*, among other business publications, reviews the performances of load and no load mutual funds. These articles frequently provide extensive data and other background information as well. Moreover, many public libraries subscribe to services that cover this subject in great detail, and there are many additional sources on the Internet.

Unless there is a strong reason to prefer a particular load fund management, no load funds should always be considered first. A load fund portfolio must grow annually about 2% faster than a no load fund portfolio for investors in each just to be even at the end of a five year period.

Mutual Funds A mutual fund is an investment company, usually established by an advisory firm, designed to offer the fund's shareholders a specific investment objective. Anyone buying shares in the fund becomes a part owner and, agreeing with the fund's investment objective, wants to participate in the effort.

Eight New EFT Funds Introduced

To manage the company, the shareholders elect a board of directors to oversee the operations of the business and the portfolio. Normally, the advisory firm that organized the company is selected as the investment advisor and operations manager. For this service, the firm is paid an annual fee (typically about one half of one percent of net assets) that will vary according to the size of the fund.

It is often assumed that the investment advisory firm is the "owner" of the fund. Actually, the shareholders own the fund and may decide to hire another investment advisor if the fund's performance is unsatisfactory.

Many advisory firms manage more than one mutual fund, and each fund in this "family" usually has a different investment objective. Often, with just a quick telephone call, an investor can switch money from one fund to another to achieve a different investment objective or to pursue a new investment strategy. In fact, this is one big reason to prefer mutual funds rather than ETFs. The biggest question otherwise is, how talented is the manager?

All mutual funds are closely regulated by the SEC. A "prospectus" that explains the fund, its investment objectives, and the risks must be made available to all potential investors.

Aside from the sales fee, or "load," as discussed earlier, mutual fund investors should be aware of any special charges against the fund's assets for marketing and advertising (sometimes referred to as "12b 1" plans). The ratio is excessive whenever 12b 1 expenses exceed 0.5% of assets.

As stated earlier, the mutual fund stands ready to buy back (redeem) or sell shares at their net asset value (NAV) at any time. If it is a well-known or popular mutual fund, its per share value is sometimes quoted in the financial section of a newspaper.

The value of each share is entirely dependent upon the value of the securities in the portfolio. For this reason, investors should be familiar with the largest holdings.

There are six basic types of mutual funds:

- *Common stock funds.* These funds invest almost entirely in equities (common stocks), although their objectives vary considerably. "Growth funds" are seeking capital appreciation by selecting companies that should grow more rapidly than the general economy. "Aggressive growth funds" buy shares in small or more speculative growth companies for maximum capital appreciation. "Growth and income

"There are two rules to remember about investing—First, never lose money; second, never forget Rule #1."

funds" seek long-term capital appreciation along with income. "Index funds," a popular type in recent years, buy representative stocks simply to match the market indexes.

- *Special-purpose funds.* These funds attempt to satisfy certain investment interests, such as participation in technology, gold, or energy. They can also use futures, options, and short selling to meet more aggressive objectives. In addition, funds of this type can be used as a method for hedging portfolios in bear markets.
- *Income funds.* These are portfolios consisting of bonds and common stocks as well as preferred stocks. Income fund managers try to obtain satisfactory interest and dividend income for the shareholders.
- *Bond funds.* Bond funds seek high income and preservation of capital by investing primarily in bonds and selecting the proper mix between short term, intermediate term, and long term bond maturities. In recent years, tax free municipal bond funds have been popular.
- *Balanced funds.* These funds buy both common stocks and bonds based on a popular belief that conditions that are unfavorable to com-

mon stocks are often favorable to bonds and vice versa.
- *Money market funds.* These offer their shareholders a means of participating in the high-quality, short-term instruments of the money market, including CDs, Treasury bills, and commercial paper.

The Investment Company Institute classifies mutual fund objectives into sixteen categories:

- Aggressive growth funds
- Growth funds
- Growth and income funds
- International funds
- Global funds
- Precious metals/gold funds
- Balanced funds
- Income funds
- Option/income funds
- Corporate bond funds
- U.S. government income funds
- GNMA or Ginnie Mae funds
- Long term municipal bond funds
- Single state municipal bond funds
- Money market mutual funds
- Short term municipal bond funds

Clearly, mutual funds can be classified in many ways, and there is really no limit. New and different funds are being formed almost every day, and the way they do business has become more imaginative.

ANALYZING MUTUAL FUNDS

As a general rule, the larger the mutual fund, the less capital appreciation one should expect relative to the market. For the more aggressive investor, the optimum size of a common stock fund is $100 million to $2 billion. Of course, there have been a few notable exceptions to the size rule. Two familiar management companies, T. Rowe Price and Vanguard, for example, have managed sizable portfolios with great success. Also, and importantly, the advent and universal acceptance of ETFs has added to redemptions of mutual funds.

As with individual company equities, management is an important consideration, and the process of identifying a well-managed mutual fund is much the same. First, look at the fund's performance over the last five or ten years and compare it to that of other funds with similar objectives. Become familiar with the people who make up the investment committee and how long they have been with the fund.

Next, consider what management is doing today. What are the fund's largest areas of investment? What holdings are being increased or reduced? And what percentage of the fund is in cash, considering the current state of the market? Remember, portfolio managers, like most investors, are subject to emotions and can be notoriously poor market timers.

Finally, what has management been saying in its reports and to the press? And have its comments been consistent with the fund's stated longer-term objectives?

The challenge for the mutual fund investor is selecting an investment company that is capable of superior performance, taking into consideration the fund's investment objectives (and there are online services).

For investors who have a limited amount of time to spend on their portfolios and who want greater diversification, mutual funds are worth considering. But here, too, the old Wall Street saying still holds true: "Investigate before you invest."

EXCHANGE-TRADED FUNDS (ETFS)

Currently, there are more than 800 ETFs, up from just a handful in the mid-1990s, and today's stockbrokers have found ETFs to be extremely helpful in rebuilding their "books" of business. The severe cutbacks in the financial community have resulted in shrinking research departments. So, to meet the challenge, brokers have been actively using ETFs in their quiver of investment tools.

If the client is seeking direct participation in semiconductors, an ETF exists specifically for that purpose. If the client is looking for a leveraged way to play a bull market, there is an ETF available for that need. If the client is bearish and believes that stock prices are headed south, there is an ETF investment for that, too.

However, it should be remembered that with ETFs, as with individual stocks, "There is no such thing as a free lunch." Money can be lost here just as easily as in individual stocks. For example, in the year 2008, the ProShares Ultra Dow 30 (DDM, a highly leveraged way to be long the Dow Jones Industrial Average) declined a whopping 62%, while the DJIA dropped "only" 34%. Of course, there were bearish-oriented ETFs that gained in value over the same period. As with equities, one must make the proper investment choices.

The exchange-traded fund was pioneered by the American Stock Exchange and then gained its popularity in 1990 on the Toronto Stock Exchange. The first major ETF in the United States was the Amex SPDR in 1993.

Exchange-traded funds are based on an index that is usually determined by an independent company, such as Standard & Poor's, State Street, or the editors of the *Wall Street Journal*. And an ETF attempts to maintain its portfolio in proportion to the weighted underlying assets of that index.

The principal advantages of ETFs relative to the open-ended index funds are the low "expense ratios" (typically less than 1%) and lower "turnover ratios," which tend to be more tax-favorable. On the other hand, ETFs are traded in the open market. They involve a commission cost for each trade, while many mutual funds do not have these trading costs. In general, when small sums are being invested, say, monthly or quarterly, no-load mutual funds become more attractive relative to exchange-traded funds.

Also, compared with mutual funds, the stocklike features are another advantage of ETFs. They have no minimums for investment; they can be sold short and traded with limit orders and stop-loss orders; and they can be bought or sold on margin. And, finally, options can be written against them. For many investors, these are important considerations.

Certain ETFs have the ability to purchase other securities or financial instruments (i.e., primarily swap contracts) to obtain additional investment leverage for

Exchange-Traded Funds

Largest 100 exchange-traded funds

ETF	Symbol	Closing price	Chg (%)
iPathDJ-AIGnts	DJP	33.58	-0.09
Diamond	DIA	84.96	-0.47
iShrBrcl20+	TLT	121.32	-0.77
iShrBrclShrtTreas	SHV	110.50	...
iShrComexGld	IAU	83.51	1.15
iShrDJSelDiv	DVY	40.31	-1.37
iShriBoxxFd	LQD	99.92	1.21
iShrMSCIEmrgMkt	EEM	24.49	-3.73
iShrMSCIPac	EPP	24.90	-0.80
iShrRu2000G	IWO	49.15	-2.38
iShrRu2000V	IWN	47.29	-1.75
iShrSPEu350	IEV	29.49	-1.31
iShrSP400G	IJK	52.91	-2.05
iShrSP400V	IJJ	48.76	-1.20
iShrSP600G	IJT	42.71	-2.40
iShrSP600V	IJS	46.27	-1.85
iShrMSCIBra	EWZ	34.79	-4.40
iShrMSCICan	EWC	16.34	-2.74
iShrMSCIGrth	EFG	43.46	-0.78
iShrMSCIHK	EWH	10.59	-1.94
iShrMSCIJpn	EWJ	9.12	-0.22
iShrMSCISK	EWY	28.39	-2.27
iShrMSCISng	EWS	7.12	-0.84
iShrMSCITaiwn	EWT	7.93	-4.23
iShrSP100	OEF	42.17	-1.29
iShrSPNANatRes	IGE	23.48	-4.59
iShrSilverTr	SLV	10.73	0.56
iShrBrcl1-3	SHY	84.63	-0.19
iShrBrcl7-10	IEF	99.26	-0.26
iShrBrclAggBd	AGG	102.53	0.54
iShrTIPSBdFd	TIP	100.73	0.72
iShrCohenSter	ICF	43.25	-2.61
iShrDJUSHlth	IYH	52.42	-0.74
iShrDJUSRE	IYR	36.47	-2.09
iShrDJTch	IYW	34.72	-1.62
iShrChina25	FXI	28.86	-5.53
iShrMSEAFE	EFA	43.06	-0.69
iShrNasBiotch	IBB	68.92	-1.36
iShrRu1000	IWB	47.36	-1.23
iShrRu1000G	IWF	35.76	-1.65
iShrRu1000V	IWD	47.70	-1.87
iShrRu2000	IWM	47.76	-1.93
iShrRu3000	IWV	50.13	-1.65
iShrRuMidGrth	IWP	30.12	-2.81
iShrRuMid	IWR	57.54	-2.49
iShrRuMidVlu	IWS	27.04	-2.31
iShrSP500G	IVW	43.33	-1.77
iShrSP500	IVV	88.04	-1.33
iShrSP500V	IVE	43.60	-2.07
iShrTr40	ILF	24.63	-5.74
iShrSP400	IJH	51.43	-1.72
iShrSP600	IJR	42.45	-1.03
MktVecGold	GDX	29.83	-2.45
RegBkHldrs	RKH	70.86	-3.62
BiotchHldrs	BBH	170.52	-0.90
PwrShrDB Agrcltr	DBA	24.33	2.57
PwrShrDB CmFd	DBC	19.92	-2.83
PwrShsWldrhll	PBW	8.45	-2.99
PwrShrWtrRes	PHO	13.64	-1.94
PwrShrsQQQ	QQQQ	29.21	-2.18
ProShrUltraFnl	UYG	5.42	-6.55
ProShrUltraQQQ	QLD	26.17	-3.89
ProShrUltraS&P	SSO	24.65	-3.22
ProShrUSFnl	SKF	116.71	5.72
PrShrsUShrQQQ	QID	68.82	3.97
ProShrUSRIEst	SRS	61.03	3.86
ProShrUlShtRus	TWM	94.22	3.54
ProShrsUShrt S&P	SDS	87.44	2.39
RydexSPEquiWt	RSP	26.51	-3.07
SP400 Spdrs	MDY	93.09	-1.81
CnsDscrSel SPDR	XLY	20.66	-2.68
ConStplSel SPDR	XLP	23.29	0.26
SPDR EngySelSct	XLE	44.63	-2.98
SPDR FnclSelSct	XLF	11.80	-3.52
HlthcarSel SPDR	XLV	25.91	-0.69
InduSelSctr SPDR	XLI	22.23	-1.55
MatrlsSel SPDR	XLB	21.95	-3.64
TechSelSctr SPDR	XLK	15.06	-1.38
UtilsSelSctr SPDR	XLU	28.20	-1.33
SPDR DJREIT	RWR	38.49	-2.01
SPDR GldTr	GLD	83.46	1.00
SPDR KBW Bnk	KBE	20.75	-3.08
SPDR S&P 500	SPY	87.06	-1.28
US NatGas	UNG	22.37	0.45
US OilFd	USO	30.63	-7.35
VangdEmrgMkt	VWO	24.20	-3.35
VangdEurPacfc	VEA	27.01	-0.30
VangdEuro	VGK	39.22	-0.91
VangdAllWldxUS	VEU	31.50	-0.54
VangdGrowth	VUG	38.28	-2.17
VangdLgCap	VV	39.11	-2.40
VangdMdCap	VO	41.95	-2.42
VangdPacific	VPL	41.82	-0.74
VangdReit	VNQ	35.53	-3.76
VangdShrtTrm	BSV	79.90	0.04
VangdSmCap	VB	41.26	-2.44
VangdSmCapValue	VBR	41.37	-2.73
VangdTtlBndMkt	BND	78.24	0.86
VangdTtlStock	VTI	43.16	-2.15
VangdValue	VTV	39.38	-2.81

their holdings. And they can engage in certain option strategies (in most cases, writing covered calls) on some or all of the fund's stocks. Also see Chapter 14.

These so-called leveraged funds (perhaps applying the term "ultra" or "enhanced") involve additional risks that come with the leverage. Such a fund's volatility is usually greater, its trading costs can be higher, and its swap contracts involve the creditworthiness of the counterparties—as investors discovered with the Lehman Brothers failure in 2008.

Leveraged ETFs (both up and down) are not recommended for most investors, since they cannot produce compounding results. These funds can be used for short-term, day-to-day trading—but not investing.

In every case, ETF investors should obtain and read the prospectus before investing in any fund. Also, it is highly advisable that the investor obtain advice on taxes and related policies from a tax professional.

The most actively traded ETF on the NYSE ARCA platform in 2008 was the Standard & Poor's Depositary Receipt (SPDR, better known as a "Spider," with the ticker symbol SPY). Trading in lockstep with the S&P 500 at roughly 1/10 the value of the target index, SPY has emerged as a very useful portfolio management tool for institutions as well as a popular passively managed fund vehicle for smaller investors.

One interesting little detail about S&P 500 ETFs: the SPDR (SPY) ETF is weighted by market capitalization, while the Rydex version (RSP) is calculated using an equal weighting. So, when comparing the two, if you favor large-cap stocks, go with SPY.

INVERSE-PERFORMING ETFS

During declining markets, the exchange-traded funds that should do better are the "inverse-performing" issues—and 2008 was a perfect example when a great many stocks were down 30% or more.

Here are two of the many inverse-performing funds that rose sharply in 2008. Both are highly leveraged, designed to outperform their underlying issues in a dramatic fashion.

- The ProShares UltraShort QQQ fund with the trading symbol QID
- The ProShares UltraShort Russell 1000 fund with the symbol SFK

These above-average performances (up more than 70%) were achieved through a combination of options, index futures, and swaps, as mentioned earlier. However, before ETFs are used in any portfolio, one should understand how they work.

A FEW MORE DETAILS ABOUT ETFS

An ETF is a basket of stocks, and its value is estimated frequently throughout the day, usually every 15 seconds. At the end of the trading session for the underlying securities (usually 4 p.m. ET when the markets close), the fund is "rebalanced" to maintain its desired leverage. And its ending market price is usually close to its net asset value (NAV)—but not always, especially with thinly traded ETFs.

So, unlike mutual funds, which are valued at NAV at the end of each day, the price of an ETF is whatever the market quote is during the day or at the close. An ETF can be bought or sold readily during the day, like any stock, but the share price is not its NAV.

In addition, over the long term, it is possible for an ETF to perform better or worse than its stated objective, mainly resulting from volatility. In its literature, ProShares, a leading manager of leveraged ETFs, demonstrates how the performance of a more predictable fund could be closer to its expected results than one that is more volatile.

Thus, the volatility of a fund can diminish the benefits of its compounding values. For example, a fund that rises 5% on Day 1, then declines 5% on Day 2 will lose 0.25% of its value over that two-day period. An ETF that is leveraged at two times will lose a full 1%. In other words, an ETF that is leveraged to *double* the performance of an index can lose *four times* as much as a result of its volatility.

So, there is an irony with leveraged ETFs. On the one hand, they can *create* a greater volatility in their issues, while, at the same time, they are being *hurt* by their volatility.

Of course, the fund's fees and expenses (typically below 1% total) are other items that will hamper investment performance. Investors should also be aware that the Internal Revenue Service (IRS) is always ready to take a cut. All ETFs are required to distribute substantially all of their *net investment income* and *capital gains* to shareholders at least annually. A fund's net investment income is derived from its holdings of debt securities, money market instruments, and/or equity securities that pay dividends.

Two S&P-related ETF charts appear on page 115. How each performed during the market decline in 2007–2008 is clear. It is important to note that the S&P short

Stock market bubbles don't grow out of thin air. They have a solid basis in reality, but reality as distorted by a misconception.

—GEORGE SOROS

fund made a distribution of $11.94 in late December. The chart was *not* adjusted to reflect that event. December 23 was the ex-date, the date of record was December 26, and the payable date was December 30.

Usually, ETFs are tax-efficient vehicles because the methods used to manage them normally produce minimal capital gains. However, when short sales and derivatives are applied in ETFs, capital gains are more likely to result, and they must be distributed to the fund holders. The resulting taxes can be onerous. Once again, the investor should consult with a professional tax advisor in such situations.

The ETFs listed here are *not* being recommended. They are merely examples of the diversity of issues available. Also, it is recommended that investors favor the actively traded funds for liquidity reasons.

MGC Vanguard's Mega-Cap 300 fund
LQD iShares quality corporate bonds
DOG ProShares Dow 30 Industrials short
GLD SPDR Gold Trust—gold bullion

USO U.S. Oil Fund—the price of oil
DDG ProShares oil and gas short
DJP iPath Dow Jones Commodity Index
FXE Rydex Eurocurrency Trust
EWY iShares MSCI South Korea

Finally, a distinction should be made between ETFs and somewhat similar financial products called exchange-traded notes (ETNs), which are structured debt instruments that are issued by a major bank or a provider as senior debt notes.

An ETN is a debt similar to a bond. The terms of this contract are determined by the structure of the ETN. Also, the investor becomes subject to the creditworthiness of the issuer. Conversely, an ETF is an asset like a stock or an index.

In recent years, exchange-traded funds and exchange-traded notes have become important investment vehicles for both individual investors and professional portfolio managers. There are a many good ETF and ETN products available today. And we can expect to see many more in the years ahead.

SPDR S&P 500 (SPY–NYSE ARCA) (2007–2008)

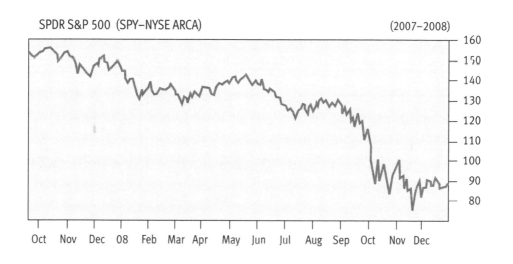

ProShares Short S&P 500 (SH–NSE ARCA) (2007–2008)

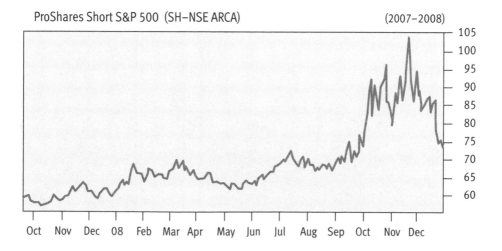

6 Growth Stocks

Introduction

The "Growth Stock Theory" of investing is not new; it can be traced at least back to the 1930s. Simply stated, this investment concept involves the purchase of shares in companies that, over the years, increase their earnings and dividends faster than the growth rate of the general economy. A true growth company has some control over its own destiny because it has the ability to finance itself internally by reinvesting its earnings in the business.

Growth stocks are appropriate for most, but not all, portfolios; they require patience and usually have somewhat greater short-term market risk as a result of their higher P/E ratios. But if the investor has a time horizon of at least four or five years and knows how to select and value them, growth stocks can be, by far, the best method of profiting from the stock market over the long term.

A few of the case studies in this section appeared in the first edition of this book nearly thirty years ago. But they are not included for the obvious benefit of hindsight; they have stood the test of time.

This chapter further defines the Growth Stock Theory and shows how companies grow. Most important, the chapter will help investors identify growth stocks and determine how much to pay for them.

Why a Growth Stock? The power of compounding values, which is frequently overlooked and usually underestimated, is brought to light by growth stock investing. A company that grows at a compound rate of 15% per year, for example, doubles its size in five years, triples in eight years, and grows to ten times its original size in seventeen years.

Perhaps the best single definition of a growth stock is, "A company that, by growing earnings over time, improves its *ability* to pay dividends." One of the best examples of this definition is Microsoft, a growing firm that increased its profits to billions of dollars before declaring its first dividend ever in 2003. Over the years, Microsoft's *ability* to pay dividends improved substantially as its earnings soared. And, to the delight of its holders, the stock price reflected its growth. See the discussion on Microsoft later in this chapter.

How does the growth stock investor benefit? Here is a highly simplified explanation:

Assume the following:

- A growth company earning $1.00 per share today increases its earnings at an average growth rate of 15% per year for twelve years.

- Each year the company pays out 30% of the earnings as a cash dividend to its stockholders.
- The price/earnings ratio of the stock today is twenty times earnings.
- The price/earnings ratio in the twelfth year is fifteen times earnings (a lower P/E ratio reflects the probability of a slower growth rate in later years).

	TODAY	YEAR 12
Earnings per share	$1.00	$5.35
Dividends per share	$0.30	$1.60
P/E ratio	20 times	15 times
Stock price	$20.00	$80.25
Current yield	1.5%	2.0%
Dividend yield on the original investment	1.5%	8.0%

A buyer of 100 shares today would be investing $2,000. The initial $30 dividend from the company, representing a yield of only 1.5%, is small compared with the higher returns other investments offer.

But, by the twelfth year, the market value of the 100 shares becomes $8,025 and the investor has received more than $800 in dividends over the years. The twelfth-year dividend check, $160, is not 1.5%, but is now 8% of the original in-

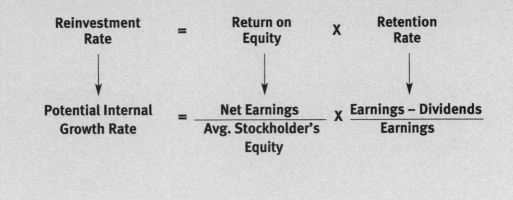

Reinvestment Rate	=	Return on Equity	X	Retention Rate
Potential Internal Growth Rate	=	$\dfrac{\text{Net Earnings}}{\text{Avg. Stockholder's Equity}}$	X	$\dfrac{\text{Earnings} - \text{Dividends}}{\text{Earnings}}$

vestment! If the company continues to grow beyond the twelfth year and the dividend is further increased in line with earnings, the return is even greater—especially when dividends are reinvested.

It is not uncommon for a long-term growth stock investor to be receiving a large return on the original investment in the form of an annual dividend check. As an example, after several years, a stockholder in Wal-Mart Stores during its most rapid-growth phase could have cashed an annual dividend check that was larger than the entire original investment! This is the power of compounding values and the advantage of growth stocks. This is also despite the fact that Wal-Mart's stock periodically declined sharply from one year to the next. Any politician who is in favor of double taxation of dividends does not understand this concept, and he or she should be voted out of office immediately.

Today, Wal-Mart Stores is the world's largest retailer. Was this rapid growth impossible to forecast years ago? No, not at all! For many years, well before it gained recognition on Wall Street, WMT was the largest holding in the well-known T. Rowe Price New Horizons Fund portfolio.

Measuring Growth For a growth company to be successful, it must earn a high return on stockholders' equity, and a significant portion of that return must be reinvested in the business. In the calculations to follow, "return on equity" is based on the average of a given year's beginning and ending stockholders' equity. Many successful growth companies, such as General Electric, have increased their growth rates through the skillful addition of outside capital. When interest rates are low, this strategy works well. But the ability to grow internally is crucial in the long run.

Reinvestment Rate	=	Return on Equity	X	Retention Rate
Potential Internal Growth Rate	=	16%	X	$\dfrac{\$4.00 - \$1.00}{\$4.00}$
12%	=	16%	X	75%

A company's internal growth rate potential is best measured by the "reinvestment rate" formula illustrated above.

For instance, if a company has a return on average equity of 16%, earns $4.00 per share, and pays an annual dividend of $1.00 per share, the reinvestment rate would be calculated in this manner:

In other words, unless this company improves its return on equity or pays out proportionately less to stockholders, it cannot grow faster than 12% per year

Johnson & Johnson Posts Increase of 18%

without assuming additional debt or selling new stock.

The reinvestment rate formula, as valuable as it is, should be used with care. A low-quality company can attain a high return on equity if stockholders' equity is small in relation to profits (perhaps the result of many unprofitable years). When return on equity and return on assets are both high, the reinvestment rate formula can be used with greater confidence.

Learning from the Past As the following examples illustrate, growth stock investing can produce favorable results if the investor is patient and owns the right stocks. And finding the right stocks is not an impossible task. The next table is from the third edition of this book. In 1960, Merck & Company, General Mills, and Procter & Gamble were already recognized growth companies. A $1,000 investment in each of these growth stocks in December 1960 would have shown these results 30 years later without the benefit of reinvesting dividends (see the 1960–1990 table).

This real-life example illustrates the "power of compounding values" referred to earlier. Between 1960 and 1990, the market value of this small portfolio advanced an average of almost 11.5%, not including dividends.

	Cost 12/30/60	Market Value on 12/30/90	Dividend Paid in 1990
Merck	$1,000	$41,420	$894
General Mills	$1,000	$24,575	$609
P&G	$1,000	$10,320	$222
Total	$3,000	$76,315	$1,725*

* 58% of the original investment.

The superiority of Merck's 1990 results compared to Procter & Gamble's outcome is accounted for by Merck's higher market appreciation (13% per year) compared with that of P&G (about 8% compounded).

Why? During that period, Merck's earnings per share advanced 14.8% per year, while P&G's per share growth averaged 9.5% annually.

Here is the same group of stocks and their twenty-year performance from 1988 until 2009:

	Cost 12/30/88	Market Value on 12/30/08	Dividend Paid in 2008
Merck	$1,000	$3,053	$161
General Mills	$1,000	$5,759	$159
P&G	$1,000	$11,535	$279
Total	$3,000	$20,347	$599*

* 20% of the original investment.

The second table shows an average annual growth rate of "only" 10%. But in this twenty-year period, there were three recessions (1990, 2001, and 2008) and two punishing bear markets (2000 and 2008).

How important are dividends to growth stock investors? See the footnote on each table. Merck has proudly paid a dividend every year since 1935, General Mills has paid one every year since 1898, and Procter & Gamble has done it every year since 1891.

Alone, this little portfolio demonstrates how important dividends can become to patient growth stock investors.

The best stock on the first table was Merck and the worst was P&G. On the second table, the best was P&G and Merck was the laggard. This is the benefit of portfolio diversification. Forecasting a "bump in the road" for a good growth company is not always easy. However, a major change in the fundamentals must be addressed. See the Eastman Kodak case presented later.

— AIR PRODUCTS VS. AIRCO INC. —

AIRCO INC. (formerly Air Reduction Co.)

	Sales	Operating Margin %	Net Income	Long-Term Debt	Return on Equity	Earnings per Share	Avg. 10-Year EPS Growth	Dividend per Share
1965	$376.8mm	12.8	$25.7mm	$124.6mm	12.6%	$2.50	4.5%	$1.25
1975	$765.7mm	12.1	$42.7mm	$187.7mm	14.0%	$3.76	4.2%	$0.95

Ten Year (1965–75) Investment Performance −25%

AIR PRODUCTS & CHEMICALS

	Sales	Operating Margin %	Net Income	Long-Term Debt	Return on Equity	Earnings per Share	Avg. 10-Year EPS Growth	Dividend per Share
1965	$121.1mm	13.7	$ 7.4mm	$ 94.0mm	11.0%	$0.70	12.4%	$0.04
1975	$699.0mm	17.0	$54.2mm	$184.1mm	19.7%	$4.02	19.1%	$0.20

Ten Year (1965–75) Investment Performance +328%

NOTE: Per share figures have been adjusted for splits and stock dividends for comparability.

Bill Gates (r.) and Paul Allen in 1981 just after signing their landmark contract with IBM for the DOS program

Note: The General Mills figures included the 1995 spin-off of Darden Restaurants.

Below is a classic case study found in the first edition that shows two very similar companies operating in the same industry at the same time to illustrate the thought process. The investor needs to see the big picture. An improving trend in profitability can enhance investment performance.

Air Products was much more aggressive than Airco in its pursuit of growth during those years. The importance of internal and external financing, and profitability, is very obvious in this case.

Air Products amplified the impact of its improving profitability and high earnings retention with additional debt to finance long-term gas sales contracts. This strategy produced superior growth for Air Products during the period. As a result, Air Products' stockholders enjoyed a far better investment performance.

Two stocks highlighted in the third edition of this book provided exceptional results in the twelve-year period 1990 to 2002: Microsoft Corporation and Dell Computer. Neither stock was an unknown entity at the time they were mentioned. In fact, the products of both companies were actually being used to create those written words.

The story of Bill Gates, today one of the world's richest men, and Microsoft is well known. Microsoft's revenues in FY 1990 totaled $1,183 million, while earnings rose 55% to $2.34 per share that year. The estimate for the June 1991 year was $3.70. On December 31, 1990, the stock was $75.25, 24.9 times its latest 12 months' earnings and 20.3 times the earnings projection. The P/E multiple was well below the growth rate of the company at the time. (The "PEG ratio" was explained in Chapter 3.)

It was Microsoft's policy to reinvest all of its profits in the company rather than pay dividends. In effect, the company was establishing its ability to pay big dividends at a later date. In the twelve-year period since 1990, Microsoft's earnings increased at a rate exceeding 31% annually!

A growth stock investor in 1990 who shared that vision would have seen 100 shares increase, after seven stock splits, to 7,200 shares by early 2003 and then finally would have enjoyed a first-ever dividend check of $576.

By 2003, Microsoft's revenues climbed to roughly $32 billion, and the company's net profit was being estimated at nearly $0.95 per share—from which that first

$0.08 per share dividend would be declared. Twelve years earlier, the company had employed 5,600 workers and had $450 million cash in its coffers. By 2003, the workforce surpassed 50,000, and the company's cash on the balance sheet was close to $43 billion.

The tale of college dropout Michael Dell is another amazing story. In the early 1980s, Dell was filling orders for custom-built personal computers from his college dormitory. By 1991, Dell was selling $546 million in computers, $397 million in the United States and other parts of the hemisphere, plus $149 million into the European market.

On December 31, 1990, Dell shares were $18.50 with an earnings estimate of $1.36 per share for fiscal year 1990–1991 and a P/E multiple of 13.6 times. Moreover, the rough estimate for FY 1991–1992 was $2.10. Like Microsoft's, the P/E multiple was not out of line with the firm's expected growth rate.

Twelve years later, in fiscal year 2002–2003, Dell's revenues reached $35 billion: $24.9 billion from the Americas, $6.7 billion from Europe, and $3.4 billion from the Far East.

During this period, the company's profits compounded at a 39.9% annual rate to about $0.80 per share (a purchase of 100 shares in late 1990 became 9,600 shares after seven stock splits, having a value of close to $257,000).

On December 31, 2002, Dell's stock price was $26.74, or 33 times current earnings, but down sharply from its $56.68 peak, hit in March 2000. At the highs of the stock market bubble, Dell sold at a P/E multiple of nearly 100 times earnings!

The Growth Cycle Almost every company faces a so-called growth cycle, and this cycle can be even more pronounced with growth stocks. That is, a company is *born*, it expands (sometimes at a very rapid pace for growth stocks), it *matures*, and then it *declines*. If management fails to act by entering new markets and developing new products before the company goes into its decline phase, the firm can die.

The single best example of this necessary "rebirth" process is the 3M Company.

Minnesota Mining & Manufacturing was founded in 1902 in Minnesota as a venture to quarry a mineral called corundum, which was to be sold to eastern manufacturers as a new, improved abrasive. The product failed. However, in the meantime, the company had converted an old flour mill into a sandpaper manufacturing facility. From that point on,

3M's growth has been the result of nothing less than a research and development (R&D) engine, producing a constant stream of new products from discoveries, either developed internally or acquired.

A perfect example of how a fundamental picture can change and dramatically affect an industry came in the late 1990s with the photographic companies Eastman Kodak and Polaroid Corporation. Decades before, both were impressive growth stocks.

Early in the twenty-first century, we find Polaroid in bankruptcy and Eastman Kodak Company working to "reinvent" itself. The firm has a substantially reduced workforce, and new technologies are now being emphasized. Clearly, digital photography, which requires no film, now has the lion's share of total photo images in a shift that began in the late 1990s. No alert growth stock investor would have been surprised. This is a case study that may well find its way into college classrooms. Here is the background.

THE RISE AND FALL OF EASTMAN KODAK

Inventor George Eastman registered the trademark Kodak in 1888. That year, the Eastman Dry Plate and Film Company introduced its first camera line, and the Eastman Kodak Company, as we know it today, was born. Its clever motto was, "You press the button—we do the rest."

The company thrived, and its hometown of Rochester, New York, also grew with it. In 1900, the first Kodak "Brownie" camera sold for $1.00, introducing a household name that continued for decades.

In 1920, Tennessee Eastman Company was organized to manufacture wood alcohol for film base. Over the years, the chemical division introduced new fibers, plastics, and coal-based chemicals.

Kodak's stock was added to the Dow Jones Industrial Average in 1930, and EK was a member of that august group for seventy-four years.

Kodacolor print film was introduced in 1942, adding to profits. By the early 1970s, Kodak was extremely profitable with its Instamatic pocket-sized cameras and film. At the time, pretax profit margins were close to 30%, superb for *any* manufacturer. Kodak's failure to compete successfully in Polaroid's instant photography market segment during that decade ultimately proved costly in both time and money.

Meanwhile, in 1975, Steven Sasson, an electrical engineer at Eastman Kodak, invented the first digital camera. Though crude in its origin, the basic concept

George Eastman (1854–1932) performed early photographic experiments in his mother's kitchen. In 1881, he and a family friend founded The Eastman Dry Plate Company, later known as Eastman Kodak Company.

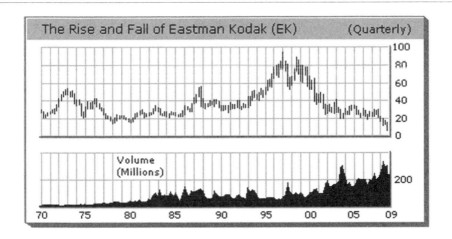

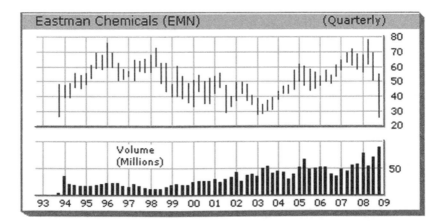

would have been Eastman Kodak's if it had wanted to pursue it. However, the company's fortunes were heavily invested in film technology, and it moved very slowly in this promising new field.

In late 1993, Eastman Kodak shareholders received one Eastman Chemicals (EMN) share, valued at roughly $26, for every four EK shares held. This gave the chemical division autonomy and added some value for shareholders.

In 1996, Kodak's first pocket-sized digital camera was introduced. But by 2000, Kodak's prospects for diminishing profits had become obvious to all, including the many analysts who had been recommending purchase of EK stock at over $70.

It should be noted that Eastman Kodak's stock has risen at least fivefold *three* different times since 1950: 1950 to 1960, 1962 to 1972, and 1985 to 1996, including the benefit of the EMN spin-off.

In early 2009, Kodak's stock price was below $5 per share. Now, almost every analyst was recommending "sell."

Will Eastman Kodak overcome its steep uphill battle and reward its shareholders once again? We will know soon enough.

These exercises, as well as other past experiences, show that successful growth companies have several characteristics in common. The investor should, therefore, be looking for a company that

- Has a product or service with increasing customer demand and is profitable enough to finance most or all of its future growth internally (that is, capable of a high reinvestment rate).
- Has a positive trend in profitability, so that, by growing earnings over time, the company improves its ability to pay dividends.
- Has a capable, imaginative management team that can turn promise into reality.

There are other related factors to consider. Does the company also have

- A growth record over the past few years? Look at revenue, facilities, and employees.
- A solid balance sheet with ample cash, little debt, and/or the management talent to use debt skillfully?
- Competitive marketing and strong service capabilities?
- A position in the marketplace that allows some product pricing flexibility? Often, the company is or will become the leader in its industry.
- Good labor relations?

- An ability to pursue new markets and add new, improved products to its line? If not, the company will most likely face maturity and, eventually, a decline.

Perspective To be successful, growth stock investors must learn to look beyond a stock's short-term price swings. Growth stocks require both patience and a long-term perspective. This is why periodic accumulation and dollar cost averaging is the best way to build a growth portfolio.

The following explains what is meant by "long-term perspective."

Imagine that it is June 1990 and you are looking at a chart in Trendline's *Current Market Perspectives* of a stock that you just purchased. The company, Wal-Mart Stores, reported a 28.6% increase in earnings in the first quarter, following a similar gain in fiscal year 1989—and a spectacular 33% gain in the prior year.

Before you bought the shares at $58, you estimated 1990 earnings to be roughly $2.25 per share, an increase of 18 to 19% over 1989—not bad for a recession year.

Your analysis points to a longer-term annual earnings growth rate of at least 15% for the next several years. If your projections prove correct, the company's per share earnings would be about $10.50 in 2001. Assuming a P/E of 18, the stock price would be close to $189. Not bad!

Your purchase price was 25.8 times your 1990 earnings projection—a P/E 1.6 times your expected growth rate. However, you acquired only 100 shares, since you felt uneasy about buying an equity that had risen 100% in the past twenty-four months.

In the few months that followed, the stock did nothing but go *down*, despite a 2 for 1 stock split shortly after your purchase.

However, you remained convinced about the company's prospects for annual growth of at least 15%. Wisely, you rejected the advice of the so-called experts who believe that "investors should immediately cut their losses if the stock declines by 8%." This rule is okay for traders, but *not* for growth stock investors. Nevertheless, *always* review the fundamentals. It is better to be averaging *up* than to be averaging *down*.

Now it is twelve years later, December 2002. Wal-Mart's stock was split 2 for 1 in 1990 and in 1993, and yet again in 1999. Your original 100 shares are now 800. In 2001, the company reported earnings of $1.49 per share—16.2% annual growth between 1990 and 2001, well in line with

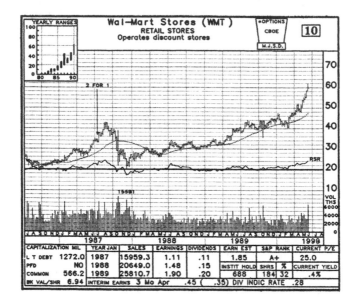

YEARLY RANGES		**Wal-Mart Stores (WMT)**			**•OPTIONS**		**10**
		RETAIL STORES			CBOE		
		Operates discount stores			M.J.S.D.		

CAPITALIZATION MIL		YEAR JAN	SALES	EARNINGS	DIVIDENDS	EARN EST	S&P RANK	CURRENT P/E
L T DEBT	1272.0	1987	15959.3	1.11	.11	1.85	A+	25.0
PFD	NO	1988	20649.0	1.48	.15	INSTIT HOLD	SHRS %	CURRENT YIELD
COMMON	566.2	1989	25810.7	1.90	.20	688	184 32	.4%
BK VAL/SHR	6.94	INTERIM EARNS 3 Mo Apr		.45	(.35)	DIV INDIC RATE		.28

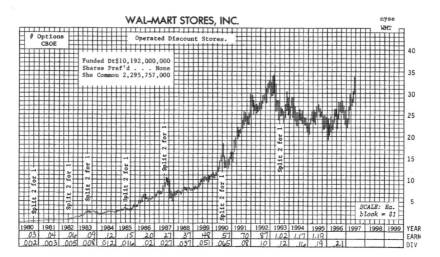

WAL-MART STORES, INC.

nyse
WMT

Options
CBOE

Operated Discount Stores.

Funded Dt$10,192,000,000
Shares Pref'd . . . None
Shs Common 2,295,757,000

SCALE: Ea.
block = $1

YEAR	1980	1981	1982	1983	1984	1985	1986	1987	1988	1989	1990	1991	1992	1993	1994	1995	1996	1997	1998	1999
EARN	.03	.04	.06	.09	.12	.15	.20	.27	.37	.48	.57	.70	.87	1.02	1.17	1.19				
DIV	.002	.003	.005	.008	.012	.016	.02	.027	.037	.051	.065	.08	.10	.12	.16	.19	.21			

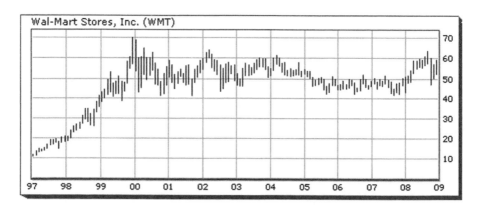

Wal-Mart Stores, Inc. (WMT)

Alexander Graham Bell (1847–1922) shown with the new telephone device he invented. Bell Telephone Company was founded in 1877.

your earlier projection. Today, your original $5,800 investment in 1990 has

- A market value of $40,408
- An annual dividend check of $240, equal to roughly 4.1% of the original investment

Notice the time frames on the Wal-Mart charts. As the years roll by, your analysis continues. One logical question to be asking at each Wal-Mart annual meeting is: Could saturation become a problem? How much longer can the company grow at a rate exceeding 10% or 12%, given its size? The questions and the analysis should never cease as long as the shares are owned.

At What Price? "What is a share of this company worth?" is the most difficult of all Wall Street questions. A precise answer cannot be found; it is simply a matter of careful analysis and judgment.

In the short term—a period of days, weeks, or months—the price of a stock fluctuates around a consensus of value based on earnings and dividend expectations. This consensus usually changes gradually—but not always. Over the long term—a few years or more—the stock price will rise or fall based on the company's actual earnings, dividends, and financial condition. This is especially true for growth stocks.

Valuing stocks is extremely complicated because investors always have alternative investment opportunities. Bonds, money market instruments, savings accounts, real estate, art, and personal business ventures are among many examples.

Therefore, an investor should make a value decision at three levels:

1. The investment environment (i.e., the potential return that all stocks offer versus alternative investment opportunities)

2. The value of the stock relative to other stocks

3. The value of the stock based on its individual merits and its growth prospects

Since the 1930s, there has been a steady decline in the purchasing power of the dollar. Most dramatic during this time were periods of accelerated inflation in 1946–1947, in 1973–1974, and in the early 1980s. Despite the gradual decline in the inflation rate since the 1980s, this long-term trend in the loss of purchasing power is not likely to be reversed, unfortunately.

Interest rates, as measured by the prime rate charged by banks, remained at a low 2 to 3% level from 1935 until 1951,

climbed gradually through the 1950s to about 5%, and maintained that level until about 1966. Since then, the prime rate has risen and fallen sharply, reaching peaks of 8 to 9% in 1969–1970, 12% in 1974, and over 20% in 1981. Of course, it has since returned to much lower levels in recent years.

Surprisingly, yields on both stocks and high-quality bonds in the fifty years from 1925 to 1975, averaged about the same—roughly 4.5%. Between 1925 and 1955, stock yields almost always exceeded bond yields, but in the years since 1955, the reverse has been true. Many observers attribute the shift since the 1940s to taxes and to a change in inflation expectations.

History also shows how a changing investment environment can affect P/E ratios. A typical stock P/E ratio in the late 1940s and early 1950s was 8 to 12 times earnings. Throughout most of the 1960s, a 15 to 19 range was considered normal. In the late 1970s, the DJIA P/E ratio dropped below 8 times earnings. Just before the stock market crashed in 1987, the ratio exceeded 20, then returned to closer to its fifty-year average of about 14 over the following three years. At the peak of the market bubble in 2000, the Dow P/E went to levels above the high of 1987. The P/E ratio for "the market," like that for in-

dividual issues, should be used with great care. A P/E of 20 has a totally different meaning when corporate earnings are projected to be rising in the years immediately ahead, as opposed to a time when earnings are expected to decline.

It stands to reason that growth equities typically command higher P/E ratios and lower yields than ordinary shares. Clearly, two stocks that have the same P/E ratio or dividend yield are not equally attractive if one is growing and the other is not.

Assuming that everything else is equal, the company that grows at a faster rate should command a higher P/E ratio. Throughout history, securities analysts and market theoreticians have worked tirelessly to devise formulas for valuing growth stocks. A well-known financial textbook, *Security Analysis*, coauthored by David L. Dodd, Sidney Cottle, and the late Benjamin Graham, presented a valuation formula based on a seven-year time horizon. Their work concluded that a company with no growth deserved, at least, the nominal P/E multiple of 8.5 times earnings, while, at the other extreme, a company growing at an annual rate of 20% could be assigned a P/E multiple of 41.5 times earnings. By 1974, it became obvious that interest rates have an influence (an inverse relationship) on P/E ratios. So the popular Graham & Dodd P/E formula was revised to read as follows:

$$P/E = \frac{37.5 + 8.8g}{i}$$

where g = the expected earnings growth rate for the next seven to ten years

i = the prevailing interest rate for Aaa bonds

37.5 and 8.8 = constant values based on experience

By using this formula and applying various growth rate and interest-rate combinations to it, a P/E ratio table can be constructed for easy reference, as shown on the next page.

To use the table, an investor must first estimate the company's annual earnings growth rate for the next seven to ten years. By crossing this growth rate with the prevailing interest rate on the table, the investor can obtain the same P/E multiple had the formula been used.

This formula has one serious shortcoming that should not be ignored, however. If the prevailing interest rate is 7% and there are two companies growing at the same rate, say, 12%, both stocks deserve a 20.4 P/E ratio, according to both the formula and the table.

However, suppose the first company has a higher return on equity and therefore is able to pay a higher dividend to its stockholders. Should both companies sell at the same 20.4 P/E multiple? Obviously not. Another factor to consider is the reliability of the growth projection, which depends on the quality of management, the sophistication of the company's products, the strength of competition, patent protection, the capital-intensive nature of the business, and so on. Thus, investors using this table to compare stock values should be prepared to make a few adjustments.

Most analysts prefer to use three- to five-year periods when studying the stock market or individual growth stocks. As mentioned earlier, Graham and Dodd used seven years. *Here, a twelve-year investment time horizon is recommended.*

Any objective analysis of growth stocks requires a time period long enough to encompass at least one to three full economic business cycles, as well as enough time to allow a company to grow. However, the time horizon should also be short enough to allow an investor to estimate the future without too much "blue sky." Thus, ten to twelve years seems to be a good time frame.

Further, whether by accident, political contrivance, coincidence, or whatever,

Price/Earnings Ratios Assuming Different Growth Rates and Interest Rates

Prevailing Interest Rate

	3%	4%	5%	6%	7%	8%	9%	10%	11%	12%	13%	14%	15%
20%	71.2	53.4	42.7	35.6	30.5	26.7	23.7	21.4	19.4	17.8	16.4	15.3	14.2
19%	68.2	51.2	40.9	34.1	29.2	25.6	22.7	20.5	18.6	17.1	15.7	14.6	13.6
18%	65.3	49.0	39.2	32.7	28.0	24.5	21.8	19.6	17.8	16.3	15.1	14.0	13.1
17%	62.4	46.8	37.4	31.2	26.7	23.4	20.8	18.7	17.0	15.6	14.4	13.4	12.5
16%	59.4	44.6	35.7	29.7	25.5	22.3	19.8	17.8	16.2	14.9	13.7	12.7	11.9
15%	56.5	42.4	33.9	28.3	24.2	21.2	18.8	17.0	15.4	14.0	13.0	12.1	11.3
14%	53.6	40.2	32.1	26.8	23.0	20.1	17.9	16.1	14.6	13.4	12.4	11.5	10.7
13%	50.6	38.0	30.4	25.3	21.7	19.0	16.9	15.2	13.8	12.7	11.7	10.9	10.1
12%	47.7	35.8	28.6	23.9	20.4	17.9	15.9	14.3	13.0	11.9	11.0	10.2	9.5
11%	44.8	33.6	26.9	22.4	19.2	16.8	14.9	13.4	12.2	11.2	10.3	9.6	9.0
10%	41.8	31.4	25.1	20.9	17.9	15.7	13.9	12.6	11.4	10.5	9.7	9.0	8.4
9%	38.9	29.2	23.3	19.5	16.7	14.6	13.0	11.7	10.6	9.7	9.0	8.3	7.8
8%	36.0	27.0	21.6	18.0	15.4	13.5	12.0	10.8	9.8	9.0	8.3	7.7	7.2
7%	33.0	24.8	19.8	16.5	14.2	12.4	11.0	9.9	9.0	8.3	7.6	7.1	6.6
6%	30.1	22.6	18.1	15.1	12.9	11.3	10.0	9.0	8.2	7.5	6.9	6.5	6.0
5%	27.2	20.4	16.3	13.6	11.6	10.2	9.1	8.2	7.4	6.8	6.3	5.8	5.4
4%	24.2	18.2	14.5	12.1	10.4	9.1	8.1	7.3	6.6	6.1	5.6	5.2	4.8
3%	21.3	16.0	12.8	10.7	9.1	8.0	7.1	6.4	5.8	5.3	4.9	4.6	4.3

Expected Growth Rate

there has been a very distinct four-year buying cycle to the stock market as measured by the Dow Jones Industrial Average. While this pattern may never again repeat, history clearly shows that, with the exception of only one instance (1930), at or near the lows of every fourth year since 1914 was a very good time to buy stocks for the year(s) to follow:

1914	1934	1954	1974	1994
1918	1938	1958	1978	1998
1922	1942	1962	1982	2002
1926	1946	1966	1986	2006
1930	1950	1970	1990	2010?

A period of three full market cycles, or twelve years, seems appropriate, since twelve-year periods play an interesting role in U.S. history. It was exactly twelve years between the U.S. entry into World War I (1917) and the beginning of the Great Depression (1929), and then another twelve years before the U.S. entry into World War II (1941). Twelve years after the end of World War II (1945–1946) was the first significant postwar economic recession (1957–1958). Twelve years later there was another recession (1970), and twelve years after that, the greatest of all bull markets began.

The Twelve-year Present Value Method is used to compare the relative values of stocks over a twelve-year period. This approach is based, as the name implies, on the present value of future earnings.

If Company X succeeds in growing at 14% annually over the next twelve years, each $1 of earnings today would become $4.82 in the twelfth year. If another firm of similar quality, Company Y, grows at 11% per year, each $1 of earnings would become $3.50 after twelve years. What is the value of the $4.82 and $3.50 today, not twelve years from now? Of course, the answer depends on the annual return the investor is seeking.

By using the twelve-year present value table shown on the next page, it can be seen that the $4.82 (14% growth) has a present value of $1.54 and the $3.50 (11% growth) has a present value of $1.12 when the investor is seeking a 10% annual return. If the investor would prefer to have a 12% annual return, the present value of Company X's future earnings is $1.24 while that of Company Y's earnings is $0.90.

To show how the Twelve-Year Present Value Method works, consider the real-life experience of an investor comparing Growth Stock A with Growth Stock B and the Dow Jones Industrial Average during the twelve-year period between one recession and the next (1990 to 2002):

12-Year Present Value Table

							Desired Return									
	4%	**5%**	**6%**	**7%**	**8%**	**9%**	**10%**	**11%**	**12%**	**13%**	**14%**	**15%**	**16%**	**17%**	**18%**	**19%**	**20%**
4%	1.00	0.89	0.80	0.71	0.64	0.57	0.51	0.46	0.41	0.37	0.33	0.30	0.27	0.24	0.22	0.20	0.18
5%	1.13	1.00	0.89	0.80	0.71	0.64	0.57	0.52	0.46	0.42	0.38	0.34	0.30	0.27	0.25	0.22	0.20
6%	1.26	1.12	1.00	0.89	0.80	0.72	0.64	0.57	0.52	0.46	0.42	0.38	0.34	0.31	0.28	0.25	0.23
7%	1.41	1.25	1.12	1.00	0.89	0.80	0.72	0.64	0.58	0.52	0.47	0.42	0.38	0.34	0.31	0.28	0.25
8%	1.58	1.40	1.25	1.12	1.00	0.90	0.80	0.72	0.65	0.58	0.52	0.47	0.43	0.38	0.35	0.31	0.28
9%	1.76	1.57	1.40	1.25	1.12	1.00	0.90	0.80	0.72	0.65	0.58	0.53	0.48	0.43	0.38	0.35	0.31
10%	1.96	1.75	1.56	1.39	1.25	1.12	1.00	0.90	0.81	0.73	0.65	0.59	0.53	0.48	0.43	0.39	0.35
11%	2.19	1.95	1.74	1.55	1.39	1.25	1.12	1.00	0.90	0.81	0.73	0.65	0.59	0.53	0.48	0.43	0.39
12%	2.44	2.17	1.94	1.73	1.55	1.39	1.24	1.12	1.00	0.90	0.81	0.73	0.66	0.59	0.53	0.48	0.44
13%	2.71	2.41	2.15	1.92	1.72	1.54	1.38	1.24	1.12	1.00	0.90	0.81	0.73	0.66	0.59	0.54	0.48
14%	3.01	2.68	2.40	2.14	1.91	1.72	1.54	1.37	1.24	1.11	1.00	0.90	0.81	0.73	0.66	0.60	0.54
15%	3.34	2.98	2.66	2.38	2.12	1.90	1.71	1.53	1.37	1.24	1.11	1.00	0.90	0.81	0.73	0.66	0.60
16%	3.71	3.31	2.95	2.64	2.36	2.11	1.89	1.70	1.53	1.37	1.24	1.11	1.00	0.90	0.81	0.74	0.67
17%	4.11	3.67	3.27	2.92	2.61	2.34	2.10	1.88	1.69	1.52	1.37	1.23	1.11	1.00	0.90	0.82	0.74
18%	4.56	4.06	3.62	3.24	2.89	2.60	2.33	2.08	1.87	1.68	1.52	1.36	1.23	1.11	1.00	0.90	0.82
19%	5.04	4.49	4.01	3.58	3.20	2.87	2.57	2.31	2.07	1.86	1.68	1.51	1.36	1.23	1.10	1.00	0.90
20%	5.58	4.97	4.43	3.96	3.54	3.18	2.85	2.55	2.29	2.06	1.85	1.67	1.51	1.36	1.22	1.10	1.00
21%	6.16	5.49	4.90	4.37	3.91	3.51	3.14	2.82	2.53	2.28	2.05	1.84	1.66	1.50	1.35	1.22	1.10
22%	6.79	6.05	5.40	4.83	4.32	3.87	3.47	3.11	2.79	2.51	2.26	2.03	1.83	1.65	1.49	1.35	1.22
23%	7.49	6.68	5.96	5.32	4.76	4.27	3.82	3.43	3.08	2.77	2.49	2.24	2.02	1.82	1.64	1.49	1.34
24%	8.26	7.36	6.56	5.87	5.24	4.70	4.21	3.78	3.39	3.05	2.75	2.47	2.22	2.01	1.81	1.64	1.48
25%	9.09	8.10	7.23	6.46	5.78	5.18	4.64	4.16	3.74	3.36	3.02	2.72	2.44	2.21	1.99	1.80	1.63
26%	10.01	8.92	7.96	7.11	6.36	5.70	5.11	4.58	4.11	3.70	3.33	2.99	2.69	2.43	2.19	1.98	1.79
27%	11.01	9.81	8.75	7.82	6.99	6.27	5.62	5.04	4.53	4.07	3.66	3.29	2.96	2.68	2.41	2.18	1.97
28%	12.09	10.77	9.61	8.59	7.68	6.89	6.17	5.53	4.97	4.47	4.02	3.62	3.25	2.94	2.65	2.40	2.17
29%	13.28	11.83	10.56	9.43	8.43	7.56	6.78	6.07	5.46	4.91	4.42	3.97	3.57	3.23	2.91	2.63	2.38
30%	14.56	12.98	11.58	10.35	9.25	8.29	7.43	6.66	5.99	5.38	4.85	4.36	3.91	3.54	3.19	2.89	2.61

Expected Growth Rate (row axis label)

Industrialist John D. Rockefeller, Sr., photographed in New York in 1894. Rockefeller (1839–1937) founded the Standard Oil Company.

Growth Stock A

Current stock price: $19
Current EPS: $1.14
Estimated twelve-year earnings growth rate: 12%
Current P/E ratio: 16.7 times earnings
Desired investment return: 10% per year

Growth Stock B

Current stock price: $26
Current EPS: $1.34
Estimated twelve-year earnings growth rate: 9.5%
Current P/E ratio: 19.4 times earnings
Desired investment return: 10% per year

Dow Jones Industrial Average

Current DJIA level: 2,625
Current EPS: 172.05
Estimated earnings growth rate: 7%
Current P/E ratio: 15.3 times earnings
Desired investment return: 10% per year

The present value of future earnings for each can be found by simply multiplying the current earnings per share by the appropriate figures found on the twelve-year present value table (Growth Stock A, $1.14 × 1.24; Growth Stock B, $1.34 × 0.95; and DJIA, 172.05 × 0.72). From these figures, an investor could have calculated P/E multiples based on the *present value* of *future* earnings rather than on *current* earnings. The results proved interesting:

Growth Stock A

13.5 times PV earnings of $1.41

Growth Stock B

20.5 times PV earnings of $1.27

Dow Jones Industrials

21.1 times PV earnings of 123.88

Using this method of comparison today, Growth Stock A was much more attractive than the Dow Jones Industrials, not less attractive, as implied by the current P/E ratios. Moreover, Growth Stock A was also much more attractive than Growth Stock B, as the stock market performance over the twelve years that followed proved:

Performance as of December 31, 2002

Growth Stock A	+458%
Growth Stock B	+223%
Dow Jones Industrials	+218%

When the Twelve-Year Present Value Method is being applied, one should also take into account any dividends received over the twelve-year period.

Investors can use the table to compare today's investment values by simply performing these same calculations with current earnings projections. However, the key to successful growth stock investing is good fundamental research and a correct analysis of the company's growth potential. Without the proper input, formulas such as these are practically useless.

STOCK MARKET MANIAS

The next chapter explores the "mania," a forever-recurring condition of excessive enthusiasm. It was apparent with Avon Products, Polaroid, and Xerox during the "Nifty Fifty" years of the early 1970s. And the dot-com bubble (the Internet and optical networking craze of 1995–2000), like the Tulip Mania in Holland, was no less absurd.

As experienced investors now realize, there can be a point when growth stocks become so overvalued that even capital gains taxes, as confiscatory as they are, should not be a deterrent to profit taking.

In 1972, Avon Products touched $140 per share, or 64.8 times current earnings.

At its peak, the total market value of Avon's stock was just over $8 billion, eight times its sales, which had just surpassed the milestone $1 billion mark. If one assumed a 15% annual growth rate for earnings per share for the twelve years that followed (actually, 10% was attained until 1979, but problems were encountered in the years after that), the stock had a multiple on present value earnings of 37.9—that is, assuming a desired annual return of only 10%! (This was calculated as $2.16 per share x 1.71.) Avon did not return to its 1972 highs until 1997, twenty-five years later! What were rational investors thinking in 1972?

In 1999, Amazon.com reached $113 per share. The 370 million shares outstanding had a total market value of more than $40 billion at the peak. By 2002, revenues were almost $4 billion and the company had attained modest profitability. Although Amazon's progress was notable, the company's profits were hardly enough to justify its peak price. By 2001, once the stock had lost 95% of its market value, investors had obviously become very discouraged. But the company's growth continued, and it is still growing today.

The story of Corvis, an optical network company, during this same period is perhaps one of the most dramatic of all. Its stock price rose to $114.75 in 2000, giving the company a total market value of more than $40 billion. Yet the firm had minimal sales and no hope for profitability in the near future. Corvis's stock price then dropped to mere pennies per share before being acquired by a (declining) company.

The price of JDS Uniphase hit $153 at its peak in 2000. With 1.4 billion shares outstanding, its market value eclipsed $200 billion while the company had yet to achieve sales of $3 per share, let alone be profitable. At about the same time, the shares of Yahoo! touched $237, for a total market value of $135 billion. Sales at the time were about $1 billion. However, unlike JDS Uniphase, Yahoo! earned a profit. Within two years, both stocks declined by more than 95%.

Even the professionals were caught up in the 2000 stock market bubble. When the stocks were near their peaks, both Yahoo! and JDS Uniphase were added to the S&P 500 Index. In fact, this was one reason why the S&P 500 Index underperformed the Dow Jones Industrial Average once the bear market hit prices in the years to follow.

Other Methods When the late Benjamin Graham, known as the "Dean of Security Analysts," was asked for his approach to common stocks, he offered the following: he wanted a stock that was selling below its working capital (net current asset value), giving no weight to the firm's plant and other fixed assets—although he realized that this approach could be limited. He also favored other conservative methods: (1) paying no more than 7 times reported earnings for the past twelve months, (2) requiring a yield of at least 7%, and (3) choosing companies with a book value greater than 120% of the stock price.

Unfortunately, growth stocks are rarely available at such attractive levels because investors also place a value on future earnings prospects, as they should.

Several top mutual fund managers in recent years have gained good reputations using an approach called "value investing," which is merely a contemporary term that describes a variation on Ben Graham's original work.

The basic idea is to buy shares of companies that have assets that are "undervalued" by the marketplace. It is important to realize, however, that unless these assets are used to produce higher earnings and dividends in future years, the idea of acquiring undervalued assets is nothing more than another application of the "greater fool theory." Buying a stock with the hope that someday a greater fool will come along and pay a higher price is not the best way to invest!

This Decade and Beyond For the growth stock investor with a sense of history and some imagination and foresight, identifying growth areas should not be a difficult undertaking. It is a continuous process of inquiry, analysis, and review, never losing sight of the "big picture," despite recent problems.

The population in the years ahead will be better educated and affluent, and will be a ready market for products and services of every type. Also, this population will be aging. People in the coming decade will be spending money on different products and services from those they bought when they were younger. In many markets, innovative entrepreneurs will create new businesses of all kinds.

Automation and the Internet will continue to change the way people accomplish their daily tasks. Health care, entertainment, and communications will remain good areas of growth to meet the needs of this group.

There are four broad concepts that hold some promise for possible investment opportunities in the coming decade.

Medical Devices. As the baby boomer generation ages, the need for medical devices should grow significantly. And unlike pharmaceuticals, where generics are a factor, pricing pressures should be less severe.

Biotechnology. Amgen and others have already proved this research concept to be valid. The problem lies with the money and time required to develop new drugs. Many biotech stocks are best avoided until the drug is well along in the FDA process—at least into Phase III testing, at the earliest.

Alternative Fuels (to Oil). There are four promising categories within this group: biofuels, wind power, solar power, and fuel cells. The primary challenge for fuel cells is one of physics.

It takes power to make power. So fuel cells, while promising, will probably never be a cheap source of energy. The technologies of wind, solar, and biofuels are all proven and should offer some profit opportunities, despite various drawbacks.

One interesting longer-term prospect for solar energy is obtaining sun power from satellites and solar ships. The possible combinations of solar and wind power, as well as power from the oceans, appear promising as well. But, again, these concepts will be somewhat longer term in their realization.

Wireless Communications. Wireless technology is already with us, of course. Some observers are talking "saturation," but the applications for wireless have just begun. New chips, devices, and services are all logical areas of opportunity.

A GROWTH STOCK LIST

All the companies listed here could offer some opportunity as growth stocks for the years ahead. Many are already established in this regard, while others only hope to be. This is not a list of recommended issues but merely a group of companies worthy of further analysis. In fact, a few possess extremely high market risk. This selection is just a starting point for growth stock investors seeking new ideas.

Technology
Adobe Systems (ADBE)
Cisco Systems (CSCO)
Cree Inc. (CREE)
Hewlett-Packard (HPQ)
Intel Corp. (INTC)
International Business Machines (IBM)
J2 Global Communications (JCOM)
Lockheed Martin (LMT)
Microsoft (MSFT)
Philips Electronics N.V. (PHG)
QUALCOMM Inc. (QCOM)
Texas Instruments (TXN)

Internet
Amazon.com (AMZN)
Google (GOOG)

Health Care
Abbot Labs (ABT)
Amgen Inc. (AMGN)
Baxter Laboratories (BAX)
Becton, Dickinson (BDX)
Charles River Labs (CRL)
Johnson & Johnson (JNJ)
Medtronic, Inc. (MDT)
Merck & Company (MRK)
Mylan Laboratories (MYL)
Pfizer, Inc. (PFE)
St. Jude Medical (STJ)
SurModics, Inc. (SRDX)

Watson Pharmaceuticals (WPI)
Zimmer Holdings (ZMH)

Consumer Staples

Coca-Cola Co. (KO)
Colgate Palmolive (CL)
General Foods (GIS)
Hershey Co. (HSY)
PepsiCo Inc. (PEP)
Procter & Gamble (PG)

Retail

Applebee's International (APPB)
Bed Bath & Beyond (BBBY)
Costco (COST)
Cracker Barrel Old Country (CBRL)
CVS Caremark (CVS)
Home Depot (HD)
Lowe's Companies (LOW)
P.F. Chang's China Bistro (PFCB)
YUM Brands (YUM)

Miscellaneous

Aqua America (WTR)
Caterpillar (CAT)
Electronic Arts (ERTS)
IAC InterActiveCorp (IACI)
Int'l Game Technology (IGT)
JetBlue Airways (JBLU)
Laboratory Corp. Amer. (LH)
3M Company (MMM)
NRG Energy (NRG)

Omnicom Group (OMC)
Rent-A-Center Inc. (RCII)
Southwest Airlines (LUV)
Verizon Communications (VZ)

As the next chapter explains, growth stock investors should be especially wary of "investment fads." An industry will sometimes flourish for only one or two years, allowing its participants to resemble true growth companies.

Examples, among many others, include boating in the late 1950s, bowling and certain electronics businesses in the early 1960s, conglomerates and computer leasing in the late 1960s, warehouse merchandising in the early 1970s, and airlines, spurred on by takeover rumors, in the late 1980s. In the last years of the twentieth century, and even now in the twenty-first, there are many areas that present opportunity, but also warrant skepticism and scrutiny.

An investor can avoid being deceived by correctly identifying the strengths and weaknesses of the industry, understanding the economics of the business, and maintaining a long-term perspective.

However, one should always keep in mind that the long-term objective of every growth stock investor is the compounding of profits and the resulting dividend potential.

7 | Manias, Fads, and Panics

Introduction

In the contemporary foreword to Charles Mackay's 1841 classic, *Extraordinary Popular Delusions and the Madness of Crowds*, a reference was made to this colloquy:

> *Have you ever seen, in some wood, on a sunny quiet day, a cloud of flying midges—thousands of them—hovering, apparently motionless, in a sunbeam? . . . Yes? . . . Well, did you ever see the whole flight—each mite preserving its distance from all others—suddenly move, say three feet, to one side or the other? Well, what made them do that? A breeze? I said a quiet day. But try to recall—did you ever see them move directly back again in the same unison? Well, what made them do that? Great human mass movements are slower but much more effective.*

We may never know the answer to the question, *"What made them do that?"* but lessons can be learned from emotional market experiences such as those described here.

This chapter will show the psychology of investing, from the Tulip Mania that began in the early 1600s to the dot-com bubble that ended in 2002. Investors who recognize a mania or a fad may not be able to profit from it, but they are far less likely to lose money in the crash that inevitably follows.

In the 1600s, "tulip mania" swept Holland.

Human Nature? "It's *greed* and *fear* that move stocks," said the savvy Wall Street trader. "When prices are rising, enthusiasm and optimism rule. When the bids dry up, a fear of losing money takes over . . . and whatever promise the future holds is put aside!"

Almost since the beginning of time, the action and the excitement of the moment have tended to stir these emotions, often to an extreme. People temporarily forget the fundamental reasoning behind the investment in the first place. When the long-term outlook does change, one can expect prices to reflect that change eventually, whether gradually or suddenly.

History offers several glaring examples of greed and fear. As always, it is very easy to be critical of others with the benefit of 20/20 hindsight. But how is it possible for someone to pay a life's fortune for a few flower bulbs? Or to invest in the cargo of a ship without knowing what the goods are or where they will be sold? Or to buy shares in a company when its profit outlook is, by any reasonable analysis, questionable at best? When these tales are told, try to imagine how these "investors" became victims of their own greed and fear. Also, consider the similarities among these experiences and the common lessons to be learned. In the end, investors who know and understand the fundamentals of the companies they own will be successful.

Tulip Mania (1633–1637) The tulip, a bulb plant with long, broad, pointed leaves and a large, brightly colored flower resembling a turban, was introduced into Europe from Turkey some time after 1550. These long-stemmed beauties rapidly gained popularity, especially among the wealthy in Holland and in Germany. By 1610, a single bulb of a new variety was said to be acceptable as dowry for a bride!

Since that time, about 100 species and at least 4,000 varieties have been identified. Indeed, these fragile flowers were a prize, and they were displayed as such—that is, until it became too extravagant to do so.

In the early 1630s, Holland's general population became much more interested in the rising market value of the Tulipe Brasserie variety than in the beauty of the flower's continuous two-month springtime bloom. In 1635, a suit of clothes could be purchased for 100 florins—only a fraction of the going price for a single Semper Augustus, at more than 5,000 florins.

From 1633 until the market peaked about four years later, it was not uncommon for people to mortgage their homes and estates merely to obtain contracts on bulbs that had never been out of the ground. And, based on experience, buyers *knew* that tulip bulbs could always be sold to other eager investors at much higher prices in the weeks or months ahead. As prices rose, almost overnight, many citizens of modest means became rich. Farmers, shopkeepers, sailors, servants—everybody enjoyed the prosperity of the tulip trade.

By this time, the wealthy no longer kept the flowers in their gardens. Instead, they sold them for an immediate cash profit. In 1636, tulips were actually traded on the stock exchange of Amsterdam, and were also publicly traded, although to a lesser extent, on the exchanges of London and Paris.

By 1637, the equivalent prices of hundreds of dollars—and in some cases thousands of dollars—for a single bulb began to raise doubts. And then, when an investment of 3,000 florins would fetch only 300 florins six weeks later, or even less a few weeks after that, contract defaults became commonplace. This was becoming a major cause of social unrest. Unfortunately, the courts found it difficult to intervene and "come to the aid of the gamblers." Within just a matter of months, a great many hard-working Dutch citizens who had been lured into trading much of their property for a handful of tulip bulbs were left in ruin. Holland's Tulip Mania and the crash that followed serve as a classic lesson that may never be forgotten!

Mississippi Scheme (1718–1720) John Law, the Scottish adventurer, gambler, economic theorist, and (at least by some accounts) financial wizard, was born in Edinburgh in 1671. At the age of only fourteen, he worked in his father's bank, and he set out for London three years later when his father died.

John Law's study of trade led to the publishing of his financial doctrines when he was in his late twenties and early thirties. His work soon gained attention among politicians. He traveled on the Continent during the early 1700s and, while in Paris, established a friendship with the Duke d'Orleans, who later became an important figure in the French government when King Louis XIV died in 1715.

In August 1717, with the support of his friend, Law created the Compagnie d'Occident (Company of the West) and obtained exclusive privileges from the government to develop the French Mississippi Valley territories in North America. He was also granted the right to collect taxes and issue money. The initial capital consisted of 200,000 shares, each valued at 500 livres (the currency predecessor to the franc).

By mid-1719, his Compagnie des Indes (Company of the Indies), as it was renamed following several acquisitions, had exclusive trading rights for other parts of the world as well—including the East Indies, China, and the South Seas. As the company's business opportunities opened up, demand for Compagnie shares increased.

Since new stock was being offered to the public in exchange for state-issued notes (billets d'état), nearly the entire population saw the opportunity to share in the promise of the Compagnie and, at the same time, retire the national debt. The government obliged and approved additional shares, which had attained a "good as money" stature. By this time, 625,000 shares had been issued, and the market price of each had risen to about 18,000 livres. Most citizens could provide a current quote, although few could explain where the new territories were actually located.

The government continued to print more money, which was readily accepted as before because it could be used to buy more shares in the Compagnie. However, the system's collapse began in early 1720 when share prices dropped sharply in the face of a developing scarcity of specie.

Coins were being hoarded, which became evident to everyone by that time, while all confidence in paper money was lost. It took years for the country to recover, and eventually the enormous debts were paid off with higher taxes.

South-Sea Bubble (1719–1720) The South-Sea Company, incorporated by act of parliament, was organized by Robert Harley, Earl of Oxford in 1711. Its purpose was the assumption of government debts in exchange for exclusive trading rights to the South Seas.

Initially, the company traded mainly in slaves with Spanish America. And even though the Treaty of Utrecht, made with Spain in 1713, proved less favorable than had originally been hoped, investors anticipated more positive developments. After all, the gold and silver deposits in South America were thought to be vast.

John Law's successes in France in the latter part of the decade did not go unnoticed by the public or the politicians, who began deliberations on the matter in January 1720. Also, the fact that King George I was governor of the company inspired confidence in the venture.

Between the time when the House of Commons opened discussions on authorizing new stock in January and the passage of the bill by the House of Lords in early April, amid rumors and speculation, the stock rose from 128.50 to over 300. The stock price was about 300 (quoted as a percentage of capital) when the bill received final approval, although, unknown to most investors, many influential people in government had a financial interest in its passage. By May, after two successful subscriptions and a price rise to about 400, most people were convinced of the merits of the investment. The stock continued to climb, reaching 1,000 in early August.

The success of the South-Sea Company in 1719 and 1720 led to many "bubbles," as they were aptly called, throughout Great Britain. And the speculative fever that swept the country encouraged ventures of all types. Among others, there were bubbles seeking capital for buying and selling goods, purchasing land, importing furs, and various insurance schemes.

The beginning of the end for the South-Sea Bubble came in August 1720, once word spread that Sir John Blunt, the company chairman, and a few others had sold their stock. This shook investors' confidence, and the decline that began quietly that month accelerated. By the end of September, the price had plunged to under 130. The ramifications of this crash were less severe than the debacle that occurred in France at the same time. However, this was not reassuring to those citizens who had used their South-Sea investment as collateral for other business dealings. In most cases, they, too, found themselves financially destroyed.

The South-Sea Company survived until 1853, even though most of its rights were sold to the Spanish government in 1750.

The 1929 Stock Market Crash The "Roaring Twenties" came to a quiet halt on September 3, 1929. The steadily rising stock market, with its well-publicized gains, especially late in the decade, seemed to confirm a popular notion that the United States had entered a "New Era"—a time of "permanent prosperity," and one that might never end. The rapid rise in prices between late 1921 and September 1929, and the violent crash and bear market that followed, are used today as a classic benchmark whenever market observers discuss the emotions of "greed" and "fear."

For some investors during the 1920s, a financial panic was not a totally new experience. The stock market had shut down for nearly two weeks in 1873, and

October, 1928 Presidential candidate Herbert Hoover

many could recall when J. P. Morgan almost single-handedly halted the panic of 1907. Also, the sharp 46% drop between 1919 and 1920 had not been forgotten.

But almost everyone agreed that the 1920s were very different. This was the new age of the consumer. Radios, air conditioners, washing machines, and automobiles were all being purchased with "buy-now-and-pay-later" plans. By 1929, consumer credit was helping the average family enjoy the prosperity of the day. Business was good, profits were up, and stocks, which were also being purchased on credit, were soaring.

Even though stock prices were reflecting investor optimism, as they normally do, there were also several behind-the-scenes factors that contributed to the high equity valuations and to the vulnerability of the stock market in late 1929.

MARGIN ON EQUITIES

Stocks could be bought on 10% margin in 1929. Any investor could purchase shares having a market value of $10,000 with only $1,000 of capital. When stocks advanced, the profits generated were being used to purchase additional shares. This leverage, investors soon learned, worked very much in their favor when

stocks were rising—and greatly to their detriment when prices were falling.

Perhaps most surprising was the magnitude of the change in stock market credit. In January 1928, total brokers' loans had reached $3.8 billion. A year later, the figure had risen to $5.3 billion, and it continued soaring to a peak of $6.8 billion in early October 1929. Of course, with the crash, equity credit also declined and was back to $3.4 billion by the end of the year.

STOCK MANIPULATION

The late 1920s saw notorious stock price manipulation. Much activity that was considered legal then is no longer permitted today. In 1929, investor "pools" were formed to trade stocks. The pool would buy the shares, use media contacts to spread favorable news or rumors, and then "paint the tape" with large, meaningless trades among themselves. This would draw attention to the stock, allowing the pool to sell the shares, usually at much higher prices, to an unsuspecting public.

One of the most infamous manipulations of the time was the RCA pool headed by broker-specialist Michael J. Meehan. The pool managed to push up

Allied Chemical	General Foods	Paramount Publix
American Can	General Motors	Radio Corporation
American Smelting	General Railway Signal	Sears Roebuck & Co.
American Sugar	Goodrich	Standard Oil (N.J.)
American Tobacco	International Harvester	Texas Corporation
Atlantic Refining	International Nickel	Texas Gulf Sulphur
Bethlehem Steel	Mack Trucks	Union Carbide
Chrysler	Nash Motors	U.S. Steel
Curtiss-Wright	National Cash Register	Westinghouse Electric
General Electric	North American	Woolworth

RCA's stock price by almost 50% between the March 8 and March 17, 1929. Then, on the very next day, March 18, the pool sold its entire holdings and divided the profits—about $100 million, by today's standards.

The trading activities, rumored or real, of William Durant, Jesse Livermore, and others were popular topics of discussion in brokerage houses across the country.

Periodically, experienced market observers of the day, including Roger Babson and Bernard Baruch, would warn of the consequences of the speculative market environment. Unfortunately, few people took the warnings seriously because both men had been repeating similar messages for up to two years before the early September peak.

THE 1929 FED

In the months between late 1927 and June 1929, the nation's personal income and industrial production rose steadily. At the same time, wholesale prices (now called "producer prices") remained flat or were declining, as they had been doing for several years following the inflationary consequences of World War I. In addition, President Hoover, in keeping with the mood of the nation's working class, fa-vored a continuation of high tariffs and protectionism. Meantime, the Federal Reserve Board encouraged easier credit.

On March 22, 1929, investors were relieved when the Federal Reserve failed to take action, thus encouraging further speculation. Yet observers seemed unaware of the consequences of the Fed's move in July when it raised the discount rate from 5 to 6%. And it was clear to some that personal income and industrial production were no longer rising. During the two months between the actual peak in the economy in August 1929 and the October crash, personal income and wholesale prices were declining, and industrial production was actually plunging.

Following the crash, the discount rate was quickly returned to 5%, and many declines followed in 1930. By October of that year, production had fallen 26%, personal income 16%, and product prices 14%. In terms of the creation of new money, it can be said that the Federal Reserve was very much "behind the curve" during the 1930 to 1933 period. The death of Benjamin Strong (the New York bank governor and chairman of the newly created Open Market Investment Committee) in 1928 led to a diffusion of leadership when the Fed needed it most.

CORPORATE PROFITS

From 1926 through 1929, the earnings of the Dow Jones Industrial Average climbed 33%, from about 15 to 19.94. Earnings remained strong year to year going into the last quarter of 1929. However, a slowdown was evident in some areas as early as the third (September) quarter of 1929, and the fourth quarter, normally higher than the third, was slipping. A substantial decline in profits occurred in 1930 and in the year following. The Dow Jones Industrial Average posted a loss for the entire year 1932. Not until the third quarter of 1948 did the Dow post earnings greater than it did in 1929.

CORPORATE DIVIDENDS

More than 60% of DJIA company profits were paid out to shareholders in 1929. And in the four years that followed, 1930 through 1933, dividends paid, although lower in each successive year, exceeded the actual earnings of the companies.

Chronology: The 1929 Crash

The Dow Jones Industrial Average began 1927 at roughly 150 and climbed steadily throughout the year, but stalled at 200 late in the last quarter. That mark was finally shattered on December 19, 1927. The Dow then advanced to 300 by November 1928. In just five days in early December, the Dow retreated 15%, but it then rallied to close out 1928 at exactly 300. Volatility was becoming more prevalent, but it was more or less accepted by the public.

Volume on the New York Stock Exchange was picking up as well. During the sharp swing in December of 1928, daily volume reached approximately 5 to 6 million shares. In late 1928, and through most of 1929, a monthly total of 80 to 100 million shares was typical. Saturday trading, which was the practice during this period, saw volume of roughly half the activity of a weekday.

On January 24, the NYSE celebrated a membership increase from 275 to 1,375.

Between January 1 and June 1, 1929, the Dow Industrials fluctuated between 280 and 333. Exactly twenty-one weeks before the October crash, the Dow began its final climb from 290 to its 386.10 peak on September 3. From that day on, a steady decline consumed the entire month of September. The Dow would not see 386 again until 1954, about 25 years later!

October 24, 1929 (Black Thursday)

On Wednesday, October 23, the Dow closed at 305.85 in a busy session of

A crowd gathered at the corner of Wall and Broad on "Black Thursday" October 24, 1929.

6,369,000 shares. Early Thursday, the market rallied 7 points, and then a wave of selling hit the exchange. At its lowest point, the Dow had reversed 40 points, or 13%, before closing at 299.47, down only 6.38 (2%) on the day. Volume totaled a record 12.9 million shares.

It can be said that "Black Thursday," as it soon became known, marked a "day of awareness" for 1929 Wall Street. The record trading activity that day was more than 50% greater than the March record, and Wall Street's back offices struggled to keep up. The new high-speed ticker tape ran hours behind, and the paperwork was still being sorted and corrected on Friday.

On Saturday, activity returned to normal, and the financial community seemed to believe that the worst had past. The Dow closed Saturday's session at 298.97.

On Monday morning, a story in the *New York Times* hit on many of the concerns of the day. The subtitle to the article was:

*Wall Street Hums on the Day
of Rest to Catch Up on Work*

Wall Street, usually as deserted and quiet on Sunday as a country graveyard, hummed with activity yesterday as bankers and brokers strove to put their houses in order after the most strenuous week in history, in which all previous records for the exchange of securities on the New York Stock Exchange, the Curb Market, and over the counter were broken.

The article explained in a colorful way how weekend sightseers gazed curiously at the stock exchange building and, here and there, picked up from the street a vagrant slip of ticker tape, as visitors would seize upon spent bullets as souvenirs from a battlefield. An NYSE official was quoted as saying that the members, many of whom were on the job Sunday morning, "have the physical work well in hand." And the article continued:

There will, nevertheless, be great interest in today's stock fluctuations and those of subsequent days this week, or until the last vestige of the market upheaval has disappeared.

Possibly, now that the nervousness has passed and holders of stocks or prospective holders of stocks have the opportunity to delve into the merits of their securities, especially in the points of earnings, dividends and outlook, the forecast may safely be made that it will be the best of stocks which will give the best accounts of themselves, no matter what the condition of the market.

U.S. Steel announced that its directors would be meeting on Thursday, leading many to believe that an important, positive announcement could be forthcoming.

It would not surprise Wall Street in the least to see several leading corporations adopt a policy of greater liberality to their stockholders during the balance of the year, in view of the crisis which has developed and passed. Money is expected to continue cheap and plentiful.

Business in most lines, according to all of the faro metric indices, continues good and record Christmas trade is expected because of the high rate of employment. Ratios of operation in basic lines are not as high as in late summer and early fall, and the edge has been dulled measurably. On the other hand, the general state of trade compares favorably with this time last year, and corporate earnings as a whole, for the complete year, will show gains, it is expected, of be-

tween 20 and 25 per cent, over the full year 1928.

Stocks of all sorts, those that have been selling at five times earnings, at ten times earnings, and those that have been selling at 75, 100, and even in extreme cases 150 times earnings, are now expected to engage in a quiet era of readjustment, in which the earnings will determine their worth, rather than the market value governed by the anxiety of speculators in all parts of the country to own them.

Monday, October 28, 1929

The Dow opened on a gap down at 295, three points lower. The popular blue chip U.S. Steel opened at $202¼, off 1¼. Upon reflection on Sunday, many were expecting some organized support at the open. They were disappointed. Prices plunged during the remainder of the session. Tuesday's *New York Times* described the action:

There was but one brief respite during the day. At 1:10 P.M. news tickers reported that Charles E. Mitchell (broker, President, National City Bank) had just entered the Morgan offices. Wall Street jumped to the conclusion that another banking

conference was on, and stocks steadied momentarily.

During the day most brokerage offices simply gave up posting prices on their chalkboards. The ticker was so late that prices put on the boards had no meaning by that time. In effect, *fear* ruled the day.

"Steel," as it was then called, closed down 17½ at $186, off almost 9% from Saturday and 29% below its $262 September high.

Monday's session closed down 38.33, or almost 13%, on 9.2 million shares. On Monday, $14 billion of total market value had vanished. Lower prices, some observed, were fueled by the stop-loss orders placed weeks earlier and by margin calls that "went out by the thousands."

Tuesday, October 29, 1929

The opening bell on Tuesday saw a flood of sell orders—immediately prices were lower. By the end of the first half hour, 3.3 million shares had traded hands. Soon stocks were being sold at whatever bid was available. Everyone wanted to sell.

From the opening bell, Steel plunged nearly $20 to $166½, down 11%, before closing at $174, down $12. Late in the day, the company's board of directors declared an extra $1 per share dividend.

The losses were widespread among all shares. Air Reduction closed at $120, off $25; General Electric at $222, down $28; International Telephone at $71, down $17; and Sears at $95, down $16¼. DuPont's action was typical for those hectic days. The stock closed on Tuesday at $116, off $34 ($50½ below Saturday's price) and 46% below its high set in September.

Union Carbide & Carbon (UK), listed in 1926, was a popular stock at the time. In mid-September, it reached $140. On Black Thursday, UK's high was $106 and its low was $90. On Saturday, October 26, its price was near $102, the level at which it opened for trading on Monday. UK hit a low of $81 that day and $66 on Tuesday, a 35% drop in two days. By 1932, UK had fallen to $15½, exactly 89% below its 1929 high, a price that was not seen again until April 1955.

At Tuesday's low, the DJIA hit 212.33, down 48.31 (18.5%) from Monday's close, 29% below Saturday, and 45% below its September 3 peak. Most issues enjoyed a recovery late in Tuesday's session. The Dow ended its two-day panic, closing Tuesday at 230.07. The day's volume totaled 16,410,030 shares, a record not eclipsed for nearly forty years.

On Wednesday, newspaper headlines were screaming ... *Variety*'s was a classic.

AFTER THE 1929 CRASH

The emotional wave of selling finally ended on October 29, although stock prices did move lower, hitting 195.35 on November 13 before a healthy five-month rally began. By April 1930, the Dow Jones Industrial Average had climbed back to 300, the precise point from which it had crashed in late October. But by that time, the deteriorating fundamentals had become more obvious. It was then that the bear market took hold, and it extended until July 8, 1932, when the average hit its final low at 40.56.

The 1929 crash and the 1930–1932 bear market that followed had a devastating impact on individual stocks. U.S. Steel hit its final low in 1932 at $22, down 92%, and did not return to its 1929 peak until May 1955. In the meantime, Chrysler declined from its 1928 high of $140 to $13 in 1930, a staggering 91% decline in just two years.

At the market peak on September 3, 1929, the P/E multiple of the Dow Industrials was 19.4 times estimated 1929 earnings and 35.0 times eventual earnings for 1930. The payout ratio was comparatively high in 1929 (64%), and the yield was 3.3%. At its low on October 29, the P/E was 10.6 and the yield had climbed to 6.0%.

Could the 1929–1932 debacle have been made less severe? Yes, most likely.

There were many major changes to the securities markets after the 1929 crash. Reforms included the establishment of the Securities and Exchange Commission (the SEC) in 1934 and the requirement of SEC filings by companies, the formation of the Federal Deposit Insurance Corporation (the FDIC), and the prohibition of pools and manipulation of stock prices.

The huge profits that Jesse Livermore realized by selling short into an extremely weak market, for example, would have been much more difficult to achieve with an "uptick" rule, option hedges, exchange "circuit breakers," and substantially higher margin requirements. By the same token, it can also be said that the emotions of greed and fear cannot be removed from the marketplace by regulation, as we witnessed once again during the crash fifty-eight years later. However, the ability now to see prices without delays reduces the great fear and anxiety that accompany the unknown.

Wars and Shocks A study of the stock market's performance following shocking developments suggests that there is no precise pattern for a market reaction, but the market's ability to anticipate is clear.

PEARL HARBOR AND
WORLD WAR II

It can be said that World War II was a factor that helped end the Depression of the 1930s. It altered the unemployment picture dramatically and eventually added to the activity of the nation's economy.

The surprise attack on December 7, 1941, produced a sudden but relatively mild reaction. At the time, most issues had experienced a five-year bear trend up to that point . . . and some experienced an immediate bottom. The majority, however, continued in a downtrend until May 1942. In general, most stocks performed very well between 1942 and 1946. The DJIA rose more than 70%.

One interesting observation regarding World War II: the stocks of military suppliers such as Grumman, for example, rose, as one would expect. Between 1942 and 1945, the company's earnings climbed sharply from $2.16 to $11.28 per share, and the stock advanced 500%. Yet, many consumer stocks such as PepsiCo, with relatively flat profits during the period, climbed even more dramatically. Airlines and utilities also did well.

One of the biggest winners during World War II was Chadbourn Gotham, Inc., a manufacturer of women's hosiery.

When the Japanese bombed Pearl Harbor in December, the stock was priced below $2 with earnings per share of $1.43. In early 1946, the stock peaked at $43. However, by the time earnings finally peaked at $4.88 per share in 1948, the stock had already lost its luster and had returned to the teens.

The years 1937 to 1942 represented a no-growth period for most companies, with little earnings progress being made while the battles were being fought. But the stocks rose in anticipation of a postwar profit boom. Deere & Co. was a good example: In 1942, the stock was $20 with $3.52 earnings per share. By 1946, Deere shares were $58, but earnings were only $2.48. By 1949, the stock had slipped to $40, yet profits had risen to an astounding $12.40 per share.

The nation's war experiences since World War II have produced mixed investment results. The wars in Korea, Vietnam, and, more recently, the Middle East did affect daily market fluctuations, each one more quickly than the one before it. In recent years, minute-to-minute reports have been seen on television right from the battlefield.

The terrorist attack of September 11, 2001, resulted in a market shutdown for several days, and it eventually caused dis-

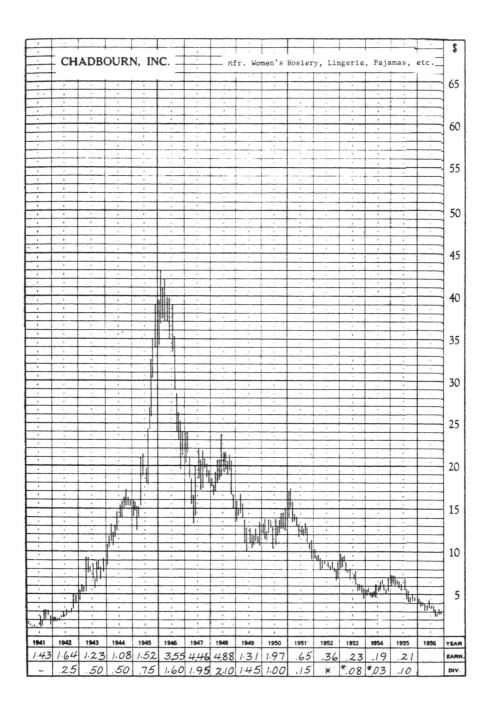

CHADBOURN, INC.   Mfr. Women's Hosiery, Lingerie, Pajamas, etc.

YEAR	1941	1942	1943	1944	1945	1946	1947	1948	1949	1950	1951	1952	1953	1954	1955	1956
EARN.	1.43	1.64	1.23	1.08	1.52	3.55	4.46	4.88	1.31	1.97	.65	.36	.23	.19	.21	
DIV.	—	.25	.50	.50	.75	1.60	1.95	2.10	1.45	1.00	.15	*	*.08	*.03	.10	

locations within many segments of the economy.

The 1987 Stock Market Crash The economic circumstances and fundamental footing for businesses in 1987 were very different from those in 1929. But the technical similarities between the two periods were striking. First, the fundamentals.

1987 BACKGROUND

The investment environment in the seven years immediately preceding the 1987 crash was as favorable as the years prior to the 1929 crash, if not more so. Inflation and interest rates, which peaked in 1980 and 1981, respectively, had been declining steadily. Even though wholesale prices had been climbing, they were not much higher than they had been five years earlier.

In late 1986, industrial production began climbing at a much faster pace than in the prior two years. By the third (September) quarter of 1987, industrial production was growing at an annual rate of almost 6% and showed no signs of slowing.

During the year 1986, the Fed reduced the discount rate from 7%, set in early March, to 6.5% in late April, to 6% in early July, and then to 5.5% in late August. This trend was reversed when the Fed raised the discount rate from 5.5% to 6% in early September 1987—déjà vu?

From an investment standpoint, 1987 was very different from 1929 in two respects:

First, when the Dow Industrials peaked in 1929, stock yields were just over 3% and bond yields were about 4 to 5% (a spread of less than 2%). In contrast, the competition for investment funds was actually greater in 1987. Yields on equities were below 3%, while bond yields had advanced to over 10% by September, reflecting a fear that inflation might be rekindled. So, with the spread close to 7%, stocks in 1987 were far less attractive relative to bonds.

Second, in 1987, unlike in 1929, there was little or no evidence that corporate earnings and dividends would be declining anytime soon. In 1987, stock prices appeared high, but, although a shift to bonds could take place at any time, there did not seem to be any fundamental reason to do so.

Still, by early October 1987, the technical stage was set.

TECHNICAL PICTURE, 1987 VS. 1929

The charts shown on the next page illustrate the weekly closing prices for each pe-

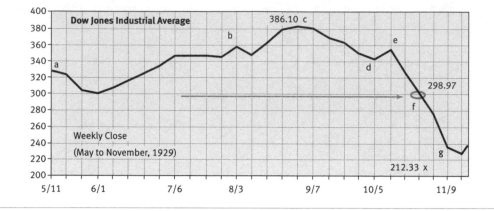

Dow Jones Industrial Average

386.10 c

a

b

e

d

298.97

f

Weekly Close

(May to November, 1929)

g

212.33 x

400
380
360
340
320
300
280
260
240
220
200

5/11   6/1   7/6   8/3   9/7   10/5   11/9

riod. As a reminder, for most of the 1929 era, the markets were open for trading six days a week, Monday through Saturday. In 1987, trading was occurring five days a week, Monday through Friday, as it is today.

Most historic accounts refer to the "1929 Stock Market Crash" as the panic that hit the markets on Tuesday, October 29. As the earlier discussion shows, however, the actual crash was a two-day event that began Monday, October 28, and merely continued into the following day, just as it did in 1987.

Compare the DJIA charts shown. In both cases, the intraday market highs (386 in 1929 and 2,747 in 1987) were just over 2.5 times the DJIA level of 36 months earlier. In 1929, the P/E ratio was 19.4, up from about 10 at the end of 1926; and in 1987, the P/E was 20.7, up from almost 11 at the end of 1984. In other words, in both cases, earnings grew and P/E multiples expanded at very close to the same rate.

At the high in 1929, the DJIA yield was 3.3%. In 1987, it was 2.6%.

In 1929, and again in 1987, the top was formed with a distinct pattern, labeled "a" through "g." In both cases, the high ("c") was 18%+ above the peak of "a." In 1929 and in 1987, the actual high of "c" was hit on a Tuesday. Exactly six weeks later, the high of "e" was attained.

Again, in both cases, prices dropped sharply for two weeks. On Saturday, October 26, 1929, the DJIA ended its second week at 298.97 and opened down with a gap on Monday (at "f"). In 1987, the second week ended on Friday, October 16, at 2,247 and also opened Monday with a gap down. The intraday crash lows were 212.33 on Tuesday, October 29, 1929, and 1,616 on Tuesday, October 20, 1987.

In both cases, 1929 and 1987, the gaps that occurred on Monday marked exactly halfway between "c" and "g"—and both occurred 21 weeks after the trough of "a."

At the October 29, 1929, low (45% below "c"), the P/E ratio had dropped to 10.6, while the yield had risen to 6.0%. In 1987 (at 41% below "c"), the P/E had dropped to 12.1, while the yield had risen to 4.4%.

This is a significant technical pattern, and it has been observed at other times, albeit less severely. Yet, although the two patterns are similar, the crash in 1987 was mostly *technical*. The event 58 years earlier was *fundamental*.

Fads Wall Street investors are a forward-thinking lot. And their ideas often lead to viable concepts—but these concepts can be taken to an extreme. It seems that every decade the community will em-

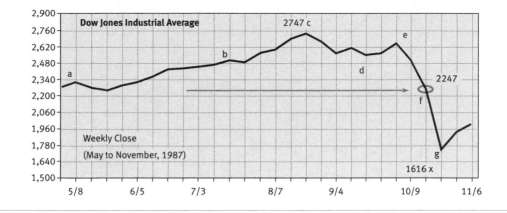

Dow Jones Industrial Average — Weekly Close (May to November, 1987)

brace a promising new investment theme and then look for its "pure plays."

Once this new concept is accepted by a larger audience, the story has become well known and valuations become excessive. Unfortunately, in the years that follow, the initial earnings projections are rarely achieved; or if they are, this doesn't happen for many years. But the excitement and momentum can produce a thrilling ride. Like manias, fads usually end the same way every time—with a "blow-off." When profit projections are revised or delayed, usually for valid reasons, investors begin to review and analyze the data and their assumptions much more carefully. Once this happens, earnings estimates are reduced and doubts about the concept itself begin to develop.

By the time it is obvious to the crowd that even the lowest, most conservative projections are not likely to be attained, the stocks have already begun their plunge. After the selling ends, the stocks are usually abandoned, sometimes for years. In most cases, a complete "cycle" will take years, depending on the madness and the degree of earnings disappointment.

Often the leading companies within the group do produce impressive growth records for a time, with one or two viable long-term investments emerging. Marginal firms will usually either be acquired or fail.

Here are some of the most notable fads over the past fifty years or so.

LEISURE-TIME STOCKS (1957–1961)

Brunswick Corp., AMF, Outboard Marine

The leisure-time stocks enjoyed great popularity in the late 1950s. Brunswick and AMF were the leaders in bowling. Also included were boating issues: Outboard Marine, Glasspar, NAFI (later Chris-Craft), and others.

Between 1957 and 1960, the shares of Brunswick Corp., adjusted for splits, rose from about $3 in early 1957 to almost $75 in March 1961. BC's earnings progression after 1955 was also very impressive: $0.39; $0.69; $1.07; $1.71; and $2.28. Earnings peaked at $2.56 per share in 1961. By 1964, however, profits had returned to breakeven levels, and the stock price was once again well below $10.

CONGLOMERATES (1962–1967)

Litton Industries, Gulf & Western, IT&T

The art of merging lower-quality and/or lower-multiple companies into a larger entity to attain "synergy" and an apparent growth record has been an everlasting fad on Wall Street, with mixed results.

FERTILIZER STOCKS (1964–1967)

Freeport Sulphur, Texas Gulf Sulphur

Sulphur (now usually spelled sulfur) and fertilizer stocks were a rage in the mid-1960s. As often happens, when playing commodities, investors can forget that prices can be hurt by additional supply.

THE "NIFTY FIFTY" (1970–1974)

The excessive valuations attained by a relatively small group of growth stocks, dubbed the "nifty fifty," contributed to the devastating market debacle of 1972–1974. These stocks included Avon Products, Polaroid, Xerox, IBM, and 3M, among others. Supposedly, these companies had reliable earnings streams that could be projected years into the future. Not so. At the same time, there were several individual groups that gained attention by other aggressive investors. Included were recreational vehicle stocks such as Winnebago and Fleetwood.

In fact, not many Wall Street fads turned from a "Cinderella" into a "Queen of the Ball" and back to a "Cinderella" as fast as this one did. Adjusted for splits, Winnebago's stock rose from $4 in 1970 to a high of $48 in 1972. By the end of the following year, when gasoline prices and supplies became a factor, the stock had returned to $4.

BIOTECHNOLOGY (1989–1992)

Amgen, Chiron, Genentech, Biogen

Except for the astounding dot-com stocks years later, no industry with such modest immediate earnings prospects ever raised as much new seed capital as this one did. Biotech IPOs were being spawned weekly in early 1991.

Their rapid rise and fall between 1989 and 1992 was noteworthy, since the year-long shakeout effectively separated those companies that had the most promising and lasting earnings prospects from those that did not. It was the Food & Drug Administration's "efficacy challenges" to products by Xoma and Centocor that changed investor sentiment at that time. Yet many biotech companies since have had drugs approved and have developed into viable, rapidly growing pharmaceutical companies in their own right.

Amgen, for example, rose from an adjusted $8 in early 1990 to almost $80 in 1992 as earnings soared from $0.04 per share to $0.67 and then to $2.43 per share in the same time frame. The stock's 50% decline in 1993 in sympathy with the industry's shakeout did nothing more than provide an excellent buying opportunity for investors who had done their homework.

The Dot-Com Bubble (1995–2000)

The Internet mania that came to a sudden halt in 2000 is labeled the "granddaddy of all stock bubbles." The dollar losses in millions of portfolios resulting from the dot-com bubble easily exceeded $1 trillion.

A later chapter in this book, "The Internet," explains the fascinating story behind this extraordinary method of communication. Why investors became so enamored is now very clear. In effect, imaginations ran amuck without any realistic understanding of the potential profitability—or the lack thereof.

The bubble was fueled by enthusiasm for numerous products and services that could eventually be developed using the Web: software sales, Internet service providers, search engines, portals, Web services, Web site auctions, Web sales, and business-to-business networks were among the many ideas to be developed. In addition, the Internet system would require greater capacity and speed. Thus, billions—or maybe trillions—of dollars of network equipment would be needed. By 1995, the investment concept was born.

The big question was: "Who will profit?"

Eventually, the answer became clear to most Internet investors: "Not everybody!"

Netscape Communications was founded by young visionary Marc Andreessen and a savvy millionaire entrepreneur, James Clark. Netscape was an early leader in the field with advanced browser software called Navigator. Revenues increased rapidly, and the company's initial public offering on August 8, 1995, was the most successful ever up to that time.

In only four months, the stock advanced from the IPO price of $28 to $171 per share. At its high, the company's shares attained a market value of more than $6.5 billion, or roughly 80 times 1995 revenues! Many seasoned observers held that Microsoft's momentum as a chief competitor was the turning point for Netscape, which was eventually acquired (after a plunge of 80%) by America Online. AOL emerged as a dot-com survivor as a result of its acquisition by media giant Time Warner. However, to this day, many questions still plague the AOL franchise. At the high, its market value exceeded $350 billion.

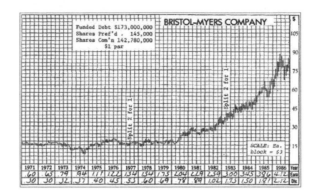

Amazon.com's story is one of an evolving strategy by its flamboyant founder, Jeff Bezos. The venture began as an online bookstore and eventually expanded into many of the merchandise categories of big department stores, including toys, clothing, electronics, and other products. The company is now recording earnings progress, and it has definitely survived the burst of the bubble.

Cisco Systems has been John Chambers's success story of sorts. The stock rose from under $1 to $82 (adjusted) before losing more than 80%. Yet Cisco, with an aggressive acquisition program, became a $20 billion enterprise—and a profitable one at that.

Overall, eBay Inc. has been one of the few dot-com companies to continue to grow and to earn good profits. Like Amazon.com, eBay has developed its forte (auctions) into a well-known Internet franchise.

Yahoo!'s rise from under $1 to $125 (prices adjusted), being added to the S&P along the way, and then its slide to under $5 makes this equity one of the true dot-com bubble "classics." Fundamentally, Yahoo! has since lost its leading position to Google and has become part of the "second tier" in the Internet search engine market.

JDS Uniphase was tagged as one of the leading suppliers of Internet products. Like Yahoo!, it became a mutual fund darling and was added to the S&P 500 once its market value ballooned above $150 billion.

One of the great ironies of the Internet Mania was the number of "conservative investors" who were unknowingly hurt by it. Once an Internet stock was added to an index, such as the S&P 500, index holders who had never owned it going *up* rode it going *down*.

Hundreds of other Internet stocks were less fortunate and went bankrupt. Many others are still struggling to survive today. Here are just a few of the many past highflyers that have since been reduced to penny-stock status or worse:

Avanex Corp.: fiber optic-based products. High: $273 ($19.0 billion).

Corvis Corp.: networking equipment. High: $115 ($41.3 billion).

Drugstore.com: Internet-based drugstore. High: $70 ($4.7 billion).

Homestore.com: a service for real estate professionals. High: $138 ($16.2 billion).

Bristol-Myers Squibb (BMY) as it is now called, had three 2-for-1 stock splits after 1986 (in 1987, 1997, and 1999).

At the end of 1986, BMY was selling at the equivalent of $8 per share vs. today's depressed price. (Note that BMY's annual dividend today is $1.24 per share.)

The 1997–2005 Real Estate Bubble Last, but certainly not least, there was the Great Real Estate Bubble that inflated U.S. home prices for nearly a decade until 2006—and we are still feeling its effects today. This once-in-a-generation experience will be explained fully in the next chapter, "From Wall Street to Main Street."

It should be noted that this was not this nation's first bout with rampant real estate speculation. It also occurred to a lesser degree in the late 1970s, when there was mounting concern about inflation. Perhaps the most visible comparison in history was the real estate bubble, mainly in Florida, that began in the early 1920s. And this mania was a terrific subject for jokes at the time. Groucho Marx had a good one:

> *"That's right, 800 wonderful residences will be built right here . . . any kind of home you want. You can even get stucco. Oh, how you can get stucco!"*
> —From the movie, *Coconuts*

The 1926 bubble ended badly. But there was a major difference between the Florida land craze in 1926 and the one that hit the United States eighty years later. At that time, the "Roaring Twenties" bull market in stocks was unaffected. In 2006, the real estate bubble affected the entire financial system of the United States. In fact, the effects and its retrenchment were felt globally!

Conclusion There is a certain degree of logic to the stock market and to the psychology that rules it when one takes into account the emotions of greed and fear. When these two imponderables are better understood, it is even possible to profit from the event.

In late 1972, Bristol-Myers's shares were $70 with EPS of $2.60. Two years later, the stock was 50% lower and the earnings figure was $3.76. The P/E had dropped from 27 to 9 within twenty-four months.

Twelve years later, BMY was earning *four times* as much and paying a cash dividend of $8.48 annually (note the adjustments for splits on the chart). Once the P/E multiple had partially recovered, those who had sold in panic had a very good reason to be unhappy: the stock had tripled and was still rising! In effect, they let their emotions rule and temporarily disregarded the fundamentals.

The same emotions that drove the price of tulips down in 1638—the fear of losing more money—led investors to sell BMY shares that offered a measurable value.

STOCK MARKET BUBBLES:

"Musical chairs without the music."

The lesson is very simple. Over time, those investors who recognize the emotions of the day for what they are, and who have done their homework, are likely to enjoy much greater success in the stock market.

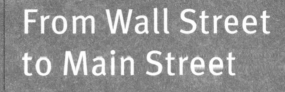

8 From Wall Street
to Main Street

Introduction

The 1997–2005 real estate bubble and its consequences touched the lives of almost every citizen. This so-called perfect storm proved to be the ultimate illustration of how closely Main Street and Wall Street are intertwined, and its effects are lingering to this day.

At no time in history was more personal wealth destroyed—and in such a short time frame. Before this event, when historians talked of financial debacles, 1972–1974 and 2000–2002 were the foremost contemporary examples. Of course, the depression that followed the market crash in 1929 might be comparable to the latest calamity, but that occurred before most of us were born.

One particularly distressing characteristic of this recent event was the extraordinary amount of greed and naïveté exhibited by nearly everyone who participated.

This chapter will examine the various links, similar to dominoes, between Wall Street and Main Street, as well as the causes of the bubble and the remedies that followed in its wake. Also analogous to the 1930s, many valuable lessons were learned from the experience—once again leading to greater oversight and future safeguards.

> *Don't gamble. Take all your savings*
> *and buy some good stock and hold it*
> *'til it goes up, then sell it. If it don't go*
> *up, don't buy it.*
>
> —WILL ROGERS

The 1997–2005 Real Estate Bubble The seeds of the "Great Real Estate Bubble," as it is likely to be called in the years ahead, were sown in the late 1990s, during the Clinton presidency. But the imbecilities of regulators and politicians, Republicans and Democrats alike, knew no bounds, and the crisis was allowed to propagate.

The initial concept was a noble one: to further the "American Dream"—that is, to offer everyone, rich or poor, an opportunity to own an affordable home.

Yet, as early as 1999, there were warnings and indications that a significant problem could be brewing. The tip of that iceberg is now well known as the "subprime" market. Home buyers with less than prime credit, with a much higher risk of default, were rapidly becoming a greater portion of the overall mortgage market.

Fannie Mae In 1968, the Federal National Mortgage Association (FNMA), founded thirty years earlier, became a publicly owned company. The shares began trading on the New York Stock Exchange, sporting the ticker symbol FNM.

FNMA, or "Fannie Mae," as it is called, was created immediately after the depression to provide liquidity for home ownership, and thus maintained a portfolio of mortgages insured or guaranteed by the FHA, VA, or Farmer's Home Administration. These mortgages would be bought from savings institutions, thus freeing up funds so that new mortgages could be granted.

Fannie Mae would buy the mortgages in the secondary market, bundle them, and then sell them to investors as "mortgage-backed securities" (MBS) to be traded in the open market.

After its initial public offering, Fannie Mae's activities would no longer be an item in the federal budget. The public offering was a resounding success, and the stock soared sixfold over the next four years.

In 1970, the government created the Federal Home Loan Mortgage Corporation (Freddie Mac) to support conventional mortgages and to provide competition for Fannie Mae, which was then also permitted to deal in conventional mortgages. This move established a healthier and more efficient secondary mortgage market.

A more complex form of the mortgage-backed security, mentioned earlier, is the "collateralized mortgage obligation." These bonds, simply referred to as CMOs, are issued by Freddie Mac and private firms. With CMOs, the pooled mortgages are divided into "tranches,"

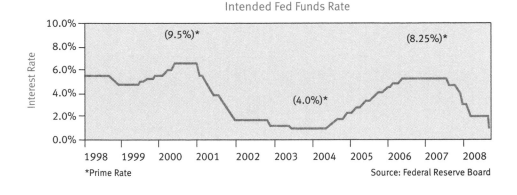

Intended Fed Funds Rate

(9.5%)*

(8.25%)*

(4.0%)*

*Prime Rate

Source: Federal Reserve Board

each having its own level of risk, rate of interest, and maturity date (ranging from a few months to twenty years).

CMOs are generally backed by savings and loan associations, mortgage companies, and the consumer loan divisions of large banks. Potential CMO investors include banks, insurance companies, hedge funds, pension funds, mutual funds, and government agencies. For investment benefits, CMOs that meet certain size and credit requirements can be insured by Fannie Mae and Freddie Mac against delinquencies and defaults.

Considering the quality and diversification of CMOs, the rating agencies usually give them AAA ratings. With CMOs, the risk of prepayment is reduced, thus making them more attractive investments. So, when subprime mortgages entered the spotlight, the question became, "Should a basket of bad apples be awarded the same credit rating as one good apple?"

In 1999, as the stock prices of both FNM and FRE reached high levels, warnings were surfacing about the deterioration of their portfolios and subprime holdings.

The oversight of Fannie and Freddie has been the responsibility of Congress and the Department of Housing and Urban Development (HUD). In late 2003, the Bush administration proposed transferring oversight responsibility to an independent agency. Barney Frank, the ranking Democrat on the Republican-led House Financial Services Committee, opposed this, saying that it would lessen the ability of poorer families to get affordable housing. Regulation remained negligent.

Both Fannie and Freddie made patient, long-term shareholders very wealthy. As the business flourished, an original FNM investment of $1,000 in 1968 became an astounding $270,000 when the stock peaked in late 2000. Likewise, Freddie Mac shares also performed spectacularly.

The money was flowing. By 2003, Fannie Mae had total assets of $1 trillion, and Freddie Mac reported $803 billion. But from that point on, both stocks began to falter. In mid-2007, their shares were selling at roughly the same price levels as in early 1999. The politicians in charge once again assured investors that everything was okay.

Lower Interest Rates To help the nation cope with a threatening recession just as President Clinton was leaving office, the Federal Reserve Board began reducing interest rates in February 2001.

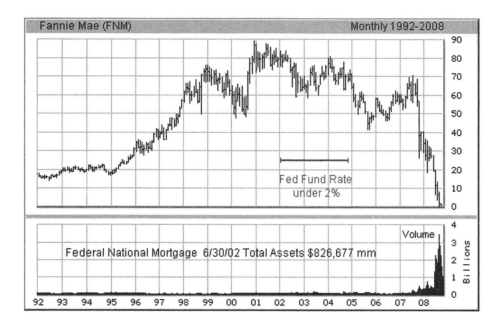

Fannie Mae (FNM)   Monthly 1992-2008

Fed Fund Rate
under 2%

Federal National Mortgage 6/30/02 Total Assets $826,677 mm

Volume

Billions

92 93 94 95 96 97 98 99 00 01 02 03 04 05 06 07 08

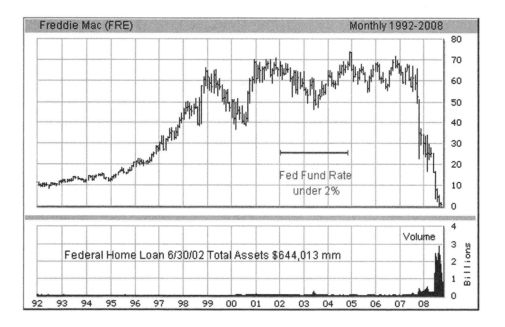

Freddie Mac (FRE)   Monthly 1992-2008

Fed Fund Rate
under 2%

Federal Home Loan 6/30/02 Total Assets $644,013 mm

Volume

Billions

92 93 94 95 96 97 98 99 00 01 02 03 04 05 06 07 08

Under the guidance of Chairman Alan Greenspan, the fed funds rate target was steadily cut from 6.5% in January 2001 to 1.0% in July 2003. See the chart given here.

For exactly 36 months, from December 2001 to December 2004, the fed funds rate stood at 2.0% or lower. The lenders responded, and mortgage rates dropped.

According to Freddie Mac, for the same December 2001 and 2004 dates, 30-year fixed-rate mortgages were 7.07% in 2001 and 5.75% in 2004, with the lowest rate being 5.23% in June 2003. Of course, the rates on 30-year adjustable-rate mortgages (ARMs) were lower, at 5.82% and 4.18%, respectively, and the lowest rate for an adjustable-rate mortgage during this mania (3.50%) also occurred in June 2003.

Mortgage lenders were indeed climbing aboard the gravy train by offering low "teaser rates" for adjustable-rate contracts. This meant that for the first few or several months, ARMs rates could be substantially below normal, but they would "balloon" to much higher rates later. Alluring interest costs were feeding the mania.

The Boom in Housing Prices In the 2001–2005 period, low interest rates and rising home values presented financial opportunities for everyone. It suddenly became easier for buyers to finance new and existing homes. Also, homeowners were refinancing at record levels, tapping into their home equity, which was increasing rapidly as home prices rose. It was soon apparent that consumers were using their homes as if they were ATM machines.

The chart on the next page shows how house prices have changed over the long term. It is also interesting to note that the sharp increase in the index began in 2000, about the same time that the stock market peaked before its two-year slide. It is likely that some stock market funds were also being invested in real estate.

Home values advanced about 9% per year between 1997 and 2005. The rise was amazing, unprecedented, and truly historic.

By 2005, the median house price in the United States had increased to approximately $240,000, depending upon the study used. And in some sections of California, New York, Florida, and elsewhere, median prices were reported to be $400,000 or higher.

But, clearly, the soaring prices of houses were outstripping the ability of consumers to buy them—even at low interest rates. Real median household income rose only slightly between 1997 and 2005, and still remained under $50,000 (next page).

Between 1997 and 2007, House Prices Far Outpaced Household Income

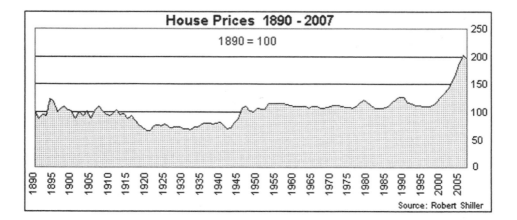

House Prices 1890 - 2007

1890 = 100

Source: Robert Shiller

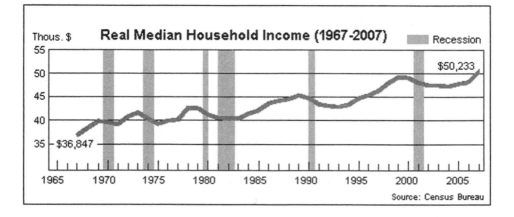

Thous. $ **Real Median Household Income (1967-2007)**   Recession

$50,233

$36,847

Source: Census Bureau

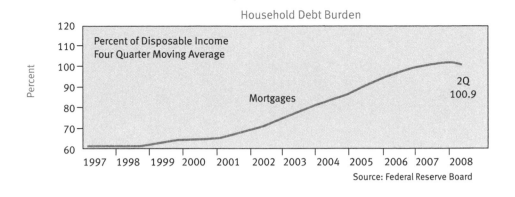

Household Debt Burden

Percent of Disposable Income
Four Quarter Moving Average

Mortgages

2Q
100.9

Source: Federal Reserve Board

In late 2005, the Great Real Estate Bubble reached its apex.

"The Perfect Storm" Because of the Fed's action on interest rates, many people hold Alan Greenspan directly responsible for the bubble. But to be fair, this story is much more complex.

The terrorist attack on September 11, 2001, was an instant blow to the economy and to consumer confidence. Adding to the anxiety, the stock markets were closed for six days. The Federal Reserve Board decided that a period of low interest rates was the best course of action at that time.

Oil was another problem. In 1998, the average monthly price for a barrel of oil was just under $12. The quote rose to over $23 in 2001, and it continued to rise to about $50 per barrel in 2005. At the pump, the price of gasoline advanced from $1.06 in 1998 to $2.76 in 2005. In effect, the consumer was being hit by an invisible tax, and not all of the proceeds were being returned to the economy.

Looking back at 2006 and 2007, according to the Federal Reserve Board, about 18% of personal income was being consumed by mortgage payments, related insurance, and taxes. Moreover, by 2007, mortgage debt was equal to 100% of disposable income (the household debt burden). Clearly, the consumer was overextended.

For the past thirty years or longer, U.S. consumers have been hailed as the backbone of economic growth. However, during this period, citizens were saving little and living well beyond their means. Now, suddenly, they were buying houses or cashing in their home equity.

In August of 2005 at Jackson Hole, Wyoming, Mr. Greenspan said in one of his preretirement speeches that "history had not dealt kindly" with investors (in this case, real estate investors) who appeared to be buying assets (in this case, houses) as if they were a one-way bet and ignoring the possibility that prices could eventually fall.

Also, the signs of a classic bubble were everywhere. Single-family homes and condos were being purchased with no money down, people with only modest incomes were speculating in the housing boom, and a new TV program was born entitled, *Flip this House!*

This was, indeed, "the perfect storm."

Trouble When house prices drop, the greatest dilemma for homeowners is the negative effect on home equity. For example, an equity amount of 20% is slashed in *half* when the selling price of the house drops by only 10%. This implies that a great many, if not most, of the people who bought homes between 2004 and 2006 had little or no equity, or even negative equity, by 2008. And this can be very discouraging when the monthly mortgage payment is rising and disposable income is under pressure.

Higher interest rates in 2005–2006 proved to be the proverbial "nail in the coffin."

Understandably, a substantial increase in delinquencies and foreclosures took place in 2007, when 1.5 million foreclosure procedures were initiated. This disquieting trend continued through 2008 and 2009. With this event, investors in mortgage-backed securities became very alarmed about the value of their holdings, and rightly so.

Beginning in late 2007, credit rating agencies, such as Standard & Poor's and Moody's, began downgrading MBS investments—roughly $3 trillion in 2008, by this author's estimate. Thus, a cryptic term became widely used on Wall Street: "toxic assets." Regrettably, investors were also losing confidence in the process that the agencies used to rate these investments.

For "sophisticated" investors, under normal circumstances, the merit and value of any holding are usually indicated by its rating and market price. In this case, the markets collapsed and no one had a clue.

One Mortgage Bankers Association survey taken in late 2007 indicated that subprime loans accounted for only 14% of total first-lien mortgages, but they represented 55% of total foreclosures—and 78% of those were adjustable-rate mortgages. And at that time, 7.5 million first-lien subprime mortgages were outstanding.

While most homeowners were continuing to pay their mortgages on time and never faced the possibility of foreclosure, the spillover was felt in every neighborhood.

The New Landscape The crisis in the MBS markets produced many victims. In 2008, the Federal Reserve Bank of New York provided an emergency loan to Bear Stearns, the 84-year-old investment bank. When this failed, the firm was acquired by JPMorgan Chase. During the same year, the investment house of Merrill Lynch was sold to Bank of America. And Lehman Brothers, an investment bank founded in 1844, was allowed to go bankrupt. This was the largest-ever American bankruptcy.

Barclays PLC of Great Britain acquired many of Lehman's North American operations, while most of its overseas sub-

Aaron Burr (1756–1836)

sidiaries were purchased by Japan's Nomura Holdings, Inc.

The two independent investment banks remaining, Morgan Stanley and Goldman Sachs, opted to become commercial banks. With this, they became subject to more stringent regulation.

In mid-September, 2008, the government's Federal Housing Finance Agency (FHFA) announced that Fannie Mae and Freddie Mac, which owned or guaranteed about half of the $12 trillion mortgage market, were being nationalized under the FHFA. Today, the government owns about 80% of each.

Following Lehman, the rating of the world's largest insurer, AIG, was reduced from AAA, which led to its "nationalization."

Government vs. Business People, especially politicians and those who have "special interests," tend to forget that the U.S. economy is based mainly on a form of democratic capitalism. When corporations are publicly owned, as most large and powerful companies are today, they are run by executives who are elected.

When a democracy functions as intended, people elect politicians to represent them in government. And, as shareholders, people elect boards of directors to represent their business interests in corporations. Ever since this nation was founded in the eighteenth century, these two factions have been either cooperating or adversarial. But the confrontations have been healthy and the democracy has functioned well.

In September 1799, Aaron Burr, soon to be the third vice president of the new United States, founded The Manhattan Company to bring fresh water to that island and to create the nation's second bank at 40 Wall Street. "The Bank of The Manhattan Company," a precursor to JPMorgan Chase, was essentially established at that time to compete with Alexander Hamilton's Bank of New York. But, more important, banks were helping the new government to become financially solvent and to survive during those early years.

In 1907, the failure of the third-largest trust company in New York, the Knickerbocker Trust Company, precipitated a nationwide panic and a run on regional banks by their depositors. Historians credit J. P. Morgan's leadership for the restoration of confidence in the system. It should be noted that this event occurred about six years before the centralized banking system of the Federal Reserve, the so-called lender of last resort, was created.

Sold as war bonds in denominations of $25 to $10,000 from 1940 to 1980.

During World War I, and especially during World War II, business and government worked closely to defeat the enemy. Auto factories, for example, were transformed into military production lines. To aid in the war efforts and to help control inflation at the time, the government issued Liberty Bonds (WWI) and War Bonds (WWII) that were purchased by both Wall Street and Main Street.

In October 1962, President Kennedy held a televised press conference to chastise U.S. Steel and the steel industry as a whole for a proposed 3.5% ($6 per ton) price increase. The president declared, "If this rise in the cost of steel is imitated . . . it would increase the cost of homes, autos, appliances, and most other items for every American family." Shortly thereafter, the steel companies rescinded the increase.

The government "bailouts" that occurred in the wake of the real estate bubble are, of course, contemporary examples of how Wall Street and Main Street are linked.

Challenged Industries Growth stocks and the inherent benefits of holding them are explained in Chapter 6. But not all companies are capable of growing to the sky. Any companies that cannot cope with the new competition they will inevitably face will suffer and eventually die out.

In the late 1930s, messenger boys were ubiquitous, delivering Western Union telegraphs just as FedEx drivers deliver packages today.

Throughout the 1940s, 1950s, and 1960s, typewriters were standard office equipment. Today, a computer linked to the Internet sits on almost every desk.

In the 1990s, silver halide photography, pioneered by Eastman Kodak, was rapidly replaced by digital imagery. Rochester, New York, changed forever.

The Autos In the decades immediately following World War II, a worker in the automobile industry could anticipate a satisfying lifelong career. With the support of trade unions, good wages, generous overtime, attractive health and retirement benefits, plus seniority provided a comfortable employment package.

The nation's increasing dependence on foreign oil was evident as far back as the mid-1970s. Yet in 1998, when oil prices began climbing once again, Toyota was investing in hybrid automobiles that were capable of 45 miles per gallon, while General Motors promoted enormous Hummer jeeps that offered only 30% of that fuel economy.

In 1957, General Motors' Chevy was
a preferred car by young drivers.

In 1957, Toyota entered the U.S. market
with the Toyopet Crown.

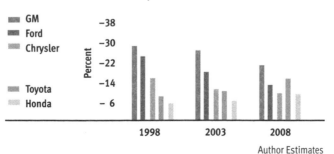

U.S. Market Share—Top Five Auto Manufacturers

Legend:
- GM
- Ford
- Chrysler
- Toyota
- Honda

Percent axis: -38, -30, -22, -14, -6

Years: 1998, 2003, 2008

Author Estimates

Chevrolet Malibu

Price Range: $17,900 – $23,750
Body Style: Sedan
Sum Up: Can it finally compete with Camry and Accord?

Rating: ★ ★ ★ ☆ ☆

Toyota Camry

Price Range: $19,580 – $26,130
Body Style: Sedan
Sum Up: The median of the median

Rating: ★ ★ ★ ★ ☆

All of a sudden, everybody noticed that GM had become one of the world's largest health-care providers with its huge legacy costs. The glaring need for change was ignored, and the necessary sacrifices were not made. Main Street, especially Detroit, suffered the consequences. But General Motors shareholders were also crushed. In just eight years, between 2000 and 2008, GM's stock price plunged 97%, and,in 2009, the company declared bankruptcy.

Throughout the entire ten-year period between 1998 and 2009, the "Big Three" domestic producers steadily lost market share to overseas companies, especially Toyota. Concurrently, higher gasoline prices encouraged the purchase of small and midsized cars at the expense of trucks and the larger, more profitable, but less fuel-efficient SUVs.

In late 2008 and early 2009, Main Street was using the buzzword "bailout." The automobile industry became a media target, and Wall Street was certainly not in any position to help. Because the auto industry is greatly dependent on the availability of credit, the government had to either step in or let the Big Three fail. The ramifications were clear.

To say that the American automobile industry has been an abject failure would be unfair. For example, like the VW Beetle, which gained mass popularity during the 1950s and 1960s, Chrysler's PT Cruiser successfully appealed to a "maverick" personality. While good gas mileage was not a feature of the PT (about 20 mpg), the car was never without an enthusiastic following.

In recent years, many critics, including the media, have focused on the problems of the auto industry, but offered little or no mention of the potential. For example, it should be noted that by the year 2015, there will be at least 4.6 billion people on this planet between the ages of 20 and 65—and less than 15% of this group will own a car. Is this hyperbole? Yes, but a great opportunity exists nonetheless.

Greed and Atrocities For more than two centuries, our nation has confronted many societal breakdowns, but the bouts of greed and narcissism that permeated our society—including Wall Street—during the first few years of the twenty-first century were utterly appalling.

Even the Tulip Mania, described in an earlier chapter, could never match the avarice of this recent period. Greedy real estate speculators, mortgage brokers, adjusters, lenders, and the gluttonous managers of venerable companies were all guilty as charged. Not to be excused was

> *Only when the tide goes out do you*
> *discover who's been swimming naked.*
> —WARREN BUFFETT

the naïveté, incompetence, and stupidity of politicians and investors alike.

In 2001, Enron became the "poster child" for willful corporate fraud and corruption. With revenues reported to be near $100 billion at the time, the firm was accused of financial fraud. The "Enron scandal" was only one of several at that time. These abuses led to the "Sarbanes-Oxley Act of 2002," which, ironically, contributed to the financial collapse in 2008. Its newly created Public Company Accounting Oversight Board forced a more stringent "mark-to-market" requirement for banks. Since then, those rules have been eased somewhat.

One of the most appalling examples of Wall Street greed in recent years was revealed when the CEO of a large, failed investment bank appeared before the House Oversight Committee in early October 2008. His attempts to justify a $482 million multiyear compensation package, awarded to him by a committee that he himself had an early role in appointing, was troubling to most observers. In the end, the firm's shareholders paid a dear price.

Throughout history, whenever economic difficulties arise, misdeeds emerge from the woodwork. Such was the case in December 2008. An investment manager with top credentials, Bernard Madoff, was unable to meet redemptions for the funds that he managed. Mr. Madoff was accused by the FBI of operating an investment business that was deemed to be nothing more than a Ponzi scheme. The total losses to his customers, which included charities, hedge funds, banks, and wealthy investors, were estimated at tens of billions of dollars.

Bailouts, Bankruptcy, and Worse Understandably, the general public does not want tax money to be used to "bail out" incompetently managed financial institutions. However, the connection between Wall Street and Main Street is much more far-reaching than just public assistance. This is not a "we" and "they" relationship as the media portray it.

CHAIN REACTIONS

As the auto industry demonstrates, of the ties between Main Street and Wall Street, perhaps the most visible is in the realm of interest rates and consumer credit. The public is financially pinched when mortgage and financing rates climb and when credit card rates become even more usurious.

If the Federal Reserve Board responds to jubilant consumer demand by raising bank interest rates, stocks typically come under pressure, and the investing public feels the result. Thus, rising interest rates can quickly become a vicious, finger-pointing cycle. But it works both ways.

The credit crisis in 2008–2009 once again illustrated the interdependence between Wall Street and Main Street. During the past crisis, we saw a proactive government and a forceful Federal Reserve Board. For example, the expansion of the "Term Asset-Backed Securities Loan Facility" (TALF) by the Federal Reserve Board in 2008–2009 was designed to help market participants meet the credit needs of households and small businesses that were exposed to asset-backed securities, student loans, auto loans, credit card loans, and loans guaranteed by the Small Business Administration (SBA).

Another contemporary example would be a chain reaction in oil prices. If OPEC votes to cut production to "firm up" oil prices, speculators, using their leverage in the futures market, can push oil prices upward as the cartel intended—and oil companies often benefit. Meanwhile, the prices of gasoline and the feedstock costs of oil-based products move up as well. So, once again, Main Street is ultimately affected, and "conspiracy" immediately becomes its battle cry. Of course, that roar turns back to silence when prices decline.

Sometimes the interrelationships between Wall Street and Main Street are much less obvious than these examples depict.

More Oversight and Transparency Following the economic calamity of the 1930s, many new regulations were put into place. We saw greater vigilance, improved oversight, and increased accountability.

Now, as the 2008–2009 experience becomes another page in history, further regulations can be expected over time. Indeed, it is in the best interest of both Main Street and Wall Street that these excesses not be repeated.

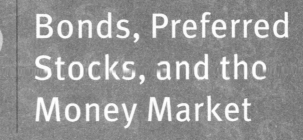

9 Bonds, Preferred Stocks, and the Money Market

Introduction

Sophisticated investors tailor their investment portfolios to meet their individual financial needs. They realize, too, that an individual's needs change with time—that an elderly widow has a different financial objective from a young business executive who is just starting a family.

Many investors find that they require more current income and greater safety of principal than can be expected of a portfolio invested entirely in common stocks. This chapter will explain several alternatives, including bonds, preferred stocks, and issues of the U.S. government. It will also explain the Federal Reserve System and touch on the meaning and content of the "money market," where short-term credit instruments and negotiable paper are traded.

Bond trading has changed since the early 1900s.

Bonds Explained News commentators frequently conclude their daily reports with a description of the day's stock market activity, but there is seldom, if ever, any mention of bonds. Widely regarded as the most conservative type of investment, bonds generally do not experience the dramatic day-to-day price changes that make for exciting reporting. Yet the bond market is actually larger than the stock market. In recent years, a majority of new corporate financing has been accomplished through bonds. Further, it has been estimated that nearly as many individuals own bonds as own common stocks.

Bonds are issued (sold) by corporations, state and local governments or their agencies, the U.S. government, foreign governments, and federal agencies. Professional bond traders use one-word designations for the bonds of each type of issuer, which are, respectively, corporates, municipals, governments, and agencies.

Although each type of bond has certain unique characteristics, bonds in general have one basic function: they are formal IOUs in which the issuer promises to repay the total amount borrowed on a predetermined date. In addition, for the use of the money, the issuer will also compensate the bondholder with, typically, semiannual interest payments at a fixed percentage rate during each year the bond is owned. In the language of bonds, the total amount to be repaid is called variously its "principal amount," "face value," or "par value." The repayment date is known as the "maturity date," the interest rate is the bond's "coupon," and the period of time the bond is outstanding is called its "term." All this information is printed on the face of the bond.

In the past, nearly all bond certificates came with coupons attached. The coupons were periodically clipped from the bond and presented for payment. This is, in fact, the derivation of the term "coupon," which became synonymous with the fixed interest payment. Bonds can be issued in "registered" form (the owner's name is registered with the corporation, and interest payments are mailed directly to the bondholder) or "bearer" form (the bond is presumed to belong to whomever possesses it). Most corporates are now registered bonds, while municipals are still issued as bearer bonds.

A bond certificate, then, is a certificate of indebtedness spelling out the terms of the issuer's promise to repay. Sometimes this promise is reinforced by collateral, such as equipment or property, but usually bonds offer only the "full faith and

Bonds	Current Yield	Volume	Close	Change
Dole 7 7/8 13	7.9	115	99.88	0.50
Duke Eng 6 7/8 23	6.8	38	101.50	0.75
Duke En 6 3/4 25	6.8	84	98.63	−1.00
FstData 6 5/8 03	6.6	23	101.00	unch
FstData 2s 08	cv	3	105.13	−1.25
FordCr 6 3/8 08	6.3	67	99.38	−0.63
GBCB 8 3/8 07	8.4	9	99.25	0.38

credit" of the borrower (bonds of this type are called "debentures"). Thus, obligations issued by the U.S. government are regarded as the safest investments available. After all, as the saying goes, only the government has the ability to print money!

A corporate certificate of indebtedness contrasts sharply with a common stock certificate, which signifies ownership. If the company prospers, its common stockholders can expect to share in the expanding profits through a combination of dividend increases and a higher stock price. Bondholders cannot share in the company's growth; they can expect only repayment of the principal amount and the fixed annual interest payments. If the company fails, however, the bondholders and owners of preferred stock, which resembles bonds in many ways, must be paid in full before the common shareholders get a cent. For this reason, bonds and preferred stock are known as "senior securities."

Bonds are issued with various face values or "denominations," usually set at $1,000 a bond. When the bond trades in the open market, however, its price is quoted at ⅒ of its value. Thus, a bond selling at par, or $1,000, would be listed as 100; a bond selling above par or, in other words, at a "premium," say $1,100, would

be shown as 110. A bond trading below par, or at a "discount," say $880, would appear as 88. Bonds trade at fractional prices, but are noted in dollars and cents and rounded up when it is appropriate.

Thus, a bond priced at 88⅛ corresponds to a dollar value of $881.25. A bond at 105⅞ is the same as $1,058.75. If the change during the day happened to be ⅛, it would appear as $0.125 and would be rounded to $0.13 as it would appear in the bond table.

Government bonds are traded in a similar fashion, but their fractions are expressed in thirty-seconds. A government bond selling for 90.12 means 90¹²⁄₃₂, which reduces to 90⅜ or a dollar equivalent of $903.75.

Shown here is a typical excerpt from a corporate bond table that appears on the Internet or in daily newspapers.

Consider the bond of Duke Energy, a well-known energy company, as an example. Reading from left to right, the investor learns that the bond was issued by Duke Energy, that it pays an annual interest rate of 6¾ percent, matures in 2025, and, on this particular day, carried a "current yield" of 6.8 percent, which will be explained shortly. The remaining figures describe that day's trading. They tell the reader that $84,000 of this specific issue

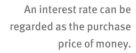

An interest rate can be regarded as the purchase price of money.

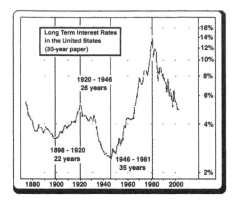

traded that day. The final trade of the day was at 98.63 (98.625), which was 1 point ($10.00) lower than the final price recorded in the preceding trading session.

The investor may wonder why bond prices fluctuate at all, since the bondholder has been promised full repayment at maturity. This question can best be answered within the larger context of interest rates—the key to understanding bonds.

An interest rate can be regarded as the purchase price of money. Basically, when there is high demand for money by business, consumers, and governments, and the supply is limited, as it is during a period of economic expansion, the cost of money (expressed by the interest rate) rises. When demand is slack and money is freely available, as it is during an economic slowdown or recession, interest rates tend to fall.

There is no single interest rate, but several. These include the prime rate, the interest rate that banks charge their most creditworthy borrowers; the federal funds rate, the interest rate charged on loans made between banks that are members of the Federal Reserve System; the Federal Reserve discount rate that member banks pay on funds borrowed from their Federal Reserve Bank; and money market rates (including issues of the U.S. govern-

ment such as Treasury bills). Although there are frequently differences between the interest-rate levels of various issues, all rates tend to move together (note the chart). At any given time, interest rates reflect not only current conditions, but also investors' expectations of future trends.

Yields The issuance of new bonds is dictated by economic conditions and expectations. As rates change, the return (referred to as "yields") that investors expect from bonds that are already trading in the open market must be adjusted so that the bonds remain competitive and attractive to investors. Since the annual interest payment is fixed throughout a bond's life, the adjustment must be made through the price of the bond itself.

Like the yield on common stocks, the current yield on a bond is found by dividing its annual interest payment by its price (with stocks, the expected annual dividend is divided by the price). When a bond is bought at par, or face value, its current yield is, obviously, identical to its coupon rate. However, if it is purchased at any other price, its current yield will be more or less than its coupon rate. As the example illustrates, the yield on a $1,000 par value bond paying $90 can decline or rise in response to a change in the price of

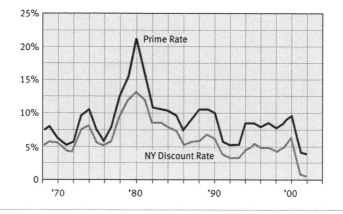

the bond. A bond's price and its yield always move in opposite directions.

1. When the bond price is at par:

$$\frac{\$90}{\$1,000} = 9.00\%$$

2. When the bond price rises, its yield declines:

$$\frac{\$90}{\$1,100} = 8.18\%$$

3. When the bond price declines, its yield rises:

$$\frac{\$90}{\$900} = 10.00\%$$

Price, then, is the basic adjustment mechanism that ensures that the yield on a bond conforms to the general level of interest rates. To repeat, even though bondholders receive full face value at maturity, a bond's price will fluctuate during its life for a very simple reason: if all other factors are equal, an investor would never buy an existing bond from another bondholder if comparable new issues being offered elsewhere were providing higher returns.

While bond prices normally do not swing as widely or as rapidly as common stock prices, potential bond investors should nevertheless realize that bond prices do fluctuate. If a bond must be sold before its maturity date, it is possible that

the bondholder will receive less than face value, and perhaps substantially less.

The term "current yield" was adequate to explain why and how bond prices change, but the most important measure of a bond's return to the long-term bondholder is called the "yield to maturity."

At par, a bond's yield to maturity equals its current yield and its coupon rate, but if a bond is purchased at a premium or at a discount, its yield to maturity will be either less or more than its current yield. At any price other than par, the yield to maturity differs from and is more accurate than the current yield. It recognizes that, in addition to the annual interest payments received during the life of the bond, the bondholder will also receive a capital gain or loss at maturity if there is a difference between the purchase price and the face value.

Yield to maturity computes the compound annual interest gained or lost on this difference, assigns (or, more exactly, "amortizes") a portion to each year of the bond's remaining life, and expresses the result as a single annual percentage rate. In effect, if a bond is purchased at a discount, the yield to maturity is greater than the current yield. If a bond is bought at a premium, the yield to maturity is less than the current yield.

6½%

Yield	18-6	19-0	19-6	20-0	20-6	21-0	21-6	22-0
4.00	132.46	133.05	133.63	134.19	134.75	135.29	135.83	136.35
4.20	129.38	129.90	130.41	130.91	131.40	131.88	132.36	132.82
4.40	126.39	126.85	127.30	127.74	128.17	128.59	129.00	129.41
4.60	123.50	123.90	124.29	124.67	125.05	125.41	125.77	126.12
4.80	120.69	121.03	121.37	121.70	122.02	122.34	122.64	122.94
5.00	117.97	118.26	118.55	118.83	119.10	119.37	119.62	119.88
5.20	115.33	115.57	115.81	116.05	116.27	116.49	116.71	116.92
5.40	112.77	112.97	113.16	113.35	113.54	113.72	113.89	114.06
5.60	110.29	110.44	110.60	110.75	110.89	111.03	111.17	111.30
5.80	107.88	108.00	108.11	108.22	108.33	108.44	108.54	108.64
6.00	105.54	105.62	105.70	105.78	105.85	105.93	106.00	106.06
6.10	104.40	104.46	104.53	104.59	104.64	104.70	104.76	104.81
6.20	103.27	103.32	103.37	103.41	103.45	103.50	103.54	103.58
6.30	102.17	102.20	102.23	102.26	102.28	102.31	102.34	102.36
6.40	101.08	101.09	101.11	101.12	101.13	101.15	101.16	101.17
6.50	100.00	100.00	100.00	100.00	100.00	100.00	100.00	100.00
6.60	98.94	98.93	98.91	98.90	98.89	98.87	98.86	98.85
6.70	97.90	97.87	97.84	97.81	97.79	97.76	97.74	97.72
6.80	96.87	96.83	96.79	96.75	96.71	96.67	96.64	96.60
6.90	95.86	95.80	95.75	95.70	95.65	95.60	95.55	95.51
7.00	94.86	94.79	94.72	94.66	94.60	94.54	94.48	94.43
7.10	93.87	93.79	93.72	93.64	93.57	93.50	93.43	93.37
7.20	92.90	92.81	92.73	92.64	92.56	92.48	92.40	92.33
7.30	91.95	91.85	91.75	91.65	91.56	91.47	91.39	91.30
7.40	91.01	90.90	90.79	90.68	90.58	90.48	90.39	90.30
7.50	90.08	89.96	89.84	89.72	89.61	89.51	89.40	89.31
7.60	89.17	89.03	88.91	88.78	88.66	88.55	88.44	88.33
7.70	88.27	88.12	87.99	87.85	87.73	87.60	87.49	87.37
7.80	87.38	87.23	87.08	86.94	86.81	86.68	86.55	86.43
7.90	86.51	86.34	86.19	86.04	85.90	85.76	85.63	85.50
8.00	85.64	85.47	85.31	85.16	85.01	84.86	84.72	84.59
8.10	84.79	84.62	84.45	84.28	84.13	83.97	83.83	83.69
8.20	83.96	83.77	83.59	83.42	83.26	83.10	82.95	82.81
8.30	83.13	82.94	82.75	82.58	82.41	82.24	82.09	81.94
8.40	82.32	82.12	81.93	81.74	81.57	81.40	81.24	81.08
8.50	81.51	81.31	81.11	80.92	80.74	80.57	80.40	80.24
8.60	80.72	80.51	80.31	80.11	79.93	79.75	79.58	79.41
8.70	79.94	79.73	79.52	79.32	79.13	78.94	78.77	78.60
8.80	79.18	78.95	78.74	78.53	78.34	78.15	77.97	77.79
8.90	78.42	78.19	77.97	77.76	77.56	77.37	77.18	77.00
9.00	77.67	77.44	77.21	77.00	76.79	76.60	76.41	76.23
9.10	76.94	76.70	76.47	76.25	76.04	75.84	75.65	75.46
9.20	76.21	75.97	75.73	75.51	75.29	75.09	74.90	74.71
9.30	75.49	75.25	75.01	74.78	74.56	74.36	74.16	73.97
9.40	74.79	74.54	74.29	74.06	73.84	73.63	73.43	73.24
9.50	74.09	73.84	73.59	73.36	73.13	72.92	72.71	72.52
9.60	73.41	73.15	72.90	72.66	72.43	72.22	72.01	71.81
9.70	72.73	72.47	72.21	71.97	71.74	71.52	71.31	71.12
9.80	72.06	71.79	71.54	71.30	71.06	70.84	70.63	70.43
9.90	71.40	71.13	70.87	70.63	70.39	70.17	69.96	69.75
10.00	70.76	70.48	70.22	69.97	69.73	69.51	69.29	69.09
10.20	69.48	69.20	68.94	68.69	68.44	68.22	68.00	67.79
10.40	68.25	67.96	67.69	67.44	67.19	66.96	66.74	66.53
10.60	67.04	66.76	66.48	66.22	65.98	65.74	65.52	65.31
10.80	65.87	65.58	65.31	65.04	64.79	64.56	64.33	64.12
11.00	64.73	64.44	64.16	63.90	63.65	63.41	63.18	62.97
11.20	63.62	63.33	63.05	62.78	62.53	62.29	62.07	61.85
11.40	62.54	62.25	61.96	61.70	61.45	61.21	60.98	60.77
11.60	61.49	61.19	60.91	60.64	60.39	60.15	59.93	59.71
11.80	60.47	60.17	59.89	59.62	59.37	59.13	58.90	58.69
12.00	59.47	59.17	58.89	58.62	58.37	58.13	57.91	57.70

The "yield to maturity" can be
found quickly by a computer
or on a bond values table.

Although in practice, a bond's yield to maturity is usually calculated today by computer programs and calculators, it can also be approximated by using a bond value table. The bond value table gives the yield to maturity at various maturities, coupons, and prices. The yields are expressed in whole percentages and smaller measurements known as "basis points." A basis point is $\frac{1}{100}$ of 1%. In other words, 100 basis points are equal to 1%. For example, a bond yield of 7.63% is 5 basis points less than a bond yield of 7.68%. Page 192 shows a sample table from a bond value book.

As an example, if a 6½% 2024 bond (currently selling at, say, 85 with a current yield of 7.6%) was being considered, the buyer would first locate the 6½% coupon rate, shown in the upper left-hand corner of the page. Next, the investor would locate the price closest to the expected purchase price in the column of prices appearing under the actual number of years to maturity; in this case, 2010 (today) to 2031, or 21 years. The price 85.00 falls between the prices 85.76 and 84.86, which, in the far left column, correspond to yields of 7.90% and 8.00%. A more exact yield can be found by interpolation. Therefore, because the bond price is now selling at 85 (below par), the

yield to maturity is greater than the 7.6% current yield.

Besides providing a more accurate picture of a buyer's potential return, yield to maturity also makes it possible to compare bonds of varying maturities and coupons. But even yield to maturity cannot be used blindly because a bond may be "called" before reaching its maturity date, which can change the yield significantly.

Calling "Calling" a bond means that the issuer exercises a right stated on the face of the bond to retire the bond before its maturity date. Most bonds are now issued with call provisions. The right to call a bond gives the issuer greater flexibility to respond to changes in the general level of interest rates. For example, if a corporation had issued bonds with a 10% coupon during a period of high interest rates, and if interest rates subsequently declined to a level where the same bond could be issued with an 8% coupon, it would be to the corporation's advantage to retire the 10% bonds and issue new bonds at 8%. In fact, the annual interest savings can be so significant, often measured in millions of dollars, that issuers usually redeem the bonds at a premium above face value. Typically, the premium amounts to one

Ratings are important to both borrowers and lenders.

year's annual interest. Thus, a $1,000, 10% bond might be called at $1,100.

Most bonds are not subject to a call provision until a specified number of years, say five or ten, have elapsed. After that period, the bonds can be called at any time at one specified price, or the issuer can stipulate a declining scale of prices, one for each year remaining after the first call date.

In addition to the optional call method, many bonds and preferred stocks are also retired through the use of a "sinking fund."

Once the fund is established, the issuer must set aside a certain number of dollars each year for periodic retirements. This enhances the security of the remaining bonds. (When new bonds are being issued, investment bankers often say they are "floating" a new issue; so it is understandable that a bond retirement fund is called a "sinking" fund.) The bonds or preferred stock to be retired each year can either be called at a specific price or be purchased in the open market. Occasionally, the sinking fund payments are allowed to accumulate while earning interest, so that the entire issue can eventually be retired at one time.

Any investor who ignores a call feature could be subject to an expensive surprise.

If bonds are called unexpectedly, a bondholder might get the principal amount back sooner, but lose what may have been an attractive yield. In some cases, the bondholder may even lose part of the principal. This would occur if a bond had been purchased at a substantial premium, but was called at a price close to par. For these reasons, the potential bond buyer should carefully examine call and sinking fund provisions with a broker or bond dealer to better understand the risks involved.

So far, it has been shown that bond selection must include a consideration of the type of issuer, maturity, coupon, yield, and call features. There is yet another important factor that must be included—a bond's "rating."

Ratings Ratings measure the probability of a bond issuer's repaying the principal amount at maturity and meeting the scheduled interest payments. Viewed another way, ratings rank issues according to their perceived risk of default. They are computed and published by objective, independent organizations. The two best-known rating agencies are Standard & Poor's Corporation and Moody's Investors Service Incorporated. Their ratings are available on a subscription basis and in a

S&P Lowers Debt Rating

variety of publications that can usually be found at a local library or brokerage office.

Together, the two agencies rate most of the publicly held corporate and municipal bonds. In addition, Moody's rates many Treasury and government agency issues. However, the agencies do not rate privately placed bonds, unless they are asked to do so on a fee basis. In recent years, nearly 50% of all bond issues have been placed privately, which simply means that investors, usually institutions, have purchased the bonds directly from the issuer without any public distribution. Although preferred stocks have ratings that appear identical to bond ratings, they are not directly comparable because bonds represent debt and preferred stocks are a form of equity (ownership).

The rating agencies use a simple system of letters to indicate their judgment of an issue's safety of principal and interest payment stability. Standard & Poor's ranks bonds from highest quality to lowest by using the first four letters of the alphabet in groups of three, as follows: AAA, AA, A, BBB, BB, B, and so on through D.

Bonds carrying a D rating are in default. Investors commonly refer to the highest rating as "triple-A." Moody's uses a similar system, stopping at C, as follows: Aaa, Aa, A, Baa, Ba, B, Caa, Ca, C. Some of the bonds in Moody's C categories could be in default.

When appropriate, both agencies use other symbols to further refine a given rating. Thus, Standard & Poor's might add a plus or a minus sign to a rating. For example, an A+ rating is a shade higher than an A rating. In its municipal bond ratings, Moody's uses A1 and Baa1 to indicate the highest-quality bonds falling within those two specific categories.

In both systems, ratings from triple-A through B carry the same meaning. Thus, Moody's opinion of an Aa bond is basically identical to Standard & Poor's opinion of its AA bond. Furthermore, both systems clearly have a boundary line established with the BBB and Baa ratings, which are the first categories indicating that the bonds have some speculative investment characteristics. Bonds above BBB are believed to be safe investment candidates for both individuals and institutions. They are also commonly referred to as "investment grade." Bonds below BBB should receive careful analysis because they are inherently more speculative.

But ratings are more than interesting academic notations. They are gauges of risk, and, in the marketplace, investors demand greater returns as risk increases.

Thus, the lower an issuer's rating, the greater the annual interest payments demanded.

Since ratings can translate into millions of dollars of interest savings, the rating agencies are understandably thorough in researching their opinions. Each agency employs a staff of securities analysts who examine the financial condition, operations, and management of a given issuer. They also study specific documents, such as the bond's "indenture," which describes certain legal and technical details of the issue.

Perhaps the most important factor is an evaluation of the company's future earnings potential, which calls for analytical techniques like those used in appraising common stocks. In general, bond analysts test an issuer's strength under adverse business conditions with the objective of determining the safety of principal and interest payments. After a rating is given, it is reviewed periodically and sometimes changed to reflect any improvement or deterioration in an issuer's overall condition.

Convertible Bonds Convertible bonds, as these debentures are commonly called, are usually subordinate to other debt. However, they have all the features discussed thus far—a par value, coupon rate, maturity date, and yield, and often a rating and a call date. But they differ from other bonds in one important respect: they can be converted into a specific number of shares of the issuer's common stock.

Convertibility closely links the price performance of the bond with that of the underlying common stock. Thus, although a convertible bond offers some of the relative safety of principal and interest characteristic of so-called straight, or nonconvertible, bonds, they usually fluctuate in price more widely and more rapidly as a result of the convertible feature. In this sense, convertible bondholders participate directly in the changing business fortunes of an issuer, whereas other bondholders cannot.

If the common stock is selling above the conversion price, the convertible bond will tend to move more closely with the common. When the stock is below the conversion price, the bond's market price will tend to more closely reflect the prevailing interest rates and the company's ability to maintain the bond's interest payments. In short, convertible bond buyers usually give up some safety and interest in exchange for potential capital gains.

Corporations select convertibles to raise additional capital for several rea-

A convertible bond is one of the most
complicated securities to use effectively.

sons. Convertibles, as opposed to a new common stock issue, limit the dilution of existing stockholders' equity. Convertibles also offer tax savings to the issuer because interest payments on convertibles, like those on other bonds, are deductions before federal income taxes, whereas cash dividends are paid from after-tax earnings. Finally, the interest rates on convertibles usually provide a higher yield than equivalent common stock dividends but lower than the yields on comparable straight bonds. If interest rates in the conventional bond market are high, an issuer can frequently obtain a lower rate by offering the convertibility feature as a sweetener.

Convertibles may offer an attractive opportunity for capital gains as well as income, but they also place greater demands on the investor's analytical resources. Several new terms and calculations, which will be presented in the hypothetical example to follow, must be understood before convertibles can be used effectively.

Consider a 7% convertible subordinated debenture with ten years remaining to maturity that is convertible into common stock at $40. The bond is currently selling at 90 ($900). The underlying common stock is selling for $32 a share.

The investor first must determine the maximum exposure to loss by calculating the bond's price as if it were selling as a straight bond. This price, often called the "investment value," is usually computed by the same organizations that publish bond ratings. The investment value is the price that causes the bond's yield to maturity to equal the yields offered by straight bonds of similar quality and maturity. Suppose that our bond carries a Baa rating (convertibles rarely receive higher), and that straight bonds in this category are currently yielding 9%. The appropriate calculations indicate that our bond must sell for approximately $835 to yield 9%.

The investment value represents the theoretical downside risk, the floor beyond which the bond's price should not fall in the current market environment. Again, it is theoretical and is based on comparative values that are subject to change. In this case, however, it does tell the investor that without its convertible feature, the bond could decline roughly 7% from the purchase price to its value as a straight bond.

Next, the convertible buyer will want to compare this risk with the possible reward.

Since the $1,000 bond is convertible into common stock at $40, the investor

Disney Plans
Zero-Coupon

knows that each bond has a "conversion ratio" of 25. In other words, at the $40 "conversion price," each bond can be exchanged for 25 shares of common stock ($1,000 divided by $40 = 25). Although the bond is convertible at $40, the stock is actually being bought at $36 because the conversion privilege is being obtained at a discount. This price is called the stock's "conversion parity price." It is obtained by dividing the bond's actual purchase price by the number of shares that will be received upon conversion ($900 divided by 25 = $36). Viewed another way, the investor is at the breakeven point at the conversion parity price. As the stock price advances beyond conversion parity, the bond's value should follow in step with at least an equal percentage move. In this case, the conversion parity price of $36 is roughly 12% higher than the stock's current price of $32.

From the breakeven point, the buyer now explores the potential gain that might ultimately be realized. The investor should have some reasonable profit target in mind. Assume that, after a thorough study of the issuer's business and prospects, the bond investor concludes that the common stock will rise to $50. At $50 per share, the bond would be worth $1,250 (25 shares × $50 per share =

$1,250), representing a profit of nearly 40% on the $900 investment. In addition, the investor receives a steady stream of interest payments.

The sophisticated convertible buyer attempts to limit risk by selecting a bond where

- The current price is close to the investment value.
- The conversion parity price is close to the common stock's current price.
- The common stock is expected to appreciate considerably.

Rarely, however, are actual situations as clearly defined as this example. A convertible bond can be a complicated security.

ZERO-COUPON CONVERTIBLE BONDS

This unique variation of a subordinated convertible bond emerged as a popular instrument many years ago. The "zero" convertible, also referred to as a Liquid Yield Option Note (or "LYON"), is a convertible bond that is priced at a deep discount. The bondholder receives no ("zero") annual interest payments, but is promised a face-value payment at maturity.

Zero convertibles are attractive to the issuer because the implied interest payments may be deducted from taxable income. Although bondholders are required to pay taxes on the implied interest they receive, they benefit from the convertible feature. To date, these bonds, which are usually convertible into the issuer's common stock at any time, have been used most successfully by growth companies to raise funds for expansion.

If an investor believes that long-term interest rates will be trending lower in the year(s) ahead, buying zeros might be a leveraged way to participate.

Zeros tend to be more sensitive to interest-rate swings because the bond's interest payments are reflected in the discount. Some speculators use twenty-year or thirty-year "stripped" Treasury bonds (called Treasury strips) to play interest-rate moves. While these zeros are not convertibles, of course, they can produce considerable profits or losses if interest rates fall or rise by just a small amount.

Investing in zero convertibles requires special care for two reasons:

1. Zeros often have a call feature at the discretion of the issuer. An investor should never purchase a zero without first calculating how much might be lost if the bond is callable and is redeemed unexpectedly.

2. A zero will be sensitive to the price movement of the equity into which it is convertible. If the price potential of the stock appears limited, the zero will probably be less attractive in the marketplace relative to other bond opportunities.

Municipal Bonds Municipal bonds are issued by states, cities, towns, political subdivisions, or authorities, such as housing authorities and bridge and tunnel authorities. They are usually issued to finance new construction for such diverse purposes as hospitals, bridges, tunnels, and sports stadiums.

Municipal bonds differ from straight corporate bonds in three ways. First, and most important, the interest on municipals is exempt from federal income taxes. Furthermore, if the investor lives in the state of issue, the interest is usually exempt from state and local taxes as well. This tax-exempt feature sets municipal bonds apart from all other bonds and explains why municipals are frequently called "tax-exempts." Note the useful calculation shown here.

Second, municipals are usually issued with "serial" maturities as opposed to the "term" maturities characteristic of corporate bonds. Serial maturity means that a portion of the total issue matures each year until the entire issue has been retired. Unlike sinking fund retirements, each year of a serial issue has its own interest rate or is priced to provide a specific yield.

For example, a state could issue $145 million of fifteen-year triple-A general obligation bonds at a net interest cost of 4.86%. The bonds might be reoffered to investors on the following partial "scale," as the series of yields is known: 2011 priced to yield 3.70%, 2012 to yield 3.90%, 2013 to yield 4.10%, and continuing with a 5.20% yield in 2023. Of course, the higher rates in later years reflect inflation expectations.

Third, most municipals are issued in $5,000 principal amounts, whereas corporate bonds usually have a $1,000 principal amount. In addition, municipal bonds are traded entirely in the over-the-counter market, unlike corporate bonds, which are also listed on some of the national exchanges. An investor who is interested in a specific issue must consult a bond dealer for a price. Municipal prices are usually not quoted in daily newspapers. The dealers themselves frequently consult the Blue List of Current Municipal Offerings, a daily publication, which gives pertinent data such as price and yield on available offerings. Although municipals usually have a $5,000 princi-

pal amount, their prices are nonetheless quoted as if the principal amount were $1,000 (i.e., at 100 or some premium or discount to 100).

There are several types of municipal bonds. Most common is the "general obligation bond," where the issuer promises its full faith, credit, and taxing power to ensure that the principal and interest payments are made on time. These general obligation bonds are considered to provide the greatest security and, as a result, usually have the lowest yields. "Revenue bonds" are backed only by the earning power of the facility constructed with the proceeds of the bond issue. Other types include general obligation bonds with a provision limiting the amount of taxation that can be applied, as well as special tax bonds and industrial revenue bonds.

In general, because of the tax-exempt feature, municipal bonds have interest rates several percentage points below the going rate on corporate bonds of comparable quality. In other words, a municipal bond will often provide the same after-tax yield to an investor as a corporate bond priced to yield several points more. The benefit of this tax-exempt feature improves as an investor's annual taxable income and tax bracket increase. For example, the tax rate for a husband and wife filing a joint return with a $65,000 taxable income is about 21%. To equal a 7% municipal bond yield, they would have to find a corporate bond yielding about 8.8%. A family earning $100,000 would be paying taxes at a higher rate, close to 24%, and would need to find a corporate bond yielding at least 9.2% to get the same after-tax return that a 7% municipal offers.

Preferred Stocks At first glance, many preferred stocks might appear to be bonds without a maturity date. They offer relatively attractive yields, they can be called, some can be converted into common stock, some are rated, most are issued at a stated par value (usually $100), and all are commonly listed as "senior securities." Indeed, some preferred stocks are thought to be of such high quality that their prices tend to parallel the price trends of high-quality long-term bonds.

There are, however, two important distinctions that investors should appreciate before buying preferreds:

1. **Dividends.** Although the dividend is set at a fixed annual rate, it can be changed by the issuer at any time. It can, in fact, be omitted entirely. For this reason, most investors seek a "cumulative preferred stock," which means that if divi-

dends are "passed" by the board of directors, they are allowed to accumulate and must eventually be paid when money becomes available.

2. **Claims.** As its name implies, a preferred stock has preference over the common stock in the receipt of dividends and in any residual assets after payments to creditors if the company is dissolved. But a creditor, such as a bondholder, has a legally enforceable claim against an issuer who defaults on an interest payment. A preferred stockholder has no such claim should a dividend be omitted.

"Participating" preferred stocks enable the owner to share in any extra dividend payments, although most preferreds are "nonparticipating," which limits the annual return to the fixed annual dividend payment.

Corporations have favored bonds over preferred stocks as a method of raising new capital. Preferred dividends are paid from after-tax earnings, whereas bond interest is paid from earnings before taxes. Thus, preferred stocks can be more expensive for the corporation.

A preferred stock is a blend of the characteristics of a bond and a common stock. It can offer the higher yield of a bond; it has priority over the common in equity ownership, but it does not have the safety of a bond, and its participation in the company's growth is limited.

Preferred stocks are usually bought for income. The investor should strive for high income with greater safety (a preferred with little debt ahead of it) or high income with growth (a preferred that is convertible into common stock). Otherwise, it is probably better to own either the bond or the common stock.

U.S. Government Securities The federal government, much like state and local governments, also uses debt obligations to finance various projects and programs. Three types, generally differentiated according to maturity range, are used most frequently. They are: Treasury "bills," with maturities up to and including one year; Treasury "notes," with maturities between one year and seven years; and U.S. government "bonds," with maturities between seven years and thirty years. There can be exceptions to this general classification, however. For example, there are ten-year notes.

Government securities offer the investor

- Maximum safety of principal, since they are backed by the word of the government itself

- Competitive yields, although seldom equal to the yields on less-secure corporate bonds
- A high degree of liquidity through active trading in secondary markets, both listed and over-the-counter
- Limited taxation because they are free of state and local taxes, although not from federally imposed taxes

Today, Treasury securities are no longer issued in paper form as depicted in the photograph. All Treasury securities are now in electronic book-entry form.

Treasury bills, commonly called "T-bills," account for the bulk of government financing. They are sold by the Treasury at a discount through competitive bidding. A weekly auction is held for bills with three-month and six-month maturities. Monthly auctions are held for the remaining two maturities— nine-month and one-year bills. Treasury bills are issued in five denominations from $1,000 to $1,000,000. The return to the investor is the difference between the purchase price and the bill's face value received at maturity.

Most Treasury securities can be purchased through a program called TreasuryDirect. Bills can be sold in the secondary market before maturity. Indi-

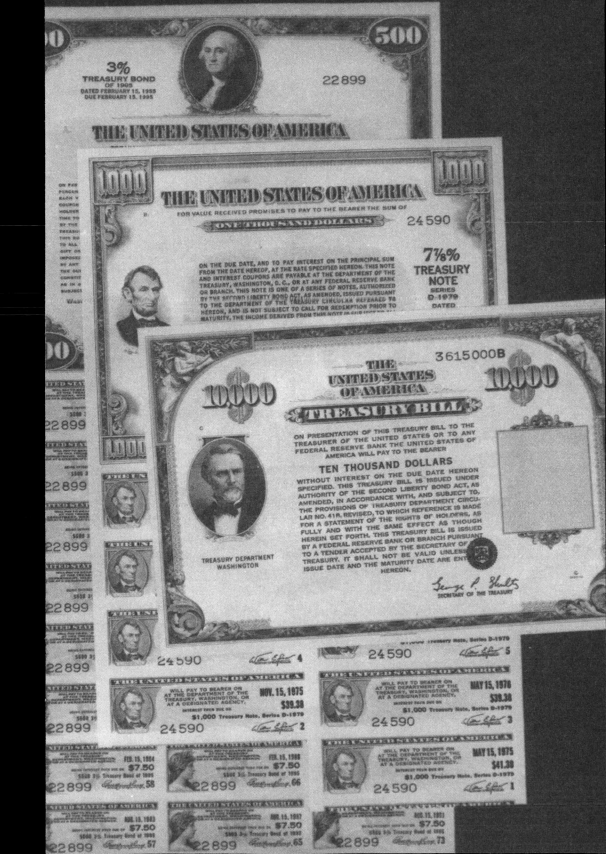

viduals can purchase bills directly at no charge either from a Federal Reserve Bank or from the Bureau of the Public Debt by sending a certified personal check or cashier's check for the bill's face value to

Bureau of the Public Debt
Securities Transactions Branch
Washington, D.C. 20226

Better yet, investors can now transact business using this Internet Web site:

www.publicdebt.treas.gov

Bills can also be purchased for a fee from certain commercial banks, government securities dealers, and brokerage firms.

As discussed shortly, T-bills are the major vehicle used by the Federal Reserve System in the money market to implement national monetary policy.

Treasury notes have become increasingly popular with individual investors for three reasons. First, they are usually issued in $1,000 denominations, the same as a minimum T-bill investment. Second, their longer maturities usually offer higher yields than T-bills. And, finally, notes are now being issued more frequently. The Treasury sells various securities, including notes, at more than 150 auctions held throughout the year.

Notes have a fixed rate of interest that is payable semiannually, and they can be purchased without charge at issuance from Federal Reserve Banks or their branches, or directly from the Treasury. Investors can also buy them for a fee from some commercial banks, brokerage houses, and other government securities dealers.

Government bonds can also be purchased without charge at issuance directly from the Treasury and Federal Reserve Banks, and in low denominations. In many ways, they resemble straight corporate bonds. They have fixed rates of interest and fixed maturity dates, and, before 1985, they were callable.

No thirty-year bonds have been issued since October 2001.

The government likes to say that if U.S. Treasury bills, notes, and bonds are the world's safest investments, then the Treasury Inflation-Protected Securities are the safest of the safest because their ultimate value cannot be diminished by inflation. These "TIPS," as they are called, are like other notes and bonds. Interest payments are received every six months, and a payment of principal is made when the security matures. However, the principal value is adjusted for inflation (using the CPI), and at maturity the bond is redeemed at its adjusted principal amount or the original par value, whichever is greater. The fixed rate of interest is applied not to the par amount of the security, but to the inflation-adjusted principal. TIPS can be purchased three times each year. A ten-year note is auctioned in July and then reopened in October and January.

Many investors were first exposed to government bonds through the famous Series E savings bond used during World War II. Savings bonds, unlike Treasury bonds, are not "marketable securities" (that is, they do not have a secondary market). Today, the "Series I savings bond," the second of two types of inflation-indexed government securities, is available with face-value denominations of $50, $75, $100, $200, $500, $1,000, $5,000, and $10,000. The I-bond has an interest return that is a combination of a fixed rate, which applies for the life of the bond, and the inflation rate. For example, the November 2009 I-bond might offer 1.60%, plus 2.46% as an inflation hedge (CPI-Urban adjusted; see the appendix), for a total return of 4.08%. Cashing in a Series I bond before five years has a three-month earnings penalty, and I-bonds are exempt from state and local taxes (federal income tax is deferred until the bond is cashed).

Nearly twenty other government agencies issue short-term notes, debentures, and participation certificates to finance their specialized operations. Most "agencies" have maturity dates, fixed interest rates, and face values, but are rarely callable. Unlike the direct obligations of the U.S. Treasury, however, only a few agencies are backed by the federal government. As a result, they usually offer higher yields than Treasury issues.

The best-known agency issues are sold by the Federal National Mortgage Association, the Federal Home Association, and the Government National Mortgage Association, commonly called "Fannie Mae," "Freddie Mac," and "Ginnie Mae," as discussed in the prior chapter. These are corporations that were created by Congress to support the secondary mortgage market.

In general, these agencies improve the market for certain types of mortgages. Their mortgage-backed securities are sponsored, but not guaranteed, by the U.S. government.

The Money Market The securities that make up the capital market primarily serve investors and borrowers who have a time horizon extending beyond one year. But many investors have surplus cash that they want to employ for shorter time periods,

even as short as overnight. Similarly, many borrowers need to raise money quickly for only short-term use. In both cases, the money market provides the ideal solution.

The money market is actually made up of several individual markets, one for each type of short-term credit instruments. Thus, there are markets for Treasury bills, commercial paper, negotiable certificates of deposit (CDs), and bankers' acceptances (drafts drawn on banks to finance international trade on a short-term basis). In addition, commercial bank borrowings from each other at the "federal funds rate" and commercial bank borrowings from the Federal Reserve Banks at the "discount rate" are also considered important parts of the money market. Unlike the other transactions, however, neither method of bank borrowing creates "negotiable paper" (marketable promissory notes pledging the return of principal at maturity and fixed interest payments in the meantime).

In any case, all transactions have maturities within one year, and most are ninety days or less.

Although each credit instrument is different, the rates tend to move closely together.

Investors, including commercial banks, state and local governments, some individuals, large nonfinancial businesses, foreign banks, and nonbank financial institutions, are drawn to the money market for three basic reasons in addition to attractive yields:

1. It is a liquid market that is capable of handling large sums with a small effect on yields.

2. It offers a high degree of safety of principal because issuers, in general, have the highest credit ratings. Investors should realize, however, that certain credit instruments can never be considered completely risk-free. When Penn Central went bankrupt in 1970, for example, it had almost $100 million in commercial paper outstanding.

3. Money market maturities are short, and thus there is little risk of loss resulting from interest-rate changes.

Borrowers, in turn, including the U.S. Treasury, commercial banks, and nonfinancial corporations, seek the market's attractive rates, which are generally below bank loan rates even to prime borrowers.

By far, the most important participant in the money market is the Federal Reserve.

THE FEDERAL RESERVE SYSTEM

On December 23, 1913, President Woodrow Wilson signed the Federal Reserve Act establishing the Federal Reserve System (also referred to as the "Fed"). Its original purpose was to improve the nation's financial system by providing a stable monetary framework. Thus, the country would have a more elastic currency, facilities would be available for discounting commercial paper, and there would be improved supervision of banking. The primary concern of the Federal Reserve System was, and is today, the flow of credit and money—although, since its formation, its responsibilities have been broadened considerably.

Generally speaking, the Federal Reserve System consists of (1) its Board of Governors, (2) the Federal Open Market Committee (FOMC), (3) the twelve regional Federal Reserve Banks and their branches, (4) the Federal Advisory Council, and (5) the 5,500+ commercial banks that are members of the system and all other institutions that are subject to its rules. The Fed is, in effect, a bank for individual banks and their lender of last resort.

The Fed's Board of Governors is located in Washington, D.C., and is the system's top administrative body. There are seven board members, each appointed by the president and subject to confirmation by the Senate. The members are appointed for fourteen-year terms, with one term expiring every two years. The president also appoints the chairman and vice-chairman of the board from among the members for four-year terms that may be renewed.

The Federal Reserve's principal function is monetary policy, which it controls with three tools:

1. Open market operations

2. The discount mechanism

3. Changes in reserve requirements

Since the 1930s, open market operations have clearly been the Fed's major instrument. However, raising or lowering the discount rate (i.e., the cost of borrowing from the Fed) and changing the reserve requirements (i.e., shifting the allocations of required and nonrequired reserves of depository institutions) are also useful tools.

Through its Open Market Trading Desk at the New York Federal Reserve Bank, one of the twelve regional banks, the Fed implements the decisions of the Federal Open Market Committee (a twelve-member body that meets about every three weeks).

The chairman of the Board of Governors is also the chairman of the FOMC. The six other board members, along with

CD Yields Are Steady at Major U.S. Banks

the president of the Federal Reserve Bank of New York and four rotating Federal Reserve Bank presidents, make up the Open Market Committee. The primary function of the FOMC is to determine the amount of securities to be purchased or sold by the Federal Reserve System. These securities are primarily Treasury bills, notes, and bonds. Also bought and sold are federal agency obligations and bankers' acceptances.

By selling and buying these various money market instruments, the Federal Reserve contracts or expands the reserve positions of the commercial banks that are members of the system. The resulting changes in member banks' reserve balances affect the member banks' ability to make loans and acquire investments. If the Fed wants a tighter monetary policy, which can produce higher interest rates, securities are sold to reduce member bank reserves.

Securities are bought by the Fed, which will increase member bank reserves, when it wants an easier monetary policy. In this way, the Federal Reserve influences the monetary and credit conditions of the entire country—and it affects the international community as well.

When the Fed makes an open market operations decision, it must take conflict-ing factors into consideration. Assume, for example, that it wants to pursue an easier monetary policy because the nation's unemployment rate is rising and lower interest rates are needed to stimulate the economy. The Fed simply bids up the price of securities high enough to purchase them from banks, bond dealers, or individuals. Will its move to ease stimulate inflation? How will the nation's exports and imports be affected? Will it become more difficult for the Treasury to sell its securities to refund its debt when the lower yields are compared with the returns available in other parts of the world? It is easy to see why each policy move by the Federal Reserve has its supporters and its critics.

Rates on money market instruments are generally scaled upward from the Treasury bill rate on comparable maturities. Otherwise, they could not compete with the nearly riskless and highly flexible government security.

Yields on negotiable certificates of deposit (CDs), for example, are usually several basis points higher. CDs are issued by banks. They are receipts for funds deposited with a bank for a predetermined period of time on which the bank agrees to pay a specific rate of interest. A certificate of deposit returns principal and interest to the owner at maturity, but it can also be sold in the secondary market should the owner need the money before maturity.

Certificates of deposit are especially popular with large corporations, which use them in cash management as a backup to Treasury bills.

Maturity dates are usually selected to suit the needs of the purchaser. They range between one and eighteen months, but most CDs mature in four months, and they are issued in denominations from $25,000 to $10 million. In the secondary market, dealers usually trade in $1 million denominations.

Commercial paper is another money market instrument, although there is no secondary market. This instrument, sold in denominations from $5,000 to $5 million or more, is simply a short-term promissory note that creditworthy businesses use in place of bank borrowing because, traditionally, it has been less expensive.

Tax anticipation bills, bankers' acceptances, and loans to and repurchase agreements with government securities dealers are also considered money market instruments. However, Treasury bills, CDs, and commercial paper make up the bulk of money market transactions.

Money market instruments, along with bonds and preferred stocks, play an important role in the world of investments. For many investors, they can be either an effective complement or a valuable alternative to common stocks.

10 | The Internet

Introduction

Since the early 1980s, the computer has entered the lives of most American families in one way or another. And since 1991, no technological development has been more significant to this new computer-savvy community than the Internet.

The personal and business applications of the Internet are far more extensive than even the greatest visionary could have imagined at the time the World Wide Web was first opened up to the general public.

Today, we take most of the Internet's capabilities for granted as just part of our daily lives. E-mail, online shopping, telephony, music, video, games, and other applications are continuing to expand the popularity of this new medium. And no field has benefited more from the Internet than Wall Street. One can almost say that the Internet has developed into Wall Street's modern-day "Curb Market."

This chapter will offer some background and explain why this revolutionary medium became the subject of the dot-com bubble. It will address the application of the Internet from the investor's standpoint, and it will show how the Internet can be used in both fundamental and technical analysis, as well as being a direct link to Wall Street.

Tim Berners-Lee opened the Internet to the public on August 6, 1991.

History of the Internet Tim Berners-Lee is credited with creating the World Wide Web while working at the European Particle Physics Laboratory (CERN) in Geneva, Switzerland. The Oxford graduate was seeking a means of collaboration among physicists and other researchers in the high-energy physics community. His proposal, entitled *HyperText and CERN*, was written in 1989.

Three new technologies were soon incorporated into his proposal: HyperText Markup Language (HTML), used to write Web documents; HyperText Transfer Protocol (HTTP), used to transmit the pages; and a Web browser client-server program to receive, interpret, and display the results at each Web site address.

One important concept of his proposal involved a client software that allowed users to access information from many types of computers. The line-mode user interface, called the World Wide Web, was completed in 1989, and Berners-Lee's files were made available to the public for the first time on August 6, 1991. At that time, all documents were stored on one main computer (called a "Web server") at CERN.

By year-end 1992, there were more than 50 Web servers, most of them located at universities and research centers.

By mid-1999, the number of servers had grown to nearly 800,000, and by 2001, there were over 20 million.

It was 1990 when Tim Berners-Lee, using a NeXT computer, wrote the first Web browser-editor, later called "Nexus." Three years later, another pioneer of the Internet, Marc Andreessen, as an undergraduate at the University of Illinois, developed the graphic interface browser named "Mosaic." This software was the forerunner to the popular Netscape browser called "Navigator." (Netscape was eventually acquired by America Online as Microsoft's Explorer captured more of that business.)

By the end of 1993, various browsers could access about 600 Web sites. There were close to 10,000 sites by 1995, about 100,000 by 1996, and about 650,000 in early 1997. There are more than 100 million today.

The Internet has forced companies to adjust. The Web has added yet another leg to the marketing stool, making the business environment more competitive. And every day access is becoming faster and easier.

Internet access was originally achieved through a dial-up system using a modem. In 2003, roughly 65% of the 72 million U.S. Internet households were dial-up and 35% used the faster "broadband" access. More recently, the reverse has been

Michael Dell formed a computer company from a venture he started in his college dormitory. Dell's success today is due, in part, to the Internet.

true—more than two-thirds of the roughly 90 million Internet households are broadband. The remainder are dial-up. This trend will very likely further the acceptance of new products and services over the Internet.

Dell Computer is a perfect example of how companies today are using the Internet to further their business. Dell's sales are made both to other businesses (80%) and directly to consumers (20%). Dell applies what is called a "direct business model." It sells customized products, mostly by using a combination of a direct sales force, an 800 number, a catalog, and the Internet.

With progress come problems, and as the Internet grows, there have been and will be challenges. Today, the three most prevalent threats to the productivity gains of the Internet are

- Virus attacks—criminal programs that spread among unsuspecting users and disrupt normal Internet activity.
- Terrorism—acts that purposely shut down systems for a time.
- Spam—unwanted advertising that clogs e-mail servers, wastes time, and destroys user productivity.

Today, billions of Internet e-mails are being sent worldwide every day, and, by some estimates, more than one-third is "junk mail."

Most experts agree that the Internet will overcome these problems in time. However, more effective measures will have to be developed in the years ahead, especially as wireless modes become more popular.

Investing and the Internet The World Wide Web has become Wall Street's newest curbstone meeting place. Here, individual investors can find an untold wealth of information and services, often free of charge. Yesterday's dirt path leading to the buttonwood tree is today's computer software program, referred to as the "browser."

Now, with just a few keystrokes or a click or two of the mouse, an investor can find a Web site that offers information, products, or services to meet almost any need.

With the help of so-called search engine directories, such as Google, Yahoo!, "Bing," and others, a Web site address, called the Universal Resource Locator (URL), can be found quickly and with little effort. Want to purchase another copy of this book for a friend? Use a search engine to find an Internet bookstore (Amazon.com is among the largest currently). Go to the Internet bookstore's Web site

An aseptic room at Johnson & Johnson Laboratories during the early days of a great company, circa 1910

and enter the book's title. After that, purchase is easy.

One of the most interesting and practical Web sites developed for active investors in recent years is the U.S. government's www.publicdebt.treas.gov. At this Internet location, visitors can enter the "virtual lobby" to buy or sell Treasury bills, notes, and bonds online, from 8 a.m. to 8 p.m.

THE COMPANY'S WEB SITE

To illustrate the simplicity and utility of this worldwide communication network for investors, here is how a visitor might search for fundamental information on, say, Johnson & Johnson. The traditional analytical approach outlined earlier can be used, of course. But the World Wide Web can greatly speed the research process.

First, the investor needs the company's URL address. A quick visit to Google, or some other search engine and entering the company's name, "Johnson & Johnson," will provide a URL. Immediately, the investor learns that the company's URL is JNJ.com. The company decided to use its stock symbol as its URL. General Motors did the same. General Motors's Web address is "GM.com."

Frequently, the investor can learn the company's URL without searching. For example, if the investor types the company's name, "JohnsonAndJohnson," immediately after the Internet designation http://, the browser will automatically connect the investor to the company's Web site, JNJ.com.

Once Johnson & Johnson's Web site appears on the screen, a series of tabs or buttons can be clicked on to direct the investor to any one of a number of locations. They might include "Company Products," "Careers," or "Investor Relations." From this location, the investor can then go to

- Company background and historical data
- Annual reports and proxies
- Dividend history and the company's dividend reinvestment plan, if any
- Financial reports
- SEC filings
- Recent news releases
- JNJ's pharmaceutical "pipeline"
- Past corporate presentations
- Webcast archives
- The latest stock quote or chart
- Requests for other information

Most company Web sites today, including Johnson & Johnson's, provide far more data and information than could

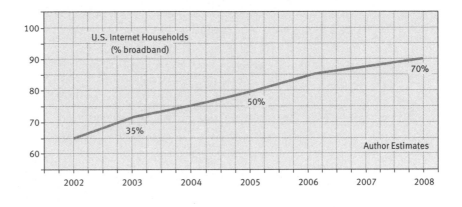

U.S. Internet Households (% broadband)

35%

50%

70%

Author Estimates

have been obtained from many different sources years ago. For example, one of the major brokerage firms recently featured Johnson & Johnson at its Pharmaceutical and Medical Devices Conference, where the company made a presentation. From JNJ's Web site, the investor can listen to this Webcast and view the slides that were used during the presentation. In effect, the extraordinary power of the Internet now allows every investor to participate directly in the complete investment process.

Nearly all company investment information, other than securities analysts' reports, can be obtained *free* from the corporation using the Internet. In most cases, it should not be necessary for the investor to pay for, or subscribe to, information that is often found elsewhere on the Web. The company's Web site is *the* place to start.

Additional examples of how the Internet can be used for research can be found in Chapter 4, "Reading the Financial Pages."

THE SEC AND OTHER SOURCES

In addition to a company's Web site, there are many other Internet locations where an investor can collect information on nearly every public firm. Other than re-

search reports from brokerage firms, the investor can access documents filed with the SEC through an entity called Edgar Online—directly from the SEC with no charge. Go to SEC.gov and search the Edgar company filings. The most important submissions to the Securities and Exchange Commission include

- 10-K—the complete annual report
- 10-Q—the complete quarterly report
- 8-K—unscheduled material events, such as an arbitration judgment or some similar action
- 4—changes in beneficial ownership
- 13-D—a statement of ownership, or merger terms and similar information

ONLINE SERVICES

Current stock prices can be found on the Internet or through some "Internet service providers" such as America Online, Microsoft Network (MSN), and others. Accessing the Web using these services typically requires a low monthly fee. Thus, users can experience Wall Street through attractive and well-constructed sites that present current prices, charts, and ample abbreviated fundamental data. But this is not always an inexpensive approach.

NASDAQ Securities - Company List

A B C D E F G H (I) J K L M N O P Q R S T U V W X

Name	Symbol	Market Value (millions)

Intel Corporation · INTC · 8,869.2

InfoQuote
Summary Quote
News
Charting
Extended Trading
Company Financials

We are the world's largest semiconductor chip r ... nue. We develop technology products, primarily integrated circuits ... as computing ar Integrated circuits are semiconductor chips etc ... ed electronic swi platforms, which we define as integrated suites of digital computing technologies tha reincorporated in Delaware in 1989. Our Internet address is www.intel.com. ... More

Usually, the latest 10k report

Once they are online, individual investors can conduct their own research and then monitor their stock portfolios on a regular basis, either independently or through these services. Usually stock prices are made available with a fifteen-minute lag from real-time prices (a situation that is satisfactory for most investors who are doing preliminary research).

Perhaps one of the best free charting and corporate news site found on the Internet is "BigCharts.com," available through a Dow Jones service, Market-Watch.com (well known on the Web for its financial news).

Investors who need real-time data or up-to-the-minute quotes for trading purposes will discover that additional fees are usually required. If the investor opens an online brokerage account, all stock prices are, of course, real-time.

Quote.com offers an excellent online charting service called "LiveCharts." Like so many interactive services of this type, its operation seems to be slowing as it becomes more popular. Nevertheless, this Web site (noted here because it works satisfactorily, it is reasonably priced, and it has been in business for several years) is worth a visit. The Quote.com service offers a good comparison benchmark for other services.

Beyond the simple task of providing stock prices and charts, some Web sites can be a link to library-quality information, especially on products and product markets. More often than not, these sites are associated with industry magazines and newsletters.

In addition, "bulletin boards" and "chat rooms" are available for open forums and discussions with other investors who have similar interests. Once in a while, other investors, perhaps those who are knowledgeable about certain products, companies, and markets, can stimulate and challenge. Of course, they can also very be misleading. Information from unofficial Internet sources should always be used with caution.

In the late 1990s, a great many Internet "scams" were uncovered and prosecuted. Among them was a young man who used the Internet as a platform to promote certain stocks for his personal benefit. Another notable case involved false press releases. Punishment was sure and swift.

Technical Analysis Almost every financial newspaper and magazine has advertisements for charts and charting services, often with free demos.

Among the most popular is the excellent charting service DecisionPoint.com. Also,

Investor's Business Daily provides daily graphs and other analysis data at the site Investors.com. Reuters has a charting service called MetaStock. Of course, most of these sites are directed toward traders rather than investors. There are many good (and bad) and reasonably priced (or expensive) services available to compare, either from independent sources or from brokers.

There have been many software packages developed in recent years to exploit the readily available data from the Internet. In 1996, this author introduced a program called The Wall Street Trader that was designed to produce short-term technical indicators, using mainly intraday or daily data from the Chicago Board Options Exchange. (The Wall Street Trader software helps identify the market's short-term swings; it is featured at the BullsOrBears.com Web site.) The indicator is described later in Chapter 13, "The Principles of Technical Analysis."

With programs like this, investors are not necessarily concerned with the application of real-time data. Most users, who are called "swing traders," have investment horizons of only days or weeks, and they are primarily interested in *daily* data.

Brokerage Firms Years ago, the Net was mostly the domain of the online and discount brokers. This is no longer true. Almost all brokerage firms today have a presence on the Internet, and they are now similar in many ways. Investors have the ability to obtain real-time quotes, have access to research reports, and, of course, can buy and sell securities online with a response time of under a minute.

Trading commission schedules vary, but normally, as one would expect, active online customers will pay substantially less using a discount broker. An independent investor can expect to pay $10 to $15 for a round-lot (100-share) transaction, perhaps up to thousands of shares. And the fees and commissions might be even lower as activity increases.

The so-called full-service brokerage firms (and a few discount brokers in a more limited way) can offer a broad range of capabilities on their Internet sites. A typical Web site might include some or all of the following:

SERVICES

- Account executive referrals
- Online record keeping
- Money transfer
- Account protection
- Extended hours trading
- Wireless and touch-tone services

Give a person a fish and you feed him for a day; teach that person to use the Internet and he won't bother you for weeks.

—ANONYMOUS

Also, some site sections could be devoted to various calculations, such as time and risk, living yield curves, finding net worth, and bond calculations.

TYPES OF ACCOUNTS

- Individual trading
- Margin
- Bank
- Corporate
- Custodial
- Estate
- Joint
- Retirement
- Trust

PRODUCTS

- Stocks
- Bonds
- Annuities
- CDs
- IPOs
- ETFs and mutual funds
- Money markets
- Unit investment trusts

Most major brokerage firms today are targeting the "wealth management" market. This also means, of course, that investors should expect to pay fees for whatever products and services they need. Fee and commission schedules are sometimes posted on the Web site. If they are not, a simple inquiry will answer the question.

Conclusion Today hundreds of millions of wireless handsets are in use, and many now also include a pocket PC capability. When this is coupled with the millions of servers, desktops, laptops, and notebooks already in use, it requires little imagination to see the unlimited possibilities that the Internet holds for all of us in the future.

Like home addresses, Internet Web site addresses can change. Therefore, listing any URL in this book presents a problem. It is likely that many of the Web site addresses that are listed here may not exist a year or so from this writing. Nonetheless, here is an alphabetical list of a few worthwhile sites to visit. Among the features they offer are quotes, news, market activity, and investor tools. Also see "Sources."

http://

- BigCharts.com
- BullsOrBears.com
- businessweek.com
- cboe.com

- cnbc.com
- conference-board.org
- cumber.com
- economywatch.com
- esignal.com
- federalreserve.gov
- finance.yahoo.com
- gold-eagle.com
- hussmanfunds.com
- investopedia.com
- johnmauldin.com
- kitco.com
- marketwatch.com
- money.cnn.com
- moneycentral.msn.com
- nasdaq.com
- news.yahoo.com
- nyse.com
- nyt.com
- pimco.com
- quote.com
- SEC.gov
- smartmoney.com
- stockmarketbeat.com
- stratfor.com
- ticker.com
- wsj.com
- zacks.com

Introduction

No changes over the past thirty years have been more startling than those that we have seen in the areas of international politics and finance.

The implosion of the former Soviet Union and the unification of Germany marked the termination of the so-called Cold War. Today, the United States is the dominant military leader, and this nation has thus been assigned a greater responsibility in the "new world order."

In only a few decades, Japan, with a population less than half that of the United States, became the second-largest economy in the world. Then, all of a sudden, the Japanese, with many of the world's largest banks and industrial companies, endured an economic contraction and deflation unlike anything any country had seen since the 1930s. Now, China, a communist country, could soon be assuming the second spot in the world's economic hierarchy.

And as we now move further into the twenty-first century, it appears that future events will be no less dramatic. The dastardly attack on the World Trade Center, as well as other radical Islamic and rogue terrorist threats, have served notice that the benefits of this new world order will not come easily or without major challenges.

Unlike the economic recessions witnessed from time to time since World War II, the downturn that began in 2008 has been global and monumental in scope. Indeed, a full recovery will take time. Yet, despite the many problems that still linger, there are great opportunities for businesses and investors in the worldwide arena. In fact, there are many reasons investors can be optimistic about the years ahead.

Instantaneous communications and global, 24-hour trading capabilities are no longer science fiction. The ongoing integration of global financial markets will be taking Wall Street investors far beyond the canyons that meet at Broad and Wall.

This chapter will explore the subject of worldwide investing and discuss the longer-term promises and risks in this new arena.

Perspective Since the 1940s, most of the world's other economies have prospered greatly as a result of U.S. government decisions and the policies of the Federal Reserve System. Japan rose from the ashes of World War II without the considerable burden of a military complex buildup or Cold War competition from the Soviet Union. And in the years immediately after the war, West Germany, aided by the Marshall Plan and limited military obligations, saw a substantial recovery. West Germany has enjoyed solid and healthy growth since its independence in 1955 and its reunification in 1990.

In addition, U.S. financial institutions and businesses invested huge sums of money in the economic development of other countries, not always with satisfactory returns. The recent wars in Iraq and elsewhere in that region are additional examples of U.S. altruism, as other nations, some of them even more dependent than the United States on oil from the Middle East, have benefited from America's initiatives and spending.

This is not to minimize the economic achievements of the Japanese, the Germans, and others. Their educational efforts, investments, competitive products, and hard work have produced meaningful results, even considering their more recent problems. On balance, their economies have prospered, and they have created attractive environments for investing.

The U.S. dollar (the world's principal monetary unit to date), the Canadian dollar, the euro, the British pound sterling, the Japanese yen, and other currencies are convertible into one another at exchange rates determined by free market forces. Domestic inflation rates and productivities, balances in trade accounts, relative interest rates, political events, and many other factors all contribute to the supply and demand forces between currencies on the world markets.

Therefore, when a foreign investor buys a share of IBM, the value of that stock in an overseas portfolio can fluctuate in two ways. First, the price can rise or fall based on the supply of and demand for that stock on NYSE Euronext. Second, its value to the foreign stockholder can move up or down, depending upon the exchange rate of the investor's currency versus the dollar. Thus, a Japanese investor in U.S. equities would monitor the yen-to-dollar relationship, a German would monitor the euro-to-dollar rate, and so on.

The same holds true for a U.S. investor who buys shares in a non-U.S. enterprise. That company's sales and profits, balance sheet values, and stock price would all be denominated in the local currency. Of course, the U.S. holder would calculate the stock's portfolio value in U.S. dollars.

Thus, a decline in the U.S. dollar relative to other currencies will increase the value of an investment in a foreign company, since more dollars will be required in exchange when the foreign investment is later converted back into dollars. Conversely, if the dollar rises relative to other currencies, the dollar-denominated value of the foreign investment will decline.

But investors in foreign stocks should not overlook the other side of the equation, either. If the dollar is rising in value, a foreign company will benefit if a large portion of its product line is exported to the United States. That is to say, its products will become more attractively priced in U.S. markets. Obviously, currency fluctuations are important in worldwide investing, but the relationship is never simply black or white. An analysis of the company is still necessary.

Besides currencies, there are other external items to consider in worldwide investing: global politics, economic trends, unpredictable taxes, and the possibility of expropriation, to name a few. In analysis, it should be noted that accounting, auditing, and reporting standards in overseas markets have been less stringent than those in the U.S. markets, adding further to the risks of foreign investing. And finally, stocks in foreign companies can be less liquid, which makes ETF shares that much more appealing. In short, to be successful in this arena, one must maintain a broader perspective than otherwise.

The Global Marketplace The marketplace for stocks and bonds is becoming more global every day. Millions of shares of many major U.S. companies are now traded daily on foreign exchanges. Similarly, U.S. investors, including mutual funds and other institutions, are finding it progressively easier to invest in companies abroad.

By the end of this decade, NYSE Euronext, the Chicago Board Options Exchange, Nasdaq OMX, and others will be operating in various capacities twenty-four hours a day. Today, it is possible for any U.S. or foreign investor to buy or sell any popular stock at nearly any hour of the day or night, depending only on the location where the shares are being traded at that particular moment—Tokyo, London, New York, or elsewhere.

However, it is unlikely that today's most dominant markets will become so integrated that they lose their identity. London and Tokyo prices for IBM will still be largely determined by New York trading. Similarly, the prices for Hitachi in London and New York will continue to be dictated by the expected supply and demand in Tokyo.

The Japanese Stock Market The Tokyo Stock Exchange (TSE) was first opened in 1878, mainly for trading government bonds and gold and silver currencies. Stocks, which gained popularity in the 1920s and 1930s, now represent more than 90% of all TSE transactions.

Since its postwar reopening in May 1949, the Tokyo Stock Exchange in Tokyo's Kabutocho financial district has experienced substantial growth. By year-end 1989, just before it began its multi-decade decline, the total value of the Japanese market reached more than $4 trillion. In terms of the Nikkei Stock Average (an average of 225 of the nearly 2,300 TSE-listed stocks), equity values rose sixfold in the 1980s alone. During the decade, the Nikkei average, as it is called, climbed from 6,536 in 1980 to its peak of 38,916 in December 1989. This climb began a mere twelve years after the market's restructuring in 1968, when Japan first required its brokers to be licensed by its Ministry of Finance. That year, the Nikkei was approaching 1,700!

In the 1990s and in the early years of this decade, the Japanese stock market has suffered greatly. The Nikkei dropped to under 10,000 once again (see the chart given here), and the steep decline in the Tokyo Stock Price Index, called the "TOPIX," has been no less dramatic.

About 70% of the companies listed on the TSE are included in the first of the exchange's three sections, or groups. About 1,600 companies with larger capitalizations dominate the first section, whereas more thinly traded stocks are commonly found in the second group. In effect, the first tier accounts for more than 85% of

all TSE shares traded. The third group, called "Mothers" (market of the high growth and emerging stocks), contains the final 122 issues.

The TOPIX, a composite index of all common stocks listed in the first section, measures the change in market value from its base on January 4, 1968. The TOPIX is also divided into more than thirty subindexes, allowing ETF investors to examine and buy the market's industry groups as well.

The Tokyo Stock Exchange enjoys a modern facility that it calls the "TSE Arrows," which includes an exhibition plaza, a museum, an information terrace, and a media center, as well as the market center.

The operations of the TSE differ from those of the NYSE in several respects. There are two distinct two-hour trading sessions in Tokyo each day, Monday through Friday. The morning session, called *zenba*, extends from 9 a.m. until 11 a.m. [7 p.m. to 9 p.m. Eastern Daylight Time (EDT)], and the afternoon trading session, called *goba*, operates from 10:30 p.m. to 1 a.m. EDT.

All but a few of the most active stocks on the TSE are traded electronically rather than through specialists. Moreover, most Japanese trading is accomplished through only a small group of brokerage firms and their affiliates, with Nomura and Daiwa being the two most dominant. It was not until 1985 that U.S. and other overseas brokerage firms were permitted to participate in the Japanese markets. Also, it should be noted that a small group of insurance firms and banks accounts for a large percentage of the daily volume on the Tokyo Stock Exchange.

In recent years, the volatility of the stock market in the United States prompted the NYSE to impose trading limits (popularly called "circuit breakers"). Actually, TSE rules have limited daily stock volatility (10% to 20%) for decades. Some market observers credit the circuit breaker as one of the reasons why stock declines in Japan were more modest during the crash of the global markets in 1987. In fact, many TSE stocks never traded during those hectic October days.

As in the United States, companies must meet certain size, profitability, and shareholder requirements to be listed on the Tokyo Stock Exchange. The companies on the TSE can be categorized into numerous business segments: fishing, mining, paper, chemicals, rubber, textiles, and so on.

In general, the list can be described as industrially oriented, and most of these businesses are well diversified. In the

United States, however, service companies are much more prevalent. To an analyst, the contrast is striking.

Four other exchanges in Japan make up the balance of Japan's stock market activity: the Osaka Securities Exchange, with more than 1,000 companies listed; the Japanese overthecounter market, which is relatively small with 200 issues; and two other small regional exchanges.

A FEW SPECIAL RISKS IN JAPAN

Throughout the 1987–1990 period in particular, some market analysts were especially critical of Japanese investing. The comments were many, but consistent: "A stock crash waiting to happen." Only a few of these critics were surprised by the Japanese stock market crash that began in early 1990. And it was largely set off by a collapse in real estate, similar in several ways to the U.S. experience recently.

Throughout the 1980s, the Japanese had apparently read Will Rogers's advice: "Buy land, 'cause He ain't making any more of the stuff." Japanese real estate, even beyond office space, was being quoted by the square foot. The islands measure 146,000 square miles, just under the size of California. This is equivalent to about 1.2 square miles for every 1,000 people. Crowded? Yes. But this hardly explains why Tokyo commercial real estate was being quoted at an average of $6,000 per square foot, with many reports of substantially higher prices. Japan's vastly overpriced real estate represented a drag on its banking industry and stock market—and it still does to some degree today:

- Japanese banks were known to lend money aggressively, with land being pledged as security. Critics contended that much of this money had been invested in the stock market.
- A large portion of commercial loans by Japanese banks was used to finance real estate purchases.
- Bank assets, even to this day, include substantial stock holdings.
- Frequently, a company's "hidden assets" (the value of its real estate holdings) were used to justify the price of its shares on the stock market.

Also, for years, analysts called Japanese stocks overpriced based on the traditional measures of P/E ratios (multiples of over 60 were not unusual), yields (returns of under 1% were typical), and profit margins, which were well below reasonable standards in the United States.

Defenders of those seemingly high prices explained that the accounting rules

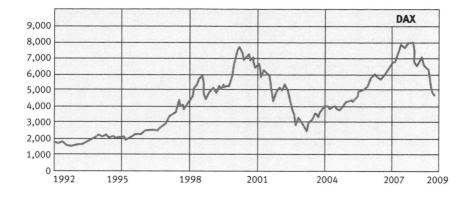

were different in Japan—depreciation is more liberal, and not all profits are consolidated. They also pointed to the faster growth rate of earnings, and, again, to the "hidden assets" of real estate. Also, it was not unusual for companies to include non-operating profits from trading in the stock market (Japanese businesses frequently invest in their suppliers as well as in other companies). However, lower stock prices lately have cured much of this problem.

Finally, it should be noted that in the United States, full disclosure of financial details is encouraged. Japanese managements make an effort to conceal noteworthy items whenever possible. In the United States, the shareholders, as the owners of the business, are held in high esteem. This is not necessarily so in Japan. Many Wall Street observers were surprised when, a number of years ago, astute investor T. Boone Pickens bought a major interest in Japan's leading automotive component producer, Koito Manufacturing. Pickens's futile attempts to change Japanese tradition should be a lesson to anyone who is interested in this market.

Most stocks on the TSE trade in 1,000-share units. And, as in the United States, ETF shares have become readily available. Any TSE issues that are not trading in the United States must be purchased, either directly or indirectly, through TSE member firms.

Even in the face of the declining market, Japan's economic growth continued, but it has been stagnant since 1995. Throughout the remainder of that decade and into the new century, Japan has struggled. Today, Japan remains a net exporting country (oil is its main import), and its GDP is roughly $4.5 trillion, second in the world only to the United States. As indicated earlier, within the next few years, we can probably expect China to overtake the Japanese in that number two position.

Leading Japanese companies that have grown and prospered globally include Toyota Motor, Honda Motor, and Hitachi Ltd. Tracking the progress of these companies is easily accomplished, and they could help investors recognize the trends in Japan at any given point in time.

Germany The reunification of the Federal Republic of Germany (West Germany) and the German Democratic Republic (East Germany) brought together a country of more than 82 million people in an area roughly the size of Nevada.

Germany is now the fourth-largest economy in the world, with a gross national product about 25% that of the

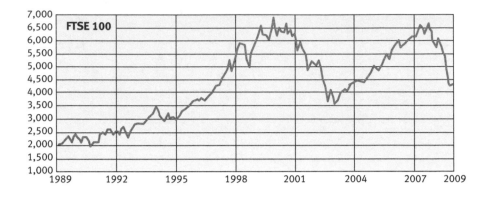

United States—larger than that of the United Kingdom, but now smaller than that of China. In terms of its exports, Germany's volume is not too different from that of the United States, but its imports are much less.

After the fall of the Berlin Wall in 1989 and the reunification that was declared official on October 3, 1990, Germany encountered a period of digestion. At the time, many economists predicted years of problems and hardships, as East Germany, which had been struggling for decades, was merged into the far more prosperous and better-managed West German economy.

East Germany, with its 14 million citizens (or 17% of the total), was contributing only 8% of overall economic activity. East Germany had roughly one-half million young, lower-paid workers who needed work. But as productivity gained, they saw cheap labor come in from Poland and the Czech Republic. Today, the challenge is banking.

German domestic sales remained flat through most of the 1990s; the transition was slow, and the country's growth has been mainly export-driven—depending greatly on the economic health of its customers. Germany's principal exports have been machinery, autos, chemicals, and electronics. Like most countries that rely on exports, Germany has been substantially affected by the recent economic problems, although less so than some other parts of Europe.

There are eight stock exchanges that constitute the German bourse. The largest is Deutsche Börse Group's Frankfurt Stock Exchange, with the lion's share of all trading activity. The FSE lists about 6,800 companies. Many of these companies are international.

Trading hours for the exchange have been extended to allow trading in both Europe and the U.S. markets.

Also worth noting is the Stuttgart Stock Exchange, located in southwestern Germany.

Traditionally, German public participation in the stock market has been relatively modest, and Germany's capital markets are still fragmented, despite constructive efforts by the Bundesbank. However, as the chart given here illustrates, the German stock market tends to move in tandem with other world markets.

The most widely followed indicator of stock market activity is the weighted German stock index, the Deutscher Aktienindex (DAX), simply referred to as the "DAX 30." Like the Dow Jones Industrial Average in the United States, the DAX entered a bull market in 1982 and rose to new

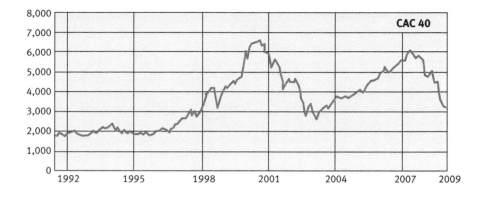

heights in 2000. The DAX declined more than 30% in the 1987 stock crash and more than 60% in the 2000–2003 period. As the chart also shows, the DAX has done well over time—but, like other global markets, the DAX has suffered markedly as a result of the recent recession.

Among the more popular investment names in Germany over the past few years have been Siemens, Volkswagen, Henkel, Schering, and Heidelberger Zement.

The London Stock Market In October 1986, London's International Stock Exchange experienced a changeover to its present methods of operation, and the media euphuistically termed the event "Big Bang." However, for Great Britain, a country of tradition, this was, indeed, a major undertaking: foreign firms were admitted to trading, fixed brokerage commissions were eliminated, and a new technology was introduced.

Since Big Bang, trading on the International Stock Exchange has been virtually all-electronic in upstairs rooms rather than on the floor, as it had been done for centuries. Together with the Unlisted Securities Market, formed in 1980, and the Third Market, this exchange has been leading Europe and the European Union into the twenty-first century.

Years ago, the exchanges in Paris, Amsterdam, and Brussels formed an alliance called Euronext. That group is now part of NYSE Euronext. Also, an earlier planned merger between the London and Frankfurt exchanges was later dropped. But both are clear indications of the ongoing trend in global finance.

London's 8½-hour trading day begins at 8 a.m. (3 a.m. Eastern Daylight Time) and ends at 4:30 p.m., 3½ hours after trading has begun in New York.

Among the most important companies in Great Britain are GlaxoSmithKline, BP plc, Unilever, Barclays plc, and Lloyds Banking Group plc.

China Not long ago, *Understanding Wall Street* was translated and published in the Chinese language (there are also Spanish and Russian editions of this book). This is but one more indication of the expanding global interest in stocks, particularly from the most unlikely locations.

With a land mass nearly the same size as that of the United States, and more than 1.3 billion people (about four times the population of the United States), China has become a major global competitor. During the 1990s and into the twenty-first century, the growth rate of the Chinese economy was about 10% per

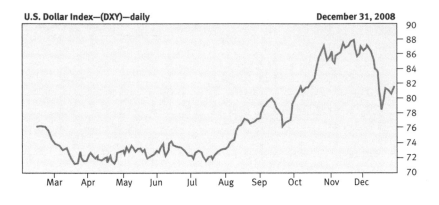

year. China's annual growth rate over the next few years could be 5% to 7%—despite the recent global recession.

Even though China's population growth rate is continuing to drop, the country will still be adding a number equal to the entire population of Florida each year. This represents both a challenge and an opportunity for businesses worldwide.

As an example of the potential from China, economists are predicting that automobile sales in that country could pass 10 million cars annually within the next several years—still modest by Western standards. But with only 35 million privately owned vehicles on the road there, it can be said that the market for automobiles in China is very similar to what it was here in the 1920s.

China's GDP per capita is now a meager $3,200 (about $6,000 on purchasing power parity), which compares to about $47,000 in the United States. Yet, China's GDP is already ranked number three in the world, just ahead of Germany, the United Kingdom, and France.

Of course, the risks of investing in China will remain extremely high as long as the government is communist. However, investors who are willing to assume this great risk might find some rewards there, too.

For those who are interested in overseas markets, the opportunities to invest in all but the most remote parts of the world are there—tempered by the risks, of course.

Other Stock Markets There are many other international stock markets, including several that are never mentioned in the news. Most U.S. investors are familiar with the exchanges in Canada (Toronto and Montreal), where mining and industrial shares are actively traded every day; and some may know of the exchanges in Mexico, France, Australia, and Israel. But how many follow the activity in Iran, Thailand, Nigeria, Peru, or Nepal? Many years ago, a stock exchange in Russia would have been the punch line to a joke. Today, it is not.

ADRs "American Depositary Receipts" ("ADRs") offer a way for U.S. investors to buy or sell shares in overseas companies without trading in markets outside the United States. An ADR is a negotiable receipt for stock in a foreign company. Typically, the shares are held in a bank in the issuer's country, and a correspondent bank in the United States creates ADRs, which are then traded in the open market in lieu of the stock. About two-thirds of the 150 or so ADRs available are listed on Nasdaq. Most of the others are on the NYSE. Investors should be familiar with ADR terms at the outset.

Normally, but not always, one ADR is created for each share held. In addition, ADRs issued prior to 1983 were not required to be registered with the SEC, and, therefore, some companies might not be obligated to disclose certain financial information. Finally, the shares might or might not be "sponsored" by the issuing company. If so, the ADRs would have voting rights and the holders would receive financial reports; otherwise, they would not.

Among the more active ADRs in recent years, which trade in the overthe-counter market, have been Reuters Holdings (Great Britain) and De Beers Consolidated Mines (South Africa). GlaxoSmithKline (Great Britain) and Sony Corp. (Japan) have been two popular ADRs on the New York Stock Exchange.

Multinational Companies One good approach to worldwide investing is buying shares in U.S. multinational companies. Many major companies listed on the New York Stock Exchange derive sizable portions of their annual earnings from overseas markets. Procter & Gamble, Johnson & Johnson, Exxon, 3M, and many other U.S. companies have meaningful earnings contributions from overseas. And, at least to some degree, these firms are adept in hedging their currency risks.

Close analysis of their 10-K reports will tell which companies participate with what products and where. Over the past decade or so, profit participation from the Far East has been deemed an investment positive. More recently, this is less true because so many of these countries have been affected by the downturn in the United States that began in 2008.

Also, profits from foreign operations can be both good and bad. There are many past examples. Xerox's worldwide profits once grew at a very rapid pace, largely because of the profit contributions from its overseas businesses, especially Rank Xerox in Europe and in Japan. In contrast, years ago, Disney investors were disappointed by the highly uncertain profit contribution from its theme park in France. And there was a time when Black & Decker's Great Britain facility was a constant drain on its consolidated profits. Foreign results can, indeed, be important.

Closed-End Funds A number of closed-end "country funds," as they are often called, have been formed to offer direct participation in certain regions. Like other closed-end funds, they are traded on exchanges and tend to advance or decline based on their portfolio values, as well as the supply of and demand for their shares in the open market. Unlike mutual funds, however, these shares trade independent of their net asset value (NAV).

Three country funds that are listed on the New York Stock Exchange exemplify the emotion and volatility that seem to be normal for investments of this type. These comments are *not* recommendations.

The "Mexico Fund" (MXF) made its debut on the NYSE in June 1981 and promptly declined from $12 to about $2 as the fortunes of Mexico rapidly faded at that time. The fund's price recovered nicely, then produced other extremely volatile cycles in the years since. MXF investors have experienced a range of $10 to $40 more than once.

Apart from normal market fluctuations, moves in this fund often reflect political events, oil prices, concerns about U.S. loans to Mexico, currency rates, Mexican inflation, and any number of other factors.

The "European Equity Fund" (EEA) was originally listed on the NYSE as the "Germany Fund" in July 1986 at about $10.

When the reunification of Germany first caught Wall Street's attention in September 1989, the fund's price rose from below $9 per share to $25 in less than six months. The excitement of this dramatic event eventually faded, so the fund's manager, Deutsche Bank Group, broadened its scope to encompass central European and Russian equities.

The "New Germany Fund" (GF), also managed by Deutsche Bank Group, has a more German-focused portfolio. It, too, was launched to satisfy the demand for participation in the reunification effort. Since 2000, the performance of the New Germany Fund has been somewhat better than that of the European Equity Fund.

Of course, lately, most country funds have been selling at the lower end of their trading ranges as a result of the insidious worldwide recession that began more recently.

As with all closed-end funds, investors should monitor both the fundamentals of these funds and the level of premium or discount to their asset values. It seems clear that market awareness is a key ingredient in successful country fund investing.

Exchange-Traded Funds (ETFs) Nowhere has the introduction of ETFs had a greater impact than in the global arena. And there are extensive choices. As with all funds, it is important for investors to obtain and read each prospectus, which

"After a sharp fall, money returns to its rightful owners."

outlines the fund's objectives, risks, and other information.

An excellent place to begin the analysis of international ETFs is the Nasdaq Web site (nasdaq.com), where summaries for each of the numerous Nasdaq-listed funds are readily available.

A typical ETF report on the Nasdaq site shows a chart for the last four or five years, a review of the fund's objectives, a specific breakdown of its sectors, its Morningstar rating, its past annual performance, and its top holdings and how they have changed within the portfolio recently.

Here are some randomly selected issues:

- iShares MSCI Emerging Markets Index
- iShares S&P Europe 350 Index
- iShares MSCI Hong Kong Index
- iShares MSCI Japan Index
- iShares S&P Latin America 40 Index
- iShares MSCI Malaysia Index

International Mutual Funds For those who would like to invest only in a certain group of countries or in a particular region, an international or global mutual fund is another vehicle. The advantages of professional management are even more compelling in this area than with domestic mutual funds. Among the benefits are

- Contact with an overseas management is nearly impossible for individuals, but easier for fund managers.

- The mutual fund analysts are likely to be more aware of accounting anomalies.

- The risk of missing negative, local news items can be minimized when there is an active management at the helm.

The descriptions found in the funds' prospectuses are usually stated in general terms, although some can be very specific. "International" refers to nondomestic investments, whereas "global" usually means investments anywhere in the world—including domestic stocks.

Unlike closed-end funds, as mentioned earlier, the prices of these investment companies directly reflect their net asset values at any given time. Moreover, like domestic mutual funds, international and global funds can be either load (with a sales charge) or no-load. And the best-known fund "families" should be considered first.

12 Gold and Silver

Introduction

One learned economist, paraphrasing the influential John Maynard Keynes, disparagingly referred to gold as a "barbaric relic." This pragmatic fellow could not understand why gold rose from $253 an ounce in 1999 to over $1,000 only nine years later. "After all, it has limited utility, it's expensive to store, and it doesn't offer any interest income. Who would want to own it?" he asked. He was serious, but one thing was clear—his college major was not history.

The answer was simple: gold is the closest to an ideal medium of exchange and "store of value" known to man. It is malleable, ductile, and easily divided into accurately measured quantities. Its quality is consistent; it does not rust, tarnish, or corrode; it is practically indestructible. Also, gold is attractive and relatively scarce. And, finally, it is recognized and accepted by almost everybody. It's "as good as gold," as they say.

This chapter examines gold, and also silver, from an investor's point of view.

Gold Soars

Background Gold is first known to have been used in central and eastern Europe as far back as 4,000 BC, as well as in Egypt in 3,000 BC. Gold does not react to oxygen and remains free of tarnish and rust. The gold death mask of King Tutankhamen, entombed in 1352 BC, was found in perfect condition when the tomb was unearthed in 1922.

Although no one knows for certain, it has been estimated that about 90% of all the gold mined throughout human history is still in existence and that more than 125,000 tons (4 billion troy ounces) of gold are aboveground and available to be traded in the marketplace. If this is so, all the gold in the world would fit into one large, four story house.

For about one hundred years, from the early 1500s until the early 1600s, consumer prices in England increased relentlessly. Throughout this period, the prices of food, fuel, and clothing advanced fivefold. And, during this same period, the price of an ounce of gold also increased steadily. By 1620, the year *Mayflower* landed at Plymouth, Massachusetts, one ounce of gold had appreciated to the equivalent value of about $17.56 (with a purchasing power considerably more than today, of course).

In 1792, the U.S. currency was established as a viable form of legal tender, backed by both gold and silver ("bimetallism"), and for many years, the two metals traded at a ratio of 16 to 1. In 1835, a little more than two hundred years after the Pilgrims landed, gold was discovered on Cherokee land in Georgia. That year, the value of gold was approximately $20.67 per ounce.

President Andrew Jackson ordered government funds to be withheld from the United States Bank and placed in state banks in 1836. Many of these banks, particularly in the West, engaged in speculation, made unwise loans, and issued bank notes without sufficient specie (metal) backing. Concerned, the president then issued his Specie Circular of 1836, which instructed federal land agents to accept only gold and silver in payment for public lands. Many banks were unable to meet the demand for specie and closed their doors, and a financial panic followed in 1837. Yet the state-controlled banking system continued for another seventy-six years until the Federal Reserve System, headed by the Federal Reserve Board, was established on December 23, 1913.

Regarding the development of the gold market, a major turning point occurred with the discovery of gold at Sutter's Mill

on the American River in California in January 1848. It has been said that 92% of all gold produced has occurred since that event.

In 1851, gold was found in Australia, and South Africa had its first year of gold production in 1884. By the end of that century, South Africa had passed the United States to become the world's leading gold-producing country.

The Civil War produced a substantial disruption of the country's monetary order. In 1862, "greenbacks," which had no specie backing, were issued. Like the worthless "Continentals" issued by the Continental Congress in 1775, this new fiat money inflated the prices of almost all commodities—including gold, which nearly doubled in value at that time. Later, the attempted withdrawal of the notes led to a substantial decline in economic activity and commodity prices. Along with the overexpansion of the railroads, this was a major cause of the depression of 1873.

By 1880, gold had returned to its stated value of $20.67. Shortly thereafter, new gold discoveries in South Africa, Australia, and Alaska, along with improved methods of mining, made it possible to increase the nation's money supply. Also, the period from 1873 to 1896 marked the beginning of the demonetization of silver, a program that was officially completed in 1964 when the Treasury minted its last silver coins. The United States was officially returned to the gold standard when Congress passed the Gold Standard Act in 1900.

The 1896–1920 period saw inflation, attributed largely to the demands of World War I. During this time frame, commodity prices quadrupled, while gold remained at its fixed price of $20.67. In 1920 and into 1921, commodity prices declined sharply, business activity slowed, and the stock of money contracted. By 1922, the economy was improving. The money stock resumed its growth, commodity prices stabilized, and businesses were again profiting and growing. The price of gold was the same.

Following a sharp decline in land values in 1926 and the stock market crash of 1929, commodity prices resumed the decline that began in 1920. The money stock contracted, and business activity and profits began to drop. The first banking crisis (of three) occurred in late 1930, when public confidence in the banking system waned. Bank failures, initially in the Midwest, led to widespread withdrawals of public deposits.

A second banking crisis occurred in mid 1931, and later that year, Great Britain abandoned the gold standard. Following numerous statewide "bank holidays," President Roosevelt declared a nationwide banking holiday in March 1933, which continued for a week. Gold redemptions and gold shipments to foreign countries were also suspended. The Gold Reserve Act of 1934 took the United States off the gold standard, and the stated value of one ounce of gold was raised from $20.67 to $35.00.

The gold reserves system on which money supply was based ended officially with the Bretton Woods Agreement in 1947. Not surprisingly, U.S. gold reserves soon began to decline as central banks turned in their dollars for the precious metal. The nation's gold stockpile of 700 million ounces after World War II declined to less than half that amount by the time sales were suspended in 1968. After the window closed, gold was allowed to seek its own price level in the marketplace, like silver or any other commodity.

History tells us that gold does not create (nor can it prevent) business cycles. It is, however, a viable hedge against the problems that result from excessive investor speculation or from the mismanagement of the economy. From the day the first grain of gold was discovered, it has been a universally accepted treasure and a viable medium of exchange. People turn to it during periods of uncertainty and concerns about the economy, or when they see that a fiat currency is rapidly losing its value.

The arguments in favor of a "gold standard" are compelling, since gold is a valid check against currency debauchment. Actually, the world will always be on a "gold standard." Only governments and their policies change.

Today, the United States and other nations are using an international system of fiat money. Such systems usually fail because the monetary quantities (the amount printed) can never be held in check. Now, the major question is: "When will the present system be replaced?" The answer is not clear—perhaps not for many more years with proper management. A fiat money system will last only until its failings can no longer be tolerated. Then, as always, people will return to gold as the starting point for yet another new and better system.

A Store of Value Ardent supporters of gold, affectionately called "goldbugs," are typically colorful personalities. They often maintain that gold is undervalued. Perhaps it is. But compared to what?

The man who used his ounce of gold to purchase a good quality suit to wear in

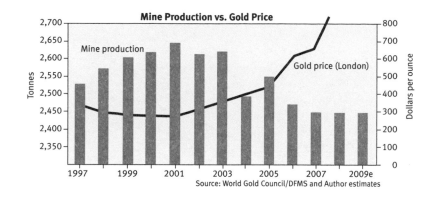

Mine Production vs. Gold Price

Source: World Gold Council/DFMS and Author estimates

1790 thought he knew what his gold was worth that day. The man who sold his ounce of gold two hundred years later, in 1990, to buy a good quality suit thought he knew what his gold was worth that day, too. And the person who bought the gold from him earlier that morning undoubtedly thought that an ounce of the metal was undervalued at $390. Inflation can be insidious.

A common mistake that many gold investors make is to expect the world to stand still from one moment to the next. One cannot assume that if runaway inflation occurs and the price of gold increases to, say, $50,000 per ounce, then that "dream house" will finally become affordable. Sadly, the home will probably be listed for sale at $25 million. But one day in the future, when the currency is stable, that same ounce of gold will probably still buy a good quality men's suit.

Today, it cannot be said that our dollar is "as good as gold." Nor can this be said of the euro, the pound sterling, the yen, or most other forms of exchange. Why? Because, unlike gold, these paper currencies do not offer a "store of value."

"Gresham's Law" Investors who are interested in the subject of gold and silver should become familiar with the mone-

tary observations of Sir Thomas Gresham during the mid 1500s.

"Gresham's Law" is an economic theory that maintains, in effect, that bad money tends to drive good money out of circulation:

When coins of equal value but different intrinsic value are put into circulation, side by side, the coin with the higher intrinsic value will be hoarded and only the coin of lower intrinsic value will be permitted to remain in circulation.

One example of Gresham's Law was the era of bimetallism during the nineteenth century, when both gold and silver were in circulation at the same time. From time to time, one would drive the other out of circulation (i.e., one would be spent and the other would be hoarded) because their relatively free market values would differ from the values being dictated by the government. This monetary concept could apply once again if gold and/or silver are ever reintroduced as specie backing for United States currency. However, specie backing will also place a physical limit on the excessive printing of money.

Supply and Demand The supply of gold is fairly constant and predictable, even

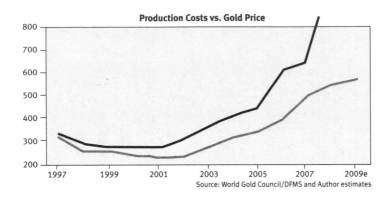

Production Costs vs. Gold Price

Source: World Gold Council/DFMS and Author estimates

though precise annual production figures are difficult to determine. A significant portion of all gold mining is done in remote, politically sensitive areas of the world. But the increment from annual production is small relative to the total aboveground stock.

In other words, the aboveground stock of gold is not likely to change substantially in the near future, since the addition to world supplies is only about 2% each year. Thus, the scarcity of the metal is well assured.

For perspective, the world's entire aboveground stock of 4 to 5 billion ounces has a total market value of about $3.6 trillion (at $800 per ounce), which is a small fraction of the nation's GDP or total national debt.

PRODUCTION AND SUPPLY

In 2008, world gold production was close to 2,450 metric tons—roughly equivalent to ten small twelve-foot moving trucks. In the United States, Nevada remains the largest producing state. But in terms of world production, the eight largest producing countries account for approximately 65% of the total. Here are the author's (perhaps a bit optimistic) estimates for 2008:

	Troy Ounces (millions)	%
Australia	9.0	11.4
China	8.4	10.6
South Africa	8.4	10.6
United States	7.1	9.0
Peru	5.8	7.3
Russia	5.1	6.5
Indonesia	4.5	5.7
Canada	2.9	3.7
Other	27.6	35.1
Total	**78.8**	**100.0**

Only about twenty years ago, world production was near 73 million troy ounces, with North America accounting for 15 million, or 21%. South Africa's production was more than 25% of world output that year, and the Soviet Union, just before its implosion, produced about 10 million ounces. Clearly, the sources of gold are not the same today.

The cost of mining gold varies from $300 to $600 per ounce, with many of the deep South African mines (10,000 feet or more) being at the upper end of the range, and the Canadian producers (1,000 feet or so) being at the lower end. The Muruntau open-pit mine, located in central Uzbekistan, is the largest of its kind and a relatively low-cost producer, but its longevity is uncertain.

The highly secure gold vault at the Federal Reserve Bank in New York

Historically, gold production has increased less than 2% annually, in line with the growth of worldwide population. Even if we assume a substantial rise in the price of gold, it is still unlikely that annual gold production will increase much, given the complexities and high costs of mining, especially in South Africa. However, there are some higher cost facilities that could be made operational if the price remains above $600 or so for an extended period. Similarly, production could be reduced if the price drops below that level. This is a highly capital intensive business, requiring hundreds of millions of dollars and three or four years, or longer, to start a new mine.

Gold is a commodity, and when it is permitted to do so, it will trade according to the basic laws of supply and demand.

Between 1933 and 1975, U.S. citizens could not, legally, own the metal without a special license, except when coin collecting. This suppressed the open market demand for gold during these years. During the 1970s, largely because of inflation fears, the price skyrocketed, hitting a peak of $870 on January 21, 1980. Tons of gold that had been hoarded for years, or perhaps even centuries, by governments and individuals were sold to the speculators. Then, largely as a result of hedging schemes, the price of gold encountered a bear market for the next twenty years, taking it to a low of $253 in 1999.

RESERVES AND DEMAND

Recent estimated gold reserves of the key member governments of the International Monetary Fund (IMF) can be seen in the following table. Central banks were selling gold, and European Central Bank (ECB) holdings became important as a result of the creation of the European Union.

	Troy Ounces (millions)
United States	261
Germany	110
IMF	103
France	83
Italy	79
Switzerland	36
Japan	25
Netherlands	20
China	19
European Central Bank	18
Russia	15
Taiwan	14

Today, the United States accounts for about 27% of all world reserves. The

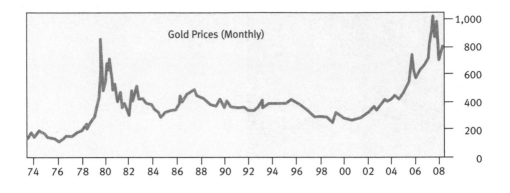

Gold Prices (Monthly)

greatest unknown continues to be the Middle East, where reserves can accumulate whenever a conversion from oil to gold takes place, as it did in the 1970s. Gold prices are influenced from time to time by central bank selling, hedging activities largely by producers, and jewelry demand, especially from India and the Middle and Far East. It is suggested that gold investors monitor the price of oil and try to anticipate trends from this region.

In recent years, the annual world demand for gold used in jewelry, industry, and dentistry has been roughly 70 to 80 million troy ounces, with jewelry accounting for 60 to 65 million, or well over 80% of this amount.

However, overall market demand for gold in the short term cannot be predicted with any confidence because investment interest in the metal (including ETFs) can change dramatically from day to day. Currency news (especially dollar-related) and world events can drive gold prices.

The Money Supply The dollar is the principal currency through which domestic and international trade is conducted. Therefore, the single most important fundamental factor for the gold investor is the U.S. currency—its quantity, its relative value, and its viability worldwide. The dollar is fiat money, dependent solely on the competence of the people printing it and the confidence of the people using it.

The U.S. money supply, as measured by M-2 and its percent change from year to year, is important. Today, the total U.S. money supply, measured by M2 (defined by the Federal Reserve as currency plus demand deposits plus deposits at commercial banks other than large CDs), now exceeds $8 trillion, up sharply from $4.9 trillion in 2000 and $1.6 trillion in 1980. The annual increase in the money supply in recent years has far exceeded the rate of growth in the nation's economy. Also, gold enthusiasts are quick to remind us that the M2 money supply is equal to roughly $30,000 per ounce of gold held at the depositories at Fort Knox and West Point.

There are other key relationships or comparisons to be made with gold. Many people monitor the Commodity Research Bureau Futures Index (CRB). Also, there is the CPI. For the past twenty-five years, CPI inflation has averaged only about 3% per year.

Gold investors are constantly aware of the U.S. budget deficit and the nation's debt. They also note that the "legal debt ceiling" is being raised regularly. The national debt now stands close to $11 trillion,

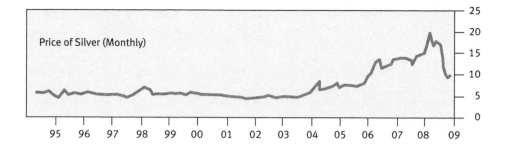

Price of Silver (Monthly)

nearly triple the $3.4 trillion of 1990. In the United States, as a percentage of GNP, debt has been climbing rapidly. In 1980, it was about 40%. In 2000, it was 54%. Today, this figure is approaching 80%.

A high debt level should be of concern because the cost of servicing that debt (i.e., the annual interest that must be paid) is added to federal outlays. The trend of lower interest rates in recent years has kept debt service from becoming an immediate problem. However, higher interest rates, for whatever reason, could very easily lead to a huge budget problem.

To finance the excess of expenditures over tax revenues (i.e., the budget deficit), the federal government must borrow by selling Treasury securities, further increasing the nation's debt—a vicious cycle, to be sure. The Fed must either refrain from supplying the funds, thus allowing interest rates to climb, or supply the funds, thereby monetizing the debt. If interest rates climb, debt service rises, further aggravating the problem. Inflation tends to lag the year-to-year change in the money supply by one or two years, especially when it is sharp and prolonged.

Silver Like gold, silver offers a "store of value" and a viable medium of exchange. Likewise, silver also has a monetary history, and it is recognized as such worldwide.

As a commodity, silver is much more abundant than gold, since its exploration and production are not dictated by its market price. Silver is mined primarily as a by-product of other metal-mining activities, most notably in Latin America and Asia.

An estimated 60 billion ounces of silver have been mined since 1800 and an estimated 40 billion since 1900. Today's annual production rate of silver is probably near 670 million ounces. This does not include silver recovery (the industry calls it "scrap"), which is now below 200 million ounces. The use (and recovery) of silver in photography has dropped dramatically in recent years. Moreover, untold quantities of silver have been hoarded for centuries in India and other remote parts of the world, and large government stockpiles of the metal stand ready to be sold at higher prices.

However, unlike gold, each year, silver has enjoyed a stable demand from industry (jewelry, electronics, and silverware). Despite the notable inroads of digital photography, which is silver-free imaging, and new silver recovery methods, a fairly steady industrial demand for this metal should continue in years to come.

The daily price quotations for gold and silver frequently move in tandem, as they should. The same monetary influences

Political Upheaval

and concerns drive the prices of both metals, although gold may lead the way.

What Are the Risks? Gold and silver advocates have been among the most vocal critics of the management of the U.S. economy. They maintain that the politicians are not capable of fiscal responsibility and that the Federal Reserve cannot contain the problem of excessive spending. The Fed, they say, will avoid high unemployment at all costs and will never be able to resist the temptation to print money in excess. They maintain that hyperinflation is a foregone conclusion.

Could these critics be wrong?

The risks of declining gold and silver prices would be substantial if the U.S. economy were to enter a period of severe recession or depression. In such an environment, producer and consumer prices would, most likely, be declining; the money supply would be contracting; interest income on savings and investments would be in demand; defaults would be commonplace; unemployment lines would be seen often; and gold and silver would be regarded as commodities. In this case, gold and silver prices would probably be going down, not up. Still, monetary upheaval could be a threat, since the government would desperately print money to offset any deflationary spiral.

Also, any legislation introduced to control government spending represents another risk for precious metals investors. The U.S. dollar will probably continue to lose value if government spending remains unchecked. A constitutional amendment to balance the budget or any legislation that might in some way limit pork barrel spending would clearly be a negative for gold and silver investors. But, could this ever happen?

Investing in Gold and Silver For those who regard inflation as the major problem in the long term, and who want to buy gold, and perhaps silver, participation is possible in several ways. There are advantages and disadvantages to each approach.

- Buying the metal directly as bullion, coins, medallions, or in other forms
- Purchasing shares in mining companies
- Investing in precious metal ETFs

In a hyperinflation environment, direct investments in gold bullion wafers (small bars) and gold and silver coins would probably outperform mining shares. At such a point of extreme circumstances, mining stocks could be subject to special government taxes and restrictions, similar to the "excess profits taxes" that oil companies faced in the 1970s. And, of course, the ownership of gold could once again be outlawed by the government, giving investors few places to hide.

Rare coins, which often attract attention when gold and silver markets are active, are frequently, and properly, cited as having performed well as long term investments. But rare coins should not be regarded in the same context as bullion coins such as American Eagles, Canadian Maple Leafs, and Krugerrands, which are priced on their meltdown bullion values. Rare coins are collectibles, almost in the same category as stamps, ceramics, and art. Coin grading, dealer credibility and competence, and comparison shopping are key elements to success in that market.

In a moderate to high-inflation period, mining stocks and mutual funds that invest specifically in companies of this type would probably be the best vehicles. The high commissions, handling costs, higher taxes, and storage fees associated with buying the metal outright can largely be avoided by purchasing equities. The dividends from gold-mining shares could soar. These are the only companies in the world that produce *real money* as their principal product. South African gold mining companies, which are available for investment through ADRs and mutual funds, typically sell at lower P/E ratios and offer higher dividend returns than do mining stocks in the United States and Canada. There are several well-established South African mining companies, such as AngloGold Ashanti and Gold Fields Ltd. However, many investors prefer not to buy the stocks of South African companies regardless of their prices, because of the declining trends in South African mining and the currency risks.

The possibility of political unrest, strikes, or other problems in South Africa also should not be ignored. As indicated earlier, South African gold mining represents a large portion of worldwide production. The industry once employed more than 400,000 (mostly black) miners. This number has been declining steadily over the years and is now below 200,000. Also, any significant disruption in supplies from South Africa could inflate gold prices and depress South African share prices, at least on a temporary basis.

For investors looking for broad participation in gold-mining shares, including South Africa, there is a closed end investment company, ASA Ltd., listed on the New York Stock Exchange. ASA has paid cash dividends every year since 1959.

Modern equipment operated by remote control (photo courtesy of Barrick Gold Corp.)

GOLD AND SILVER MINING INVESTMENTS

The following is an alphabetical list of the leading mining companies with activities principally in the Western Hemisphere. These are not recommendations, but only descriptions of several well-established mining participants and their properties:

Barrick Gold Corp. (ABX)

This well-managed Toronto based firm has become the world's largest gold company, with 30 operating mines and about 120–130 million ounces of proven and probable reserves.

Barrick has many producing gold mines in the United States, Canada, Chile, and Peru. Its major operations include its Goldstrike mines in Nevada and an open-pit mine in Utah, as well as other properties in Ontario and Quebec.

With its acquisitions of Homestake Mining in 2001 and Placer Dome a few years ago, Barrick's annual gold production has been expanded to roughly 8 million ounces. The Homestake properties are located in South Dakota, northern California, and Nevada, as well as in other parts of the United States and in Australia. Placer Dome added mines in the United States and Australia, while Barrick sold its

four Canadian mines to Goldcorp to help finance the huge $10 billion acquisition.

Today, Barrick's gold production costs are in the range of $350 to 400 per ounce.

The company, which is also a producer of copper and silver, has had a good growth record overall. However, Barrick's policy of forward-selling its gold production from time to time can have both advantages and disadvantages for longer-term investors.

Goldcorp (GG)

Toronto-based Goldcorp, which once operated only two mines, one underground and one open-pit, has become an important gold producer. In 2006, Goldcorp purchased four Placer Dome Canadian mines from Barrick. Then, in late 2006, Goldcorp acquired Glamis Gold, a small, nonhedged gold producer in Reno, Nevada.

Today, Goldcorp's Red Lake, Porcupine, and Musselwhite properties in Canada, along with operations in the United States, Mexico, Guatemala, and Honduras, make it one of the leading miners in this part of the world.

The company has proven and probable gold reserves of 40–45 million ounces, with annual gold production of more than 2.3 million ounces.

Goldcorp's costs, now about $350 to $375 per ounce, are rising. This is an item

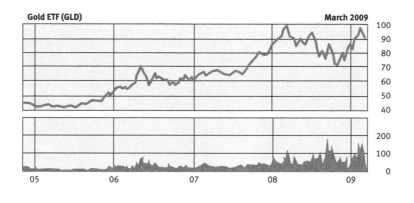

Gold ETF (GLD)   **March 2009**

that investors should monitor in the years ahead.

Hecla Mining (HL)

Hecla Mining, headquartered in Idaho, with production of 8 to 9 million ounces annually, is not even close to being the largest silver producer, but it has a long history. Its two most important properties are located in Idaho (the Lucky Friday silver mine) and in Alaska (Greens Creek). The company is now exploring in Colorado and in Mexico.

Newmont Mining (NEM)

This Denver-based firm was the world's largest gold company before it withdrew from Russia in 2006. It continues to be a key player, with substantial proven and probable reserves of 85–90 million ounces worldwide. Its production of over 5 million ounces comes from projects along the Carlin Trend in northern Nevada, as well as major properties in Australia, Peru, Ghana, Indonesia, and other parts of the world.

North America accounts for almost 40% of the firm's worldwide reserves, not including any Hope Bay possibilities in Canada. It can also be noted that Newmont's recent efforts have helped Australia become one of the world's most important gold-producing countries.

Pan American Silver (PAAS)

Pan American Silver, founded in 1994, is a growing silver producer with an expected annual output of close to 25 million ounces of silver. It has eight mines operating in Mexico, Peru, Bolivia, and Argentina.

Yamana Gold Inc. (YAU)

Toronto-based Yamana Gold, organized in 2003, has become a notable gold- and copper-mining company, especially in Central and South America. Three mines in Idaho, Nevada, and Chile were added with the purchase of Meridian Gold in 2007.

Today, Yamana has proven and probable reserves of about 15–20 million ounces, with modest production levels. Its current costs are roughly $350 to $375 per ounce.

ETFs

For gold participation, there are two ETFs that are worth investigating: GLD and GDX.

Conclusion Investing in gold and gold stocks should be a decision based on long-term considerations. In recent years, gold has regained its place as a possible hedge.

Where investing in gold and precious metals is concerned, advice is abundant—and caution is strongly advised. One should be especially careful of mail-order schemes and unscrupulous dealers who promote gold and silver as a sure way to riches or safety. Investors who fail to do their homework or who enter into transactions unknowingly are easy targets for abuse.

13 The Principles of Technical Analysis

Introduction

On Wall Street, there are two distinct approaches to the stock market. "Fundamental Analysis" is the study of all relevant factors that influence the future course of corporate earnings and dividends, and hence stock prices. This approach involves the analysis of economic data, industry conditions, company fundamentals, and corporate financial statements. In contrast, "Technical Analysis" refers to the study of all factors related to the actual supply of and demand for stocks. Using stock charts and various indicators, the "technicians," as they are called, attempt to measure "the pulse of the market" in their effort to forecast future stock price movements.

The number of investors who are using fundamental analysis successfully attests to the merits of that approach. However, technical analysis also has considerable value because, ironically, not all investors believe in it. There is an old Wall Street saying: "If everyone bought at the bottom and sold at the top, the top would be the bottom and the bottom would be the top."

An individual who understands both the fundamental and the technical approaches is aware of the strengths and weaknesses of each and is, therefore, likely to have an advantage on Wall Street.

"He who sells what isn't his'n, must buy it back or go to prison."

Here is a key point from an earlier section that is worth repeating: "As a general rule, *investment selection* and *investment timing* are inversely important. When the investment horizon is longer, selection becomes more important than timing. But timing is far more critical when the horizon is shorter." And *this* is where technical analysis is most valuable.

Investors often find it frustrating to watch a stock decline immediately after they purchase it or advance right after they sell it. Hopefully, this section will prove useful in this regard.

This chapter describes several popular technical methods, and it explains several key principles that have been successful over the years.

Bar Charts A stock chart is a picture of the stock's price history. With just a glance, an investor can quickly see the stock's past action and gain valuable perspective.

There are several types of stock charts. The most popular, called a bar chart, shows the price of a stock and its volume (the number of shares traded) over a period of time, usually measured in days, weeks, or months. A daily bar chart, for example, would show the highest, lowest, and closing prices for each day, along with the number of shares traded daily. Similarly, a weekly bar chart would show the highest and lowest prices for the entire week along with Friday's closing price and the total volume from Monday through Friday.

Online computer programs today are a great deal more sophisticated than they were even ten or fifteen years ago. Users can now construct real-time charts of all types with one-, two-, five-, ten-, fifteen-, thirty-, or sixty-minute price ranges.

Investors who want to pinpoint the best price to buy or sell a stock will find the monthly price chart a good place to begin. Then, by gradually moving down the time scale, the analysis can be "fine-tuned." A thirty-minute scale with a moving-average setting of "40," as explained shortly, can provide a good picture of a stock's daily action—especially when it is viewed in conjunction with a weekly chart.

To demonstrate exactly how bar charts are constructed, assume that a stock traded at the following prices over a period of four weeks (twenty trading days):

Date	High	Low	Close	Volume
First Week				
Mon. 2nd	29.75	28.50	29.00	13,400
Tues. 3rd	29.50	28.63	29.13	15,200
Wed. 4th	29.50	28.25	28.75	15,800
Thurs. 5th	29.00	27.88	28.50	17,500
Fri. 6th	28.63	27.00	27.50	14,300
Second Week				
Mon. 9th	29.00	26.75	29.00	40,200
Tues. 10th	29.50	28.75	29.00	16,100
Wed. 11th	30.25	29.00	30.00	29,400
Thurs. 12th	31.00	29.63	30.50	15,600
Fri. 13th	30.75	30.00	30.25	12,100
Third Week				
Mon. 16th	31.00	30.13	30.75	17,800
Tues. 17th	31.50	30.38	30.38	10,200
Wed. 18th	30.75	29.50	29.75	18,100
Thurs. 19th	30.00	29.13	29.75	15,000
Fri. 20th	29.75	29.13	29.63	13,100
Fourth Week				
Mon. 23rd	32.00	29.63	31.25	18,000
Tues. 24th	32.25	31.00	31.38	14,500
Wed. 25th	32.00	31.13	31.88	14,900
Thurs. 26th	32.50	30.75	30.75	17,300
Fri. 27th	31.63	30.38	31.50	11,700

A daily bar chart of this price information would appear as follows:

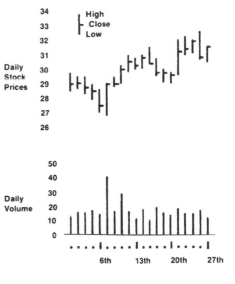

Typically, a complete daily chart displays several months (and sometimes more than a year) of daily data.

And with the Internet services available today, investors can see up-to-the-minute daily (or even intraday) charts with just the click of a mouse. But both investors and traders should realize that daily charts lack a necessary perspective and illustrate only *part* of the story.

A weekly bar chart of the same prices would simply be a condensed version of the daily chart:

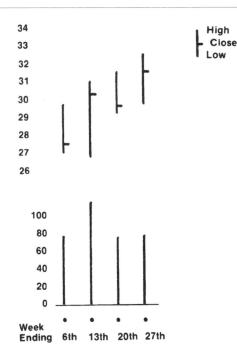

Week
Ending   6th   13th   20th   27th

A complete weekly chart would normally show at least three to five years of weekly data.

To repeat, one challenge that all investors need to overcome with charts is *perspective*, as was evident in the discussion of growth stocks in Chapter 6. For a longer-term investor with a time horizon of several years, charts with "intraday" settings, or even "daily" or "weekly" settings, have less value the further one looks into the future. Charts are mainly *short-term* tools.

Chart Patterns Once a bar chart has been constructed and maintained, over time, various patterns appear. Each tells a different story, and some are more valuable than others. "Support and resistance" patterns, for example, work well because investors have a tendency to remember past stock prices. Here are two typical support and resistance patterns and the psychological reasoning behind each:

Price Support

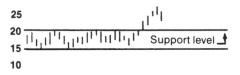

This stock traded in a price range between $15 and $20 for several weeks or months, providing ample time for many investors to buy, sell, or just observe. When the stock suddenly rose above $20, an action that is called a "breakout," each person who bought the stock was saying, "Wow, am I smart! This is a good one! If it returns to the $15 to $20 range, I'll buy more." The same can be said for the investor who sold it or who watched it rise without owning it: "What a mistake! If the stock returns to that price range again, I'll buy it!" This is called a "price support" pattern.

The story would be completely different, of course, if the breakout happened to be down, forming a "price resistance" pattern.

Price Resistance

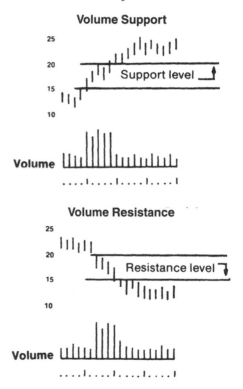

In this case, the stockholders might be thinking, "I knew I should have sold that stock! If it rallies back to $15 to $20, I'm going to sell it and use the money to buy a better stock!"

Price support and price resistance patterns have even greater meaning when the trading range is accompanied by large volume. This usually indicates that investment interest is high.

Normally, the moment the stock breaks out of its trading range—either up or down—its volume increases. If it does, and the stock continues in the same direction, the pattern can be considered quite reliable.

When a stock breaks out of a price support or price resistance pattern, the precise spot of the breakout is often called the "pivot point." Frequently, but not always, the pivot point represents half of the move before the stock returns to "test"

the breakout. This pullback can be "one final chance" for investors to buy or sell.

There are two other types of support and resistance chart patterns.

Volume Support

Volume Resistance

The increased volume, as illustrated here, highlights the accelerated trading activity at those particular price levels. For essentially the same psychological reasons mentioned earlier, support and

Panic Reversal

Head & Shoulders Reversal

Neckline

Rounding Top Reversal

Descending Triangle Reversal

Double Top Reversal

Broadening Top Reversal

Selling Climax Reversal

Test

Climax

Inverse Head & Shoulders Reversal

Neckline

S   S

H

Rounding Bottom Reversal

Double Bottom Reversal

1   2

Triple Bottom Reversal

1   2   3

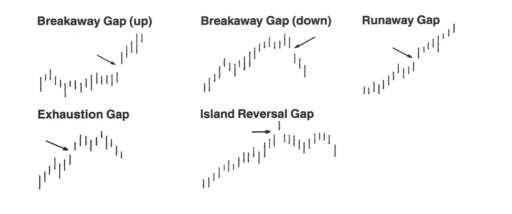

Breakaway Gap (up)

Breakaway Gap (down)

Runaway Gap

Exhaustion Gap

Island Reversal Gap

resistance levels created by volume can also influence future buy and sell orders.

Note, too, that after an extended move in a stock, whether up or down, the volume support or volume resistance pattern can mark the beginning of the end of the stock's prior trend.

Ascending and descending triangles are interesting and useful variations of the price support and price resistance patterns discussed earlier. They are so named because the direction of the breakout is frequently indicated in advance by the shape of the triangle.

Ascending Triangle

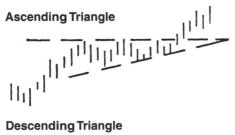

Descending Triangle

When the direction of a stock changes, specific chart patterns frequently develop as the turn occurs. Several of these so-called reversal patterns are shown on the next two pages. In some cases, they develop gradually; at other times, the reversal occurs more suddenly.

The type of reversal pattern that appears is frequently determined by the nature of the advance or decline. Usually, the faster the move, the more rapid the reversal.

A "gap" occurs when the entire trading range on a given day is above or below the trading range of the previous day. Often the result of an emotional response to an overnight news item, a gap can be the first indication of a new price trend. However, if the stock's unusual volatility is partly due to its having a small float (i.e., a relatively small number of shares available for trading), the gap can be less reliable as a chart pattern.

Bar charts are amazingly geometric. As a result, technicians frequently draw trend lines and channels to identify future support and resistance points. In so doing, an experienced chartist will not ignore the "secondary points," which are the high and low points immediately before and after each peak or trough. Here are three trend-line illustrations:

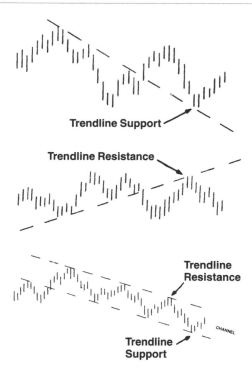

Trendline Support

Trendline Resistance

Trendline Resistance

CHANNEL

Trendline Support

Stock charts are like snowflakes—they are similar, but they are never exactly the same. With the benefit of 20/20 hindsight and hours of experimenting, an investor can apply many of the same lessons learned time after time. Still, stock patterns present two major problems:

- If the pattern has developed completely, some of the move has already occurred.

- Chart patterns are never 100% reliable.

Most technical analysts who use bar charts prefer regular-scale graph paper, which is probably best for most investors. However, technicians who are interested in stock price movements on a percentage basis can obtain a somewhat different perspective by constructing the same charts on semilogarithmic-scale paper.

Of the few chart subscription services that remain, S&P has been the best and most reliable. In one book, hundreds of charts can be seen in an easy-to-read format. And several can be found on the Internet…

The Dow Theory The Dow Theory is one of the oldest and most famous technical tools of the stock market. Its primary purpose is to forecast the future direction of the overall stock market by using the past actions of both the Dow Jones Industrial Average and the Dow Jones Transportation Average as a guide.

The Dow Theory is based mainly on the observation that market movements are analogous to movements of the sea. In other words, there are three movements in the market, all occurring simultane-

BigCharts.com

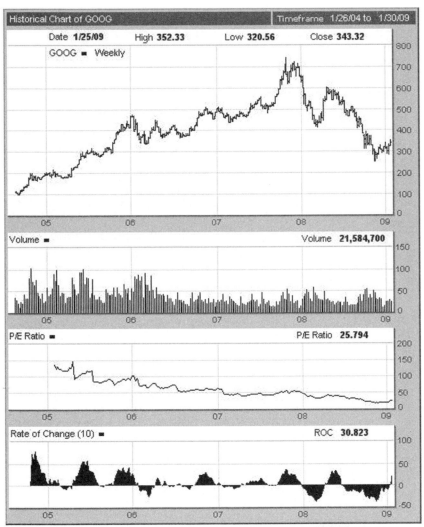

©BigCharts.com

BigCharts.com is one of the best charting services on the Internet. Much of the service is free (delayed) and the format choices are extensive. Both technical and fundamental capabilities are excellent.

StockCharts.com

StockCharts.com offers good technical capabilities with good format flexibility. The time frame choices are limited. This service is more for technical analysts, not fundamentalists. Free charts are delayed.

Quote.com Live Charts

Quote.com LiveCharts is a good fee-based service for both technical and fundamental capabilities. The format choices are good while the free service (delayed) offers only limited utility.

There is always the temptation in the stock market, after a period of success, to become careless or excessively ambitious.

—JESSE LIVERMORE

ously: hourly or daily fluctuations (ripples); secondary or intermediate movements, which take two or three weeks to a month or more (waves); and the primary trend, which extends several months to a year or more (the tide). It is this primary trend that is generally referred to as either a bull or a bear market.

According to early proponents of the theory, daily fluctuations are of little value. Secondary movements, however, are closely watched. They can retrace between one-third and two-thirds of the prior primary price change. The Dow Theory becomes useful when the secondary movements of the Dow Jones Industrial Average and the Dow Jones Transportation Average both signal a new primary trend by penetrating their previous secondary peak points. A new primary trend is not "confirmed" until both averages have produced the necessary signal.

Although most technicians believe that the Dow Theory has been successful, they do not agree on the extent of its success. The distinction between a primary and a secondary movement is not always clear. Still, many analysts find the tenets of the theory useful in their work.

The Elliott Wave Theory Like the Dow Theory, the Elliott Wave Theory uses past chart movements to forecast future price action.

The Elliott Wave Theory contends that movements in the stock market can be identified as having five steps (forming three distinct waves). Once these five steps are complete, and the top or bottom has finally been reached, investors should anticipate a new trend.

However, as with the Dow Theory, not all of the proponents of the Elliott Wave Theory agree on its interpretation at any given time. What might appear to be a third step to one student could be the fifth step to another.

Despite its obvious shortcomings and, in some cases, misleading conclusions, the Elliott Wave Theory should not be totally dismissed. There are many bright and talented technicians who are using this theory successfully in one form or another.

The Moving-Average Deviation Technicians frequently monitor a stock's progress by relating the stock price to its "moving average." A forty-week average, for example, is calculated by adding a stock's closing price for the current week to the closing prices for the previous thirty-nine weeks and dividing by forty. As time passes, this weekly average becomes a "moving average," displaying a smoothed trend of the stock's past prices.

Among the most popular moving averages are the 50-day moving average and the 200-day (or 40-week) moving average.

A stock's momentum, or rate of change, is shown by its "moving-average deviation." Using a weekly chart and a ten-week moving average of the stock price, an investor can, each week, calculate the deviation simply by dividing the last stock price in the series by the ten-week moving average calculated for that week. This approach can be especially helpful in the technical analysis of highly volatile stocks (e.g., many growth and cyclical stocks). A new price trend is often indicated by the moving-average deviation well before it actually takes place. The moving-average deviation is also a good measure of an "overbought" or "oversold" condition, which can result when a stock moves too far too quickly. A weekly moving-average deviation chart is shown in the next column.

Calculating a ten-week moving average of the deviation figure and plotting it on the same (lower) scale will sometimes help the investor gain a longer-term perspective and avoid being "whipsawed" by excessive short-term activity.

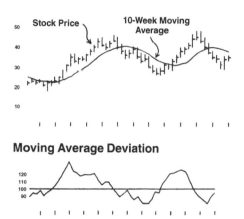

Moving Average Deviation

Technician Gerald Appel is credited with developing what is called the "MACD" (the moving-average convergence/divergence). This calculation involves three exponential moving averages, instead of one or two. The MACD is displayed as two separate lines that fluctuate above and below a baseline. The second line is set at a longer time frame than the first (usually twice as long).

"Stochastics" is a popular technical tool that measures the price velocity of a particular stock or market index. The investor sets a range, and stochastics measures where the price is relative to that range (i.e., a stochastic of 100% means that the price is currently trading at the extreme high of the range; at 0%, the price is trading at the extreme low of the range). A moving average of the indicator is also used to smooth this otherwise volatile indicator.

Relative Strength The two most popular forms of relative strength are the calculations used by *Investor's Business Daily*, a relative price strength rating for individual stocks that it calls the "RS Rating" and the "Relative Strength Index" (the RSI), developed by J. Welles Wilder, Jr.

The *Investor's Business Daily* RS Rating measures a stock's relative price change in the previous twelve months compared to those of all other stocks, and *IBD* is impressed when a stock's RS Rating is above 80.

Based on the way the Worden service calculates the RS Index, a stock is declared to be "overbought" when it has an RSI of 70 or more and is considered "oversold" when the RS Index falls below 30.

Beta Many professional portfolio managers use a form of technical analysis in their attempt to measure a stock's market risk or sensitivity by calculating its "beta coefficient." Beta is a measure of the percentage change in the price of a stock relative to the percentage change in a market index.

Usually beta refers to the stock's relationship to the S&P 500 Index (i.e., the S&P Index = 1.00). A typical electronics stock, for example, might have a beta of 1.60, which means that the stock can be expected to move up or down by as much as 60% more than the general market. Conversely, an electric utility might have a beta of only 0.80 or less, which suggests that the stock is expected to be 20% less volatile than the general market.

Portfolio managers often try to outperform the market by placing high-beta stocks in the portfolio when the market is expected to advance and by using low-beta stocks when they think the market outlook is less promising.

The major drawbacks to beta analysis are that beta never remains constant, and that predicting its future direction can be hazardous. For example, bank stocks were once thought to be low-beta issues, which has not been the case in more recent years. Thus, the beta formula must be monitored and must not be taken too literally.

Point-and-Figure Charts Quite different from bar charting is another method called "point-and-figure" analysis (P&F). Although a point-and-figure chart cannot measure time precisely and does not

"If everyone bought at the bottom and sold at the top,
the top would be the bottom and the bottom would be the top."

show volume, two important features of bar charts, P&F does have its advantages. Its construction is simple and, once understood, a point-and-figure chart is easy to maintain and read. As with bar charts, an investor should spend at least several hours experimenting with old charts before putting any theories into practice.

Prior to starting a point-and-figure chart, examine the past price range and volatility of the stock. It is necessary to determine the appropriate denomination or "reversal" to be used on the chart. A high-priced stock (e.g., $50 or above) usually requires a 2-point, 3-point, or perhaps even a 5-point reversal. A medium-priced stock (say, in the $20 to $50 range) is probably best represented by a 1-point, a 1.50-point, or a 2-point reversal chart. A 0.50-point or a 1-point reversal is frequently used to chart low-priced stocks. Any one of these reversals will work on the same stock, but the chartist must decide which is most effective. With point-and-figure charts, the stock moves in only one direction at a time—either up or down. It does not change direction until a "reversal" of the desired amount occurs.

Once the scale has been drawn, mark the beginning price on the chart. If the price advances thereafter, place X's on top of one another. If the price declines, use O's and place them below one another. These symbols are used merely to identify the price direction. When the stock's direction changes by the required amount (the reversal), move to the next column. Do not place a new "X" or "O" on the chart until the exact price has been hit. With the passing of time, a P&F chart will show alternating columns of X's and O's.

For example, shown here is a 2-point reversal chart built from this string of prices: 29 (start), 32.75, 29.63, 33.25, 30.13, and 34.88.

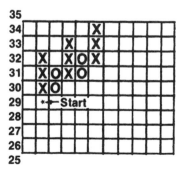

Point-and-figure charts, like bar charts, can show price support levels and price resistance levels.

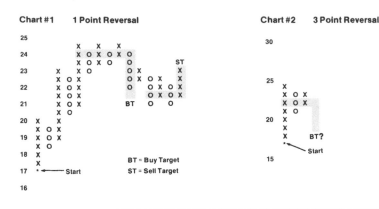

Chart #1   1 Point Reversal

```
25
24              X     X     X
23              X O X O X O
        23      X O X O     O              ST
                X   X O        O X          X
22      X O X              O X O X          X
        X O X              O   O X O X
        X O X                  O X O X
21      X O X        BT        O   O
        X O
20  X     X
        X O X
19  X O X
        X O
18  X
        X                    BT = Buy Target
17  • ←——— Start              ST = Sell Target

16
```

Chart #2   3 Point Reversal

```
30


25
        X
        X O X
        X O X
20      X O
        X
        X              BT?
        •   ←——— Start
15
```

In addition, "breakouts" are easy to detect using the point-and-figure method:

Bullish

```
                    X ←—— Breakout
        X     X     X
        X  O  X  O  X
        X  O     O
        X
```

Bearish

```
        X     X     X
        X  O  X  O  X  O
        X  O     O     O
        X                 O ←——Breakout
```

Many technicians use point-and-figure charts to predict how far a stock can advance or decline. There are several techniques, although none has been found to work every time.

The charts labeled #1 and #2 at the top of the page illustrate one approach. Both charts are constructed from this same string of prices: 17 (start), 20.38, 18.13, 20.75, 19.63, 23.25, 21.50, 20.25, 24.63, 22.75, 24.75, 23.13, 24.75, 22.00, 23.13, 20.75, 22.50, 20.63, and 23.25.

According to point-and-figure practitioners, the greater the frequency of reversals at a certain level, the greater the stock's potential rise or fall from that level. As the 1-point reversal chart demonstrates, the base indicating the 21 buy target has a count of six (shaded) across the 24 line. Six blocks below is the 21 price objective. Similarly, the sell target of 23.50 is the result of a base count of four (shaded) across the 21.50 line. The base to be used in the measurement can be found at the foot of the breakout, regardless of whether the chartist is looking for a buy or a sell target.

Point-and-figure charts can do many things. They can help an investor spot breakouts and new price trends. They can help identify support and resistance areas. Sometimes they can provide price objectives. But, for most investors, because it does not include volume, this charting method is best used as an adjunct investment tool to confirm or challenge other technical and fundamental work.

Japanese Candlestick Charts One interesting variation of modern-day bar charts is the ancient Japanese candlestick method of technical analysis. Actually, it is similar to bar charts, as explained earlier, except that opening prices are also included. In other words, the opening, high, low, and closing prices all appear on the chart, rather than just the high, low, and close. The result is a chart notation that looks much like a candlestick.

Here is an example of how a candle-stick chart illustrates a day when the closing price is lower than the opening price—and how it would be shown on the standard bar chart:

High for day
Opening price

Closing price
Low for day

This is how the candlestick chart would appear when the closing price is higher than the opening quotation:

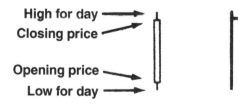

High for day
Closing price

Opening price
Low for day

There is much more to this approach, of course, but the chart patterns are basically the same. The Japanese descriptive terms can be both interesting and exotic: gaps are referred to as "windows," and an intraday reversal can be called a "shooting star," a "hanging man," or a "hammer." The clever Japanese often name each symbol for its graphic appearance.

Japanese candlestick charts are a colorful way to view the stock market. However, most experienced technicians dismiss candlesticks as a complex tool for an art that is best kept simple. And in technical analysis, it is important not to miss the forest for the trees.

Technical Indicators Suppose a baseball player at bat happened to notice that almost every time the pitcher wiped his hand across his shirt, the next pitch would be a fast ball. The batter might still strike out, but with this knowledge, he has a better chance for a hit. Analysts rely on technical indicators in much the same way. The use of these statistical tools as an aid in stock market timing is perhaps the most interesting and intellectually stimulating part of technical analysis.

There are literally hundreds of technical indicators. Most of them are derived from four primary sources:

1. Business data

2. Analysis of investor activity

3. Market action

4. Nonrelated coincidental factors

The indicators explained in the following pages have been fairly reliable in the past. Few, if any, work perfectly at every turn in the stock market. For this reason, an investor should maintain a portfolio of indicators, or perhaps establish a composite index of several indicators.

MONEY SUPPLY INDICATORS

Many Wall Street professionals believe there is a correlation between stock prices and the expansion or contraction of the nation's money supply. Indeed, a study of the six-decade period since the end of World War II strongly suggests a definite correlation, especially if inflation is also taken into account. When the money supply is increasing at a fairly steady rate, and inflation is low and of little concern, stock prices tend to rise. On the other

hand, either a contraction in money supply growth or an increase in the rate of inflation, or both, can be considered a distinctly unfavorable development.

The Money Supply Indicator is calculated monthly. It shows the year-to-year percent change in M2, adjusted for the year-to-year percent change in the Consumer Price Index (CPI).

To calculate the indicator, the percent change in M2 and the inflation impact (as measured by the percent change in the CPI) are added to or subtracted from 100. For example, if last month M2 increased 6.5% over the same month a year ago and the Consumer Price Index increased 4.0% in the same period, the money supply indicator would read 102.5 for that month (100 + 6.5 − 4.0). On the other hand, if M2 advanced 3.0% while the CPI increased 5.8%, the indicator would only be 97.2 for the month (100 + 3.0 − 5.8).

In the late 1940s, the Money Supply Indicator was frequently under 100 because the rate of inflation was greater than the growth of the money supply. Corporate profits advanced, but stocks remained dormant. Throughout most of the 1950s, the indicator fluctuated in the 100 to 104 range. At that time, the money supply was increasing modestly while the inflation rate remained low. Stock prices rose.

In general, stocks can be vulnerable when the indicator declines, but seem to do well when it is steady or rising. An investor should be especially cautious when the indicator is declining while stock prices are advancing. This occurred in 1972 and again in mid-1987, prior to substantial market declines shortly thereafter. Conversely, if the indicator is rising sharply when stocks are declining, the market could be nearing a turn for the better.

The Money Supply Indicator can be a reliable tool during uncertain economic periods when money supply and inflation rate figures are in the limelight . . . which seems to be most of the time.

There is another money supply indicator that is easy to calculate and is also worth following. By subtracting and plotting the difference between M3 and M2, one can create another indicator that shows a fairly good correlation with stock prices. The Federal Reserve defines the difference between these two money stocks as "institutional money funds, and certain managed liabilities of depositories (that is to say, large time deposits, repurchase agreements and Eurodollars)."

THE EPS/T-BILL YIELD RATIO

One of the best methods of measuring the relative value of stock prices compared to other investment opportunities is the ratio of the S&P 500 earnings per share yield to the three-month T-bill yield. This monthly ratio is easy to calculate and to maintain. It is constructed in the following manner:

1. Divide the latest twelve-month earnings per share for the S&P 500 Index by the monthly average price of the index for the current month. The result is called the "earnings yield."

2. Divide the "earnings yield" by the average yield on the three-month T-bill for the same period.

If the ratio is 0.90 or lower, it is most likely a good time to sell stocks. When the ratio is 1.20 or greater, it is usually a good time to buy stocks.

SHORT INTEREST

At about mid-month, the New York Stock Exchange and other markets announce their short interest figures. These are shares that have been borrowed and sold by investors who believe that the same shares will be available for repurchase later at lower prices. Although a large short interest indicates that many investors anticipate lower prices, it also represents potential buying power. In years past, the NYSE short interest was a popular and reliable market indicator—especially when short-sale figures were looked at in relation to the number of shares traded.

The Short Interest Ratio is a measure of this relationship. It is calculated by dividing the NYSE short interest total by the average daily volume over the same period.

Historically, when the average daily volume exceeded the short interest figure (i.e., a ratio of less than 1.00), the indicator reading would be bearish. A short interest ratio of 1.00 to 1.60 was regarded as neutral, and a ratio of more than 1.60 was bullish. For many decades, when short interest was at least double the average daily volume (when the ratio was 2.00 or more), it was generally a good time to buy stocks.

As a result of arbitrage and hedge fund activity, the short interest ratio has recently climbed to much higher levels than it did in years past. The ratio has been distorted by professional short-selling funds that hedge their short positions with stock options.

Also, there are those who bloat the short-sale figures with special dividend-capture or tax-avoidance strategies. In recent years the ratio has ranged between 3 and 5 and bears little resemblance to the original indicator. It can no longer be regarded as a reliable technical tool.

ODD-LOT INVESTORS

It is a widely accepted rule on Wall Street that the "odd-lot" investor (defined as a buyer or seller of less than 100 shares) is almost always wrong. Yet, a close study of odd-lot behavior does not bear this out entirely. The record clearly shows, for example, that odd-lot investors were heavy net buyers at the market lows of 1966 and 1970, and were aggressive sellers at the highs in 1968 and 1972. Also, odd-lot investors correctly used the 1987 stock crash as an opportunity to buy.

Nevertheless, small investors, like all participants who monitor the market's fluctuations and day-to-day activities, are motivated by greed and fear—and do tend to buy or sell incorrectly during times of extreme optimism or pessimism. One of the best barometers of this emotion is the Odd-Lot Short-Sale Ratio.

The ratio is calculated by dividing odd-lot short sales by total odd-lot sales. These New York Stock Exchange statistics can be found in newspapers and on the

"When they raid the house, they take all the girls . . . but the madam and the piano player get bailed out first."

Internet. The weekly totals, two weeks old but more complete, are summarized each weekend in *Barron's*, the popular weekly financial newspaper.

When the ratio reaches or exceeds 3.0%, the indicator is considered to be positive. When the ratio declines to 0.7% or less, the reading is negative.

It can be argued that stock options have diminished the reliability of this technical indicator and that the numbers are small, rendering the ratio irrelevant and not worthy of the time required to compile it. Still, odd-lot activity does seem to offer consistency.

"MEMBER" SHORT-SALE RATIO

Although two weeks old, the weekly NYSE round-lot statistics that appear in *Barron's* are a useful technical indicator. In addition to total shares purchased, sold, and sold short, this weekly report also shows the number of shares purchased, sold, and sold short for member accounts (a descriptive term that is no longer used).

The specialists, floor traders, and "off-the-floor" traders involved in trading for their own accounts are among the most astute people on Wall Street.

When trading firms' short selling is high relative to total short sales, the indicator is bearish. Conversely, when these trader shorts are proportionately less, the indicator is bullish. The ratio is calculated weekly by dividing all shares sold short for member accounts by total short sales for the same period. The indicator is negative when member short selling is 82% or more of the total and is positive when the ratio is 68% or less.

Technical analysts also use the Specialists' Short-Sale Ratio, which is calculated in almost the same manner. However, this indicator may be less reliable than the overall member ratio because specialists are sometimes forced to go short. Traditionally, when specialists' short sales reach or exceed 60% of total short sales, the ratio is bearish; when the level drops to 40% or less, it is bullish. Still, the principal argument against the use of this indicator is, as with the Member Ratio, the lag time of the data reports.

THE WST RATIO

By far, the most reliable and effective technical indicators are found among stock option statistics. Options players are typically traders, they are highly receptive to short-term stories, they are highly emotional, and, most important, they are wrong more often than they are right.

Put and call options, which are explained in detail in the next chapter, are contracts that provide investors with an opportunity to buy or sell a stock or an index at a specific *price* and at a specific *time* in the future. A "call" contract is purchased when the stock is expected to rise. A "put" is bought when the stock is expected to decline.

In 1996, the Wall Street Trader, a simple, inexpensive two-screen program, was first published by BullsOrBears.com. Thus, the WST Ratio was so-named.

The WST Ratio is a sophisticated measure of index option activity. This indicator can be computed using Chicago Board Options Exchange (CBOE) intraday data, although the official daily WST Ratio figures are published only once—at the end of each trading session. When the ratio is below 38.0, put buyers far outnumber call buyers, and the reading is *bullish*. When the ratio is above 62.0, the call buyers dominate, and the reading is considered *bearish*.

The WST Ratio is a short-term indicator for predicting market swings of typically not more than one to three days. The twenty-day moving average of the ratio offers good predictive value for the intermediate term (a few weeks or more).

The twenty-day moving average is bearish in the 50s and is bullish in the 30s.

A reading of higher than 55 is very bearish, and one in the low 30s is very bullish. This indicator often coincides with important market reversals. See the chart on the next page.

THE CBOE VOLATILITY INDEX (VIX)

One of the most widely watched numbers today is the CBOE "VIX" (the Volatility Index), which is computed throughout the session and published by the CBOE at the close. The VIX measures the level of implied volatility of the U.S. equity market using real-time S&P 100 (OEX) index option bid and ask quotes.

By itself, the VIX has limited value as a technical indicator, but it does show in broad terms the state of the market's emotion. The VIX will rise sharply to a peak when the market is in great despair, and it normally displays a low volatility when prices are near or at their highs.

For years, a "normal range" for the VIX was considered to be 20 to 25. Then it spiked into the 40s near the lows of the 2002 bear market. The lower end of the 10 to 25 range became the "norm" in 2004, 2005, and 2006. Then readings began to rise in late 2007 and displayed historically high readings of 80 or more on

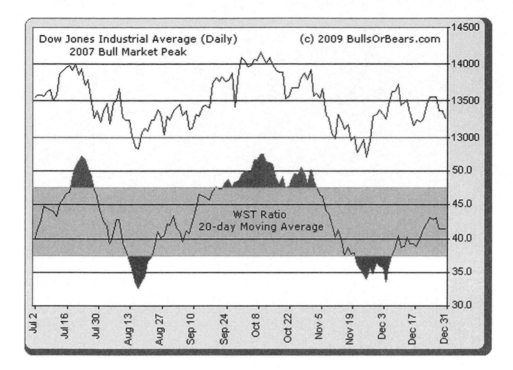

Dow Jones Industrial Average (Daily) (c) 2009 BullsOrBears.com
2007 Bull Market Peak

WST Ratio
20-day Moving Average

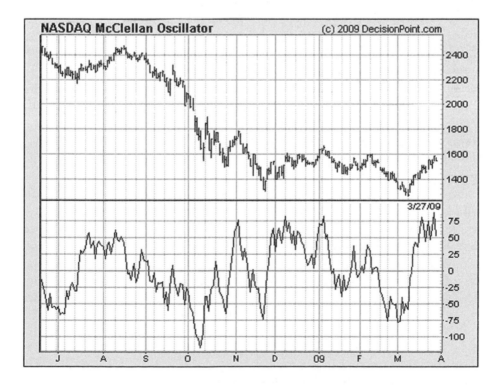

NASDAQ McClellan Oscillator (c) 2009 DecisionPoint.com

3/27/09

five or six different days in October and November of 2008. Clearly, this was one of the most volatile periods for the stock market since 1929, and the VIX displayed it dramatically.

There is another similar volatility index for the Nasdaq (the VXN, pronounced "vixen"), and it moves in a manner identical to the more widely followed VIX.

MARKET BREADTH

One widely followed technical indicator is called the Arms Index. Named for its creator, technician Richard Arms, the Arms Index measures the current condition of the market by relating the ratio of NYSE daily advancing and declining issues to the ratio of the volume of shares rising and falling on the NYSE. As a general rule, an Arms reading of less than 1.00 suggests buying demand, and a reading above 1.00 indicates selling pressure. Another very useful tool is a ten-day moving average of this index. Still another useful tool is the McClellan oscillator.

THE McCLELLAN OSCILLATOR

Guy Ortmann, one of the most accurate technical analysts on Wall Street today, has found great success using the McClellan Overbought/Oversold Oscillator to help determine the level of risk in the overall equity markets. Developed by Sherman and Marion McClellan in 1969, it evaluates the rate at which money is entering or leaving the markets and, as a result, reflects short-term "overbought" and "oversold" conditions. Calculations are made for both the NYSE and Nasdaq markets.

The daily calculation for each exchange is computed by subtracting the number of declining issues from the number of advancing issues and dividing the result by the total number of advances and declines. The thirty-nine-day EMA (exponential moving average) of the daily calculation is then subtracted from the nineteen-day EMA.

Readings greater than +75 are associated with an overbought market (i.e., a relatively large amount of stock has been purchased in a short time frame), while readings of –75 or lower suggest an oversold condition (a large amount of selling within a short period of time). The more intense the readings become, the greater or lesser the degree of market risk implied. Very high readings tend to coincide with short-term market tops, while very deep readings are typically found at short-term market bottoms. There have been periods when the McClellan has produced extreme readings of plus or minus 200. See page 281.

Essentially, the McClellan oscillator is another breadth tool that reflects the basic law of supply and demand in the equity markets. In the case of an uptrending McClellan reading, more and more money is being funneled into the markets as an increasing number of shares are bought. This results in an increasing amount of the potential supply of stock that could be sold at some point in the future. Conversely, as the oscillator declines and moves deeper into an oversold condition, the supply of stock for sale is reduced. As the theory goes, with less stock available for sale, as money flows back into the markets, stock prices could turn and once again trend up.

Other Technical Observations The use of indicators in technical analysis is limited only by one's imagination. These are several other ideas that technicians use:

- Customers' margin debt on the New York Stock Exchange. A rising amount of margin debt is considered positive; a declining amount of margin debt is negative.

- Studies based on the inverse relationship between commercial paper rates and stock prices.
- The total market value of NYSE stocks as a percentage of the nation's gross national product. In the past, a ratio below 40% has been positive, and one above 70% has been negative.
- An analysis of personal buying and selling activity by company executives. These figures are reported to the SEC and are especially worth noting when three or more officers sell within a month of each other without any "insider" buying. The same rule applies to buying, but it is somewhat less reliable. Stock options are often a factor.
- The market value of $1 of dividends (the inverse of stock yields). Using the Dow Jones Industrial Average as a benchmark, the market has been fully valued at or above 30 times each dollar of dividends and at attractive levels at or below 15.
- The cash holdings of mutual funds as a percentage of total fund assets. A 10% level or higher is thought to be positive, while a level of under 6% is deemed unfavorable.

The statistical sources for these and most other technical indicators are plen-

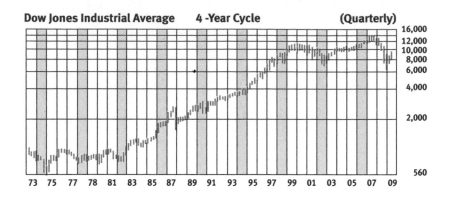

Dow Jones Industrial Average   4-Year Cycle   (Quarterly)

16,000
12,000
10,000
8,000
6,000
4,000
2,000
560

73 75 77 78 81 83 85 87 89 91 93 95 97 99 01 03 05 07 09

tiful. There are numerous online sources, and most local libraries offer a variety of publications with business and economic data. Once all past figures have been collected, keeping the indicators current is an easy task.

Many market analysts are convinced that there are other, unexplained forces that influence stock prices. For example, over the years, there have been distinct seasonal trends. Traditionally, the best months for rising prices have been January, July, November, and December. The worst months have been February, May, June, and October. This explains why buyers in May and June hope to see a "summer rally" and why October buyers look for the so-called year-end rally.

Short-term traders with years of experience are aware that, on balance, Mondays have been "down" days, while Fridays have been "up" days. Also, when the market declines on Friday, there seems to be a notable tendency for prices to decline further on Monday. Perhaps the "weekend warriors," as they are called, become fearful and review their charts over these two days.

Are there stock market cycles? Some technical analysts think so. In fact, the first two of the following points were mentioned in the inaugural edition of *Understanding Wall Street* more than thirty years ago, and they are still worth noting today.

- Every "5 year" since 1905 has been a year of rising stock prices (1915, 1925, 1935, 1945, 1955, 1965, 1975, 1985, 1995, and 2005).
- Historically, the lowest price of every fourth year since 1930 has been followed by notably higher prices the following year (i.e., 1934, 1938, 1942, 1946, 1950, 1954, 1958, 1962, 1966, 1970, 1974, 1978, 1982, 1986, 1990, 1994, 1998, 2002, and 2006).

It should be noted that prices can drop below these low points at some future time. Consider, for example, the lows of 1970 vs. 1966 or 1974 vs. 1970—and, of course, the year 2006, when the prices of many stocks were much lower in later years. Still, each four-year cycle represented a decent buying opportunity for traders and investors alike.

- Finally, there is a very distinct seventy-one-year pattern of highs and/or lows beginning with the 1903–1974 correlation. Other dates worth noting: 1911–1982, 1916–1987, 1919–1990, and 1929–2000 highs, with both cycles ending thirty-four months later.

"Don't fight the tape."

Market observers are forever arguing whether technical analysis is more of an "art" than it is a "science" (and some might insist that it is no more than "voodoo"). The answer lies in the eye of the beholder.

If these three cycle patterns are to be taken seriously, the period 2010–2015 should be a very exciting time for many investors.

Looking into the future, market psychology may never be understood, much less predicted, but a good technical analyst is one step closer to channeling it.

14 | Stock Options and Other Derivatives

Introduction

When the term "derivative" is used, most investors immediately think of stock options, a subject that is explained later in this chapter. Yes, stock options are derivatives that many investors use often, but they are only one of several financial instruments whose value is determined in part from the value and characteristics of another asset (securities, commodities, real estate, mortgages, and so on). Derivatives can also be based on an index (of interest rates, exchange rates, the stock market, or something else).

The growth of derivatives since the late 1990s has been nothing short of amazing.

This chapter will discuss what continues to be the most arcane (and maybe, for some observers, alarming) segment of Wall Street—especially considering the economic turmoil in recent years.

Today, exchange-traded options on equities are only a small but very useful portion of this colossal world within the overall investment arena.

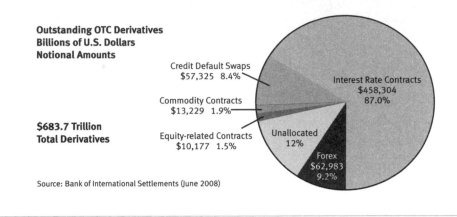

Source: Bank of International Settlements (June 2008)

Probabilities It is often said that horse racing is "the poor man's stock market." The fact that many owners of racehorses are among the richest people in the world is another story for another day.

However, when you visit the racetrack and horse 4 shows 3-to-1 odds on the tote board, this means that the public estimates the probability of 4 winning the race to be 25%. On the other hand, if horse 7 is posted at 15-to-1, this horse is being given a much smaller chance of winning—only about 6%. There is a simple mathematical formula to calculate these figures.

If you buy hurricane insurance to cover the cost of rebuilding your house, it is quite likely that your insurance policy will be more expensive in Florida than in North Dakota. Similarly, home insurance against tornado damage will probably be more expensive in Kansas than it would be in, say, Maine. Insurance companies have very precise statistical tables to determine their risks and the probabilities of these occurrences.

Most derivatives are born out of the need for some investors to avoid risk. And, like insurance, they are driven by probabilities.

What is the probability that this event will occur? Could this currency rise while another one falls? What is the chance that

this company will go bankrupt or not meet its obligations? Or, as we witnessed in an earlier chapter, what is the probability that this mortgage will go into default?

The overall derivatives market is enormous—so large, in fact, that it towers above the combined total output of all the countries in the world. However, it is important to know that derivatives involve a "notional" amount. If we add up the value of every house that is insured, this would be the total notional value. So, to be fair, based on probability tables, the notional total is not necessarily a realistic measure of the aggregate risk.

The graphic shown here presents the derivative arena worldwide. Among the segments illustrated, credit default swaps have been the fastest-growing and most dynamic. As explained shortly, this could represent an area of greater risk when the economic environment is especially difficult.

Interest-Rate Swaps By far, the largest segment of the worldwide derivatives market is "interest-rate contracts." Again, for perspective, remember that the gross domestic product (GDP) of the United States is "only" about $15 trillion.

While interest-rate swaps have many applications, one of the most common is that of mitigating the exposure to inter-

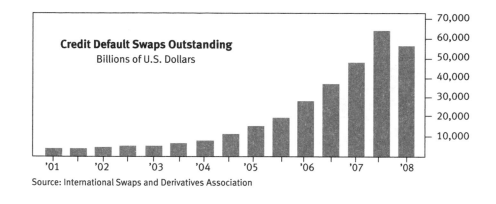

Credit Default Swaps Outstanding
Billions of U.S. Dollars

Source: International Swaps and Derivatives Association

est-rate fluctuations. When a company is vulnerable to interest-rate fluctuations, these changes could be very harmful financially under certain conditions. By swapping interest rates, and thus going from a floating obligation to a fixed obligation, or vice versa, a company can alter its exposure to this business risk.

Interest-rate risk originates from rates that fluctuate. The party who pays the floating rate benefits when rates fall. This is analogous to owning an adjustable-rate mortgage (versus a fixed-rate mortgage) when interest rates are declining.

Foreign Exchange Forex is an important segment of the derivatives market, especially for central banks, large banks, corporations, currency speculators, governments, hedge funds, and others.

The Forex market is both large and liquid, with various parties buying one currency in place of another. An important activity is hedging, and a particularly essential factor is the LIBOR (London Interbank Offered Rate). Roughly comparable to the target federal funds rate in the United States, the LIBOR rate is a reference for a large number of financial instruments (e.g., currencies, interest-rate swaps, inflation swaps, variable-rate mortgages, and so on).

In 2008, *Euromoney* magazine in London conducted its annual "FX Poll," which placed Deutsche Bank in Germany, UBS AG in Switzerland, and various large banks in the United States and Great Britain among the dominant currency traders that year.

Credit Default Swaps CDSs, as they are often called, are credit-risk derivatives traded between two counterparties. The buyer makes a series of regular payments to the seller, similar in some respects to an insurance policy. In exchange, the seller will pay a compensating amount if a certain credit instrument (typically a bond or a loan) goes into default.

Unlike the buyer of an insurance policy, however, the buyer of a CDS does not necessarily own the property. If the buyer owns the credit instrument, then the credit default swap can be viewed as a "hedge" against failure.

The "spread" (or price) of a CDS is the annual amount the buyer pays over the life of the contract (ending sooner if the credit instrument goes into default). The spread is usually expressed in terms of a percentage of the notional amount. For example, if the spread is, say, 40 basis points (0.4%), a buyer purchasing $10 million of protection will be paying

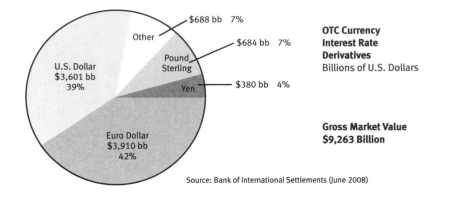

$688 bb 7%

Other

$684 bb 7%

Pound
Sterling

U.S. Dollar
$3,601 bb
39%

Yen

$380 bb 4%

Euro Dollar
$3,910 bb
42%

**OTC Currency
Interest Rate
Derivatives**
Billions of U.S. Dollars

**Gross Market Value
$9,263 Billion**

Source: Bank of International Settlements (June 2008)

$40,000 annually to the seller. Needless to say, when the risk of default is great, the spread is high, and vice versa. The spread is inverse to creditworthiness.

Like most derivative instruments, the credit default swap can be used for speculation, hedging, or arbitrage.

Since the invention of credit default swaps in 1997, the popularity of these derivatives has been explosive. See the previous chart. Credit default swaps have been used by MBS and CDO investors to insure against credit risk. It is also interesting to note that the first decline in the number of outstanding contracts occurred in early 2008.

If a large default or failure occurs, as in the cases of Washington Mutual and Lehman Brothers in 2008, auctions (organized by the International Swaps and Derivatives Association) can be used to settle very large volumes of contracts.

Referring to the earlier discussion of the housing bubble and the fate of Fannie Mae and Lehman Brothers, the final value of Fannie's credit obligations remained high, whereas Lehman had little value at the end.

Before commencing the discussion of equity-related contracts in the next section, a distinction should be made between "options" and "futures." Both are contracts that rise or fall in value based on price changes for the underlying asset. When stock options are explained later, the differences between the two will become clearer.

An options contract grants the buyer the *right*, but not the *obligation*, to establish a position granted by the seller of the option. A futures contract gives the holder the *obligation* to make or take delivery under the terms of the contract. Both, of course, are derivatives.

Introducing Stock Options On April 26, 1973, options, as we know them today, began trading on the Chicago Board Options Exchange (CBOE).

Up to that time, options had been trading quietly in the over-the-counter market for at least one hundred years. Some people hailed them as the new way to make quick profits in any type of market, while many others dismissed them abruptly as just another form of outright gambling. However, options should be recognized for what they are: an additional investment tool and a means of managing risk for knowledgeable investors and seasoned speculators.

The growth of the options market has been notable. The average daily contract volume on the CBOE was close to 10,000

CBOE Total Annual Volume (000)

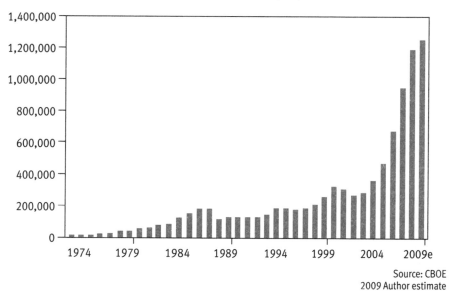

Source: CBOE
2009 Author estimate

Options Industry Annual Volume (000)

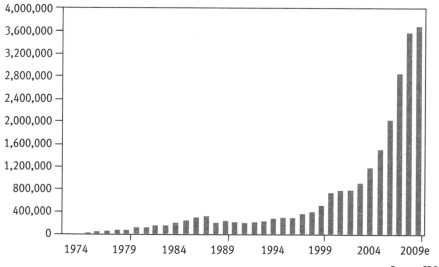

Source: CBOE
2009 Author estimate

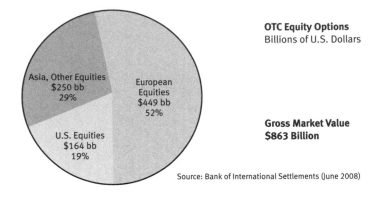

OTC Equity Options
Billions of U.S. Dollars

European Equities $449 bb 52%

Asia, Other Equities $250 bb 29%

U.S. Equities $164 bb 19%

**Gross Market Value
$863 Billion**

Source: Bank of International Settlements (June 2008)

contracts in 1973. Today, the CBOE trades about 1 billion contracts annually—roughly one-third of the industry annual total of 2.8 billion. The CBOE and the International Securities Exchange (ISE), combined, represent more than 60% of the total. Also, today, most CBOE (and all ISE) trading activity is performed electronically, as opposed to the "open-outcry" method.

The mechanics of put and call options, suggestions for valuing them, and the methods for using them in a risk-manageable manner are among the highlights of this chapter segment.

Background for Options A stock option is a contract that gives the owner the right to buy or sell a specific number of shares (usually 100) of a given stock at a fixed price within a definite time period. The stock involved is referred to as the "underlying security," the fixed price is called the "striking price" or "strike price," and the date the contract expires is called the "expiration date." In return for the privileges granted by the option, the buyer pays a "premium," another name for the option's "price." It is not a down payment. It must be paid in full in cash. The premium is the only variable in any option contract; all the other items are fixed.

And, like the price of a common stock, the premium is an equilibrium price that reflects the judgments of all buyers and sellers in the market at any given time.

An option conveying the right to buy stock from the option's seller (the "writer") is known as a "call" because it allows the buyer to call stock away from the writer. An option conveying the right to sell stock to the writer is termed a "put" because it allows the buyer to put stock to the writer. Either action by the buyer is known as "exercising" the option. Once an option has been written, the writer must abide by its stated terms. However, the writer can extinguish this responsibility, as explained later.

Stock options are currently traded on most of the national exchanges, including the Chicago Board Options Exchange and the International Securities Exchange. All are closely regulated by the SEC.

The next page shows how option information is displayed in a newspaper—if any newspaper still provides it. Only the most active options are likely to appear, although *Barron's*, a weekly financial paper, continues to offer a fairly complete listing. However, today, most of this information is found online—on the CBOE Web site, for example—but in much the same format. This illustration

LISTED OPTIONS QUOTATIONS

Tuesday, January 28

Composite volume and close for actively traded equity and LEAPS, or call or long-term options, with results for the corresponding put or call contract. Volume figures are unofficial. Open interest is total outstanding for all exchanges and reflects previous trading day. Close when possible is shown for the underlying stock or primary market. XC-Composite. p-Put. o-Strike price adjusted for split.

NOTICE TO READERS

The number of listed options quotations presented in the Journal has been pared to the top 100 most-active issues, from the top 350 issues. This recognizes the prevalence of online availability of these data. For full market coverage, go to the Online Journal at WSJ.com.

OPTION/STRIKE		EXP	-CALL- VOL	LAST	-PUT- VOL	LAST
AllgEngy	10	Jul	2501	1.30	2500	2.20
Altria	12.50	Feb	2074	0.20	40	4.40
38.38	40	Feb	1685	0.65	3142	2.20
Amazon	22.50	Feb	1868	0.80	2171	1.70
A E P	25	May	2024	1.85	10	3.10
Amgen	55	Feb	2690	0.60	110	3.90
51.59	55	Apr	1847	2	52	5.10
BP PLC	35	Jul	5	3.50	2000	3
36.49	40	Jul	2076	1.55	...	...
BankNY	25	Apr	1002	2.20	2206	1.90
BostSc	45	Feb	4511	0.35	6	4.20
Celgene	22.50	Mar	1735	1.10	460	2.10
CienaCp	7.50	Mar	2024	0.45	15	1.75
Cisco	12.50	Feb	401	2.05	2997	0.25
14.22	15	Feb	7535	0.50	490	1.25
14.22	15	Mar	5145	0.80	420	1.55
14.22	15	Apr	5376	1.05	28	1.80
14.22	15	Jul	1871	1.75	1050	2.50
Citigrp	35	Feb	2659	1.75	4745	1.40
CocaCola	40	May	91	3.50	7771	2.40

OPTION/STRIKE		EXP	-CALL- VOL	LAST	-PUT- VOL	LAST
32.66	35	Mar	8951	0.75	12	3.10
32.66	35	Jul	1709	1.70	...	...
Gen El	25	Feb	2209	0.35	273	2.10
23.15	25	Jun	2174	1.35	24	3.30
HomeDp	22.50	Feb	1846	0.25	243	2.20
IMS Hlth	25	Feb	12860	0.05	7278	9.10
Intel	17.50	Feb	12259	0.35	230	1.70
16.01	17.50	Apr	2329	0.95	287	2.35
16.01	20	Jul	1740	0.85	11	4.80
I B M	75	Feb	448	6.50	2026	1.50
80.11	80	Feb	3667	3.20	2930	3.20
80.11	85	Feb	2120	1.15	245	6
80.11	85	Mar	1782	2.40	42	7.20
In Pap	35	Mar	1992	2.05	...	...
JPMorgCh	25	Feb	6731	0.55	387	2.10
23.51	25	Mar	4360	1.10	6315	2.50
23.51	30	Mar	3058	0.20	5	6.20
JackinBox	15	Mar	...	...	1920	0.40
JnprNtw	10	Feb	2136	0.30	305	1.05
KLA Tnc	35	Feb	684	2.05	2568	2.25
			983	2.40	2893	2.70
			3648	1.60	1926	2.85
			4067	3.50	355	4.60
			3113	0.70	34	11.60
			2221	0.30	301	16.20
			6	4.10	12319	0.35
			3337	2.20	19248	0.40
			7931	1.50	8982	0.70
			35762	0.95	7362	1.15
			8448	1.55	1859	1.60
			39864	0.55	6359	1.70
			26519	0.30	2749	2.45
			3036	0.65	250	2.70
			6636	0.30	7	4.60
			...	...	2520	0.90
			3	3.60	2650	4.80
			...	...	5305	0.50
			3574	2.05	2327	2.05
			1760	7.60	1760	3
			82	3	2183	1.05
			113	4.60	6394	2.55

OPTION/STRIKE		EXP	-CALL- VOL	LAST	-PUT- VOL	LAST
37.09	40	Mar	2116	1.35	43	4.40
Sanmina	5	Apr	5500	0.35	...	...
Sears	25	Feb	507	2	7513	1.35
SiebelSys	7.50	Feb	253	1.40	3759	0.20
Starbcks	25	Apr	4036	0.55	35	2.60
Texasinst	17.50	Feb	3982	0.30	263	1.60
16.00	17.50	Apr	3972	1.05	20	2.70
Tycolntl	17.50	Feb	1871	0.30	622	1.60
UPS B	60	Feb	1791	2	987	1
VeritasSf	15	Feb	10	3.70	2526	0.30
18.72	17.50	Feb	1021	2.10	2768	0.90
18.72	20	Feb	11964	0.85	4078	2.05
VerizonCm	35	Feb	239	2.30	2518	1.25
36.05	35	Jul	11	4	3815	3.50
ViacmB	35	Feb	5286	4.10	406	1.20
37.85	37.50	Feb	1940	2.40	1488	1.95
Yahoo	20	Feb	1962	0.50	157	1.90
18.63	20	Apr	3209	1.45	20	3

Volume & Open Interest Summaries

AMERICAN

Call Vol:	355,652	Open Int:	28,738,079
Put Vol:	181,456	Open Int:	21,476,934

CHICAGO BOARD

Call Vol:	531,599	Open Int:	41,862,861
Put Vol:	330,219	Open Int:	31,649,974

INTL SECURITIES

Call Vol:	373,393	Open Int:	35,543,282
Put Vol:	301,672	Open Int:	26,696,411

PHILADELPHIA

Call Vol:	161,115	Open Int:	42,765,925
Put Vol:	93,472	Open Int:	24,337,804

PACIFIC

Call Vol:	147,276	Open Int:	37,427,770
Put Vol:	119,947	Open Int:	27,728,623

TOTAL

Call Vol:	1,569,035
Put Vol:	1,026,766

OPTION/STRIKE		EXP	-CALL- VOL	LAST	-PUT- VOL	LAST
AllgEngy	10	Jul	2501	1.30	2500	2.20
Altria	12.50	Feb	2074	0.20	40	4.40
38.38	40	Feb	1685	0.65	3142	2.20
Amazon	22.50	Feb	1868	0.80	2171	1.70
A E P	25	May	2024	1.85	10	3.10
Amgen	55	Feb	2690	0.60	110	3.90
51.59	55	Apr	1847	2	52	5.10
BP PLC	35	Jul	5	3.50	2000	3
36.49	40	Jul	2076	1.55	...	...
BankNY	25	Apr	1002	2.20	2206	1.90
BostSc	45	Feb	4511	0.35	6	4.20
Celgene	22.50	Mar	1735	1.10	460	2.10
CienaCp	7.50	Mar	2024	0.45	15	1.75
Cisco	12.50	Feb	401	2.05	2997	0.25
14.22	15	Feb	7535	0.50	490	1.25
14.22	15	Mar	5145	0.80	420	1.55
14.22	15	Apr	5376	1.05	28	1.80
14.22	15	Jul	1871	1.75	1050	2.50
Citigrp	35	Feb	2659	1.75	4745	1.40
CocaCola	40	May	91	3.50	7771	2.40

shows price information from a previous trading session for each class of options, and also the closing prices of the underlying stocks.

A "class" is made up of all options, both puts and calls, covering the same underlying security. Thus, the options for Cisco and for Citigroup, as they appear in the table, each constitute a class.

Several expiration dates can be given for each strike price. The tables here show the call and put options for the stock of Cisco Systems, trading on the Nasdaq system and currently priced at $14.22. For most options, such as Cisco's, expiration dates are spaced over the next three consecutive months—in this example, February, March, and April. In this case, the example also shows figures for July. Expiration dates are usually spaced at three-month intervals to as far out as nine months, the most distant expiration date now available.

The February "series" will expire in the third week of February, and the tables will always be amended accordingly. Thus, when the Cisco February series ends, the tables will begin showing March, April, and May expiration dates. Depending upon the exchange and, of course, the time of year, the option tables also show other consecutive series combinations. It is pos-

sible for options to be available and not be listed in a newspaper. It depends on the level of activity and the degree of interest.

New options are introduced when the price of the underlying security advances or declines. This will usually occur at 2½-point intervals for stocks trading below $25 a share, 5-point intervals for stocks trading between $25 and $200 a share, and 10- or 20-point intervals for stocks trading above $200. For instance, if Cisco's common stock, last traded on the NYSE at $14.22, as indicated to the left, were suddenly to advance to about $19, new options would probably be offered with a strike price of $22.50 and the same expiration dates. (The 20s already exist, but they are not being shown in the table).

Sometimes, no options are traded at an existing strike price for a given expiration date, and a "—" notation or "0" will appear in the volume column. But again, new options are introduced only when there is a new expiration date, or when the stock price moves far enough to warrant a new strike price.

Each data source, using its own method, summarizes the previous trading day's statistics for the options in each series. In this case, for example, the interested options investor learns that the trades in the Citigroup February call op-

tions with a 35 strike price took place at a premium of $1.75 per share of the underlying stock. Since each option contract covers 100 shares of the underlying stock, to compute the actual dollar cost of a single option of any series, the premium listed in the table must be multiplied by 100. In this case, the premium would be $175.00 for one Citigroup February 35 call. This cost does not include commissions and taxes.

Obviously, these figures would have the same meaning in every instance if puts were being discussed rather than calls. Also, published newspaper prices and volumes might differ slightly from online figures, depending on the exact time the data were collected by the news agency at the close of the trading session.

Today's market contrasts sharply with the early days of options trading. In the 1920s, for example, most options activity took place in a small restaurant on New Street in New York's financial district. Each day, a small cadre of options traders turned the restaurant into their own office, dining room, and afterhours club. They arrived early and set up shop near the public telephone booths. Their pockets jingled with change for what was then a nickel telephone call. Some of the more prosperous brokers employed messengers who crisscrossed the Wall Street area trying to bring buyers and sellers together.

However, matching a buyer and a writer was usually difficult and often impossible. It was a process that invariably required several telephone calls and exasperating negotiation to formulate terms that were agreeable to both the buyer and the writer. If an options investor decided the contract was no longer useful, it was even more difficult to sell it to someone else in a secondary market. The CBOE redefined options trading when it standardized the terms of an option contract and created the first regulated exchange. Prior to that time, options had not been exchange-traded.

The original trading floor of the CBOE was housed in a small room adjacent to the Chicago Board of Trade's main trading floor and later moved upstairs at the CBOT when that exchange "doubledecked" its mainly grain futures–focused trading floor. The CBOE later built its own ten-story building across the street from the CBOT.

There are currently eight oval trading posts on the floor of the CBOE. Posts 7 and 8 are devoted only to OEX and SPX trading. The exchange uses a "hybrid" system of both electronic and open-outcry trading. Subsecond pricing information

Option certificates are not widely used but they are available.

on each option traded at the post appears on display units. These data include the last premium trade, the current bid and ask quotation, and the underlying trading information for each stock, index, or ETF.

When a trade is completed by the floor traders, the results are quickly recorded, and the new trading information appears on the screens above almost instantly. The data are simultaneously available electronically to brokerage firms and customers throughout the world.

Today, the majority of CBOE trades for options on the related stocks, indexes, and ETFs are completed electronically, although larger, more complex orders are often transacted using the open-outcry method. By contrast, the International Securities Exchange (ISE) is 100% electronic.

The Options Clearing Corporation serves as a giant bookkeeping operation, recording the actions of all buyers and sellers from the seven options exchanges.

After the orders are matched on the trading floor, the Options Clearing Corporation acts as the buyer to every seller and the seller to every buyer. It severs the relationship between the original writer and the original buyer. This combination of the Options Clearing Corporation and the active secondary market makes it possible for an option owner to sell at any time and for an option writer to terminate the responsibility to deliver or accept stock at any time. The owner of an option instructs a broker to sell it in much the same way that a common stock would be sold. This action is called a "closing sale transaction." The writer terminates the responsibility to deliver or accept stock through a "closing purchase transaction," also called "buying in."

In this transaction, the writer buys an option that is identical in all respects to the option originally written, except for the premium. The outstanding option is then offset at the Options Clearing Corporation with the option purchased in the closing purchase transaction. In each case, the profit or loss of either the writer or the buyer is determined by the difference between the original premium paid or received and the premium paid or received in the closing transaction. If one investor liquidates a position as writer or buyer, it has no effect on the other investor. That is, if a call writer liquidates a position in a closing transaction, the owner of the call may still exercise it at any time.

Today, option trading is linked among the seven exchanges by an electronic network to ensure the SEC's "best execution" rules.

	Stock			Call Option		
April	Bought 100 shares @ $40	$ 4,000		Bought	1 July 40 Call @ $4	$ 400
June	Sold 100 shares @ $46	4,600		Sold	1 July 40 Call @ $7	700
	Trading Profit	$ 600		Trading Profit		$ 300
	Less approximate commissions	135		Less approximate commissions		50
	PROFIT	$ 465		PROFIT		$ 250
	Net Return on Original Investment Before Taxes	11.6%		Net Return on Original Investment Before Taxes		62.5%

Buying Options For buyers, options offer leverage with a predetermined risk. The option's cost is its premium, and this premium is usually only a small fraction of the underlying stock's market price. Thus, the buyer participates in any price change in the stock without having to buy the stock itself, which would require a substantially greater investment. Furthermore, the buyer knows that the maximum possible loss is the total amount of the premium.

In practice, most option buyers expect to profit from an increase in the premium. They are not interested in exercising the option to acquire the stock itself, but are attracted by capital gains leverage and the limited capital exposure.

Here is a simplified explanation of how an option buyer can make or lose money on an option trade.

After studying the fundamental and technical characteristics of the ABC Company, a speculator concludes in late April that the company's common stock price will increase substantially in the next three months. The stock is selling for $40 a share.

The trader could either buy the stock outright or buy a call on the stock. Since purchasing the stock would require an immediate outlay of $4,000 (excluding commissions) for 100 shares, the trader decides to take advantage of the inherent leverage of options and purchases a July ABC 40 call for a premium of 4.00 ($400 for 100 shares). The July expiration date was selected because, as the trader reasoned, the underlying stock would advance soon.

By late June, the stock price has increased 15% to $46, while the option has advanced to 7.00, a gain of 75%. At this point, the trader might want to sell the option in the secondary market to capture the 3-point increase in the premium. The comparison given earlier shows how one can profit either by owning the stock directly or by buying a call. The degree of risk, however, is greatly different between the two.

The absolute dollar profit from the call option was less than that from the stock; however, compared to the capital invested, the call option produced a greater profit at a much greater risk.

If the investor had misjudged the stock's potential and it had declined rather than advanced, the maximum loss would be the entire initial premium of $400. Even though the stock could drop by more than the premium amount, the call buyer's loss is still limited to $400. Although the buyer might be able to reduce this loss by selling the call in the secondary market for whatever value remained, any loss to the call owner is an immediate out-ofpocket cash loss. On the other hand, the owner of stock has only a "paper loss" and can hold the shares for future recovery.

If the trader in this example expected the stock's price to drop sharply in the same short time period, the premium for a July ABC 40 put would have increased in value as the underlying stock declined. Puts are calls turned upside down. And, like calls, puts offer leverage and limited loss of capital, but in reverse. Puts are appropriate in a declining market as opposed to the traditional method of profiting from falling stock prices by selling stock short. Stated differently, a put option is to a short sale as a call option is to buying the stock "long."

Under current margin requirements of 50%, selling short 100 shares of ABC at $40 in late April would have required a margin deposit of at least $2,000. If, two months later, the stock had dropped 15% to $34 as expected, the trader would have a profit of $600, or 30%.

The purchase of an ABC July 40 put in late April at 4 would have produced a 75% profit in the same period if the premium had advanced to 7 as the stock declined (excluding commissions and taxes).

The put limited the buyer's potential loss to the amount of the premium, whereas the short seller's risk was theoretically unlimited. Moreover, puts give the option trader greater psychological staying power. For example, if the stock had advanced before beginning the anticipated decline, the short seller might have been tempted to cover prematurely. On the other hand, the put buyer, realizing that the total possible loss was limited to $400, could have endured the advance more easily.

It should be noted, however, that if the stock remained steady and did not decline to $34 until August, the short seller would still have made a 30% profit, whereas the put would have expired worthless.

Speculators beware! When you buy a call or put option, *three* things can happen during the life of the option—and *two* of them are *bad*!

Writing Options Option sellers are called "writers" in a carryover from the early days of over-the-counter trading, when the details of each contract had to be carefully written out by hand. Today, option writing is standardized, but the term remains.

An option writer's primary purpose is to earn additional income through the premiums received from option buyers.

This income can be a plus to the overall return on a portfolio. Premium income can also provide a "cushion" against an adverse move in the underlying stock—but only to the extent of the premium.

Assume that an investor who owns CDE Company stock at a cost of $50 writes a CDE 50 call and receives a premium of $5.00. If the stock does not move and the option expires worthless, the entire 5-point premium can be considered additional income. If the stock advances, it can be called away, which means that the investor is, in effect, selling the stock for $55. The writer's maximum profit, therefore, is limited to the premium amount.

The premium also hedges the stock against a decline to $45. If the stock drops by more than the premium, the investor will suffer a loss, as before. Obviously, writing covered calls increases the total rate of return on a given portfolio only if the underlying stock neither increases nor decreases by more than the amount of the premium.

While all option purchases require a full cash payment, option writing involves more complex accounting. Most writing takes place in a margin account. The options written may be "covered" or "uncovered" (also called "naked"). For a covered call, the writer deposits with the broker the exact number of shares of the underlying stock that would need to be sold if the option is exercised. A covered call writer can choose between delivering the stock that is on deposit or delivering stock that was bought in the open market when the option was exercised. Some writers who have a low cost on the stock they already own might select the latter method to avoid paying a large capital gains tax at that time.

A naked call (a call written against cash) can be written only in a margin account. A broker requires that sufficient funds to purchase stock in the open market if the option is exercised be on hand at all times. A put is covered only when it is offset share for share by a long put having an equal or greater exercise price. The margin requirements for writing uncovered puts and calls are identical. Whenever a margin account is used, the investor should compute the transaction's ultimate rate of return based on the amount of capital deposited.

Naked call writing has much greater risk than covered call writing. If the stock either remains steady or declines, naked calls can produce large returns on the margin deposited. But if it advances, every point beyond the amount of premium initially received will be an out-of-pocket loss to the writer when the call is exercised. The naked call writer, like the investor who sells stock short, could have unlimited losses, but with greater leverage.

Some option investors who are eager to increase their premium income mix covered and naked calls in a strategy known as "variable hedging." The variable hedger writes more than one option for each 100 shares owned. For example, an investor who owns 100 shares of EFG Company at $40 writes three EFG 40 calls for a premium of $4 each, or a total premium income of $12. By definition, one call is covered and two are naked. The $12 premium could offset a substantial decline in the stock owned to $28. However, if the stock were to rise, each 1-point advance beyond $46 would increase the variable hedger's loss by $2 until the calls are finally exercised. At $46, the $12 premium offsets the $6 increased cost for each share of stock underlying each naked call.

The variable hedge, then, has two breakeven points, and the hedger will make a profit at any price between them. In this example, the two points were $28 on the downside and $46 on the upside. Each additional option written extends the downside breakeven point but lowers the upside breakeven point. More premium income is received, but the investor is also

exposed to the huge risk inherent in writing naked calls. This high risk combined with the difficulty of predicting shortterm price changes makes writing naked calls hard to justify. Even if it appears certain that the stock will collapse, writing naked calls is not the best method of exploiting the expected decline. Either shorting the stock outright or buying a put will produce greater profits from a steep price drop because the writer's maximum profit is always limited to the premium.

All writers can buy in the option at any time rather than waiting for the expiration date. For example, a covered GHI Company 50 call has been written for a $5 premium. The underlying stock, which the writer owns at $50 a share, advances to $55, and the premium advances to $7.00. If the stock appears to be headed higher, the writer could buy in the option at $7.00. This closing purchase transaction would produce a $2 loss on the option trade, but would leave a $5 unrealized gain in the stock with the potential for greater profits if it continues to advance as expected.

Put writers, like call writers, hope that the premiums they receive will mean additional income. Since put writers agree to *buy* stock rather than *sell* stock, the contracts they write are not covered by

	XYZ Calls at 40 Strike Price Stock Price	XYZ Puts at 40 Strike Price Stock Price
In-the-money	Over 40	Under 40
At-the-money	40	40
Out-of-the-money	Under 40	Over 40

stock, as they are with call writers. Although it is possible to write covered puts, as mentioned earlier, most puts are uncovered and are written against cash. Actually, if a put and a call have identical premiums, exercise prices, and expiration dates, the covered call writer and the uncovered put writer will have the same maximum dollar risk and reward after the options are written. *If the options are exercised, the premium that a put writer receives reduces the purchase cost of the stock, just as the premium from writing a covered call is part of the proceeds of the sale.*

Put writing, like call writing, also finds its greatest utility when the underlying stock neither increases nor decreases by more than the amount of the premium.

For most investors or traders who are considering options, *writing* them is preferable to *buying* them. It allows the trader to be on the most profitable side of the transaction—the side on which *time* is an *ally*, not an *adversary*.

Thus, for this reason, writing covered calls and writing naked puts (but strictly against shares that the investor intends to purchase anyway) are the two best and most consistently profitable applications of stock options. In both cases, they can add to the profitability (the return) of a portfolio.

Investors who are intrigued by the idea of writing covered calls should find the CBOE S&P 500 Buy/Write Index (BXM) of interest. Introduced in 2002, the BXM is a passive, total return index designed to outperform the S&P 500 in flat and declining markets. This is due to the premium income. Of course, the index will typically underperform the primary index in extended bull markets.

In the following illustration, notice the relative performance for the twelve-month period 9/1/07 to 9/1/08. However, to avoid confusion, indexes and option strategies will be discussed in greater detail later.

Premium Valuation At any given moment, the amount of an option's premium is a function of the following:

1. The relationship or expected relationship between the current price of the underlying stock and the option's strike price

2. The amount of time remaining before the expiration date

3. The volatility of the underlying stock

4. The dividend of the underlying stock

5. The level and direction of short-term interest rates

These factors are built into the premiums of all options, and if they change, the level of the premiums will also change.

In practice, once the underlying stock and its probable direction have been identified, there is still the problem of selecting one option out of the many available to obtain the best combination of risk and reward. To do this, the option buyer must begin by answering two questions:

1. What is the extent of the stock's expected move?

2. In what time period will the stock make its expected move?

Stated simply, option premiums in the same class are two-dimensional. There is a vertical dimension involving the stock price/strike price relationship, and there is a horizontal dimension involving time. By answering the two questions, the options investor will be better equipped to cope with these two dimensions.

THE VERTICAL DIMENSION

The relationship of the stock price to the strike price determines whether an option is "in the money," "at the money," or "out of the money," as the table given on page 303 illustrates.

A call is in the money when the stock price is *above* the strike price, at the money when the stock price and the strike price are *identical,* and out of the money when the stock price is *below* the strike price. Puts are described with the same terms, but in reverse.

An in-the-money call option is said to have "intrinsic value" in the amount that the underlying stock is above the strike price. Thus, in the previous example, with the stock selling at $44, the intrinsic value of a 40 call would be $4.00. The term "intrinsic value" is used to denote the value that can be captured immediately by exercising the option and selling the stock.

Just as "intrinsic value" is used when evaluating the premiums of in-the-money options, the term "price concession" is used for out-of-the-money options. Price concession, also called "extrinsic value," is the opposite of intrinsic value. It is the amount by which the stock is *below* the strike price. A call with a $40 strike price would have a price concession of $2 when the stock is $38. Neither intrinsic value nor price concession is fixed. Their amounts depend upon the current price of the underlying stock and thus will change as the stock's price changes. Both "intrinsic value" and "price concession" also apply to put options, but, again, in reverse.

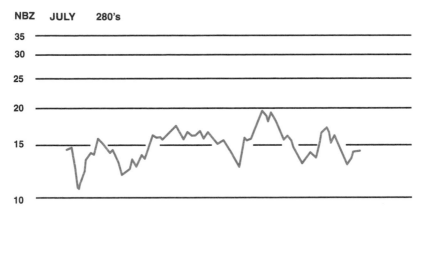

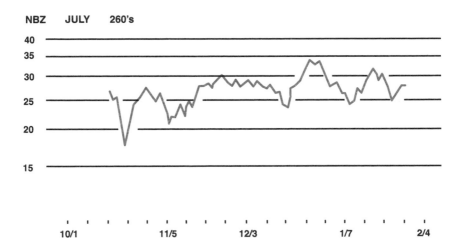

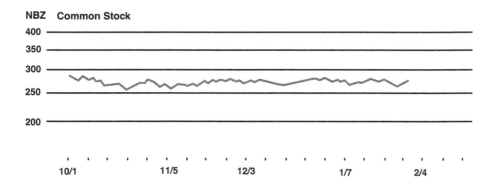

NBZ   Common Stock

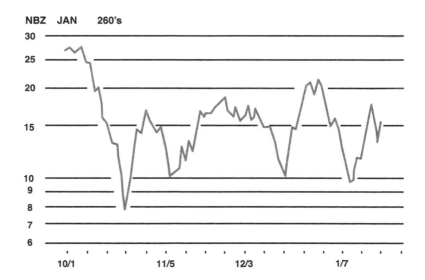

NBZ   JAN   260's

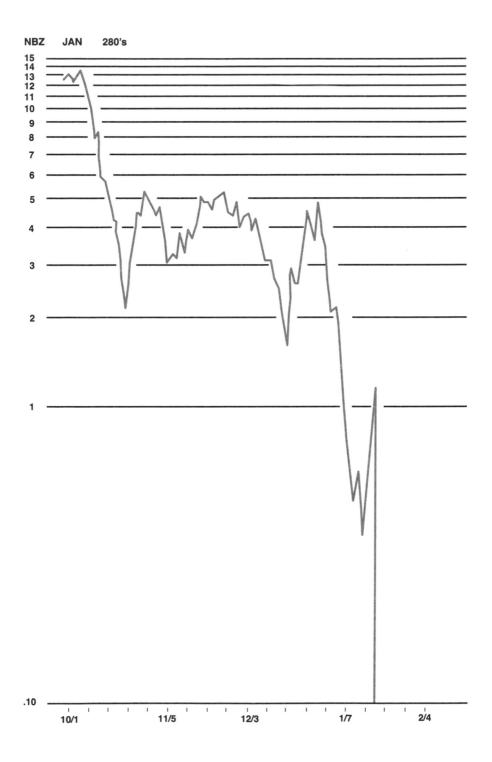

XYZ Company Call Option @ 40

	Stock Price	Price Concession	Intrinsic Value	Premium	% of Stock Price	Time Cost	% of Stock Price
	52	—	12.00	13.375	25.7%	1.375	2.6%
	50	—	10.00	11.75	23.5	1.75	3.5
	48	—	8.00	10.00	20.8	2.00	4.2
	46	—	6.00	8.125	17.7	2.125	4.6
	44	—	4.00	6.375	14.5	2.375	5.4
	42	—	2.00	4.50	10.7	2.50	6.0
Strike Price	40	—	—	3.25	8.1	3.25*	8.1
	38	2.00	—	1.75	4.6	3.75	9.9
	36	4.00	—	1.125	3.1	5.125	14.2
	34	6.00	—	0.50	1.5	6.50	19.1
	32	8.00	—	0.25	0.8	8.25	25.8
	30	10.00	—	0.125	0.4	10.125	33.8
	28	12.00	—	0.06	0.2	12.06	43.1

* The greatest amount of "real" time cost.

Unfortunately, intrinsic value and price concession do not entirely explain this vertical dimension. A trader who buys a call option for $5.00 when the stock is selling at $3 above its strike price is paying $2 above the intrinsic value of the premium. *This $2 is the cost of the time remaining in the contract.* In other words, the difference between the premium and the intrinsic value is the option's "time cost." Time becomes less important as the stock price moves higher and as the intrinsic value increases.

Conversely, when the stock price declines below the strike price, the premium is purely time cost, since the option has no intrinsic value. Although, on the surface, the premium appears low, there is a hidden time cost (the price concession).

Unlike the intrinsic value when the option is in the money, price concession is not included in the premium. Even though price concession is only a theoretical time cost and not a "real" time cost, it should not be ignored.

The table at the top of this page shows that there is less risk and less reward for the XYZ call buyer the further the stock price is above the strike price. It also shows greater risk and greater reward the further the stock price is below the strike price. As the option acquires intrinsic value, it loses leverage. The relatively larger premium reduces the option's sensitivity to further increases in the price of the underlying stock (i.e., the option's reward). At the same time, the presence of intrinsic value also reduces risk.

Similarly, as price concession increases, risk also increases because the probability of the option's ever attaining intrinsic value decreases. The reward potential also increases because a small premium investment could produce dramatic gains if the stock were to advance substantially.

The further the stock is from the strike price, either up or down, the more the stock must move to justify the option price. And the probability of a stock's moving, say, 10% in the course of a few months is much greater than the probability of its moving 30% in the same time period.

For these reasons, the buyer should choose an option that provides the best combination of a low premium and a low time cost as a percentage of the underlying stock's price. As the table suggests, the most favorable cost combination is generally found in a narrow band slightly above and slightly below the strike price.

The charts on the previous pages illustrate the first three months of daily trading of The NewBrite Lighting Company

Analyzing a security involves an
analysis of the business.

—Benjamin Graham

(NBZ) July 260s and July 280s from October through January.

Throughout this period, the July 260s were consistently in the money and the July 280s were consistently out of the money. In these early months, the percentage moves of the July 280s were greater than those of the July 260s. With both options having, or nearly having, intrinsic value, traders turned their interest to the option with the lower premium because they could participate in the stock's move for less money.

How far out of the money should an option buyer go to obtain greater reward? The answer depends on the extent of the stock's expected move. Traders do not recognize an option's potential for attaining intrinsic value until the stock has moved closer to the strike price. In the meantime, other options in its class with strike prices closer to the stock price will have outperformed it. This also explains why the volatility of a stock is a very important consideration in the valuation of option premiums.

The fate of an expiring out-of-the-money option can be seen by comparing the charts showing the expirations of the NBZ January 280s and the NBZ January 260s. The stock price was $275 when both expired in January.

THE HORIZONTAL DIMENSION

An option is a "wasting asset" because the time remaining up to the expiration date has a value that diminishes day by day. Clearly, an XYZ option with an expiration date that is only two weeks away is worth less (and should have a smaller premium) than another XYZ option with the same strike price but not expiring for six months.

It has been shown that a premium includes a time cost that varies according to the stock price/strike price relationship. This time cost also varies according to the time remaining. Hence, the horizontal dimension. For this reason, it is necessary to ask, "In what time period will the stock make its expected move?"

The crucial value of time can be seen by comparing the previous charts showing the early months of the NBZ July 260s and the last few months of the January 260s. They traded side by side briefly at the same time. Each had the same strike price and the same intrinsic value or price concession at that given moment, but the premium for the July 260s was consistently $10 or more above that for the January 260s. Understandably, the January option was also much more sensitive to the stock's price swings.

Now, using the vertical and horizontal dimension concept, the investor can compare all options in the same class.

Consider the following real-life example, although the name has been changed.

On November 10, the common stock of XYZ Corporation closed at $47.75. An interested trader who believed that the end of the stock's decline was near glanced at the option tables. The following calls were available:

	January	April	July
XYZ 45	3.63	n/a	n/a
XYZ 50	1.13	2.13	2.63
XYZ 55	0.25	0.75	n/a
XYZ 60	no tr	0.25	0.75

The trader reasoned that the stock price would rebound 10% to 15% within the next two or three months. The analysis proved correct, but which option would have produced the maximum gain?

Two months later, on January 4, XYZ closed at $53.63, up 12%, and the XYZ call premiums closed as follows:

	January	April	July
XYZ 45	8.75	n/a	n/a
XYZ 50	3.88	4.88	5.50
XYZ 55	0.44	1.69	n/a
XYZ 60	no tr	0.31	0.88

From November to January, the XYZ calls increased by the percentages indicated below:

	January	April	July
XYZ 45	141%	—	—
XYZ 50	244%	129%	110%
XYZ 55	75%	125%	n/a
XYZ 60	—	25%	17%

The best results would have been obtained by purchasing the XYZ January 50s—the option with the strike price just above the stock price and with the shortest time period.

Many seasoned option buyers carry this idea a step further in a process called "walking up" an option. After the largest part of the premium's advance has been captured, the option is sold and the initial process is repeated over again. If the XYZ trader, for example, had expected the stock to continue its advance by another 10% to 15% in the January–April period, the January 50 calls would be replaced by the April 55 calls, available on January 4 for $1.69. The trader would hold the option either until the stock was no longer expected to rise or until it crossed above the strike price, allowing the trader to walk up again.

This example enjoyed the benefit of 20/20 hindsight. In practice, correctly predicting a stock's short-term price change is considerably more difficult, often impossible. In fact, had the XYZ investor bought the April 55s, the outcome would have been disappointing.

Option buyers will find it easier to compare premiums than to value them on an absolute basis. While there are numerous sophisticated formulas and theories designed to compute theoretical premium values, even the professional floor traders and market makers of the leading options exchanges temper these theoretical values with their trading senses. *Option buyers know how much can be lost, but they cannot say exactly how much might be made.*

Writers are in a somewhat better position to make value judgments because the premium received can be considered an investment return that can be compared with the returns on other available short-term opportunities. *Option writers know how much can be made, but they cannot say exactly how much might be lost.*

The premium that a writer receives is basically compensation for

1. Accepting the risk that the underlying stock could move adversely prior to the expiration date

2. Agreeing to support the option written with a reserve of either stock or cash during the option's life

The premium compensation, expressed as an annual rate of return on the capital invested, will obviously be subject to change as the market environment changes. When interest rates rise and alternative investment opportunities become more attractive, a writer should either expect a greater return or consider placing the capital elsewhere. And the reverse is true when interest rates and other investment returns are declining.

There is significantly greater risk in writing an option than in buying a Treasury bill, for example. Clearly, an option writer should demand much greater compensation. But whether the compensation must be double the Treasury bill rate or triple the rate before an investor is motivated to write options will depend on that investor's perception of the risks and rewards involved. Some traders will simply accept a more modest return than will others.

Since option prices are equilibrium prices, a potential writer can quickly calculate what other option writers are demanding (and what buyers are paying) by reviewing the daily option quotations.

A writer, like a buyer, is usually faced with several strike prices and expiration dates. From these choices, the writer must select the option offering the best combination of risk and reward. For writers, as for buyers, this combination will most likely be found in the option that has a strike price slightly above or slightly below the current price of the underlying stock because the writer will obtain the largest amount of "real" time cost within this band.

The importance of real time cost is most evident when a covered call is written. In this instance, the writer's only possible net profit is, in fact, the amount of real time cost. For example, assume that an investor buys IJK Company stock at $60 and, attracted by the large premium, writes an IJK 50 call for $12. If the option is exercised immediately, the writer will deliver the stock at $50. The $10 loss in the stock will be offset by the premium's $10 of intrinsic value. The writer's profit will be $2, or the premium's "real" time cost. If the stock had dropped to $50 and the option expired worthless, the net profit would also be $2. Of course, if the stock drops by more than the total premium, the covered writer has a loss.

A writer's risk and reward combinations are the reverse of a buyer's—the more in the money the option is when it is written, the greater the risk and reward; the more it is out of the money, the less the risk and reward.

The latest alterations in the tax laws changed the Internal Revenue Code sections that affect writers and other option investors. The combined impact of new and preexisting tax laws on the economics of any options trade should be carefully reviewed by every options player with an accountant or tax advisor.

Reducing Risk One of the major attractions of options is their versatility. They can be used individually or combined in various ways to create strategies that modify an investor's risk/reward ratio. Many of these strategies are based directly on the relationships presented earlier. One very popular approach, called "spreading," involves the simultaneous purchase and sale of options on the same underlying stock. Of the numerous spreads available, two are frequently used in option investing: the vertical spread and the calendar spread.

THE VERTICAL SPREAD

A vertical spread is formed by simultaneously buying (going long) and writing (going short) options on the same underlying stock with identical expiration dates but different strike prices. In a calendar spread, the options used have the same strike price but different expiration dates.

A premium is paid going long, and a premium is received going short. Spreading takes its name from the "spread" or numerical difference between the two premiums. If the amount the investor pays is more than the amount received, the difference is called a "debit" and the investor is said to have "bought" the spread. A spread is "sold" with a "credit" if the premium received is greater than the premium paid.

In the earlier example, a vertical spread created by going long NBZ January 260s for 7.88 and shorting NBZ January 280s for 2.13 would have been bought at a debit of 5.75. Reversing the transactions would yield a 5.75 credit.

If a spread is *bought,* the difference between the two premiums must expand for the trader to profit. But if a spread is *sold,* the difference must narrow. The increase or decline in the premium difference will depend on the movement of the underlying stock and, of course, the passage of time.

Vertical spreads and calendar spreads can be designed to exploit either an increase or a decline in the price of the underlying stock. But "bullish" vertical or calendar spreads generally offer better risk/reward characteristics than "bearish" spreads.

The theory behind both types of spreads emphasizes the sensitivity of time cost to the expiration date and to the strike price, two familiar relationships explained earlier.

In a bullish vertical spread, the trader hopes to replace time cost with intrinsic value in the long option with the lower strike price. As the stock advances toward the higher strike price of the short option, and the expiration date draws near, the time cost of the long option will become an increasingly smaller percentage of the total premium. The short option, however, will reflect only time cost, since the stock has not crossed the higher strike price. As expiration approaches, the time value of the short option will decline rapidly and, unless the stock goes above the strike price, the option will ultimately expire worthless. In practice, however, the price change of the underlying stock rather than the disappearing time cost might be the predominant influence. In addition, spreads are frequently closed out before expiration.

In late October, when NBZ was selling at $256.50, a bullish vertical spread could have been bought as follows:

NBZ Bullish Vertical Spread

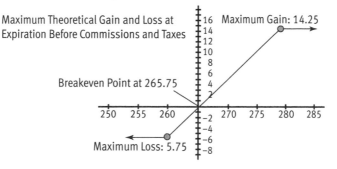

Maximum Theoretical Gain and Loss at Expiration Before Commissions and Taxes

Breakeven Point at 265.75

Maximum Gain: 14.25

Maximum Loss: 5.75

Action	Option Series	Premium
Buy	January 260s	7.88
Sell	January 280s	2.13
		5.75 Debit

In late December, when the stock was 280, the spread could have been closed out at the following premiums:

Action	Option Series	Premium
Sell	January 260s	21.38
Buy	January 280s	4.88
		16.50 Credit

This spread, then, gave the investor a gross profit of 10.75 (the difference between the 16.50 ending credit and the 5.75 beginning debit), for a return of 87% on the 5.75 net investment before costs. Of course, in hindsight, a trader can say that it would have been more profitable to purchase the January 260 call option alone. However, the point of spreading is to reduce the risk of a simple long or short position. By buying the spread for 5.75, the trader reduced the capital at risk by nearly 30% from the 7.88 premium for the single January 260 call. And for this additional security, the trader accepted the certainty of a smaller reward.

With vertical spreads, both the maximum loss and the maximum theoretical profit at expiration can be determined from the outset. With bullish vertical spreads, the maximum profit is limited to the difference between the strike prices and the net premium paid. Should the underlying stock decline, the maximum loss would be the net premium paid. Thus, in the NBZ spread, the maximum gain could have been 14.25, the difference between 260 and 280, or 20, less the net premium paid of 5.75. Even if the underlying stock were to advance beyond the higher strike price, the gain could not be greater than 14.25 because the loss on the short option would offset the gain on the long option. And if the stock dropped below the lower strike price, the loss could be no greater than 5.75, since both options would expire worthless. These profit and loss boundaries are illustrated in the graphic. In addition, the chart shows that this spread would "break even" at 265.75, which means that the long option must acquire 5.75 of intrinsic value to offset the opening debit.

In a bearish vertical spread, the option with the lower exercise price is sold and the option with the higher exercise price is bought. As a result, the maximum theoretical profit at expiration will be the net premium received, and the maximum potential loss will be the difference between the exercise prices minus the net premium received.

When selecting a vertical spread, the investor should follow these guidelines:

1. The underlying stock should be able to reach or exceed the higher strike price in a bullish vertical spread, or to decline to or below the lower strike price in a bearish vertical spread.

2. The debit, expressed as a percentage of the difference between the two strike prices, should be kept as small as possible in a bullish spread. The credit in a bearish spread should be as large as possible. Attractive percentages might be 30% or less for a bullish spread and 70% or higher for a bearish spread. In each spread, a lower debit or a higher credit brings the breakeven point that much closer.

3. Perhaps stocks selling for $50 or more should be considered first, since the difference between the premiums will be $10 or $20 and commissions might be lower than for stocks selling below $50.

THE CALENDAR SPREAD

While vertical spreading emphasizes the interrelationships of stock price and strike prices (i.e., the vertical dimension of options), the theory of calendar spreading stresses the importance of time (the horizontal dimension). In a calendar spread, the investor initially selects the appropriate strike price and then builds the spread by using two of the three expiration dates in whatever combination produces the greatest reward. In most calendar spreads, one option with a closer expiration date is sold short and another option with a more distant expiration date is bought long. Almost all calendar spreads will begin with a debit, since the longer-term option will always have a larger premium than the nearer-term option. As time passes, however, the spread between the two premiums should widen, allowing the investor to buy back the short option for significantly less while selling the long option for only slightly less than its purchase price.

The calendar spreader understands a simple fact of option valuation presented earlier, namely, that an option that is approaching expiration loses time cost far more rapidly than an option with several months of life remaining. This is particularly true for an expiring out-of-the-money option, a condition dramatically illustrated on the chart of the expiring NBZ January 280. The calendar spreader

The Options Trading Room at the Philadelphia Stock Exchange

hopes that the short option will share a similar fate.

A successful calendar spread might resemble the following example. In late June, these quotations appear in the options table on the Internet:

NYSE Strike					
Option	Close	Price	Jul	Oct	Jan
KLM	$58.75	60	1.50	4.00	5.00

The trader, believing that the underlying stock will remain relatively stable, buys a calendar spread for a debit of 1 by selling short a KLM Oct 60 at 4.00 and going long the KLM Jan 60 at 5.00. During the next several months, the stock has a series of small gains and losses but stays close to the strike price. Just before the October expiration, with the stock selling for $59, the October option is quoted at 0.50, while the January option is quoted at 3.50, since it still has three months of life remaining. At this point, the trader successfully closes out the spread with a credit of 3. The trader's initial $100 risk was able to produce a $200 gain (the difference between the closing credit and the beginning debit), even though the underlying stock remained steady.

However, if the underlying stock had had a large move, either up or down, most likely the spread would have ended with the loss of nearly the entire debit. The spread must widen for a calendar spread to be successful, but as the stock moves further away from the strike price, the spread will narrow.

Calendar spreads should be appraised with the following requirements in mind:

1. The underlying stock should be expected to trade in a narrow band slightly below or slightly above the strike price. The effect of large unexpected moves in the underlying stock will always be greater than the effect of diminishing time cost. As noted, large moves either up or down may force the spread into a loss.

2. The short option should have a large "real" time cost, which, again, will be found in the option with a strike price close to the price of the underlying stock.

3. The initial debit should be small relative to a realistic projection of the spread's potential gain. In other words, it is ill advised to risk an opening debit of, say, 4 if the spread's ultimate gain will be a net credit of 1.

MNO Company
Straddle

Bought			Sold			Profit/Loss		
April 50 Call	@	$4.00	April 50 Call	@	$10.50	Profit	+	$6.50
April 50 Put	@	$3.50	April 50 Put	@	$ 0.50	Loss	–	$3.00
Total Premium			Total Premium			Total Gross		
Paid		$7.50	Received		$11.00	Profit		$3.50

Although vertical and calendar spreads can produce nice gains, their effectiveness is hampered by three major drawbacks:

1. **Commissions.** A commission is paid every time an option is bought or sold. Opening and closing transactions on a typical vertical or calendar spread can, therefore, result in four commission charges. Even though commissions were excluded for simplicity in the examples of spreads just presented, the investor should always include this cost when computing any spread's potential gain or loss. In any spreading strategy, it is usually best to use several options. For example, the commission expense for five short and five long options should be proportionately smaller than the expense for only one short and one long. Any spread that yields a profit, only to have much of it consumed by commissions, is rightfully known as an "alligator" spread.

2. **Volatility.** Judging the short-term price movement of the underlying stock is essential to the success of all option activity. Unfortunately, this is not as easy as it seems. Without knowing the volatility of the stock, this task becomes even more difficult.

3. **Exercise.** The spreader may receive an exercise notice against the short option at any time. The probability of exercise increases as the underlying stock gains intrinsic value. Exercise radically alters the risk/reward ratio, which was the basis for the spread's creation. It leaves the investor with a simple long position. Depending on the circumstances, the spreader may respond to an exercise notice by

- Exercising the long call and delivering the stock
- Buying stock in the open market
- Delivering stock borrowed from the broker by shorting the stock and maintaining the long call as a hedge

HEDGING

Options can be used as a hedge to reduce risk in much the same way that an insurance policy can provide protection against a catastrophic loss. If an investor owns stock and does not want to sell it, even though it may decline in the near future, a put option could be bought as a temporary hedge.

Investors should carefully review the tax consequences of any hedge beforehand. In certain instances, the holding period of the stock owned could be al-

Here are simple graphics to demonstrate the profit and loss characteristics of each of these strategies:

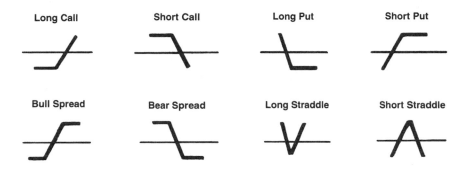

| Long Call | Short Call | Long Put | Short Put |
| Bull Spread | Bear Spread | Long Straddle | Short Straddle |

tered. Nevertheless, hedging a long position is sometimes worth considering.

The benefits of a short-sale hedge involving the purchase of a call against an ordinary short-sale position might be more compelling. The short seller is mainly concerned with the potential "unlimited loss" that could result if the price of the shorted stock were to soar. A short "squeeze" is particularly unnerving because additional capital is required when the stock is covered at higher prices—as opposed to owning a declining stock outright. Short-sale hedging can be especially effective during a bear market, when call premiums are often depressed.

Puts and Calls Combined Unpredictable corporate events can often place investors in a precarious position. They believe, or sense, that the price of a given stock is about to change substantially, but they do not know whether it will rise or fall. Such a situation might occur if a pending lawsuit is about to be resolved. If the company wins, its stock might rise sharply, but if it loses, the stock could drop precipitously. While many investors wait on the sidelines for the smoke to clear, a risk-conscious options investor might immediately use a strategy known as a "straddle."

A straddle consists of an equal number of puts and calls purchased or written simultaneously with identical strike prices and expiration dates. It enables the buyer to profit from a major price change in either direction, while limiting the risk to the total combined premiums paid. Conversely, straddles produce substantial premium income for straddle writers who take the contrary view that the stock price will change little, if at all.

Assume that in early January, the stock of the MNO Company has been trading steadily at $50 a share awaiting certain corporate developments that could conceivably alter the price dramatically either up or down. An option buyer who is convinced that a major price change will occur within the next three months, yet is unsure of its direction, concludes that a straddle will be profitable. The MNO investor buys, simultaneously, an April 50 call for 4 and an April 50 put for 3.50. By early April, the stock has advanced 20% to $60 a share. The call premium is now priced at 10.50, while the put premium has fallen to 0.50. If the straddle is now "unwound," that is, terminated, through closing sale transactions, the options investor would have a $3.50 ($350) gross profit on the initial $7.50 ($750) investment, as shown in the illustration.

Depending on the amount of time remaining, it might be better to risk expiration rather than selling the put. It could regain some value if the stock were to drop suddenly.

Of course, the call could be exercised to acquire the stock, which would then be sold to capture the profit. In practice, however, most straddles terminate in closing sale or purchase transactions.

If the stock had declined sharply instead of rising, the put would have been profitable, but not the call. A closing sale or exercise of the put would produce results virtually identical to those obtained from the profitable call.

This basic example provides the straddle buyer with several important guidelines:

1. The total premium establishes the straddle's "breakeven points." The underlying stock must rise or fall by an amount equal to the combined premium before any profits can be realized. In the example just given, the breakeven points were 57.50 and 42.50 because the initial premium was 7.50, or 15% of the stock's price. The stock had to move at least 15% in either direction before the straddle would be profitable. It is, therefore, important for the investor to keep the total premium as low as possible and the terms of the contracts realistic.

2. A straddle involves "round-trip" commissions on two options. As in other option strategies, such as spreading and variable hedging, multiple commission charges must be computed accurately. Commission costs can easily turn a profitable trade into a loss. In addition, the trader should consult a tax advisor to anticipate the tax effects of any trade.

3. While the prospect of a double premium is enticing, a potential straddle writer should remember that a sharp move can produce a substantial loss. If the writer does not own the stock and it rises sharply and the call is exercised, the writer will have to purchase the higher-priced shares in the open market. If the stock declines and the put is exercised, the investor might have to produce a large and immediate cash payment to pay for the put stock.

The simple graphics shown here demonstrate the profit and loss characteristics of several popular strategies.

Puts and calls can be combined in several other ways to create various risk and reward strategies, as in the "strip" (two puts and one call) or the "strap" (two calls and one put). The possibilities are almost endless, and their names are no less esoteric—long butterfly, short butterfly, long strangle, short strangle, ratio call spread, ratio put spread, call ratio backspread, put ratio backspread, and the box or conversion.

These and other exotic methods should be avoided until the use of individual puts and calls becomes second nature. And, even then, each new idea should be scrutinized carefully, with special emphasis on tax consequences, margin requirements, and commissions. An investor might find that in some instances, simply buying or selling an unadorned put or call is more effective than creating the complex web of a supposedly advanced strategy.

Index Options In recent years, the use of options has grown far beyond individual equity applications. Options are being offered on interest rates, currencies, and now, most important, stock indexes. With options on indexes, an investor can buy or sell calls or puts on groups of stocks or industries in the same way options are used for individual stocks.

These stock groups can be small and specialized, such as the index on the semi-conductor stocks (the SOXX), or can be large, highly diversified market indexes, such as the S&P 500 Index (the SPX), the S&P 100 Index (the OEX), or the Dow Jones Industrial Average (the DJX).

Today, largely because of increased activity by hedge funds, the SPX alone now accounts for more than 150 million contracts, or about 15% of the annual total of the CBOE.

Also, option contracts can be applied to ETFs. Among the most popular of these are the Nasdaq 100 Trust (QQQ), the S&P 500 Spider (SPY), and the DJIA Diamonds (DIA), which offer more leveraged ways to play market swings. In short, the investors and traders of today have a broad range of opportunities to buy or sell the "market," or segments of it, to hedge or to speculate, with varying degrees of risk.

The next page illustrates how the table for the OEX could appear in a newspaper; it is roughly similar to the way the numbers are displayed on the CBOE Web site. The table is also similar to those for individual stock options. On this day, the OEX close was 426.68. The strike price closest to it is called the "central strike" (the 425s), and any options above or below this are either "in the money" or "out of the money."

Index Options

SP100 — Close 426.68

P/C Strike	Feb Vol	Feb Last Price	Mar Vol	Mar Last Price	Apr Vol	Apr Last Price
c390	40	49	....	....	....	....
c400	....	....	2	43^{30}	....	....
c420	108	17^{50}	....	....	....	....
c425	154	14^{20}	....	....	....	....
c430	296	11^{60}	13	19^{20}	....	....
c435	464	9	2	19	....	....
c440	1174	7^{20}	7	17^{50}	....	....
c445	1129	5^{40}	....	....	....	....
c450	2285	4	47	10^{10}	....	....
c455	824	2^{80}	3	8	....	....
c460	1291	2^{10}	38	6^{80}	....	....
c465	399	1^{70}	6	6	....	....
c470	620	1^{10}	65	4^{90}	....	....
c475	1108	0^{75}	4	4^{30}	....	....
c480	615	0^{50}	52	3^{30}	10	6^{30}
c485	140	0^{40}	....	....	....	....
c490	1170	0^{25}	20	2^{05}	....	....
c495	15	0^{20}	....	....	....	....
c500	286	0^{15}	121	1^{20}	1	3
c505	35	0^{10}	....	....	....	....
c510	200	0^{15}	....	....	....	....
c515	63	0^{05}	....	....	....	....
c520	158	0^{05}	300	0^{45}	110	1^{35}

P/C Strike	Feb Vol	Feb Last Price	Mar Vol	Mar Last Price	Apr Vol	Apr Last Price
p300	210	0^{05}	208	0^{60}	201	1^{40}
p320	....	....	150	1^{15}	....	....
p340	100	0^{25}	103	1^{95}	10	3^{60}
p350	60	0^{50}	....	....	....	....
p360	22	0^{75}	2	4	....	....
p370	781	1^{30}	1	5	....	....
p380	359	1^{95}	202	6^{80}	....	....
p390	312	3^{20}	3	9	....	....
p395	261	3^{90}	....	....	....	....
p400	1509	4^{70}	147	11^{50}	146	15
p405	147	6	....	....	....	....
p410	577	7	6	14	....	....
p415	108	8^{30}	....	....	....	....
p420	699	10^{30}	68	18	26	22^{90}
p425	340	12^{50}	10	20^{20}	....	....
p430	1124	14^{80}	22	22^{60}	9	26
p435	407	17	19	23^{30}	....	....
p440	198	20^{10}	24	27^{20}	6	29
p445	1	21^{20}	1	29^{50}	....	....
p450	54	28^{10}	109	33^{20}	....	....
p455	55	32	....	....	....	....
p460	152	36^{10}	55	40^{70}	4	39
p465	1	35^{60}	....	....	....	....
p470	86	40^{90}	....	....	....	....
p480	25	50^{70}	....	....	....	....

Program Trading This section would not be complete without saying more about this volatile market influence. Automatic, or algorithmic, trading (often called just "algo" trading) can account for half, or more, of all trades on any given day.

Algo trading is used widely by hedge funds, pension funds, and mutual funds, among others, with many investment strategies.

Program trading is defined as "strategies that involve the purchase or sale of fifteen or more stocks with a market value of $1 million or more." Algo trading cannot be detected by simply reading the morning newspaper, although these statistics are published. However, most investors can see the volatility and random swings that result every day.

One better-known example of program trading is "index arbitrage," which involves the purchase or sale of a basket of stocks in conjunction with the sale or purchase of a derivative product such as futures or options. The objective is to capture the difference between the two prices.

Flexible Products As we have seen in the case of equities, there will also be new products in the options arena. For example, the CBOE recently introduced what it calls "FLEX products," whereby users have the opportunity to select option terms, including strike prices, and expiration dates for any day of the month. Moreover, this applies to both indexes and equities.

Stock Options—Conclusion Stock options present a special challenge. The investor must judge not only whether a stock is going to go up or down, but when and roughly by how much.

It has been demonstrated that puts and calls can be used in any type of market. They can be used alone or in various combinations to create numerous risk and reward opportunities. But for the vast majority of investors reading this book, the two best and most consistently profitable applications of options are

- Writing covered calls
- Writing naked puts as a less expensive way to buy shares that would otherwise have been purchased

Yet, in the final analysis, successful option investing ultimately rests on the accurate assessment of the underlying investment potential of the stock or index in question. After all, this is one of the primary reasons for this book!

15 | Personalities of Wall Street

Introduction

The history of Wall Street provides an endless number of distinctive personalities. These are the newsworthy individuals who have attained investors' attention for one reason or another. They could be the investment tycoons of their day, prominent industrialists, influential financiers, money managers, or celebrities, self-made or otherwise. Whatever actions these people took, or whatever comments they made, usually had an immediate impact on the markets. In today's parlance, they are called the "movers and shakers" of their time.

Many of the individuals highlighted here are known by name, but their significance, their contributions, and sometimes their notoriety have not always been fully recognized.

This chapter will describe a number of these interesting personalities and attempt to portray their contribution to the evolving investment landscape and to the lore of Wall Street.

Alexander Hamilton

The Early Days During the incubation days of Wall Street, few people had more influence than *Alexander Hamilton* (1755–1804). This was a man of conflict from the day he was born until the day he died. Even his exact birth date (1755 or 1757) is in dispute to this day. Throughout his life, given the mores of his time, Hamilton was haunted by the fact that he was born out of wedlock in the British West Indies. His political views had detractors, and even his abrupt death was the result of conflict.

As an avid reader with a keen interest in finance and commerce, young Hamilton attended Kings College (now Columbia University). What the man accomplished within his short life span of less than fifty years was remarkable.

Hamilton was a militia volunteer and gained attention as a member of George Washington's staff before commanding battalions that led to the British surrender at Yorktown. He was soon a New York representative to the "Congress of the Confederation." In 1784, he founded The Bank of New York, and he was later a New York delegate to the Constitutional Convention.

George Washington appointed Hamilton as the first secretary of the treasury in 1789, and during his five years in this position, much of the initial financial structure of the new government was put in place. The events during his reign included the founding of the nation's first stock exchanges: the Philadelphia Stock Exchange in 1790 (now part of Nasdaq OMX) and the New York Stock Exchange, organized in 1792. That same year, the shares in the Bank of New York became the first corporate stock to be traded on the New York Exchange.

Alexander Hamilton was said to have been an expert with dueling pistols. An expert? Maybe not.

The Nineteenth Century The Civil War and the years just before and immediately after were notable as a result of the innovation and industrialization that occurred during that period. Despite the deadliest war in its history, the young nation made enormous strides during the nineteenth century.

John Jacob Astor (1763–1848) was born in Germany, moved to London, and then came to America just after the Revolutionary War.

Initially, Astor was a trader of furs before his interests turned to real estate in New York City. In 1804, Astor purchased the remaining sixty-two years of a ninety-nine-year lease in Manhattan from Vice President Aaron Burr.

Cornelius Vanderbilt

In the decades just before the Civil War, Astor was establishing himself as a real estate mogul by buying land and then leasing it to others for development.

During his later years, Astor was a patron of the arts, and when he died in 1848, he was known as the nation's wealthiest man.

The Trinity Church cemetery at the intersection of Wall Street and Broadway, Astor's burial site, holds many other notable figures in U.S. history: Alexander Hamilton and his wife, Elizabeth; Revolutionary War General Horatio Gates; William Bradford, a colonial printer; and Robert Fulton, credited with the invention of the first commercially successful steamship.

Also well known in the Astor family was his great-grandson, John Jacob Astor IV, who perished on the RMS *Titanic* in April 1912.

While John Jacob Astor was building his real estate empire, *Cornelius Vanderbilt* (1794–1877), known as "Commodore," was beginning his fortune in New York.

Vanderbilt, born in Staten Island, became interested in shipping at an early age. Although he never finished school, by 1812, when he was only eighteen years old, his modest shipping enterprise of schooners had a government contract to supply the forts around New York.

Within thirty years or so, Vanderbilt's fortune had become substantial. He was operating about one hundred steamships that plied the Hudson River. Ships of this type were a new development at that time.

However, the Commodore became more visible to Wall Street when his interests turned to railroads in the 1830s and 1840s.

In the early 1860s, Vanderbilt acquired the New York & Harlem Railroad, and then the Hudson River Railroad, followed by the New York Central Railroad in 1867. Later, combined, they formed the New York Central and Hudson River Railroad.

Very telling of the Commodore's nature is the following rude quote written to former business associates in 1853: "You have undertaken to cheat me. I won't sue you, for the law is too slow. I will ruin you."

At the time, railroads had become essential, and in the 1860s and 1870s, much of Wall Street's attention was focused on the Erie Railway and the great struggle for control between Cornelius Vanderbilt and three other significant financiers of the day: James ("Diamond Jim") Fisk, Daniel Drew, and *Jay Gould* (1836–1892).

Gould was born in Roxbury, New York, in Delaware County. Later, his keen interest in the subject led him to become a broker of railroad stocks. And he, along with Jim

John Davison Rockefeller

Fisk, another broker (who was employed by Daniel Drew), won the battle for Erie, but then later lost control of it in 1873.

While Cornelius Vanderbilt could have been called ruthless in his business dealings, his adversaries, Drew, Fisk, and Gould, could have been charitably referred to as "notorious."

In addition to their fight for control of the Erie Railway, Gould and Fisk attempted to corner the gold market in 1869.

A few years later, Gould gained control of the Union Pacific and a controlling interest in the Western Union Telegraph Company.

Jay Gould's association with Diamond Jim ended abruptly when Fisk, thirty-eight, was shot to death by his girlfriend's newest lover.

Not all of Wall Street in the nineteenth century was mired in unseemly and sordid affairs. For example, *Charles H. Dow* (1851–1902) was reputable in every way. He was born in Sterling, Connecticut, and, like many in his generation, never finished school.

Dow was a reporter, initially with a news agency, and one of the three principal founders of Dow Jones & Company in 1882. The new firm published daily, handwritten, messenger-delivered bulletins that it referred to as "flimsies."

In the following year, the firm began publishing what was then called the *Customers' Afternoon Letter*, which included the early versions of the Dow Jones stock averages. Initially, the average included 14 stocks. Soon there were two averages, the Dow Jones Railroad Average of 20 stocks and the Dow Jones Industrial Average of 12 stocks. On July 8, 1889, the letter became the *Wall Street Journal* at a price of two cents per copy. The cost for an advertisement was twenty cents per line. Soon, the *Journal* became one of the nation's most influential news sources.

At the time Dow's publishing efforts were taking hold, one of the most newsworthy figures was *John Davison Rockefeller* (1839–1937), the second of six children, born in Richford, New York. The town's name was certainly appropriate, because J. D. Rockefeller amassed an enormous fortune. He was the world's first billionaire.

Early in his business career, having a talent for numbers, Rockefeller began work as an assistant bookkeeper for Hewitt & Tuttle, a commission merchant business in produce and commodities. In 1859, with a partner, he started an independent firm in that field, and gradually his fortune grew when commodity prices rose as the Civil War approached.

John Pierpont Morgan

Edwin Drake's oil strike near Titusville, Pennsylvania, in 1859 was a catalyst for Rockefeller's interest in oil refining in 1862. In 1865, the twenty-six-year-old bought out a few of his partners and gained complete control of their oil refining business for a reported $72,500. In 1870, when the Standard Oil Company of Ohio was formed, the firm was doing about 10% of the country's refining.

The fact that the New York Central and the Erie Railway lines were serious competitors worked greatly to the advantage of the Standard Oil Company at the time.

In the early 1870s, Rockefeller and one of his most important partners, Henry Flagler, who later became a developer and railroad tycoon, obtained the support of banks to undertake a major consolidation of oil refiners. By the end of the decade, Standard Oil controlled almost all of the refining activity in the United States.

In 1882, the Standard Oil "trust" (in effect, a corporation of corporations) was created. However, the trust was ruled illegal in 1911, and the government dismantled it into thirty-four independent companies. It can be said that, to date, as a percentage of GDP, John D. Rockefeller accumulated more wealth than any other American in history.

During the nineteenth century, the industrialists held most of Wall Street's news interest. Yet, over the entire history of Wall Street, no financier was ever more influential than *John Pierpont Morgan* (1837–1913). He was the titan among financial giants at the turn into the twentieth century, and his legacy endures to this day.

Born in Hartford, Connecticut, Pierpont, as he preferred to be called, was educated in Boston and in Europe, where he learned to speak French and German.

Initially, he joined the London branch of his father's banking house and then worked in New York as an agent for his father's company. In 1871, he joined the Drexels of Philadelphia to form Drexel, Morgan & Company. After Anthony Drexel's death in 1895, the company was reorganized to become J. P. Morgan & Company, with branches in London and Paris to market American securities in Europe.

In the 1870s, Morgan was involved in raising millions of dollars to help railroads reorganize and build and to help the country pay off the huge debts resulting from the Civil War. J. P. Morgan's involvement in the railroads continued into the 1880s after the deaths of Cornelius Vanderbilt, Daniel Drew, and Jim Fisk. By the late 1880s, Morgan's railroad holdings were considerable. And his contributions to other areas of American business were also extensive:

Henrietta "Hetty" Robinson Green

- In 1878, he financed the Edison Electric Illuminating Company.
- In 1892, Morgan arranged the merger of the Edison General Electric Co. with a major competitor, Thomson-Houston Company, to create General Electric Company.
- In 1901, Morgan bought Rockefeller's iron-related business and added it to the United States Steel Corporation, which he formed in March of that year.

Although J. P. Morgan's business activities alone made him the most dominant Wall Street financier of all time, his considerable influence and power were best illustrated by his actions to keep the U. S. government solvent during the depression that began in 1893. Railroads had overbuilt, banks were failing, and unemployment was soaring.

In 1895, President Grover Cleveland asked Morgan for help when the U.S. Treasury's gold supply was being depleted at an alarming rate. The credibility of the entire government was at stake.

According to historians, J. Pierpont Morgan single-handedly turned the tide by creating a syndicate to buy government bonds with European gold.

And again, during the Panic of 1907, six years before the Federal Reserve System was established, Morgan stepped in to help the entire country. By pledging his money, and convincing others to do the same, he managed to stabilize the nation's struggling banking system.

Mark Twain referred to the years between the late 1870s and the Panic of 1893 as "the Gilded Age." Industry flourished, and great wealth was created by industrialists and financiers, including Andrew Carnegie (steel), John D. Rockefeller (oil), Cornelius Vanderbilt (railroads), and, of course, noted international financier J. P. Morgan. There were also the so-called robber barons, which might have included Daniel Drew, Diamond Jim Fisk, and Jay Gould.

Unquestionably one of the most colorful personalities of that era was *Henrietta "Hetty" Robinson Green* (1834–1916), who was known for her investment acumen and her excessively miserly habits. She gained the dubious nickname "Witch of Wall Street." Observers have also referred to Hetty as a banker and a "nasty lady" who became one of the richest women ever.

Her investments varied from "greenbacks" to lending money to Vanderbilt's New York Central Railroad. She was also

Irving Fisher

William C. Durant

a lender of last resort to the City of New York to keep the city solvent during the Panic of 1907.

Actually, the term "colorful" might be a misnomer, since she was rarely seen in any color other than black, and her clothes were worn until they were tattered.

Over the years, she cleverly parlayed her inheritance of several millions of dollars into great wealth with one philosophy: conservative investments and substantial cash reserves to back up every action.

Hetty Green once said, "There is no great secret to fortune-making. All you have to do is buy cheap and sell dear, act with thrift and shrewdness, and be persistent."

The Twentieth Century Many interesting observations can be made regarding this volatile 100-year period. One of them was that a brilliant and popular economist can be a hero one day and a goat the next.

Perhaps the best example was the highly respected mathematician and economist *Irving Fisher* (1867–1947). His writings were viewed as practical, easy reading for people with an interest in the subject of money, interest rates, and the economy. Many of his superb theories and formulas have since been acknowledged by several generations of economists.

Irving Fisher was born in Saugerties, New York. Later, he earned the first Ph.D. in economics ever awarded by Yale. He remained there as an economist in the years after, and he also became a celebrity of sorts during the 1920s.

In addition, Fisher was an inventor, and his success led to personal riches at that time.

As talented as he was, Fisher's reputation was badly tarnished when, just before the market crashed in 1929, he proclaimed, "Stock prices have reached what looks like a permanently high plateau."

Fisher lost much of his wealth and further damaged his reputation when he continued to assure investors in the early 1930s that prosperity would return quickly. It didn't.

Like the Gilded Age, the so-called Roaring Twenties produced many flamboyant personalities. One of the most notable was *William C. Durant* (1861–1947). "Billy," as he was called, was an industrialist, a racing enthusiast, and a fearless gambler rolled into one.

Born in Boston, Durant was the grandson of William Crapo, the governor of Michigan at the end of the Civil War. Billy quit high school to work at his grandfather's lumberyard.

Jesse L. Livermore

In his twenties, Durant became a partner in a manufacturer of horse-drawn carriages. Within ten years, the Durant-Dort Carriage Company was dominant in its field.

In 1904, Billy was asked to join the Buick Company, a manufacturer of horseless carriages. In 1908, he incorporated General Motors, raised capital, and then used stock to acquire Buick. Soon after, he acquired the Olds Corporation of Lansing, and then a financially strapped company in Pontiac, Michigan. By 1910, his numerous dealings had left him financially overextended, and he lost control of his company to bankers.

A year later, Billy Durant formed a new auto manufacturer with a partner, Louis Chevrolet. He eventually bought out his partner and then regained control of GM in 1916. Soon, Chevrolet Motor Company was a division of General Motors. But, once again, Durant lost control of GM for the final time to Pierre du Pont in 1920.

Relentless, Billy formed Durant Motors in 1921, and his new company manufactured automobiles until the economic depression led to its failure in 1933.

However, throughout most of the 1920s, news reporters and stock speculators were always asking, "What's Billy buying today?"

In his later years, Durant was managing several bowling alleys in Flint, Michigan, not far from the Buick complex that he had built.

Another notable figure during the Roaring Twenties was *Jesse L. Livermore* (1877–1940).

He was born in Acton, Massachusetts, and left home before graduating from school.

Livermore was interested in the market, and at fifteen, he started as a "chalk boy," posting stock prices at a Paine Webber brokerage office in Boston.

Eventually, he became a successful stock trader, and was once quoted as saying, "The point is not so much to buy as cheap as possible, or go short at top price, but to buy or sell at the right time."

Livermore was best known for his timely short sales in 1907 and again in 1929. At his peak, he was reportedly worth close to $100 million. Everyone wanted to be like The Boy Plunger. But after the crash, the rules were changed. Journalists could no longer promote stocks blatantly, insiders were not permitted to profit as they had once done, and short sales had to be made on an uptick. Driving a stock's price down was no longer legal. For Livermore, the game lost its allure, and he shot himself in 1940.

Gerald Tsai, Jr.

There were several other newsworthy people during this period: *Roger Babson*, who had been consistently warning of a pending market crash; *Charles Mitchell*, head of the National City Bank, who calmed investors' fears in early 1929; and *Michael J. Meehan*, the NYSE specialist for RCA, a very popular stock of the day.

One of the greatest investment advisors in the twentieth century, or perhaps of all time, was *Thomas Rowe Price, Jr.* (1898–1983).

Price was born in Linwood, Maryland. He graduated from Swarthmore College in 1919, majoring in chemistry, but he found a greater interest in numbers and in finance.

He began his Wall Street career when he joined a Baltimore-based brokerage office (later, Legg Mason) and rose to become its chief investment officer.

In 1937, Price founded his own investment advisory firm, Price Associates, which later became T. Rowe Price & Associates. His investment philosophy was very basic: to find stocks that have superior investment characteristics, and that are expected to grow, over the long term, faster than the general economy.

In 1950, Price introduced the first of many mutual funds, *The Growth Stock Fund*, but without any sales commission. Price was a pioneer of the no-load mutual fund concept.

Throughout his career, Rowe Price was widely quoted as a "market guru," although he never aspired to be one.

Contrary to Price's desire for companies that grow from within, "conglomerates" gained attention during the 1960s, when "growth" was attained by combining unrelated companies into one entity.

The leaders of the popular conglomerate fad were *Harold Geneen* (International Telephone & Telegraph), *"Tex" Thornton* (Litton Industries), and *Charlie Bluhdorn* (Gulf+Western). During this time, Wall Street analysts and speculators expended considerable energy trying to anticipate the next acquisition targets of these men.

During the "go-go era" of the 1960s, the activities of money managers were being monitored closely as they ran what became known as "performance funds." These aggressive funds sought short-term capital appreciation by identifying trends early and holding the appropriate stocks as they enjoyed their greatest momentum.

This aggressive means of investing was pioneered by *Gerald Tsai, Jr.* (1929–2008). Tsai was born in Shanghai, moved to the United States in 1947, and received bach-

George Soros

elor's and master's degrees in economics from Boston University. He became a securities analyst on Wall Street in 1951.

In 1965, Gerry Tsai established the popular Manhattan Fund, further enhancing his growing reputation and following. In 1968, the successful fund was sold to CNA Financial for about $27 million in stock.

Tsai joined American Can in the 1980s and helped accelerate its move into the faster-growing financial services industry. The can operations were sold in 1986 and the company's name was changed to Primerica. It eventually became a part of Citigroup.

Finally, the twentieth century, like many periods before it, had its share of "market seers." These were typically writers of market letters who were newsworthy during troubled times, when investors were seeking guidance or a confirmation of their personal views.

Two prominent personalities with many years of news exposure were the deep-thinking *Richard Russell* and the colorful Wall Street showman *Joe Granville*. Both writers made their fair share of good and bad market calls, and they were only two of many, but Russell and Granville never seemed to be without a following.

Moving On to a New Century As Wall Street moved into the twenty-first century, the investment products were changing, but the public's fascination with talent and success never waned.

One successful, but controversial, global speculator is *George Soros* (1930–), born Gyorgy Schwartz, in Budapest, Hungary.

Controversies involving Soros center mainly on his penchant for political activism. His views and fundings are very much to the left of center. His investment success over the years has involved currencies and equities.

Soros first traded currencies as a teenager when hyperinflation hit Hungary in 1945–1946. Later, in 1952, he graduated from the London School of Economics and soon joined a merchant bank in London.

In the early 1960s he worked as an analyst at Wertheim & Company, and he was later a cofounder of the Quantum Fund. Soros gained fame in 1992 when he forced the Bank of England to devalue its currency.

Soros has written at least three books over the past twenty or so years, all predicting a global financial disaster.

Warren Edward Buffett (1930–) has been proclaimed by some as "the greatest

Warren Edward Buffett

investor of all time." The fact that he became one of the world's richest people lends some credence to the comment.

Buffett was born in Omaha, Nebraska, and, as a son of a U.S. representative, was educated in Washington, D.C. Buffett received degrees in economics from the University of Nebraska and Columbia University, where he became a disciple of the noted securities analyst Benjamin Graham.

When Buffett was in his twenties, he started investment partnerships, which led to his becoming a millionaire in his thirties.

His partnerships were merged in the early 1960s, and he then began buying stock in Berkshire Hathaway, a leading cotton manufacturer. This (OTC) company had a good balance sheet, no debt, and a small capitalization of only 1.6 million shares. This became his "investment vehicle."

Berkshire Hathaway made wide-ranging investments in numerous companies, sometimes acquiring them in their entirety.

Today, Berkshire Hathaway's holdings include investments in financial services companies (American Express and Geico), oil (ConocoPhillips), and consumer companies (Coca-Cola and Procter & Gamble), among others in various fields.

Since 1965, when Buffett began, the per share book value of Berkshire Hathaway has increased at an average compounded rate of roughly 20% per year, versus just below 9% for the S&P 500, with dividends.

This is, indeed, a very impressive record.

Sources

Dictionary of Wall Street

annual meeting A stockholders' meeting, normally held at the same time each year, to elect the company's board of directors and transact other corporate business.

annual trading license The system that replaced the 188-year NYSE tradition of selling membership "seats" in late 2005.

arbitrage The practice of buying and selling two separate but related securities to profit from the difference in their values. An arbitrage opportunity often arises when two companies plan to merge or when one security is convertible into another.

asset Anything of value owned by a company. Assets can include cash, product inventory, and other current assets, as well as land, buildings, and equipment.

authorized See "shares authorized."

averaging down The purchase of additional shares of already-owned stock at lower prices to reduce the average cost per share of all shares held.

Balance Sheet A financial statement showing the company's assets (what the company owns), its liabilities (what it owes), and the difference, called "net worth" or "stockholders' equity."

bear market An extended declining trend in stock prices, usually occurring over a time period of months or years.

beta (coefficient) The second letter of the Greek alphabet, used by Wall Street to describe the volatility of a stock relative to a stock market index (the market's beta = 1). The term is used to describe a stock's risk.

block A large amount of stock sold as a single unit. The term is most often used to describe a unit of 10,000 shares or more.

blue sky laws State laws designed to protect investors from "blue sky" (worthless) securities.

board of directors A group of people elected by the stockholders, usually annually, to exercise powers granted to it by the corporation's charter. These powers could include appointments of officers, issuance of shares, and declaration of dividends.

bond A certificate of indebtedness extending over a period of more than one year from the time it is issued. A debt of less than one year is usually called a "note." A bond is an obligation that must be repaid at a certain time. Meanwhile, the borrower pays interest to the bondholder for the use of the money.

book value The equity value of an outstanding share of stock. Book value is determined by dividing the amount of stockholders' equity by the average number of shares outstanding.

broad tape A news service used by brokerage firms and other business offices. The service provides a continuous printed stream of current business news items. The news is printed on a "broad tape" of paper.

bull market An extended rising trend in stock prices, usually occurring over a time period of months or years.

buyout See "leveraged buyout."

calendar spread An investment strategy of buying and selling options on the same underlying security, with the options having identical strike prices but different expiration dates.

call option A contract giving the holder a right to buy 100 shares of a stock at a predetermined price (called the striking price) at any time up to a predetermined expiration date. A call option is bought to profit from a rise in the stock's price.

capital gain A gain realized on the sale or exchange of securities, fixed property, or similar assets. Under current IRS rules, a capital gain is taxable.

capital loss A loss realized on the sale or exchange of securities, fixed property, or similar assets. Such a loss can sometimes be used to reduce taxes.

capitalism A profit-oriented economic system involving the private ownership of production and distribution in a competitive environment.

capitalization All money that has been invested in a business, including equity capital (common stock and preferred stock), long-term debt (bonds), retained earnings, and other surplus funds.

cash flow Loosely defined as "net income plus depreciation." The term is frequently used to describe the amount of internally generated cash that is available for dividends and/or for the purchase of additional assets.

class (of options) All options, both calls and puts, involving the same underlying security.

closed-end fund An investment company with a limited number of shares. A shareholder must buy the shares from or sell them to another person, rather than dealing directly with the investment company. Closed-end funds often sell at a market discount.

collateralized debt obligation (CDO) A type of asset-based security representing various nonmortgage bonds, loans, and other such instruments. The CDO is divided by the issuer into slices or "tranches," each having different risk, rating, and coupon levels.

collateralized mortgage obligation (CMO) A debt security collateralized by mortgages or securities backed by such mortgages. Separate pools are divided into slices or "tranches," each having its own interest and prepayment schedule. Most are rated AAA.

conglomerate A broadly diversified corporation that offers a large number of products and/or services in many unrelated industries. Rightly or wrongly, the term connotes a lack of corporate direction by management.

contango A condition in which distant delivery prices for futures exceed spot prices, often because of the costs of storing and insuring the underlying commodity. It is the opposite of "backwardation."

convertible debenture A debenture that is convertible into common shares at the option of the owner.

convertible preferred stock A preferred stock that is convertible into common shares at the option of the owner.

corner Having such complete supply/demand control of a security that its price can be manipulated. The practice is illegal today, and the term is primarily historical.

coupon A promise to pay interest when due, usually attached to a bond. When the due date arrives, the coupon is detached and submitted for payment. The term also refers to a bond's interest rate, and this is the more frequent use of the word today.

credit default swap (CDS) A derivative contract between two parties that offers the buyer some protection against the default of a financial instrument (e.g., a bond or a loan). Also see "swap(s)."

current assets Assets that are expected to be converted to cash within twelve months.

current liabilities Obligations that will be paid within twelve months.

current ratio The ratio of current assets to current liabilities. This ratio is calculated by dividing current assets by current liabilities. Current assets at, or above, twice current liabilities is considered a healthy ratio for most businesses.

debenture An unsecured (without collateral) bond issued on the good word and general credit of the borrower.

deflation The economic condition in which the prices of goods and services are falling. It is the inverse of inflation, and it involves an increasing buying power of cash and a substantially reduced amount of currency in circulation.

depreciation The estimated decrease in the value of property as a result of use, deterioration, or obsolescence over a period of time. Although depreciation does not require a cash outlay, it is a cost of doing business.

derivatives A wide variety of financial instruments whose value is determined in part from the value and characteristics of another security (the "underlying security"). Options and futures are examples.

discount The amount below the list price or face value. A bond discount refers to the excess of the face value over the bond's current market price. A bond that sells below 100 (below par) is said to be "selling at a discount."

disinflation An economic condition in which the prices of goods and services are rising, but at a declining rate, as witnessed in the 1981 to 1986 period. See the appendix.

dividend A payment to stockholders, usually in the form of a quarterly check. The dividend is declared by the board of directors, and its amount is normally determined by the level of the company's earnings.

dividend reinvestment plan or "DRIP" An investment plan involving the automatic reinvestment of stock dividends, usually sponsored by the company that is declaring and paying the dividend.

dollar cost averaging An investment approach that involves regularly buying uniform dollar amounts of a security, regardless of the price. When prices are low, more shares are bought than when prices are high.

dual listing The same security listed on more than one exchange.

earned surplus Another term for "retained earnings."

earnings The amount of profit a company realizes after all costs, expenses, and taxes have been paid. See also "net earnings."

earnings per share The net earnings divided by the average number of shares outstanding.

EBITDA A term, popular with analysts, that means "earnings before interest, taxes, depreciation, and amortization."

enterprise value A simple calculation used in security analysis to compare the value of different companies. The formula: total market value of the equity, *plus* total debt outstanding, *less* the balance sheet cash and equivalents.

equity See "stockholders' equity."

expiration date The date on which an option expires. In recent years, the expiration date has been designated as the Saturday immediately following the third Friday of the expiration month.

extrinsic value Another term for "price concession."

Fibonacci series A series of numbers, popular among technical analysts, in which each new number is the sum of the prior two (i.e., 0, 1, 1, 2, 3, 5, 8, 13, 21, etc.).

financing The sale of new stock or bonds by a corporation in order to raise capital.

float The number of shares currently available for trading. The float is calculated by deducting from the number of shares outstanding the number of shares that are closely held by individuals or institutions that are not likely to sell immediately if the stock price rises.

free cash flow Defined as "net income plus depreciation, less the total of dividends, capital expenditures, required debt repayments, and any other scheduled cash outlays." Also loosely defined as "cash flow *plus* after-tax interest *plus* any noncash decrease in net working capital."

front running The illegal practice by a specialist of buying or selling for his personal account ahead of a customer.

fundamentalist One who believes that stock prices are determined by the future course of earnings and dividends. The fundamentalist studies, among other things, the economy, industry conditions, and corporate financial statements.

futures Contracts specifying a future date of delivery of a certain amount of a tangible or intangible product. Such products might include commodities such as grains or metals, and financial instruments.

going public A term used to describe the initial sale of shares of a privately held company to the public for the first time. In more recent years, the term "initial public offering" (IPO) is used more often.

goodwill See "intangibles."

government-sponsored entities (GSEs) Government-sponsored mortgage resellers such as Fannie Mae and Freddie Mac. GSE paper is not government-guaranteed.

greenbacks About $400 million of notes (a fiat currency) that were issued by the U.S. government to finance the Civil War.

greenmail The unethical act of buying stock in a company, threatening to take control unless the company purchases the shares held, usually at a price higher than other shareholders can obtain on the open market.

gross profits Profits earned from a basic manufacturing or service operation before selling costs and other expenses are deducted and before taxes are paid.

hedge fund A managed portfolio created for 100 or fewer (usually wealthy) clients to provide various means of offsetting excessive market risk elsewhere. Hedge fund activities can involve short selling, program trading, swaps, and derivatives.

Income Statement A financial statement that presents a company's business results over a specific period of time, usually quarterly or annually. It shows, in dollar terms, all revenues, costs and expenses, taxes, and earnings.

index The measure of the combined, representative value of a group of stocks, bonds, currencies, commodities, or other interests. An index is ordinarily expressed in relation to its original "base" value.

index option A call or put option having an index (rather than an individual stock) as the underlying security. Index options are similar in many ways to listed stock options, except that exercising is settled with a cash payment rather than receiving or delivering stock.

inflation The economic condition in which the prices of goods and services are rising. It involves a declining buying power of cash and a substantially greater amount of currency in circulation. It is generally the result of excessive government spending.

initial public offering (IPO) See "going public."

insider An officer, director, or any person with access to confidential corporate information that is not available to the public.

Instinet A subscriber service for displaying tentative bid and ask quotations.

institutional investor A bank, mutual fund, pension fund, insurance company, university, or other institution that invests in the securities markets.

intangibles Nonphysical assets such as trademarks, patents, copyrights, and "goodwill" (usually the result of accounting differences after mergers or acquisitions).

interest The compensation a borrower pays to a lender for the use of money borrowed.

interim report A company report, usually quarterly, that presents a company's business results (Income Statement) for the period and usually its current financial condition (Balance Sheet). During the year, a company will normally issue three interim reports and one annual report.

intrinsic value The amount by which the current price of the underlying security is above a call option's strike price (or below a put option's strike price). An option that has intrinsic value is said to be "in the money."

"irrational exuberance" A term made famous by then Federal Reserve Board Chairman Alan Greenspan during the dot-com bubble in late 1996.

junk bonds Bonds that are issued with little or no collateral or liquidation value. Junk bonds typically offer high interest income and great risk. Bonds of this type have been popular instruments in buyouts, corporate mergers, and acquisitions.

leveraged buyout Acquiring control of a company, usually through issuing debt. Typically, the company's stock is purchased by employees or a group of investors with the help of an investment banker.

liability Anything that is owed. Liabilities can include both current liabilities and debt to be repaid in later years (e.g., bonds).

liquidate The action of selling assets or securities to obtain cash.

liquidity The ability of a stock to absorb a large amount of buying or selling without disturbing the price substantially.

load mutual fund An open-end investment company that charges the investor a fee when the investor buys the fund shares. This fee (or "load," as it is called) is used primarily to compensate the salespeople selling the fund.

long-term debt Liabilities that are expected to be repaid after twelve months.

margin account An account, typically with a brokerage firm, that allows an investor to buy or sell securities on credit. An investor can, depending on the rules, borrow up to 50% or more of the investment value.

market breadth The extent or scope of changes in stock prices. Market breadth is most often measured by the number of stocks that advanced or declined during the period and the number of shares traded.

market order An order to buy or sell at the best possible price as soon as it can be accomplished.

mark-to-market An accounting rule stating that holdings must be valued at market prices.

municipal bond A bond issued by a state, territory, or possession of the United States or by any municipality, political subdivision, or agency (e.g., bonds issued by cities, counties, school districts, and authorities).

mutual fund An open-end investment company. A mutual fund offers the investor the benefits of portfolio diversification (i.e., owning shares in various companies to provide greater safety and less volatility).

Nasdaq (pronounced "nazdak") The computerized National Association of Securities Dealers Automatic Quotation system that provides brokers and dealers with price quotations of securities traded.

net earnings or **net income** or **net profit** The profit a company realizes after all costs, expenses, and taxes have been deducted from revenues. See also "earnings."

net profit margin The profitability of a company after taxes are paid. The net profit margin is found by dividing net earnings by total revenues (sales and other income).

net worth See "stockholders' equity."

no-load mutual fund An open-end investment company that allows investors to buy and sell fund shares without paying a fee (called the "load"). A no-load fund is sold by word of mouth and advertising, since it typically has no salespeople.

odd lot Any number of shares less than a round lot. Normally, an odd lot is 1 to 99 shares, with a round lot being 100 shares or a multiple of 100 shares.

odd-lot differential A small extra charge that an investor pays if an odd lot is purchased. The amount is ordinarily $0.125 per share.

open-end investment company An investment company that buys shares in other companies. Fund holders are able to buy fund shares from or sell them to the investment company at book value. See "mutual fund."

open order An order to buy or sell a security that is still pending or on the books, but has not yet been executed. An open order will remain in effect until it is either executed or cancelled.

operating profit The profit a company earns from operations before taxes are paid. It is the remainder after deducting all operating costs from sales.

operating profit margin The profitability of a firm's operations before taxes are paid. The operating profit margin is calculated by dividing operating profits by sales.

option A contract allowing an investor to purchase or sell 100 shares of stock at a predetermined price at any time up to a predetermined expiration date.

Option Clearing Corporation (OCC) The central bookkeeping operation that issues standardized options and matches the buyers and sellers of options. The OCC is a clearing agency, regulated by the Securities and Exchange Commission.

outstanding See "shares outstanding."

paper profit A profit that has not been realized. In most cases, the term "paper profit" refers to the profit an investor has on a security that was purchased earlier but has not yet been sold.

par value In bonds, to the stated value of a bond (usually $1,000 or 100). In stocks, an arbitrary value that is used primarily for bookkeeping purposes.

pattern day trader A trader who buys and sells the same stock on the same day at least three times in a five-day period. Such a trader must maintain an equity balance of no less than $25,000 in the margin account.

payout ratio The proportion of earnings that is paid out to stockholders as dividends. For example, a company that pays a $0.25 dividend out of every $1.00 of earnings has a payout ratio of 25%.

pink sheets A daily list of over-the-counter stocks that are unable to qualify for the electronic Nasdaq exchange or an OTC Bulletin Board listing. Also, pink-sheet firms usually lack SEC filings. Pink-sheet market makers show the prior day's bid and asked prices.

Ponzi scheme A fraudulent investment ruse, named for Charles Ponzi in 1920, in which previous investors, lured by superior returns, are paid off using the money received from the most recent investors.

preferred stock A stock that has a prior claim on dividends (and/or assets in the case of corporate dissolution) up to a certain amount before the common stockholders are entitled to anything.

premium The amount above the list price or face value. A bond premium refers to the excess of the market price over the bond's face value. A bond that sells above 100 (above par) is said to be "selling at a premium."

premium (of an option) The market price of an option. This is the price that the buyer of an option pays and the writer of an option receives. The premium is determined by the supply and demand from the option's buyers and sellers as they assess the future market value of the underlying security.

pretax margin The profitability of a company before taxes are paid. The pretax margin is calculated by dividing pretax profits by total revenues (sales and other income).

pretax profits The profit a company earns before paying taxes. It is the profit remaining after deducting all costs and expenses, other than taxes, from total revenues.

price concession The opposite of intrinsic value. It is the amount by which the current price of the underlying security is below a call option's strike price (or above a put option's strike price). An option with a price concession is said to be "out of the money."

price/earnings ratio or **P/E ratio** The relationship between the price of a stock and its earnings per share. The P/E ratio is calculated by dividing the stock price by the earnings per share figure. A $45 stock with an EPS of $3.00 has a P/E ratio of 15.

private placement A stock or bond issue that is sold by a company directly to an investor (or a group of investors) without involving an underwriter or registration with the SEC.

profit margin The profitability of a firm measured by relating profits to revenues. The three most common profit margin calculations are operating profit margin, pretax profit margin, and net profit margin.

program trading Computer-driven, automatically executed securities trades (usually in large volume) of a basket of 15 or more stocks. Also, with index arbitrage, the objective is to capture the arbitrage profits available when, for example, stock indexes and their futures are being traded.

prospectus A document issued by a corporation at the time securities are offered, providing potential buyers with pertinent details and data on the corporation and the security being issued. Also see "red herring."

proxy A written authorization by a stockholder allowing a representative or someone else to vote for or against directors and business proposals at the annual meeting. The results of these votes are usually announced at the meeting.

proxy fight Two or more groups soliciting signed proxies from stockholders to gain a voting majority. It usually involves an outside group that is seeking to win control and oust the incumbent management.

put option A contract giving the holder the right to sell 100 shares of a stock at a predetermined price (called the striking price) any time up to a predetermined expiration date. A put option is bought to profit from a decline in the stock's price.

quick-asset ratio or **acid-test ratio** Current assets less inventories as a percentage of current liabilities (i.e., current assets minus inventories divided by current liabilities). Some accounting experts prefer dividing the sum of cash and marketable securities by current liabilities. A company's position is considered healthy when quick assets exceed current liabilities.

random walk A stock market theory based on the belief that stock price movements are completely random and unpredictable.

red herring A preliminary prospectus, easily identified because the cover has a red trim as a warning to investors that the document is not complete or final and the issue is yet to be priced.

Regulation T The Federal Reserve Bank regulation that sets the minimum margin requirement.

reinvestment rate The internal growth potential of a company. The reinvestment rate is calculated by multiplying the firm's return on equity by the retention rate.

retained earnings Profits that have been reinvested in the business rather than being paid to stockholders as dividends. Another name for retained earnings is "earned surplus." Retained earnings is often an important component of a company's "stockholders' equity" figure.

retention rate The percentage of net earnings that is reinvested in the company after dividends are paid to stockholders. The retention rate is the reciprocal of the payout ratio. If the payout ratio is 25%, the retention rate is 75%.

return on equity The rate of investment return that a company earns on its stockholders' equity. Return on equity is calculated by dividing net earnings by the average stockholders' equity figure.

revenues or **total revenues** A term used loosely to describe the income sources of a corporation (i.e., sales and other income) before any costs or expenses are deducted.

reverse stock split The opposite of a stock split. A 1 for 10 reverse split, for example, is analogous to receiving a dime for ten pennies. A reverse split is usually done to raise the stock's market price.

round lot A standard unit of trading or a multiple thereof. Generally speaking, the unit of trading is 100 shares in the case of stocks and $1,000 par value for bonds.

Rule 13-d An SEC rule requiring the disclosure of beneficial ownership of 5% or more of a security registered with the SEC.

sales The total dollar value of products sold. It is the number of units sold multiplied by the sales price per unit.

Sarbanes-Oxley Act of 2002 A law that addresses a wide range of accountability issues. Among them, CEOs and CFOs must certify their company financial reports, subject to civil and criminal penalties.

seat A membership unit for the privilege of trading on an exchange. Regarding the NYSE, also see "annual trading license."

secondary A large block of stock purchased by a securities firm or a group of firms for resale, usually in smaller lots at a fixed price. The stock is purchased from existing stockholders, not the company.

Securities and Exchange Commission An agency established by Congress in the Securities Exchange Act of 1934. It also administers the Securities Act of 1933 and several other investment-related acts.

senior securities Bonds and/or preferred stocks within the capitalization of a corporation. These securities are considered "senior" to the common stock.

series (of an option) Options that cover an underlying security and that expire in a specific month (e.g., the "July" series).

settlement date The date on which money or securities are due once the securities have been purchased or sold (three business days after the trade date).

shares authorized The maximum number of shares allowed to be issued under a corporation's charter. Additional shares require a charter amendment.

shares outstanding The number of authorized shares that have been issued and are now in the hands of owners.

shelf registration A registration of a new issue that can be prepared up to two years in advance so that funds can be raised when the market conditions are right.

short "against the box" A short sale involving stock that is already owned (rather than borrowing it). This technique to reduce taxes is no longer allowed.

short interest Shares that have been sold short but not yet repurchased.

short sale A trading technique that is typically used when a stock is expected to decline in price. A short sale involves selling borrowed stock, anticipating that the same number of shares can be repurchased later at a lower price. The repurchased shares are then returned to the original lender.

sinking fund An arrangement whereby a portion of a bond or preferred stock issue is retired periodically prior to its fixed maturity date.

SIPC The Securities Investor Protection Corporation, created by Congress in 1970. It provides limited protection, up to $500,000, to customers of securities firms.

soft dollars A payment, typically for research services, by using commissions or underwriting fees in lieu of cash.

spot price The price of a commodity that is to be paid for immediate delivery.

spread The difference between two values; most often used to describe the difference between the "bid" and the "asked" prices.

statement of income See "Income Statement."

stock dividend A dividend that is paid in securities rather than in cash.

stock split A division of a company's shares into a greater or lesser number. A 2 for 1 stock split, for example, is analogous to the division of a dime into two nickels.

stockholders' equity The difference between a company's total assets and total liabilities. Stockholders' equity, sometimes called "net worth," is the stockholders' ownership in the company.

stop order or stop-loss order An order to buy or sell that becomes a market order when the stock sells at or through a specific price (called the "stop price"). A stop order is typically used to protect paper profits or to limit the extent of a possible loss.

straddle An investment strategy of simultaneously buying or writing both a call and a put on the same underlying security, with the options having identical exercise prices and expiration dates.

"street" name A term that applies to securities held in the broker's name rather than in the customer's name. Securities purchased on margin are held in street name. The customer can request street name for convenience or other reasons.

striking price The predetermined exercise price of a stock option. It is also frequently called the "strike price."

swap(s) An agreement between two parties to exchange a stream of future cash flows using a prearranged formula (e.g., an interest-rate swap has one party agreeing to pay a fixed interest rate in return for receiving an adjustable rate from the other party).

TARP (Troubled Assets Relief Program) A U.S. government program involving the purchase of "troubled" assets from banks and other financial institutions to improve their financial conditions.

technical analyst or **technician** One who studies all factors related to the actual supply of and demand for stocks, bonds, or commodities. The primary tools of a technician are price charts and various technical indicators.

tender offer An offer by a company or a special group to purchase the stock of another company. Usually the tender is made at a price above the prevailing market price.

third market The buying and selling of exchange-listed stocks in the OTC market.

tout A slang term referring to a highly biased recommendation to buy a stock.

trade date The date on which a transaction takes place. The settlement date is three business days later. The trade date (no longer the settlement date) is now the cutoff point for tax purposes.

Treasury bill An obligation of the U.S. government with a maturity date that is less than one year from the date of issue. A Treasury bill bears no interest, but it is sold to the investor at a discount prior to maturity.

treasury stock Issued stock that a company has reacquired from its stockholders. The company may hold these shares indefinitely, reissue them to the public, or retire them. Treasury stock is not eligible to vote and receives no dividends.

triple witch The day on which stock options, stock index options, and stock index futures all expire simultaneously.

unit investment trust A registered load investment company that buys and holds a generally fixed portfolio of either stocks or bonds with a stated date of termination. "Units" in the trust are sold to investors.

uptick or **plus-tick** A term used to describe a transaction made at a price above the preceding transaction price.

vertical spread An investment strategy of simultaneously buying and selling options on the same underlying security, with the options having identical expiration dates but different strike prices.

VIX or **Volatility Index** A figure introduced by the CBOE in 1993 that measures the level of implied volatility of the U.S. equity market using real-time S&P 100 (OEX) index option bid/ask quotes. VXN is an identical formula for the Nasdaq 100 Index. They are calculated continuously.

volume The total number of shares traded, either of an individual security or in the entire market, in a given period of time.

warrant A certificate giving the holder the right to buy securities at a predetermined price within a predetermined time limit or perpetually. Warrants are issued directly by the company. In contrast, call options are written on stock that is already outstanding.

wash sale A fictitious and illegal purchase and sale of stock to create market activity, prohibited by the NYSE in 1817. The term also applies to the repurchase of shares within 30 days, which automatically disallows a loss for tax purposes.

when-issued The abbreviated form of "when, as, and if issued," which refers to a security that has been authorized but not yet issued.

wire house A stock brokerage firm with many branch offices linked by a communications network. The term is now primarily of historical significance.

working capital or **net working capital** The excess of current assets over current liabilities.

writer (of options) The seller of an option is called the "writer." The writer receives the premium from the option buyer.

WST ratio A sophisticated ratio of puts and calls that measures the emotions of index option traders. The WST ratio has a positive reading at or below 38.0, and a negative reading at or above 62.0.

yield The annual return on an investment (from dividends or interest), expressed as a percentage of either the cost or the current price.

yield curve The yield difference between short-term Treasury notes and long-term Treasury bonds. This indicator is watched closely by economists and analysts.

yield to maturity The yield of a bond, taking into account the bond's premium or discount and its remaining time to maturity.

Sources

Through corporate and other Internet Web sites, local public and college libraries, and brokerage firms, investors can obtain virtually all the necessary information on companies, industries, and the economy.

Once an investor learns how to use these sources on a regular basis, valuable information and data can be found quickly and easily. Better libraries subscribe to numerous resources and investment services—and some of these are quite expensive. Most individual investors can neither afford them all nor absorb them all on a regular basis. The Internet is the place to start, but a visit to your local library is almost always time well spent.

Here are just a few of the many valuable publications and services that are available to serious, independent investors.

PUBLICATIONS AND SUBSCRIPTIONS

Barron's

200 Liberty Street
New York, NY 10281
online.barrons.com

BusinessWeek

P.O. Box 8418
Red Oak, IA 51591
businessweek.com

Statistical Abstract of the United States

Superintendent of Documents
U.S. Government Printing Office
732 North Capitol Street, NW
Washington, DC 20401
bookstore.gpo.gov

The Economist

North American Office
P.O. Box 46978
St. Louis, MO 63146
economist.com

Forbes

90 Fifth Avenue
New York, NY 10011
forbes.com

Investor's Business Daily

12655 Beatrice Street
Los Angeles, CA 90066
investors.com

Kiplinger Newsletter

1729 H Street
Washington, DC 20006
kiplinger.com

The Wall Street Journal

200 Liberty Street
New York, NY 10281
wsj.com

INVESTMENT SERVICES

Moody's Investors Service

250 Greenwich Street
New York, NY 10007
moodys.com

Standard & Poor's

55 Water Street
New York, NY 10041
standardandpoors.com

Value Line

220 East 42nd Street, #6
New York, NY 10017
valueline.com

BUSINESS ORGANIZATIONS

American Stock Exchange

11 Wall Street (NYSE Euronext)
New York, NY 10005
amex.com

Chicago Board Options Exchange

400 South LaSalle Street
Chicago, IL 60605
cboe.com

Federal Reserve Bank of New York

Public Information Department
33 Liberty Street
New York, NY 10045
ny.frb.com

Financial Industry Regulatory Authority

1735 K Street
Washington, DC 20006
nasd.com

Investment Company Institute

1401 H Street, N.W. Suite 1200
Washington, DC 20005
ici.org

New York Society of Security Analysts

1177 Avenue of the Americas, #2
New York, NY 10036
nyssa.org

NYSE Euronext

11 Wall Street
New York, NY 10005
nyse.com

LEADING BROKERAGE FIRMS

Charles Schwab

120 Kearney Street
San Francisco, CA 94104
schwab.com

Goldman Sachs Group

85 Broad Street
New York, NY 10004
gs.com

Merrill Lynch (Bank of America)

4 World Financial Center
New York, NY 10080
ml.com

Morgan Stanley

1585 Broadway
New York, NY 10036
morganstanley.com

TDAmeritrade

4211 South 102nd Street
Omaha, NE 68127
tdameritrade.com

Wachovia Corp. (Wells Fargo)

1525 West W.T. Harris Blvd.
Charlotte, NC 28288
www.wachovia.com

OTHER ONLINE SECURITIES FIRMS

Dreyfus (BNY Mellon)

dreyfus.com

E*Trade Securities

us.etrade.com

Fidelity

personal.fidelity.com

Muriel Siebert & Co.
siebertnet.com

ScoTTrade
scottrade.com

Smith Barney
smithbarney.com

T. Rowe Price
troweprice.com

UBS Financial Services
ubs.com

OTHER USEFUL ONLINE
ADDRESSES

EDGAR (SEC's searchable database)
edgar-online.com

CME (Chicago Mercantile Exchange)
cmegroup.com

Fortune Magazine
money.cnn.com/magazines/fortune

Money Magazine
money.cnn.com

NYMEX (N.Y. Mercantile Exchange)
nymex.com

Securities Industry Association
sia.com

MISCELLANEOUS PRODUCTS
AND SERVICES

BigCharts
bigcharts/marketwatch.com

Briefing.com
briefing.com

BullsOrBears.com
bullsorbears.com

CNBC
cnbc.com

DecisionPoint
decisionpoint.com

John Mauldin
frontlinethoughts.com

Lipper
lipper.com

Morningstar
morningstar.com

MSN
msn.com

Quote.com
quote.com

Richard Russell
dowtheoryletters.com

SmartMoney
smartmoney.com

StockCharts
stockcharts.com

Yahoo! Finance
finance.yahoo.com

Zacks Investment Research
zacks.com

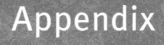

Appendix

SELECTED STATISTICS

Year	DJIA Close	DJIA Earnings	DJIA Div.	Payout Ratio	Avg. P/E	Div. Yield	% Chg. CPI
1945	193	10.56	6.69	63%	16.4	3.9%	2.3%
1946	177	13.63	7.50	55%	13.8	4.0%	8.3%
1947	181	18.80	9.21	49%	9.3	5.3%	14.4%
1948	177	23.07	11.50	50%	7.8	6.4%	8.1%
1949	200	23.54	12.79	54%	7.7	7.0%	−1.2%
1950	235	30.70	16.13	53%	7.0	7.5%	1.3%
1951	269	26.59	16.34	61%	9.7	6.3%	7.9%
1952	292	24.78	15.43	62%	11.1	5.6%	1.9%
1953	281	27.23	16.11	59%	10.1	5.9%	0.8%
1954	404	28.18	17.47	62%	12.1	5.1%	0.7%
1955	488	35.78	21.58	60%	12.1	4.9%	−0.4%
1956	499	33.34	22.99	69%	14.7	4.7%	1.5%
1957	436	36.08	21.61	60%	13.0	4.6%	3.3%
1958	584	27.95	20.00	72%	18.3	3.9%	2.8%
1959	679	34.31	20.74	60%	18.3	3.3%	0.7%
1960	616	32.21	21.36	66%	19.4	3.4%	1.7%
1961	731	31.91	22.71	71%	21.1	3.4%	1.0%
1962	652	36.43	23.30	64%	17.3	3.7%	1.0%
1963	763	41.21	23.41	57%	17.2	3.3%	1.3%
1964	874	46.43	31.24	67%	17.9	3.8%	1.3%
1965	969	53.67	28.61	53%	16.9	3.2%	1.6%
1966	786	57.68	31.89	55%	15.1	3.7%	2.9%
1967	905	53.87	30.19	56%	16.0	3.5%	3.1%
1968	944	57.89	31.34	54%	15.6	3.5%	4.2%
1969	800	57.02	33.90	59%	15.2	3.9%	5.5%
1970	839	51.02	31.53	62%	14.4	4.3%	5.7%
1971	890	55.09	30.86	56%	15.9	3.5%	4.4%
1972	1,020	67.11	32.27	48%	14.3	3.4%	3.2%
1973	851	86.17	35.33	41%	10.7	3.8%	6.2%
1974	616	99.04	37.72	38%	7.4	5.1%	11.0%
1975	852	75.66	37.46	50%	10.0	4.9%	9.1%
1976	1,005	96.72	41.40	43%	9.7	4.4%	5.8%
1977	831	89.10	45.84	51%	10.1	5.1%	6.5%
1978	805	112.79	48.52	43%	7.3	5.9%	7.6%
1979	839	124.46	50.98	41%	6.8	6.0%	11.3%
1980	964	121.86	54.36	45%	7.2	6.2%	13.5%
1981	875	113.71	56.22	49%	8.1	6.1%	10.3%
1982	1,047	9.15	54.14	n/m	100.9	5.9%	6.2%
1983	1,259	72.45	56.33	78%	16.0	4.9%	3.2%
1984	1,212	113.58	60.63	53%	10.4	5.1%	4.3%
1985	1,547	96.11	62.03	65%	14.2	4.5%	3.6%
1986	1,896	115.59	67.04	58%	15.0	3.9%	1.9%
1987	1,939	133.05	71.20	54%	16.4	3.3%	3.6%
1988	2,169	215.46	79.53	37%	9.4	3.9%	4.1%
1989	2,753	221.48	103.70	47%	11.1	4.2%	4.8%
1990	2,634	172.05	102.00	59%	15.6	3.8%	5.4%
1991	3,169	49.27	95.18	50%	57.3	3.4%	4.2%
1992	3,301	108.25	100.72	50%	30.1	3.1%	3.0%
1993	3,754	146.84	99.66	68%	24.0	2.8%	3.0%
1994	3,834	256.13	105.66	41%	14.7	2.8%	2.6%
1995	5,117	311.02	116.56	37%	14.6	2.6%	2.8%
1996	6,448	353.88	131.00	37%	16.4	2.2%	3.0%
1997	7,908	391.29	136.10	35%	18.7	1.9%	2.3%

Year	DJIA Close	DJIA Earnings	DJIA Div.	Payout Ratio	Avg. P/E	Div. Yield	% Chg. CPI
1998	9,181	383.35	151.13	39%	21.4	1.8%	1.6%
1999	11,497	477.22	168.52	35%	21.6	1.6%	2.2%
2000	10,787	485.14	172.08	35%	22.1	1.6%	3.4%
2001	10,022	369.51	181.07	49%	26.2	1.9%	2.8%
2002	8,342	385.58	189.68	49%	23.3	2.1%	1.6%
2003	10,454	519.96	209.42	40%	17.2	2.3%	2.3%
2004	10,783	588.95	239.27	41%	17.4	2.3%	2.7%
2005	10,718	476.32	246.85	52%	22.0	2.4%	3.4%
2006	12,463	728.02	267.75	37%	15.9	2.3%	3.2%
2007	13,265	199.87	298.99	n/m	65.5	2.3%	2.8%
2008	8,776	380.00e	316.40	83%e	27.1e	3.1%	3.8%

GOVERNMENT STATISTICS (BILLIONS OF DOLLARS)

Year	GDP	National Debt	Budget Surplus	Money Supply M2	+ % Chg.	Income Taxes Indiv.	Corp.
2000	9,710	5,674	236	4,911	6.0%	1,004	207
2001	10,058	5,807	128	5,418	10.3%	994	151
2002	10,377	6,228	−158	5,765	6.4%	858	148
2003	10,809	6,783	−378	6,055	5.0%	794	132
2004	11,500	7,379	−413	6,400	5.7%	809	189
2005	12,238	7,933	−318	6,662	4.1%	927	278
2006	13,016	8,507	−248	7,022	5.4%	1,044	354
2007	13,668	9,008	−162	7,417	5.6%	1,163	370
2008	14,312	10,025	−410e	8,254	9.9%	1,220e	345e

Index

in South America, 148
  strategies for investing in, 250–251
Silver halide photography, 178
Sinking funds, 194
SIPC (Security Investors Protection Corporation),
  27
Small Business Administration (SBA), 183
Small investors, 13
Solar power, 140–141
Sony Corp., 235
Soros, George, 336
South Africa, 243, 246, 251
South-Sea Bubble (1719-1720), 148–149
South-Sea Company, 148–149
Soviet Union, 225, 246
S&P 100 Index (OEX) (*see* Standard & Poor's 100
  Index)
S&P 500 Spider (*see* Standard & Poor's 500 Spider)
Spam, 215
SPDR (*see* Standard & Poor's Depositary Receipt)
Special tax bonds, 200
Special purpose funds, 108
Specie Circular (1836), 242
Speculating, 12
Spreading, 313
Spreads:
  calendar, 316–318
  of credit default swap, 291
  defined, 31
  and SuperDOT, 32
  vertical, 313–316
SPY (Standard & Poor's 500 Spider), 321
Standard & Poor's (S&P) 100 Index (OEX), 321,
  322
Standard & Poor's (S&P) 500 Index, 62, 112, 115,
  139, 277
Standard & Poor's (S&P) 500 Spider (SPY), 321
Standard & Poor's chart subscription services, 265
Standard & Poor's Corporation ratings, 194–195
Standard & Poor's Depositary Receipt (SPDR), 99,
  112
Standard Oil Company, 137, 331
State-issued notes, 148
Statement of cash flows, 42, 51
Statements of income, 8
Steel industry, 178
Stochastics, 271
Stock certificates, 12
Stock Exchange Office, 22
Stock manipulation, 150–151
Stock market activity, 64–66
Stock market crash of 1929, 149–156
  aftermath of, 156
  chronology of, 152–155
  corporate dividends, 152
  corporate profits, 152
  Federal Reserve System, 151
  margin in equities, 150
  stock manipulation, 150–151
Stock market crash of 1987, 159–160
  and circuit breakers, 34–35
  recovery from, 61
Stock options (*see* Options)

Stock power, 89
Stock prices:
  determination of, 9–10
  and options, 305, 309
Stock splits, 72–75
Stock tables, 62–64
Stockbrokers, 26, 63–64, 84–88
StockCharts.com, 267
Stockholders:
  common characteristics of, 35–36
  election of company directors by, 41
  elections by, 6
  profits for, 7–8, 72–73
Stockholders' equity, 42–44
Stocks:
  exchange-listed, 27
  fertilizer, 162
  foreign, 33
  growth (*see* Growth stocks)
  Japanese, 230
  leisure-time, 161
  mining, 250, 251
  preferred, 44, 195, 201–202
  reasons for buying, 12–14
Stop limit order, 98
Stop loss orders, 155
Stop orders, 97–98
Straddle strategy, 319–320
Strap strategy, 321
Street name, 89
Striking price, 294, 305, 309
Strip strategy, 321
Strong, Benjamin, 151
Stuttgart Stock Exchange, 232
SuperDOT, 32
Supply, of gold, 245–247
Supply and demand, 226, 227
Support and resistance patterns, 260
Sutter's Mill, 242–243
Syndicates, 25

T

T. Rowe Price Associates, 76, 109, 335
T. Rowe Price New Horizons Fund, 121
TALF (Term Asset-Backed Securities Loan
  Facility), 183
Tangible book value, 54–55
Tax anticipation bills, 209
Tax rates, 49–50
Taxes:
  on annual report, 43
  on bonds, 199–201
  increases and cuts, 77
  and investing/trading, 103–104
  and stock yields, 132
  and total return, 93
  on U.S. government securities, 202
Teaser rates, 173
Technical analysis, 257–285
  bar charts in, 258–260
  beta in, 272
  candlestick charts in, 274–275
  chart patterns in, 260–269

during twentieth century, 333
during twenty-first century, 336–337
Wall Street (film), 13
Wall Street Journal, 59, 66, 68
    development of, 330
    indication of stock splits in, 74
    mutual fund listings in, 75
Wall Street Trader (WST), 219, 280
Wal-Mart Stores, 121, 129–131
War Bonds, 178
Washington, George, 20, 328
Washington Mutual, 292
Watson, Thomas J., Sr., 139
Web sites, 216–217
Weekly bar chart, 258–260
Weisner, Jerome, 219
West Germany, 226, 231
Western Union, 178, 330
Wilder, J. Welles, Jr., 272
Wilson, Woodrow, 206–207
Wind power, 140–141
Wireless communications, 141, 220
Working capital, 44

World War I, 135, 178
World War II, 135, 157–158, 178
World Wide Web, 214
Writing options, 101, 300–304
WSJ.com, 59
WST (*see* Wall Street Trader)
WST ratio, 279–280

X
Xerox, 138, 162, 235

Y
Yahoo!, 139, 164
Yamana Gold Inc., 253
Yield to maturity, 191
Yields:
    bond, 190–193
    dividend, 9–10

Z
Zenba (morning trading session), 229
Zero-coupon convertible bonds, 198–199

About the Authors

Jeffrey B. Little, a finance graduate of New York University, began his Wall Street career in the early 1960s. Initially, he worked as an accountant in the margin department of a leading brokerage firm and additionally served as an instructor of technical analysis in a Wall Street training center. Later, as a highly respected technology analyst, he became a portfolio manager and advisory committee member for one the largest funds at T. Rowe Price Associates, a Baltimore-based global asset management firm.

Mr. Little has been a Fellow of the Financial Analysts Federation, a member of the New York Society of Security Analysts, as well as a vice president of T. Rowe Price Associates. As an Investment Analyst, he was registered with FINRA (Series 7, 86, and 87) and retired from Wall Street in late 2009.

Presently, Mr. Little is a writer and publisher of biographies and computer software in Deerfield Beach, Florida, where he and his wife, Judith, now reside.

Lucien Rhodes, an economics graduate of Dartmouth College, has several years' experience as a securities analyst and portfolio manager in both commercial and investment banking. He has been registered on the New York Stock Exchange and is a past member of the Baltimore Society of Security Analysts.

Mr. Rhodes is also a respected financial journalist. His articles have appeared in various well-known publications, including the *Baltimore Sun*, *Fortune*, *Wired*, and *INC.* magazine, where he received a national journalism award for his work. In addition to his background in finance, he is also expert in various computer technologies. In recent years, he has combined these interests to serve as an Internet consultant to financial services companies and venture capital start-ups in California's Silicon Valley.

Mr. Rhodes currently lives near San Francisco with his wife, Nancy.

UNDERSTANDING WALL STREET
Video

The highlights of this classic book are now available on DVD for your viewing pleasure. This two-hour video begins with the startup of a new business and the colorful history of Wall Street, tracing its origin as a dirt path, along with an explanation of how the markets work. You will also learn details about evaluating a company for potential investment.

This up-to-date video, explains Wall Street in its contemporary investment setting with lively graphics, appropriate video footage, and clever chapter organization.

The *Understanding Wall Street* video is perfect as a home reference or as an educational medium. It can be ordered quickly and easily with an 800 number and any one of the three major credit cards.

Thank you, but I would prefer to order by mail.

_____ copies of the new *Understanding Wall Street DVD*

Enclosed is $39.95 plus $7 shipping and handling for each video ordered.

☐ Visa   ☐ Master Card   ☐ Amex   ☐ Check or Money Order

Credit Card Number _____ Expires _____

Name_____

Address _____

City _____ State _____ Zip_____

Signature_____

Mail To:

LIBERTY PUBLISHING COMPANY, INC.
P.O. Box 4485
Deerfield Beach, FL 33442

Toll-free call for immediate service: **(800) 251-3345**
Company Offices: (954) 426-9677

Liberty Publishing Company, Inc. can also be reached at **BullsOrBears.com**.

(Florida residents please add applicable 6% sales tax. Prices are subject to change.

Orders outside the U.S. must be prepaid with international money orders, payable in U.S. dollars).